Trump and Political Theology:
Unmaking Truth and Democracy

Trump and Political Theology: Unmaking Truth and Democracy

Jack David Eller

AN IMPRINT OF THE
GLOBAL CENTER FOR RELIGIOUS RESEARCH
1312 17TH STREET • SUITE 549
DENVER, COLORADO 80202

INFO@GCRR.ORG • GCRR.ORG

GCRR Press
An imprint of the Global Center for Religious Research
1312 17th Street Suite 549
Denver, CO 80202
www.gcrr.org

Copyright © 2020 by Jack David Eller

DOI: 10.33929/GCRRPress.TrumpandPoliticalTheology

Typesetting: Holly Lipovits
Copyediting: Julie E. George
Cover Photo and Design: Darren M. Slade

Library of Congress Cataloging-in-Publication Data

Trump and political theology: unmaking truth and democracy / Jack David Eller ; foreword by Darren M. Slade
p. cm.
Includes bibliographic references (p.) and index.
ISBN (Print): 978-0-578-80730-0
ISBN (eBook): 978-0-578-80731-7
1. Trump, Donald J.—Theology.   2. Religion and politics—United States. 3. Conservatism—Religious aspects—Christianity—History—20th and 21st century   4. United States—Politics and government   5. Church and social problems—Racism—United States   I. Title.

BR115.P7   .E454   20

A Selection of Publications
By Jack David Eller

From Culture to Ethnicity to Conflict: An Anthropological Perspective on International Ethnic Conflict (University of Michigan Press, 1999)

Violence and Culture: A Cross-Cultural and Interdisciplinary Approach (Wadsworth, 2005)

Introducing Anthropology of Religion: Culture to the Ultimate (Routledge, 2007, 2014)

Cultural Anthropology: Global Forces, Local Live (Routledge, 2009, 2013, 2016, 2020)

Cruel Creeds, Virtuous Violence: Religious Violence Across Culture and History (Prometheus Books, 2010)

Cultural Anthropology 101 (Routledge, 2015)

Culture and Diversity in the United States: So Many Ways to be American (Routledge, 2015)

Social Science and Historical Perspectives: Society, Science, and Ways of Knowing (Routledge, 2017)

Inventing American Traditions: From the Mayflower to Cinco de Mayo (Reaktion Books, 2018)

Psychological Anthropology for the 21st Century (Routledge, 2019)

Advanced Endorsements

OMG. Wow. Here is an analysis of the Donald Trump phenomenon that goes deeper and wider than anything I've read. A must read no matter who the next president is because David Eller's discussion of "political theology" reveals so much about the craziness and ironic coherence of American politics.

—Mark Galli,
Former Editor-in-Chief of *Christianity Today*

In the void left by the death of God, Eller explores how the violence of language and the power of mediatic charisma can create a new politics of myth, ritual, and emotion: from this abyss Trump emerges as a figure of exception that reveals the contradictions of liberal democracies. This is a fundamental book to understand our age.

—Dr. Antonio Cerella, Kingston University, London,
Author of *Genealogies of Political Modernity*

Eller highlights the inescapable significance of political theology to late modern discourse. His work combines a rich historical survey with a penetrating analysis of religious thought in twenty-first-century America.

—Dr. Benjamin T. Lynerd, Christopher Newport University,
Assistant Professor in the Department of Political Science

Contents

Foreword

By Darren M. Slade

I had the morbid pleasure of being on the campus of Liberty University during the 2016 presidential election between candidates Donald Trump and Hillary Clinton. Significantly, throughout its existence, both the institution and its faculty prided itself on being the gatekeepers of social and personal morality. Though I was originally unfamiliar with the university's founder, Jerry Falwell Sr., and his demonizing rhetoric against those he judged to be depraved contaminants of America's "Christian" conscience, over time it was soon apparent that he, like many evangelicals I encountered, had no real interest in promoting Christlike godliness. Rather, they employed the language of religion and morality because it was expedient to do so. They had become political sycophants of the Republican Party, and they were willing to say and do anything to maintain a political, legislative, racial, and economic control over society's marginalized voices. This willingness to overlook some of the most unconscionable behavior by Republican leaders and fellow religionists was never more apparent than when I witnessed the cult-like endorsement of candidate Donald Trump from some of Liberty's faculty and theology students. The mental and moral gymnastics needed to rationalize their endorsement was beyond disturbing; it was dangerous. Indeed, these theologians exhibited the type of dangerous brainwashing that usually occurs within cults of personality.

Somehow, these self-proclaimed "salt of the earth" gatekeepers were more concerned with Hillary Clinton using a personal email server than they were with the fact that an obvious con-man had never once exhibited the type of love, empathy, grace, forgiveness, or compassion that Christ himself demanded of his followers. I listened to certain professors become visibly giddy when they first heard the chant, "Lock her up," at a Trump rally, yet they never spoke a word of condemnation when they heard Mr. Trump brag about sexually assaulting unsuspecting women. Despite Trump's obvious biblical illiteracy and lack of church attendance, these professional apologists were more than willing to view him as the embodiment of Christian values. Despite his track record for reveling in sin and debauchery, these Christian leaders still saw him as an answer to prayer. Despite his obvious bigotry, lack of integrity, emotional immaturity, and mental instability, these followers responded to Donald Trump as though he were the second coming of Christ, displaying an excitement and unconditional allegiance typically reserved for a demigod. And despite the nonstop flow of scandals and criminal behavior during his four-year administration, many of his supporters remained unmoved in their loyalty.

For most of us, it was obvious what had occurred right before our very eyes. Specialists the world over watched the formation of a genuine cult of personality develop in real time. Of course, this Trumpcult would have

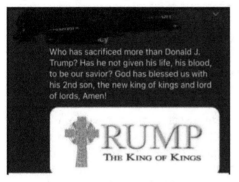

made for a very benign academic study had it not also involved surrounding the madman with unquestioning loyalists while giving him access to and authority over the most powerful military force and nuclear arsenal in the world. In a word, Trump had become their Messiah. Not surprisingly, I received a letter in the mail expressing this very sentiment from a group claiming to speak on behalf of God. The letter declared that Mr. Trump was

Screenshot of a public Facebook post from a Trump supporter on October 23, 2020. Screenshot by Darren Slade.

"God's Chosen One" and that he "Is Our Only Chance To Deter The End Of The World." As is standard in religious cults, the letter even attempted to engage in spiritual manipulation by writing, "God Says 'If You Don't Support Our President You are Committing Spiritual Treason'."

Anonymous letter received in the mail during the 2020 presidential election. Photographs by Darren Slade.

Those four years of Trump's administration left the unswindled asking what it was that made people willingly overlook such blatant corruption for so long. What was it about the "other side" that made otherwise decent people become religious zealots for a fanatical political figurehead who befriended dictators and praised tyrants? The answer, like too many things since 2016, came in the form of a Tweet. Actor Jon Voight once shared a video in July of 2020 where he pleaded the urgency for voting against Democrats:

And to have left wing behavior, left wing danger, destroying this nation, He will not allow, because my fellow Americans, God the Almighty gave all this to us, so we as a civilization with all our greatness must give back and we shall protect the USA with God, and He who understands this Liberty must protect as well.[1]

Almost four months later, Jon Voight tweeted another video where he compared the victory of President-elect Joe Biden to the work of the devil. "This is now our greatest fight since the Civil War, the battle of righteousness versus Satan. Yes 'Satan' because these leftists are evil, corrupt." Voight then went on to make the battle lines even clearer, "Let us give our trust to God and fight now for Trump's victory because we all know this ballot count is corruption like they are. So let us not back down. But fight this fight as if it is our last fight on Earth."[2]

Sadly, the Republican Party has done a good job of convincing religionists that liberals and progressivist policies are quite literally evil incarnate. A vote for Republicans is a vote for God himself whereas a vote for Democrats is a vote for Satan. Although Donald Trump was a registered Democrat from 2001–2009, he soon realized that he could dupe America's most religious by capitalizing on an inherently xenophobic, exclusionist, and dichotomistic mindset. What this rhetoric and hypocrisy demonstrated for me back at Liberty University was that most evangelicals were willing to embrace (and even imitate) a malignant narcissist's behavior all for the sake of fighting Satan's encroachment into American society. It revealed to me, as it had to many other disillusioned Christians, that these followers would, in fact, support the antichrist himself as long as he ran under the banner of the supposedly "God-loving" Republican Party. To this day, as I work with religious specialists and faith leaders all around the world, I continually hear just how ashamed and embarrassed they are to be associated with the name "Christian" *because* of President Trump and his Christian followers. But

---

[1] Jon Voight, "Faith and Trust," Twitter, July 22, 2020, https://twitter.com/jonvoight/status/1286055348973867008?s=20.

[2] Jon Voight, "We all know the truth," Twitter, November 10, 2020, https://twitter.com/jonvoight/status/1326323889417322497?s=20.

how in the world was any of this even possible in the first place? What did we all just experience with the Trump presidency?

Dr. Jack David Eller's book, *Trump and Political Theology*, provides the most definitive explanation for how it is that the Trumpcult was able to develop and spread with such fervency among the American populace. Using insights of political theory and the place of religion in permitting a sovereign to rule, Dr. Eller offers a social-scientific description for what it meant for President Donald Trump to lie so profusely and for his followers to be deceived so easily. *Trump and Political Theology* exposes just how Americans are especially susceptible to authoritarian leaders who would destroy truth and democracy in order to save face and why so many Americans would rationalize this behavior as a moral necessity. This book is primed to become one of the most significant academic examinations of Donald Trump's abysmal four-year presidency and the enablers who allowed the United States to degrade into such a lurid, loathsome laughing stock around the civilized world.

Dr. Eller's academic prowess as a world-renown scholar makes his incredible insights into the Trump era all the more important to help us understand and learn from the 2016 presidential debacle. The book invites Americans to consider the cracks in their political system, as well as the collective insecurity that would put democracy itself on the verge of collapse. As an anthropologist, Dr. Eller is suited to inform us about the human tendency toward tribalism and extremist thinking. As a religious outsider, he is suited to confront the political and religious hypocrisy expressed by those who are too blind to notice (or even care). *Trump and Political Theology* is a must-read for anyone seeking an explanation for what in the hell the world just went through with Donald Trump and why this was not (and likely will not be) an isolated event.

Preface

This book was composed in the spring and summer of 2020, during the heat of the presidential campaign and the height of the coronavirus pandemic. This preface is composed in November, the day after Joe Biden accepted the declaration of his victorious bid for the presidency, marking (presumably, ideally, ordinarily) the end of the Trump era.

If Donald Trump really does leave office on January 20, which he must do short of a stunning recount reversal or a judicial (or other) coup, does this book remain relevant? The name "Trump" as the title lead suggests that the study contained herein is primarily about Trump, but it is not. This is a study of power, its sources, and, even more urgently, its relation to "normal" practices and institutions like law, constitutions, political traditions, and democracy itself. I stress "normal" for two reasons, which are the interrelated inspiration for this book in the first place. Carl Schmitt, in his reorientation of political theology, emphasized that power or sovereignty lies precisely not in the normal but in the *exceptional*, where and when norms, traditions, laws, and even constitutions are violated. More profoundly, he argued that the exceptional is not only the death but the *birth* of the normal, that it is only in *the decision* that norms and laws and constitutions are created at all.

The second reason for stressing normal is that, however one may feel about him, both sides agree that Trump is/was not a normal politician or a normal president. Some celebrated his exceptionality as just the tonic for the country's ailment, someone to shake if not break the government. Others cringed at his antics and his authoritarian tendencies and despaired for our democracy, if not for our world. And Trump is indeed a force, for good or ill. But more importantly, more enduringly, Trump is a lens—a shocking lens, admittedly—through which to observe the inner workings of power. His conduct and his dazzling success at ignoring and trampling precedent, tradition, and law illustrate Schmitt's point exquisitely, namely the contingency and fragility of democracy, of truth, and of reality itself. As I contend in a later chapter, what Schmitt was describing was *the will*, the sovereign will, the will to power but also the will to reality.

Democracy or any other "normal" political system is not fully prepared to confront the sovereign will. It assumes a normal leader, and in normal times leaders restrain themselves by internalizing and respecting norms and rules. In exceptional times, the leader suffers no such restraint; that is what *makes* them exceptional times. And Trump has guessed the Schmittian secret: there is no one and nothing to stop him. Some of his powers are constitutionally granted, like the power of pardon, but still open to abuse. Other powers are discovered or invented, like the power of executive order or "signing statement," while there is underestimated power in the brazen lie. But when he bends or shatters the "guardrails" of democracy—ignoring Congress, packing courts, disparaging his own executive agencies, and lastly delegitimizing the electoral process itself—he exposes precisely how vulnerable and impotent those institutions are to respond. As I will say below, the only thing that can constrain such a will is an equal and opposite will, and that we do not see.

Trump did not emerge from a vacuum; there has been a long road toward an imperial presidency and Republican anti-democratic impulses (driven not least by the demographic fact that most Americans do not vote for Republicans). And Trump too shall pass. But authoritarianism and illiberal democracy—or the end of democracy—will continue to loom, even more so since he has revealed the insubstantiality and defenselessness of "normal" politics. Others no doubt will learn and exploit this lesson, the Schmittian lesson, the political theology lesson, that laws and institutions are never completely settled and secure, that the exception and the decision are perpetual and irrepressible threats, and that normal politics is relatively unarmed against the will of the populist, the authoritarian, the trickster-troll who would gleefully burn it all down.

Introduction

> The underlying rationale of politics is the quest for finality and decisiveness in the affairs of groups, ends that are permanently frustrated by the slippery and inconclusive circumstances in which that quest occurs....The fundamental thought-practice of finality is the decision.[1]

Something is wrong. Everything seems to be in decline, even upside down. Old truths dissolve into uncertainty (like Marx's solids that melted into air more than a century and a half ago), and no one understands it or knows what to do about it. Then there is Donald Trump. He violates every norm of presidential comportment, attacks every institution, violates every ethics rule, insults every rival, and disregards every standard of truth in the service of making America great again. Is he a cause or an effect of the condition—or is he the cure, as he himself and his followers believe? Is his presidency corrosive, or is it revelatory?

In the present moment, as numerous scholars have noted, there is renewed attention to the notion of "political theology" as both a diagnosis and a remedy for the malaise of modern America and of the West in general (how quaint it is to recall Jimmy Carter's appeal to malaise more than forty years ago, when the first rumbles of political/economic tectonic shifts were perceptible). For some contemporary sufferers, the therapy is a simple and literal return to/of God (whom Nietzsche may have prematurely declared dead, or who may once again have risen from the dead), of old-time religion and biblical values. Such would be merely the latest occasion of Christian revival, a venerable tradition in the United States, which has seen continuous waves of revivalism and "great awakenings" throughout its history. For very specific constituencies, like the Reconstructionists or Dominionists of the Chalcedon Foundation, this means virtual theocracy or at least biblocracy, government and society structured along (especially Old Testament) biblical lines. For others, and presumably for the majority of scholars who investigate and/or advocate it, political theology means (re)establishing a supernatural or divine ground for government and more generally for

---

[1] Michael Freeden, *The Political Theory of Political Thinking: The Anatomy of a Practice* (Oxford and New York: Oxford University Press, 2013), 22.

society—a sort of Thomistic cosmological first cause or unmoved mover—
to secure them against the peril of dissolution.

The Trump phenomenon is an apposite, even obligatory,
opportunity to reconsider political theology and the relation between religion
and society/state, and not only because of Trump's incomprehensible
support among American evangelicals despite being perhaps the most
ungodly political figure in recent memory. At the extreme, some followers
(and sometimes he himself) have likened Trump to the messiah, the savior,
the king of Israel, the very voice or hammer of God. I am not implying in the
slightest way that Trump possesses an articulate political theology, or any
other political theory, or that his campaign or his presidency represents a
conscious political theology. What I am contending is that the very
abnormality of Trump's politics lifts a veil on the operation of power—of
the nature of law and of sovereignty—in much the same way that abnormal
psychology lifts a veil on mental function. Thus, viewing the Trump
phenomenon through the lens of political theology sheds light on both, as he
exposes the profound contingency and vulnerability of the political while
also forcing us to consider religious or symbolic forces and resources
beyond the familiar Christian or theistic ones.

What is Political Theology?

At the most obvious level, the term "political theology" designates some
relation between politics and religion, as well as or in addition to an
application of theology to political questions. However, like all technical and
cultural terminology, things are never so obvious and never so settled. Jan
Assman famously characterizes political theology as the "ever-changing
relationships between political community and religious order, between
power [or authority: *Herrschaft*] and salvation [*Heil*]."[2] Saul Newman's
recent brief introduction to political theology expands on the definition to
include "the way in which political concepts, discourses and institutions—
particularly sovereignty—are influenced, shaped and underpinned by
religious categories of thought."[3]

In *The Future of Illusion*, Victoria Kahn defines political theology
quite tersely but instructively as "the theological legitimation or religious

---

[2] Quoted in Hent de Vries, "Introduction: Before, Around, and Beyond the
Theologico-Political," in *Political Theologies: Public Religions in a Post-Secular World*,
ed. Hent de Vries and Lawrence E. Sullivan (New York: Fordham University Press,
2006), 25. Original quotation in Jan Assmann, *Herrschaft und Heil: Politische Theologie
in Altägypten, Israel und Europa* (Munich: Carl Hanser, 2000), 15.
[3] Saul Newman, *Political Theology: A Critical Introduction* (Cambridge: Polity
Press, 2019), 4–5.

dimension of political authority," raising the critical issue of legitimation.[4] This issue is not at all lost on other commentators, including Newman—in fact, it will soon become central to the entire enterprise—as he grants that "the problem of political theology is a way of thinking about the foundations and legitimacy of power in modern societies,"[5] perhaps especially but by no means exclusively in modern societies. Meanwhile, Andrew March, of all places in an essay about Islamic politics, argues that political theology is "the assertion that certain concepts, gaps, and aspirations immanent in Western political theory are transferred from theology either in the form of presence or of absence"—primarily the presence/absence of a god.[6]

Political theology may be predominantly Western, but it is not exclusively modern. A pre-Christian thinker, Marcus Terentius Varro (116–27 BCE), is often credited with the first use of the term, naming *theologia politikē* or *theologia civilis* as one of the three branches of theology (and the prerogative of priests), along with "mythical" and "cosmological" or natural theologies, the realms of poets and philosophers, respectively.[7] Particularly in premodern societies, including ancient Israel, politics and theology were intimately, although not always comfortably, entangled, and as Christianity penetrated and crystallized in the Roman Empire, the tension between politics and religion became acute. The admonitions of Jesus that God's kingdom was not of this world and that believers should render to Caesar what was Caesar's and to God what was God's were simultaneously helpful and unhelpful, stipulating but obscuring the chasm between earthly and heavenly authority. As is well known, Christians were often castigated in Rome, not so much for their unconventional beliefs as their disloyal behavior. Their crime was more political (failing to revere and obey the emperor) than religious (believing in the wrong/false god), although failing to worship the old gods was potentially catastrophic too.

As Christopher Rowland warns, Christianity's "eschatological hope of God's kingdom on earth which is such a dominant thread in New Testament theology cannot allow any easy accommodation between the church, the community of those called to bear witness to the reign of God, and political powers."[8] Not that this stopped anyone, like Constantine and

---

[4] Victoria Ann Kahn, *The Future of Illusion: Political Theology and Early Modern Texts* (Chicago and London: The University of Chicago Press, 2014), 1.

[5] Newman, *Political Theology*, xx.

[6] Andrew F. March, "Genealogies of Sovereignty in Islamic Political Theology," *Social Research* 80, no. 1 (2013), 293.

[7] de Vries, "Introduction," 25.

[8] Christopher Rowland, "Scripture: New Testament," in *The Blackwell Companion to Political Theology*, ed. Peter Scott and William T. Cavanaugh (Oxford: Blackwell Publishing, 2004), 33.

subsequent monarchs, from trying. Augustine faced the challenge with kindness in his *City of God*, recognizing, contrary to many fundamentalist Christian sects today, that even if there are two cities or kingdoms—a fallen worldly one and a perfect heavenly one—nevertheless humans are citizens of both. Appreciating that humans are thoroughly social beings long before the advent of modern social science, Jean Bethke Elshtain judges that Augustine taught, "Christians are not to hunker down in the church, but to approach the world with a loving worldliness, born out of a recognition of the world's many goodnesses and blessings."[9] Truly, "earthly institutions have a real claim on us,"[10] and we would best think of ourselves as dual citizens, although the same complications with dual national citizenship today apply to dual spiritual citizenship.

We cannot possibly rehearse the entire history of political-theological thinking here, so let it suffice to say, along with Elizabeth Phillips, that there have historically been at least four eras of or approaches to political theology in Christendom:

> The first is related to theological understandings of creation, fall and human nature. Some suggest that there are basically two types of political theology: one type begins from positive possibilities inherent in God's creation and the other type begins from human limitations due to sin. A second way would be to describe distinctive approaches to political theology according to theological traditions, noting the differences between Catholic, Lutheran, Reformed, Anglican, Anabaptist and Eastern Orthodox political theologies. Third, we can note differences between political theologies by contrasting three distinct approaches within twentieth-century scholarship: Political Theology, Public Theology and Liberation Theology. Finally, it is also important to note more recently emerging schools of thought—what might be considered the second generation of political theologies.[11]

Hence, Assman's ever-changing relationships.

---

[9] Jean Bethke Elshtain, "Augustine," in *The Blackwell Companion to Political Theology*, ed. Peter Scott and William T. Cavanaugh (Oxford: Blackwell Publishing, 2004), 40–41.

[10] Ibid., 42.

[11] Elizabeth Phillips, *Political Theology: A Guide for the Perplexed* (London and New York: Bloomsbury, 2012), 31–32.

Modern Political Theology:
Carl Schmitt

Most scholars would concur that the contemporary phase of political theology is greatly beholden to Carl Schmitt whose classic 1922 *Political Theology: Four Chapters on the Concept of Sovereignty* relaunched the concept and sent it in a new direction. To fully grasp Schmitt's argument, let us look back to Thomas Hobbes, whose *Leviathan* is a work of political theology in its own right. Conceived during the convulsions of the English Revolution of the 1640s–1650s that culminated with the execution of a king and the establishment of a Protestant fundamentalist regime, *Leviathan* ponders the *reason for* and the *proper form of* organized political institutions, namely, the state. Hobbes' premise that humans are essentially selfish and violent and that without restraint their lives would be nasty, cruel, brutish, and short is only too well known. Human nature may create the *need* for, but it does not provide the form of or, more crucially, the *justification* for, the state. Hobbes expressly disallows religion as the foundation of the state, due to the very sectarian strife that tore his country apart and killed its ruler. At the same time, Hobbes finds no "Universal Reason," no absolute or natural law, that would dictate the correct form of government; for the task of politics, rationality is "impotent" and of no assistance. Yet, in the words of Otfried Höffe, "The political community (or 'commonwealth,' as Hobbes would say) must justify itself in the eyes of every individual involved. For if political authority cannot justify itself in this way, it remains nothing but a case of mere force in relation to each individual."[12]

To put it bluntly, and in terms immediately relevant to Schmitt (and hopefully increasingly clearly to Trump), Hobbes asserts that "there is not amongst Men an Universal Reason agreed upon in any Nation, besides the

Fig. 1 The title page of Carl Schmitt's 1922 *Political Theology*

---

[12] Oftried Höffe, *Thomas Hobbes*, trans. Nicholas Walker (Albany, NY: SUNY Press, 2015), 11–12.

Reason of him that hath the Sovereign Power."[13] On the principle of *sed auctoritas, non veritas, facit legem* ("it is authority, not truth, which makes the law") overtly stated in *Leviathan*, Hobbes concludes that "the law is, in fact, the order of the legislator and the order is a declaration of will," and "the civil law is a speech, defined by the will of the State, which commands the individual things that must be done."[14] Ideally, the sovereign ruler is guided by facts and logic, but he is not bound by them, and, in the end, such law or legal institution as actually exists "is an emanation of the will of the sovereign," a "command (*imperatum*)."[15] On a good day, this "artificial reason of the State presents itself as 'universal,' that is, valid for all citizens"—if not for the whole world—"and as 'shared' or—more literally—'which everyone has agreed upon.'"[16] But this agreement or consensus, which will become a "contract" for subsequent theorists like Rousseau and Locke, is a legal and cultural fiction; the sovereign is sovereign because and insofar as s/he gives or promulgates the law. Therefore, there is no law before and independent of the sovereign: "The sovereign is the only legislator and, as such, *he is not himself subjected to the law*."[17] In short, Hobbes maintains that "the sovereign (whether the king or the assembly) stands above the civil law, of which he constitutes the source (partly because, as legislator, *if he wants he can amend it*)."[18]

In this light, the political theology of Schmitt is not unprecedented. Let us first agree with Victoria Kahn that Schmitt was not defending the traditional Christian position that divinity somehow undergirds and justifies the political order; rather, in his analysis, the "absolutist state was *modeled on* but not *legitimized by* reference to the omnipotent God."[19] The question for Schmitt—and it is a more pertinent question today than strictly religious political justification—is the relation between the leader and the law. His *Political Theology* opens with the stunning but oft-quoted line, "Sovereign is he who decides on the exception."[20] This concept of the exception is absolutely central to his political theory. It does not mean emergency declarations or reactions to disaster or war; instead, it refers to the very capacity to give the law *and to take it away again*, that is, to determine when the law applies and when it does not. Law, rather than being the basis for

---

[13] Quoted in Raffaella Santi, "Legal Thought in Early Modern England: The Theory of Thomas Hobbes," *Economics World* 6, no. 5 (2018), 385.

[14] Quoted in Santi, "Legal Thought," 386.

[15] Ibid.

[16] Ibid., 385.

[17] Ibid., 387, emphasis added.

[18] Ibid., 388, emphasis added.

[19] Kahn, *The Future of Illusion*, 14, emphasis added.

[20] Carl Schmitt, *Political Theology: Four Chapters on the Concept of Sovereignty*, trans. George Schwab (Chicago: The University of Chicago Press, 2005 [1985/1934]), 5.

isions, *is the result of political decisions*, specifically the
he sovereign: "The legal order rests on a decision and not on a
\ the exception exposes the contingency of law because law
....ietely prepare for it or "subsume" it. In the moment of
exception, it becomes clear that "all law is 'situational law'":

The sovereign produces and guarantees
the situation in its totality. He has the
monopoly over this last decision.
Therein resides the essence of the
state's sovereignty, which must be
juristically defined correctly, not as the
monopoly to coerce or to rule, but as
the monopoly to decide. The exception
reveals most clearly the essence of the
state's authority. The decision parts
here from the legal norm, and (to
formulate it paradoxically) authority
proves that to produce law it need not
be based on law.[22]

Fig. 2 The title page of Thomas
Hobbes' 1651 *Leviathan*

Nor is law or the authority by which it is made a product of reason or
empiricism. Law, as Schmitt writes elsewhere, "is abstract thought, which
cannot be derived from facts."[23]

Indeed, the political decision arising only from the mind and will of
the sovereign, especially the decision to set aside the law in the first place,
"is analogous to the miracle in theology," and now we begin to approach the
theological element in Schmitt's political theology.[24] This law-giving
capacity, this potency to say the word and make it so, resembles the creative
power of the Judeo-Christian god. This leads Schmitt to assert that "all

[21] Schmitt, *Political Theology*, 10.

[22] Ibid., 13.

[23] Quoted in Arthur Bradley and Antonio Cerella, "The Future of Political
Theology and the Legacy of Carl Schmitt," *Journal for Cultural Research* 20, no. 3
(2016), 211. Original in Carl Schmitt, D*er Wert des Staates und die Bedeutung des
Einzelnen* [*The Value of the State and the Importance of the Individual*] (Tübingen:
Mohr, 1914), 37–38.

[24] Schmitt, *Political Theology*, 36.

significant concepts of the modern theory of the state are secularized theological concepts."[25] In the end, though, he laments that, in the present day under the regime of constitutional law and parliamentary/congressional legislation and case law jurisprudence—aimed at following procedure, preserving the normal, and avoiding or constraining the exception—"all tendencies … point toward eliminating the sovereign in this sense."[26] In a real way, sovereignty as Schmitt envisions it hardly exists, or at least is denied to exist.

The Problem of Legitimation

Carl Schmitt interestingly arrives where Hobbes arrived and quotes him thusly: *Autoritas, non veritas facit legem*—again, "authority, not truth, makes the law."[27] The one with jurisdiction, the position to "speak the law," whether a god or king/emperor/dictator (dictator, literally, is the one who speaks), has authority because s/he is the veritable *author* of legal and institutional reality. Either way—and this is the key—the law, and more broadly the social system, comes from and depends upon something other than and outside of itself. This is what Arthur Bradley and Antonio Cerella call the enduring "mystery of the political."[28] It is not surprising in the slightest that the political mystery would get mixed with the religious mystery.

For much of Western Christian history, and for many Christian scholars and apologists today, this mixture was explicit and literal: the Christian god was the maker and guarantor of the ultimate and eternal law, whether or not particular human political systems conformed to that law. The divine law was the standard by which all temporal law was judged, and divinity was the extra-political source and ground of political society, with its power to violate natural and moral law at will (i.e., the miracle), such natural and moral law being an act of will in the first place.

The issue, in a word, is *legitimation*: *why* should we have this law, *why* should we kneel to this king, *why* does the office of king (or president or prime minister or party chairman, *ad infinitum*) exist at all? I have argued elsewhere that one of the most important functions of religion is just such legitimation, by a variety of strategies.[29] These include *the metaphysics, the model*, and *the mandate*. An example of metaphysical legitimation would be the Hindu-Buddhist concept of karma: if it is simply a feature of reality that

---

[25] Schmitt, *Political Theology*, 36.

[26] Ibid., 7.

[27] Ibid., 52.

[28] Bradley and Cerella, "The Future of Political Theology," 211.

[29] Jack David Eller, *Introducing Anthropology of Religion*, 2nd ed. (London and New York: Routledge, 2015).

actions generate spiritual consequences, then the station of any individual (determined by that person's past actions) in a caste hierarchy or a reincarnation system is justified, as is the social order premised upon it (the caste system). The model refers to the precedent set by the actions of a founding and therefore authoritative figure, like Jesus or Muhammad or Gautama (see the discussion of myth and the paradigmatic acts of spirits and ancestors in Chapter 7). Christians commonly orient their behavior to the model provided by Jesus, sometimes directly pondering, "What would Jesus do?" The words and deeds of Muhammad (the instructions that he received from Allah and the collection of his sayings and rulings, the *hadith* of Islam) provide a still more fully-realized road map for society. Gautama, the original Buddha, set the prototype and laid down many of the rules for the subsequent Buddhist community. The mandate, quite obviously, is the express commands of founding and/or supernatural figures: if a deity said let there be light, or let there be ten commandments, or let there be (heterosexual) marriage, or let there be kings, then so be it.

The problem of the legitimation of authority occupied Max Weber as much as or more than it did Schmitt. Sociologists and political scientists well recall Weber's three forms or sources of authority—traditional, rational-legal, and charismatic. Traditional authority, generally derived from custom or habit and performed in rituals and symbols (again, see Chapter 7), and charismatic authority, experienced as an ineffable personal "gift of grace" and flowing from "revelation, heroism, or other leadership qualities of an individual," are an obvious bailiwick of religion.[30] However, rational-legal authority, encoded in formal offices and written documentation, is no stranger to religion either; the Catholic Church was and is distinguished by extensive office-holding and record-keeping. To be sure, the three versions of legitimate authority are not mutually exclusive and can and often do occur together (along with Weber's other forms of power—persuasion and coercion).

Without perhaps full awareness of the problem and the terms of legitimation, most pre-modern societies naturally turned to religion for its solution. In imperial China, the mandate of heaven secured the emperor's right to rule. In Europe, the divine right of kings achieved the same effect: if a particular person or family was the god's choice for ruler, then that person's/lineage's rule was ordained, and disobedience was tantamount to rebellion against the god. As Western history has abundantly shown, this does not assure smooth cooperation between religion and state: popes, for instance, have claimed the authority to install kings, while kings have asserted their authority to install popes. Martin Luther struggled with and

---

[30] Max Weber, "*Politik als Beruf*" (Politics as a Vocation), *Gesammelte Politische Schriften* (Muenchen, 1921). Originally a speech at Munich University, 1918, published in 1919 by Duncker & Humblodt, Munich.

vacillated on the tension of religion and state, emphasizing at one point "the priesthood of all believers and its equalization of all under the temporal authorities ordained by God" and then advocating in his 1523 *On Secular Authority* a "two kingdoms" perspective, in which Christ's otherworldly kingdom of love and justice contrasts with earthly kingdoms ruined by sin "where secular rulers have authority and must wield the sword to maintain the peace," with control over bodily but not spiritual matters.[31]

In other places and times, politico-religious authority and its legitimation were manifested in different ways. On Pacific and Melanesian islands like Tikopia, *mana* was the currency of efficacy in many undertakings. Chiefs had *mana*, as did great hunters and warriors, indeed anyone who could get things done and to whom others should defer. Arguably a noun, an adjective, and/or an adverb according to Raymond Firth, *mana* was not a property of its wielder; the "only real source of *mana* is in the spirit world. *Mana* does not mean the exercise of human powers but the use of something derived from gods or ancestors."[32]

Another common phenomenon was sacred kingship, in which the person, sometimes the very body, of the king instantiated society and rained potency upon it as he reigned over it. The Merina and Betsileo kingdoms of Madagascar are two of a great many examples where a force not unlike *mana* empowered the king. *Hasina* was a supernatural energy associated with life and reproduction, both human and natural, such as agriculture. Possessing or controlling *hasina* entitled a person to honor and authority, as the application of this mystical power facilitated the functioning of society and nature alike.[33] Among the Shilluk of southern Sudan, royal prerogatives were sanctioned by an ideology that each king was the reincarnation of the original king, participating in his primal authority. Finally, religion anchored the Japanese emperor's right to rule; the island's gods or *kami* spawned a corpus of sacred ceremonies, but this Way of the Gods also provided "the principles of imperial rule; it is a system of correct social and political etiquette; it is the ideal national morality; it is a system of patriotism and loyalty centering on emperor worship ('Mikadoism'); it is, in its pure and original form, a nature worship."[34] In the attendant mythology, the sun goddess Amaterasu-Omikami was the fount of royalty and the veritable ancestor of the human emperor; in the nineteenth century these beliefs and practices were organized into a nationalistic "state Shinto."

---

[31] Phillips, *Political Theology*, 61–62.

[32] Raymond Firth, "The Analysis of Mana," *The Journal of the Polynesian Society* 49, no. 196 (1940), 501.

[33] Maurice Bloch, *Ritual, History, and Power: Selected Papers in Anthropology* (London: The Athlone Press, 1979).

[34] Daniel Clarence Holtom, *The National Faith of Japan: A Study of Modern Shinto* (New York: Paragon Book Reprint Corp., 1965 [1938]), 5–6.

With all this religious legitimation of political authority, it is little wonder that the rise of secular regimes and democracies caused new difficulties in legitimation. When the head of Charles I rolled in 1649, negating and usurping his divine right as king—a Schmittian exception if there ever was one—the question had to be asked: on whose authority was the authority overthrown? When the United States (with its separation of church and state) and then the French revolutionary republic (with its much more virulent anti-clericalism) did away with kings altogether, not only some other form of government but some other legitimation for the government besides tradition and theology was demanded. As Schmitt bemoans, sovereignty would never be the same.

Claude Lefort analyzes this challenge in an influential essay on the alleged permanence of the theologico-political question. Especially following the American and French Revolutions, there was an inevitable and necessary project "to conceive of the state as an independent entity, to make politics a reality *sui generis*, and to relegate religion to the domain of private belief."[35] As Lefort formulates it, in the secular republic "power no longer makes any gesture toward an outside ... it is no longer articulated with any other force that can be represented, and ... in that sense, it is disentangled from the religious."[36] But now we look into the Schmittian/Hobbesian abyss: what is the authority, what is the legitimation, of any law that the secular republic passes—or of the government of the secular republic itself? Granted, there are other potential grounds for political identity and institutions than gods or supernatural forces—like "the nation" or "the people" or reason or nature or other more pestilent ones like class or race, all of which we will meet again soon—but *none of them transcends the society and its mundane politics*. There is no, at least no consistent, necessary, and absolute, Other beyond the society and the government that can serve as bedrock.

The nation/people/class/race and its founding documents like the U.S. Constitution suffice until, like a cartoon character running off a cliff, we look down and discover there is nothing solid under us. In other words, sooner or later we are due for a legitimation crisis, as Jürgen Habermas called it in the 1970s.[37] Consequentially, at almost the same moment, Jean-François Lyotard was probing the "postmodern condition" with its characteristic "incredulity toward metanarratives" or grand stories like

---

[35] Claude Lefort, "The Permanence of the Theologico-Political?" in *Political Theologies: Public Religions in a Post-Secular World*, ed. Hent de Vries and Lawrence E. Sullivan (New York: Fordham University Press, 2006), 149.

[36] Ibid., 161.

[37] Jürgen Habermas, *Legitimation Crisis*, trans. Thomas McCarthy (Boston, MA: Beacon Press, 1975 [1973]).

progress, capitalism, communism, liberalism, and of course theism.[38] Without these rocks to cling to, politics, society, even identity (since Habermas opined that a legitimation crisis "is directly an identity crisis"[39]) is stripped bare for all to see—and to doubt.

Re- (or Un-)Thinking Political Theology in the Twenty-First Century

It is easy to understand, and difficult to dispute, that in the contemporary Western world "the turn to political theology is a way of talking about the crisis of liberal democracy—a crisis of values that derives from liberalism's inability to offer a substantive defense of its own principles, including formal equality, religious neutrality, and religious tolerance."[40] Pointing the way back to political theology, Bradley and Cerella contend that the liberal tradition is subsequently "deemed (both by defenders and critics alike) to be incapable of substantiating its own ontological claims because it surreptitiously appeals to a religious excess that it cannot expunge or metabolize."[41] An added danger, which is far more than theoretical in contemporary global politics, is that, during the "assault on liberalism," democracy itself will suffer and fall either as "collateral damage" or as an intentional target of the crafty demagogue or dictator. As we will also see, though, political theology can be a defense or a weapon in that war.

Whatever the ills of twenty-first century politics, however, political theology is not the requisite prescription, if only, as we have seen, because there is no agreement as to what political theology even prescribes. Bradley and Cerella remind us that thinkers have offered it as anything

> from an unashamed apology for a pre-modern Christian philosophy (John Milbank), a theological genealogy of the modern liberal order (Giorgio Agamben), an irreducible transcendental remainder within the self-definition of the secular (De Vries, 1999), to a necessary fiction or fantasy through which we must pass in order to enter a new radically materialist politics (Slavoj Žižek).[42]

We can summarily dismiss the first offering on that list, for three good reasons. One, various pre-modern (and modern) societies and communities

---

[38] Jean-François Lyotard, *The Postmodern Condition: A Report On Knowledge*, trans. Geoff Bennington and Brian Massumi (Minneapolis: University of Minnesota Press, 1984 [1979]), xxiv.

[39] Habermas, *Legitimation Crisis*, 46.

[40] Kahn, *The Future of Illusion*, 1.

[41] Bradley and Cerella, "The Future of Political Theology," 206.

[42] Ibid., 205.

throughout history have attempted to institute a Christian government, with so little success—and so much disaster—that secularism seemed like a preferable alternative. Two, there is no consensus on what a Christian government or society would be, since (a) there is no consensus on what the relationship between Christianity and government or society should be and (b) there is no consensus *on what Christianity is*. Three, on any construction whatsoever, political theology cannot be equated with Christianity. As our all-too-brief tour of religions illustrated above, and as we will survey in more depth below, Christianity is not the only religion that could underwrite and has underwritten a political community.

This takes us to a more elemental complaint with political theology: it speciously expands "theology"—and more narrowly only Christian theology—to encompass all religion and sometimes even all symbolic or transcendent thought. We cannot, for instance, except in the most metaphorical way, regard Tikopian *mana* or Merino/Betsileo *hasina* as "theology" (if we take that term seriously as "knowledge of god[s]"), and many religions include no gods at all. It is sloppy and presumptuous to use "theology" to label this array of religious concepts; better it might be to use a more generic term like animism (the belief in spiritual beings) or animatism (the belief in spiritual forces) of which gods and their theologies are a subset (see Chapter 8). We must then come down on the side of March, again writing from an Islamic studies perspective, who holds that the term "political theology" is "something of a misnomer.... For there is often little *logos* in political theology, indeed, very little *theos*. Political theology traffics in analogies, symbols, and imputations of meaning. It does not traffic very much in formal theology."[43] Schmitt himself is a prime case of political theology without actual theology.

The situation resembles Samuli Schielke's assessment of the anthropology of Islam, that "there is too much Islam in the anthropology of Islam," in the sense that everything that people in Islamic societies do tends to be blamed on Islam.[44] Likewise, there is too much theology in this misnamed political theology, in the sense that everything that people in political communities do tends to be attributed to their god-concepts. Accordingly, Bradley and Cerella further explain that there is no unity on the supposed relationship between politics and theology (or we should say from now on, religion) in political theology:

> it seems to encompass everything from a formal, structural or homological analogy between the religious and the political, a historical,

---

[43] March, "Genealogies of Sovereignty in Islamic Political Theology," 294.

[44] Samuli Schielke, "Second Thoughts about the Anthropology of Islam, or How to Make Sense of Grand Schemes in Everyday Life," Working Papers No. 2 (Zentrum Moderner Orient, 2010), 1.

genealogical or sociological relation, a psychoanalytic lack, surplus or work of mourning, to a much stronger ontological or metaphysical sense that the religious constitutes a permanent or necessary condition of the political.[45]

Now we near the heart of the matter. Political theology does not, including in the work of Schmitt, refer to literal gods or even to religion. "Every power is transcendent; the Transcendent is power,"[46] writes Schmitt, *but not every instance of power, or of transcendence, is divine.*

How then should we conceive political theology and recover its usefulness for understanding contemporary politics? As Schmitt indicates, and as Newman explicates, "political theology is not so much a problem of religion in modern societies as a problem of *power*—not only ... the power embodied in the concept of sovereignty, but also the new forms of governmental, economic, and technological power that emerge with the modern state."[47] And power is no less mysterious, and no more or less in need of legitimation, when we add or remove god(s).

Victoria Kahn encourages us to contemplate political theology through the concept and practice of "poiesis," by which she means the Hobbesian view that "we can only know what we make ourselves."[48] From this vantage, the problem and mystery of politics is that *we humans* have created political structures—laws, offices, institutions, governments, the state itself—but we do not fully comprehend how or by what right we have done so. What is the authority, what is *our* authority? Understood this way, our political community, indeed our entire social system, is built over a Schmittian or Nietzschean void, and it gives us a bout of Nietzschean nausea to realize it. Few people, of course, ever get that far; they would be like the rare madmen in the streets announcing the death of the Christian god. But the lesson, and a salutary lesson I think, is that the entire project of political theology "is inseparable from reflection on the human capacity for creating artistic fictions, *including the fiction of a theologically grounded political order.*"[49] And this lesson is the very premise of my chosen discipline, anthropology, which teaches that all social facts are human constructions, integrated and perpetuated only because and as long as humans trust them and practice them.

---

[45] Bradley and Cerella, "The Future of Political Theology," 205.

[46] Carl Schmitt, *Glossarium. Aufzeichnungen der Jahre 1947–1951* [*Glossarium. Diaries of the Years 1947–1951*] (Berlin: Duncker & Humblot, 1991), 1801.

[47] Newman, *Political Theology*, 19.

[48] Kahn, *The Future of Illusion*, 3.

[49] Ibid., 21, emphasis added.

So we must take a broader view of political theology than the explicit religious foundations of political order. Political theology, in Kahn's words once more,

> names something more than a structural relationship between, though less than a substantial identity of, politics and theology: the persistent haunting of liberal modernity by something in excess of the law, an exception that is then analogized not only to the miracle, grace, or some other figure of transcendence but also, in the register of immanence, to mere life, creaturely life, biopower or bios.[50]

We can discern more clearly now that political theology, when done with eyes wide open, is precisely an exercise in analyzing the artistic fiction, the artifice, of politics. This analysis recruits religion, to be sure, when partisans of religion enter the field, but it also recruits religion indirectly, almost accidentally, in the form of metaphors and homologies and in the absorption of the discourse of religion. As I gather Schmitt himself recognizes when he declares that all concepts of the modern state are secularized theological concepts, the state or the sovereign is *like* a god in that it/he/she speaks the law into existence by an act of will; *like* a god (in some versions of theism but by no means all), the sovereign can breach the law in a way that is *like* a divine miracle. Or the flaw might be more a matter of confusing part for whole. For instance, in a series of publications Paul Kahn proclaims that the nature and engine of politics is sacrifice: the sovereign is "a hungry god, and we remain willing to feed it our children."[51] Now, while the sovereign and the modern secular state do ask much from us, including sometimes our lives, sacrifice is not the only or essential aspect of religion, let alone of theology, and representing political authority as a bloodthirsty god is the epitome of metaphor or poetry.

Moreover, people cannot help but use the vocabulary at hand, with its connotations and semantic ranges, so terms like power and transcendence evoke a whole religious discourse or frame for people who "speak the language" of, whose consciousness is colonized by, that religion. Thus when a new political formation like a monarchical state or a secular republic emerges, it is almost inescapable that it will adopt some of the language and imitate some of the institutional structures of the ambient religion, resulting in Bradley and Cerrella's historical/genealogical relation above. This is one way of interpreting what Andrew March means when he says that political concepts are transferred from religion *either as presence or absence*, for the absence of a god or other spirit or spiritual force is just as palpable as the

---

[50] Kahn, *The Future of Illusion*, 4.

[51] Paul W. Kahn, *Out of Eden: Adam and Eve and the Problem of Evil* (Princeton, NJ: Princeton University Press, 2007), 210.

presence for people who are culturally and historically attuned to it. In the end, March is correct when he characterizes political theology, now re-imagined, as "a call to explore the symbolic dimension of politics, the crypto-theological origins of political concepts and practices, or the ways in which certain political practices ... come to have meaning for us and other ones do not."[52]

Ironically, there is also too much *politics* in political theology, and definitely too much "state" and "sovereignty." To begin with the latter, "sovereignty" is really not part of the mainstream political debate in the United States today; except maybe for border security (e.g., Trump's wall) and membership in multilateral organizations (e.g., Trump's diatribes against the World Health Organization), Americans do not particularly worry about a loss of sovereignty. Sovereignty is, arguably, a more immediate issue in some European countries under the shadow of the European Union, and sovereignty is a central concept for many Native American peoples in their struggles with and against the American state. Indeed, as Schmitt admits—which is germane to his entire argument—sovereignty in the classical sense of Louis XIV's "*l'état, c'est moi*" no longer exists, and I am not sure that many citizens want it back again.

There is specifically too much "state" in political theology, which is to be expected in a world where the state is the dominant political form. It is not, of course, the only political form in human history and even today has no monopoly on politics or on power more generally. Nicholas Wolterstorff instructs us that the state is a "governance-authority structure" but is certainly not unique in that regard.[53] The state, it is true, enjoys "the authority to govern," but "authority to govern extends beyond governance-authority structures, and authority in general extends beyond authority to govern."[54] We might add, following Weber, that power in general extends beyond either authority or authority to govern, an insight that Michel Foucault develops into a more comprehensive model of *governmentality* or all of the ways in which our conduct is audited, disciplined, and controlled. Governmentality operates both "below" and "above" the state: at the sub- or intra-state level, corporations, educational institutions, medical facilities and many more sites exercise it, while at the super- or trans-state level, it is exercised by multi-national organizations and religions (e.g., the Catholic Church) among others. If there is anything special about the modern state, it is what Wolterstorff describes as its ideology of public governance or of "governing the public" (as opposed to managing merely the employees of a corporation or the devotees of a religion). That is, everyone within its

---

[52] March, "Genealogies of Sovereignty in Islamic Political Theology," 293–94.

[53] Nicholas Wolterstorff, *The Mighty and the Almighty: An Essay in Political Theology* (Cambridge and New York: Cambridge University Press, 2012), 47.

[54] Ibid.

territory is subject to its jurisdiction, its sovereignty, and when "the state issues a directive to the public and someone within the territorial jurisdiction of the state wishes to protest that directive, there is never a procedure for appealing to any institution other than the state itself."[55] That may be the most "divine" of the state's qualities, but it also renders political theology rather moot, as the state negates the basic political-theological claim that there is anything *outside of* or *beyond* the state to which it must explain or justify itself. The modern state, whether or not a hungry god, aspires to be a self-sufficient one.

But our argument here is not about the specialness of the state but about its very unspecialness. The same legitimation problems face pre-state as well as sub-state and trans-state political orders. Ancient and pre-modern chiefdoms and kingdoms dealt with them through devices like *mana* and *hasina* (sometimes practicing sacrifice, including human sacrifice, to display and enact the ruler's power over life and death). Political figures, parties, and institutions deriving their authority from religion, race, ethnicity, class, or any source whatsoever were and are all vulnerable to legitimation crises: all may eventually be called to the stand to justify themselves, and all will find their assertions of power to equally groundless, equally mysterious.

Just as "theology" is a proxy for religion and for symbolism/transcendence in general, "state" is a surrogate for society and social institutions taken in their totality. It is not just the state, or politics or law more broadly, that is at stake and that risks redefinition if not disintegration but any and every social institution and value, including gender categories and roles, racial hierarchies or lack thereof, language, marriage, and the rest. The scope of political theology is too narrow in focusing on government while all of the social order seems to be thrown up in the air, leaving us uncertain about what will land again and in what condition.

All of this takes us to the final point. American politics may be and probably is in a moment of crisis, but few if any Americans encounter it as quite a "legitimation" crisis. Still fewer, as noted, suffer it as a crisis of sovereignty. In fact, if anything, there is *not enough* sovereignty for many Americans, who would fix the problem with walls and bilateral treaties that "win." I am not even sure that we should call it a "political" crisis, let alone a theological or political-theological one (although no doubt theology or religion is in crisis in America too). For most Americans (and other peoples of the world), it is a more diffuse threat, a more generalized anxiety. The experience is less a loss of legitimation/sovereignty than *a loss of stability*. The world is changing, rapidly and not for the better. Things that seemed dependable a generation or two ago—like full-time jobs, pensions, Social

---

[55] Wolterstorff, *The Mighty and the Almighty*, 59.

Security, and such—are fading or already gone. Forces beyond our control, maybe beyond our comprehension, such as globalization and neoliberalism, seem to rule our lives. Other countries that were recently jokes if not nearly unreal ghosts to Americans, such as China and India, are on the rise, while vanquished enemies like Russia are resurgent again, all challenging America's "rightful" place as the dominant and richest country on earth. What was supposed to be "the American century" after victory in the Cold War (who today remembers the hubristic PNAC or Project for a New American Century?) already feels like the American senility.

In a word that social scientists use more frequently these days, life feels *precarious*. This precarity is experienced less at the level of politics and more at the level of economics and of lifestyle. It begins, in the assessment of many scholars, with work and income, or what Andrew Ross calls "the new geography of work." Since the 1970s, with initiatives of down-sizing, right-sizing, off-shoring, etc. employers have eliminated jobs while shifting costs (e.g., the cost of health care or retirement) and risks back onto employees, by providing fewer jobs, fewer benefits, and/or more irregular, contract, or part-time work (including what we have come to call, and to a degree celebrate as, the side hustle or the gig economy, like driving for Uber, renting our homes on Airbnb, or selling on Etsy). Simultaneously, for budgetary as well as ideological reasons, the state is abandoning its function of guaranteeing services and standards of living (e.g., through cutting welfare programs or rescinding regulations and consumer protections). In the estimation of Ross, precarity entails features of low-wage work increasingly intruding into the middle class; the result is heightened vulnerability for individuals and families and, too often, intensified inequality and poverty, leading to the growth of a mass "precariat" (as opposed to proletariat), a population "somehow linked by shared concerns about the insecurity of all aspects of their lives."[56]

While government has certainly not prevented it, government is not exclusively responsible for it, and the reputed "failure" of government is often a matter of expecting the state to do things that it actually cannot do. Corporations, flexing their governmentality, effectively and sometimes intentionally rip the stability from under the feet of workers. Sharryn Kasmir chronicles this phenomenon in an American Saturn automobile factory. Saturn, a subsidiary of General Motors, built a plant in Tennessee, requiring many workers to uproot from their homes and communities in northern "Rust Belt" areas. Then the company got employees to sign contracts separate from the national union, surrendering pay and benefits, while squeezing the small town of Spring Hill, Tennessee for tax relief and free services (road and sewage system). Even at that, Saturn announced that its

---

[56] Andrew Ross, "The New Geography of Work: Power to the Precarious?" *Theory, Culture, & Society* 25, no. 7/8 (2008), 34–35.

decision to build was "provisional," and sure enough in 2009 the plant was shuttered for bankruptcy reorganization, with a plan to reopen with 1,800 employees instead of the original 7,200. Meanwhile those employees had been subjected to various kinds of insecurity. The apparently generous offer of cooperation with management fostered divisions among workers while obfuscating the real divide between labor and management. Non-union subcontractors were hired, and a two-tiered wage scale was established, paying new hires less than incumbent workers. The constant threat of layoffs and plant closures, known as "whipsawing," kept workers and towns nervous, competing against each other for survival. Relocation of workers fractured relationships and communities, while shift work and long commutes strained and often broke marriages. Workers became isolated from their peers, with little socializing outside of work. And host towns realized little benefit from factories, only higher rents, property taxes, and utility costs. In the end, Kasmir concludes, Saturn—and hardly only Saturn—engaged in deliberate "geographic displacement, disorganization, and individualization."[57]

This story, which is just one of a litany of similar tales, demonstrates how far we are from issues of legitimation and sovereignty. Instead, we are deep in the domain of insecurity and a visceral sense of—to use one of Trump's favorite scare words—*losing*. From vacant factories and depressed coal towns to stagnant incomes and opioid epidemics, a large swath of America is less concerned with legitimating the state than with—to use one of Trump's most beloved words—*winning* (or increasing, just surviving). More importantly, our story of American work and American worries illustrates how unsatisfying political theology is as a solution. Even a literal return to a god as the bulwark for the political community does not and cannot address these economic and lifeworld tribulations. It is the wrong tonic for the ailment. More fundamentally, however, a god or a religion cannot provide the missing stability *because religions and gods are as essentially unstable as any other institution or concept.* If, as Michael Freeden argues in our opening epigraph, the goal of politics, and especially of Schmittian sovereignty, is *finality* by means of *decision*—that is, settling the issue or solving the problem once and for all by a decisive act of will— any such finality, whether based on politics or religion, is a chimera. Religions may proffer their gods (or other beings and forces) as the rock of ages, but rocks age and erode too. That is to say, beliefs about any particular god, say the Christian god, change over time, and gods themselves come and go (nobody much talks about securing our government, and definitely not our jobs or social status, with obeisance to Odin or Zeus). At any given

---

[57] Sharryn Kasmir, "The Saturn Automobile Plant and the Long Dispossession of US Autoworkers," in *Blood and Fire: Toward a Global Anthropology of Labor,* ed. Sharryn Kasmir and August Carbonella (New York and London: Berghahn, 2014), 242.

moment, people disagree about what gods are and want, not to mention the disparate and competing religious beliefs in a multicultural society like the United States; in other words, an appeal to the Christian god will not satisfy Muslims, Hindus, or Wiccans and vice versa. And—as history has amply illustrated—gods and all religious beliefs, offices, and institutions are vulnerable to their own legitimation crises; their authority is in no way whatsoever solid and unquestionable, and when questioned they melt into air as surely as any secular authority. So the last thing we need in a time of disbelief and distrust of grand narratives is more credulity.

Looking Forward (to Trump)

This introductory chapter has been an excursion through political theology, with few direct references to Trump, but the relevance has hopefully been evident. Trump is not a king, not even a sovereign, and certainly not a god, and the relation between Trump and religion is oblique at best. He seldom invokes a deity and cannot cite a verse of scripture. His popularity among Christians, particularly evangelicals, suggests that there is something about him that appeals to the faithful, yet he shows no signs of establishing a theocracy or even governing on Christian values (like honesty and charity). Political theology in the strict scholarly sense seems barely applicable to him and his presidency.

Yet, the deeper message of political theology, specifically of the reformed political theology that we have been fashioning here, is highly relevant and revealing. Unless they are taken for granted, accepted and believed without questioning or close inspection, the state, political institutions, and law, and the informal, ubiquitous, and crucial norms and traditions of political and ethical behavior are fragile and easily fractured. A leader with sufficient disregard, even disdain, for them—we are learning with shock and dismay—can consolidate power to ignore and overturn them, pulling the levers of government (the Department of Justice, the courts, the military) against them and against civil society (the media, the two-party system, etc.). Without external, let alone supernatural, support and justification, the state and the law prove to be defenseless against the onslaught of a Schmittian decider, one who, like a sovereign, produces political acts that need not be based on, are heedless of and are unconstrained by, "normal" law. And as both Schmitt and Hobbes apprehend that authority, not truth, drives politics, so truth is no protection against sheer political will. Instead, we get an unobstructed view of the deep non-rationality if not irrationality of politics and of society in general (that is, not driven by facts and logic but by beliefs and values, interest and identity, and emotion; sorry, Habermas, but the public sphere is not exclusively or primarily a space of communicative rationality), where truth is the hapless victim of the exceptional decider, of the perpetual disruption and interminable exception.

In the chapters that follow, we will explore the Trumpian exception in its many locations and formations, tacking back and forth between Trump specifically and political theology—or politics and religion—generally. Some chapters will deal primarily with Trump, some more tangentially, but they will all contribute to an analysis of political power in the present moment. The first chapter examines actual political theologies as they have appeared throughout American history, setting the stage for a character like Trump. This leads to the second chapter and the perennial question of whether Trump really is an exception, an aberration, or a continuation or completion of a long-term trend in American politics. No radical disjuncture or aporia from American political history, we will consider the Trump phenomenon as a "resonant rupture" at most.

To further illustrate the point, the third chapter will take an international perspective, investigating the rise and spread of right-wing populism around the world. Trump accordingly emerges as one incarnation of a global trend, related to equally global economic and cultural forces much bigger than one man or one country. The fourth chapter will subject the Trump phenomenon, which in many ways harkens back to an idyllic (if not imaginary) 1950s America, to an analysis via some of the breakthrough 1950s scholarship on authoritarians, agitators, and true believers by scholars who lived through the traumas of the mid-twentieth century.

The fifth chapter will ask a question that most observers seem to think has been definitively answered: who are Trump's supporters? But a closer inspection teaches us that the appeal of Trump, or at least a vote for Trump, is not as easily understood as we usually assume. Studying "Trumpland" with the ethnographic tools of anthropology reveals not only previously undiscovered details about its denizens but a more refined picture of how politics and identity really work. The sixth chapter turns to one of the signature traits of Trump and his regime, his and their profligate lying, and discusses some reasons why lies are good (or effective) strategy.

The final two chapters return to our reformation of political theology. In the seventh chapter we go beyond theistic propositions and "belief" to interrogate the power of myth and ritual and to relate them to Trump's public performances. And chapter eight transcends gods altogether to propose that other religious/mythical characters might tell us more about Trump the person and politician, namely the shaman and the trickster, who are precisely beings for an uncanny globalized neoliberal present. Shamans and tricksters alert us to the impermanence and abnormality of reality, urging us not to take ourselves or our leaders too seriously while learning to live with disorder and mischief. Not that this knowledge makes Trump's chicanery any more pleasant or acceptable.

1

Political Theologies American Style

We are going to impose Christian values in America again, whether
you like it or not.

—Rick Wiles,
Christian television host
and founder of TruNews[1]

Almost two hundred years ago, Alexis de Tocqueville, still the most
perceptive witness of American society and culture, noted the
omnipresence of religion in the supposedly secular republic: "The
religious atmosphere of the country was the first thing that struck me on
arrival in the United States. The longer I stayed in the country, the more
conscious I became of the important political consequences from this novel
situation."[2] Despite recognizing the political consequences of American
religiosity, he nevertheless assured readers that religion "never intervenes
directly in the government of American society."[3] Indeed, he expressly
cautioned that the alliance between religion and state tends to be
"burdensome" for religion, narrowing its appeal to one party or political
ideology. All the same, for a people deeply dedicated to individual and
national liberty, de Tocqueville reported that Americans see no contradiction
in their religiosity; rather, for them "the ideas of Christianity and liberty are
so completely mingled that it is almost impossible to get them to conceive of
the one without the other."[4]

In order to understand the relation between the election and
administration of Trump and American political theology, it is necessary
first to inquire into the nature of those theologies. That is the project of the
present chapter. The chapter is not an exploration of academic theories and
debates about political theology by American scholars. Instead, it is a

---

[1] Kyle Mantyla, "Rick Wiles: 'We Are Going to Impose Christian Rule in This
Country'," Right Wing Watch, May 17, 2019, https://www.rightwingwatch.org/post/rick-
wiles-we-are-going-to-impose-christian-rule-in-this-country.

[2] Alexis de Tocqueville, *Democracy in America*, ed. J. P. Mayer, trans. George
Lawrence (Garden City, NY: Anchor Books, 1969), 295.

[3] Ibid., 292.

[4] Ibid., 293.

sampling of some of the very many home-grown political-theological enterprises that have arisen on American soil.

I use the term "political theologies" in the plural for the plain reason that there is not and never has been a single American political theology, nor is a single one thinkable (in the U.S. or anywhere else). Both religion and politics in the United States are too diverse for any one political theology to encompass the beliefs and needs of all citizens. Try as they might to finalize political affairs in Freeden's sense, as discussed in the introduction—that is, to establish power and law on a firm and permanent footing—all of the alternatives of religious doctrine and interpretation amount to what Freeden sagely calls *competing finalities*, which defeats the whole point of conclusive political-theological settlement.[5] The possibilities for interaction between religion and government are legion, from actual theocracy to separatist (and sometimes suicidal) cults to "the sacred nation" to state establishment and support of one or more sects or denominations to disestablishment to ceremonial deism to official state secularism and the monitoring or banning of some or all religions. At some time or in some circumstances, Americans have attempted most of these strategies, and other countries in the past and present have practiced all of them.

Americans have been incredibly prolific and creative with their theologies. Philip Jenkins, a historian and author of a veritable library on Christianity, has gone so far as to opine that "extreme and bizarre religious ideas are so commonplace in American history that it is difficult to speak of them as fringe at all," including various apocalyptic and doomsday scenarios.[6] Few if any of these movements had an explicit or systematic political theology, and their religious attachments and aspirations have varied greatly, yet we will find some consistent themes across wildly different beliefs and groups. The most consistent, and most political, of these themes is enthusiastic support for "liberty" and for the instruments of American democracy, most specifically a reverential attitude toward the country's Constitution. Less happy has been the persistent linkage of the American nation with one religion (the particular group's or movement's own version of Christianity) and with one race (usually the white race).

The Problem of Political Theology
in Pluralistic America

The most basic fact shaping (or impeding) political theology in the United States is the country's dizzying religious diversity. According to a recent

---

[5] Michael Freeden, *The Political Theory of Political Thinking: The Anatomy of a Practice* (Oxford and New York: Oxford University Press, 2013), 25.

[6] Philip Jenkins, *Mystics and Messiahs: Cults and New Religions in American History* (Oxford and New York: Oxford University Press, 2000), 5.

Pew Research Center survey, many Americans continue to be Christian (70.6 percent), but this majority contains extensive variation, including:[7]

- 14.7 percent mainline Protestant (e.g., Baptist, Methodist, Lutheran, Presbyterian, etc.)
- 25.4 percent evangelical Protestant (e.g., Pentecostal, Holiness, non-denominational and often "megachurch," etc.)
- 6.5 percent historical Black Protestant
- 20.8 percent Catholic
- 1.6 percent Mormon
- 0.5 percent Orthodox Christian

Therefore, almost thirty percent of Americans do not identify as Christian, including Jews (1.9 percent), Muslims (0.9 percent), Buddhists and Hindus (0.7 percent each), New Age adherents (0.4 percent), and "nones" or individuals without religious affiliation (22.8 percent) such as atheists (3.1 percent) and agnostics (4.0 percent).

Even within this predominantly but decreasingly Christian majority, religious belief and knowledge is inconsistent. A 2016 survey by Lifeway Research (overtly advocating "biblical solutions for life") on behalf of Ligonier Ministries revealed some startling facts about American religiosity:[8]

- Only fifty percent agree strongly that God is a perfect being (sixteen percent agree somewhat—whatever that means—and twenty-five percent disagree somewhat or strongly)
- Fewer, just thirty-seven percent, believe strongly that God is the author of scripture (twenty-one percent agree somewhat, while thirty-one percent disagree somewhat or strongly)
- Less than half, forty-five percent, agree strongly that the biblical resurrection of Jesus is historically accurate (nineteen percent agree somewhat, twenty-two percent disagree somewhat or strongly, and thirteen percent are not sure)
- A mere forty percent agree strongly that Jesus is "truly God" and "truly man" (twenty-two percent agree somewhat, twenty-five percent disagree somewhat or strongly, and fourteen percent are unsure)

---

[7] "Religious Landscape Study," Pew Research Center, 2014, accessed May 19, 2020, https://www.pewforum.org/religious-landscape-study.

[8] "The State of American Theology Study 2016," Lifeway Research, September 1, 2016, http://lifewayresearch.com/wp-content/uploads/2016/09/Ligonier-State-of-American-Theology-2016-Final-Report.pdf.

- More than half (fifty-one percent) agreed strongly or somewhat that the Bible is open to interpretation as the individual chooses

And so forth.

Given all of this difference of opinion, Paul Froese and Christopher Bader infer that Americans ultimately believe in four different gods, or at least hold four different images of the Christian god in their minds. One of these deities they call "the authoritative God," a being "who is both engaged in the world and judgmental"; the second is "the benevolent God" who is "engaged, yet nonjudgmental"; the third or "critical God" is "judgmental, but disengaged"; and the fourth or "distant God" is both nonjudgmental and disengaged.[9]

This array of god-images has correlations with all sorts of other social variables. Women are much more likely to envision a benevolent god than are men; the god of African Americans is dramatically more commonly an authoritative one (over fifty percent) than is the god of whites (around thirty percent). Predictably, authoritative gods are associated with lower education and income and are found more frequently in the South. Equally predictably, and correlated with the previous factors, conservatives tend to hold authoritative god beliefs (sixty-eight percent of authoritative god believers are political conservatives), while liberals lean toward distant gods (and atheists are sixty-three percent liberal and only sixteen percent conservative).[10]

A 2018 Pew Research Center survey paints a still more complex picture of American religiosity. This research suggests a typology of seven kinds of religiosity, organized into three categories. In the "highly religious" category (thirty-nine percent) are the "Sunday Stalwarts," traditionalists who are active and involved in their church; "God-and-Country Believers" who are less active in religion and "tilt right on social and political issues" like the undesirability of immigrants"; and the "Diversely Devout" who accept not only conventional Christianity but also psychics, reincarnation, and spiritual energies. The thirty-two percent classified as "Somewhat Religious" feature the "Relaxed Religious" who may think religion is important but do not believe that regular theistic belief is necessary for a good life and the "Spiritually Awake" who gravitate toward New Age religions. Finally, the nearly one-third (twenty-nine percent) of "Non-Religious" include "Religion Resisters," liberals and Democrats mostly who

---

[9] Paul Froese and Christopher Bader, *America's Four Gods: What We Say About God—& What That Says About Us* (Oxford and New York: Oxford University Press, 2010), 24.

[10] Ibid., 60.

feel that religion is largely a negative force in society, and the "Solidly Secular" who reject religion in any form.[11]

In one last and still more elaborate typology, *The Atlantic* magazine suggests twelve "tribes," arrayed on a Cartesian plane with economic values (liberal to conservative) on one axis and cultural values (liberal to conservative) on the other. The most conservative on both scales is the "religious right," white evangelical Protestants; somewhat less conservative along both variables are the "heartland culture warriors" (white non-evangelical Christians) and "moderate evangelicals." All three of these groups voted overwhelmingly Republican in the 2004 election (the original analysis was published in 2006). In the middle are "convertible Catholics" (non-Latino moderate Catholics), Latino Christians, and "white-bread Protestants." At the liberal (and Democratic) end of the spectrum are the Black Protestants, Muslims and Jews and other, the "spiritual but not religious," the "religious left," and, at the extreme edge of cultural liberalism, the "seculars."[12]

The most comfortable way to erect a sacred canopy over this motley collection of believers (and non-believers) is what Robert Bellah famously dubs "civil religion." In his celebrated essay on American religion, Bellah proposes that "there actually exists alongside or and rather clearly differentiated from the [Christian] churches" another religion which is equally "elaborate and well-institutionalized."[13] A term borrowed from Rousseau's *The Social Contract*, this civil religion is activated on important political or ceremonial occasions. Central to civil religion is the concept of "God," "a word that almost all Americans can accept but that means so many different things to so many different people that it is almost an empty sign."[14] In fact, it may be one of the very few religious concepts that Americans do widely accept (though not the atheists), and even then, as Froese and Bader demonstrate, it is precisely an empty signifier making room for the plethora of god-images. The civil religion, Bellah notes, does not typically refer to Jesus or to other more sectarian and contentious beliefs and doctrines. As he admits, the god of civil religion "is not only rather 'unitarian,' he is also on the austere side, much more related to order, law, and right than to salvation and love."[15] Neither the civil deity nor the civil religion as a whole is "in any specific sense Christian," but neither is the civil god merely a general god, and the civil religion is not a "religion in

---

[11] "The Religious Typology," Pew Research Center, August 29, 2018, https://www.pewforum.org/2018/08/29/the-religious-typology.

[12] "The Twelve Tribes of American Politics," *The Atlantic*, accessed July 20, 2020, https://www.theatlantic.com/magazine/archive/2006/01/the-twelve-tribes-of-american-politics/304505.

[13] Robert N. Bellah, "Civil Religion in America," *Daedalus* 96, no.1 (1967), 1.

[14] Ibid., 3.

[15] Ibid., 7.

general."[16] And obviously, as a religion, this civil religion cannot be "anticlerical or militantly secular."[17]

Why does the U.S. have and need a civil religion in addition to its ubiquitous Christianity? Bellah's answer is first that the American orientation to religion—as a private and basically apolitical matter—means that no sectarian religion, even Christianity, can or should be injected into public affairs. Still, there are moments and circumstances in which a religious invocation seems appropriate if not essential. Bellah thus suggests that civil religion provides a religious sanction to which most Americans can consent. But this does not solve the problem of why a religious sanction is called for at all. His answer is that a society and its institutions require legitimation and transcendental goals. As we have seen, religion not only explains but legitimates social arrangements; in the U.S., where the people are sovereign and their will law (in theory, anyhow), civil religion provides the political-theological service of assuring that "the ultimate sovereignty" lies with a superhuman source. This both secures the goodness and value of laws and institutions and sets a standard for judging and criticizing them: "The will of the people is not itself the criterion of right and wrong. There is a higher criterion in terms of which this will can be judged; it is possible that the people may be wrong. The president's obligation extends to the higher criterion."[18] Further, the sense of transcendental goals means that American decisions and actions are "going somewhere," part of a greater plan and a greater good—literally, that Americans are doing God's work on earth. This makes their history and their policies virtuous and vital.

Even this does not entirely explain the efficacy of civil religion. It is "ceremonial" but not merely for show; like any other religion, its rituals are not empty forms but the embodiment and performance of meanings and goals. The civil religion achieves national solidarity in a way that no other, more sectarian religion quite can because it calls upon "God" as a national symbol—one that, as the greatest of all empty signs, can be filled freely with meaning by all who hear it. In other words, the very fact that the meaning or identity of "God" is not specified allows listeners and participants to hear and feel and believe whatever they want. It does not ask them to believe anything in particular but merely to believe something. As President Eisenhower seems to have understood, the message here is that "Our government makes no sense unless it is founded in a deeply felt religious faith—and I don't care what it is."[19]

However they imagine their god—authoritative, benevolent, critical, distant, or civil—Paul Froese reasons in another paper that "many

---

[16] Bellah, "Civil Religion in America," 8.

[17] Ibid., 13.

[18] Ibid., 4.

[19] Quoted in ibid., 3.

Americans understand God as a political actor; because of this, American political culture mixes religion and political language with fervor, all while keeping church and state institutions separate."[20] If that sounds counterintuitive, verging on contradictory, it will seem less so by the end of this chapter. But Damon Linker concurs, asserting that it is extremely uncommon to encounter an American theology that disputes the "basic legitimacy of American democracy," even if the theology must contort itself or democracy to maintain the affinity.[21] For the vast majority of American political theologies, from Mormonism to the Ku Klux Klan, Christian Identity, and Christian Reconstructionism or Dominionism, these churches and organizations are filled with devotees "who passionately defend American constitutional principles and political institutions but who also interpret these principles and institutions in explicitly theological terms."[22]

Benjamin Lynerd among others insists that this conception and function of religion goes far beyond Bellah's civil religion. Although characterized as "the civil religion of American evangelicals," the *republican theology* that Lynerd describes by no means restricts itself to evangelicals or to Republicans as a political party. Seldom explicitly articulated, Lynerd's republican theology (or what others like Mark Noll have similarly labeled "Christian republicanism") does more political work than Bellah's civil religion. In the American context, it

> holds that God confers the right to liberty on humanity for the purpose of its sanctification: only in free societies can citizens cultivate Christian virtue, and only a virtuous citizenry can sustain a free society. "Liberty is the parent," went a sermon of the Revolutionary era, "of truth, justice, virtue, patriotism, benevolence, and every generous and noble purpose of the soul. Under the influence of liberty, the arts and sciences, trade, commerce, and husbandry flourish and the wilderness blossoms like the rose."[23]

The point of contact between religion and republicanism (as opposed to, say, monarchy, which has certainly been the prevailing political arrangement for most of Christian history) is the notion of liberty or freedom, which republican theology claims is essential not only for the health of religion but of society in general. It is consistent, at least on the surface, with

---

[20] Paul Froese, "Religion and American Politics from a Global Perspective," *Religion* 5 (2014), 648.

[21] Damon Linker, "Political Theology in America," Cato Unbound, October 10, 2007, https://www.cato-unbound.org/2007/10/10/damon-linker/political-theology-america.

[22] Ibid.

[23] Benjamin T. Lynerd, *Republican Theology: The Civil Religion of American Evangelicals* (Oxford and New York: Oxford University Press, 2014), 6.

constitutional guarantees of religious freedom in the sense that government will not impede religion (although not necessarily in the sense that religion will leave government alone). Freedom, in short, is freedom *for* religion, which makes American republican religion a natural ally of limited government.

More, though, republican theology demands a seat for religion at the table of politics, on the premise that individual liberty is part of a system that entails "moral virtue" and the Christian faith specifically. Individual liberty conduces to social order and happiness only if those liberated individuals possess moral virtue (so that they use their freedom wisely), and moral virtue only comes from the teachings and authority (and punishments) of Christianity. In other words, freedom of the American sort will fail without morality, and morality will fail without Christianity. Christianity thus becomes the bedrock on which the American republic stands.

Lynerd traces this line of thinking to the earliest days of English settlement in North America but certainly contends that it was inherent in evangelical thought and speech by the mid-1700s and added a theological dimension to the American Revolution. For instance, John Witherspoon (1723–94) endorsed independence from England on the basis of "the righteousness of a liberated people" and "God's ultimate sovereignty over human events."[24] Benjamin Rush (1746–1813) declared that a Christian must necessarily favor republican government, on the grounds of the inherent equality of all humans under God, on the Christian kindness and humility that is anathema to monarchical and feudal societies, on humanity's God-given sociality, and on the Golden Rule that makes believers "wholly inoffensive" and accordingly fit for liberty.[25] (So much for the divine right of kings!) Founding fathers like Adams, Madison, and Washington (not to mention, much more disastrously, revolutionary France's Robespierre) purportedly appreciated the requirement for a free country to have a virtuous population (Robespierre's "republic of virtue," purchased at the blade of a guillotine).

At least as interesting as these claims is Lynerd's analysis of how free market capitalism, and eventually loyalty to the Republican Party, became part of the republican theological agenda. Beginning with the overthrow of the social gospel and its commitments to economic justice and poverty alleviation by fundamentalists who were focused on individual piety (and thereby a limited government that played no role in social justice), the rise of the Soviet Union and the late-twentieth-century Cold War "created a unique opening in American politics for a party that stood in perfect ideological contrast to global communism."[26] The Democratic Party,

---

[24] Quoted in Lynerd, *Republican Theology*, 86–87.
[25] Ibid., 91.
[26] Ibid., 160.

perceived as comparatively weak on communism (and as committed to non-traditional values like civil rights, women's rights, and, worst of all, gay rights), lost its attractiveness for many American Christians, including evangelicals, who surprisingly "had never before coalesced behind a national political party, and who began the twentieth-century split between free market and Social Gospel factions, migrated to the Republican Party on the strength of its entire platform."[27] Gradually, Christians became more Republican as Republicans became more Christian, until their natural affinities for small government and individual liberty, including free market capitalism, led to the destination that

> republican theology became Republican ideology: the New Right movement sought to scale back the welfare state and the taxes used to fund it, reduce governmental authority over schools and businesses, and appoint judges who would take a stand for traditional morals.[28]

All of these positions were wrapped in a bundle of discourse about "national decline," a decay that "could be reversed through moral, social, and political reform"—specifically, through individual liberty, moral virtue, and Christian faith, the prescription of republican theology.[29] Soon, Jerry Falwell of the Moral Majority was able to proudly announce that the policies of the Republican Party "could easily be the constitution of a fundamentalist Baptist Church."[30]

Some Political Theologies throughout American History

Even before they set foot on North American soil, the pilgrims aboard the *Mayflower* were crafting the lineaments of self-government: in the 1620 "Mayflower Compact," they agreed that their voyage, undertaken "for the glory of God" (although financed by the English merchants of the Plymouth Company), should result in "a civil body politic" for which they should "enact, constitute, and frame such just and equal laws, ordinances, Acts, constitutions, and offices, from time to time, as shall be thought most meet and convenient for the general good of the colony."[31] A decade later John Winthrop gave his memorable sermon, "A Model of Christian Charity," where he enunciated the theological mission of New England to be a

---

[27] Lynerd, *Republican Theology*, 160.
[28] Ibid, 183.
[29] Ibid.
[30] Ibid, 188.
[31] "The Mayflower Compact," MayflowerHistory.com, accessed May 20, 2020, http://mayflowerhistory.com/mayflower-compact.

paragon of Christian society for the world, "a city upon a hill," a phrase revived by Ronald Reagan in the 1980s.[32] Accordingly, religion was codified into law or "established," as in a 1648 code ordering mandatory church attendance, obligatory taxes to support the church, and penalties for those who criticized or violated Christian beliefs and regulations. The 1648 Cambridge Platform of the Massachusetts Bay Colony formally stipulated that the role of political leaders or "magistrates" was to assist and further churches; hence civil authority should use its power to punish idolatry, blasphemy, heresy, and "corrupt and pernicious opinions" in religion. By the end of the seventeenth century, a profession of Christian faith was a requirement to serve in the Massachusetts legislature.

Clearly, long before the United States was incorporated, politics and theology were tightly entangled, and the "disestablishment" of religion written into the First Amendment of the Constitution did not end that entanglement. Prior to the American Revolution, the so-called "First Great Awakening" between 1720 and 1750 re-energized American religion and gave it a distinctly American spin, characterized by a popularization of Christianity (a Christianity of the common people as opposed to institutions and elites) and emphasizing personal faith and choice between a burgeoning assortment of denominations. Throughout American history, to this day, the federal courts have been a site to adjudicate the details of the church/state relationship.

With this background in mind, we will now examine a few varieties of political theology that have appeared since the founding of the United States, all of which are still active today. Ours cannot be an exhaustive catalogue of practical American political theologies; such a task would demand a thick volume or an entire series of volumes. We cannot even hope to exhaust the specific traditions that we introduce. Rather, this representative sample considers a few of the ways in which diverse religious movements have interacted with politics and manifested the republican theology discussed above.

The Mormons:
A Divine Kingdom within the State

Approximately a century after the first Great Awakening, a second Great Awakening erupted across the land. Between 1820 and 1850, a number of movements formed, many with features of "primitive Christianity" (i.e., aiming to return to a simpler form of the faith, more consonant with images

---

[32] John Winthrop, "John Winthrop Dreams of a City On a Hill, 1630," The American Yawp Reader, accessed May 20, 2020, https://www.americanyawp.com/reader/colliding-cultures/john-winthrop-dreams-of-a-city-on-a-hill-1630.

of the original church) with names like "Disciples of Christ" or merely "Christian." Another recurring and related trait was communalism, sometimes giving rise to separatist communities without private property, such as the United Society of Believers (also known as Shakers). A third common element was a kind of spiritualism or transcendentalism that involved prophecy, esoteric knowledge, and specialized states of consciousness such as trance and possession. So many such movements emerged in and swept across western New York that the region has been called "the burned-over district," and one of the most successful and lasting movements born from the flames of the burned-over district was the Church of Jesus Christ of Latter-Day Saints, the Mormons.

Originating from revelations to Joseph Smith in upstate New York in the 1820s, including golden plates that supposedly contained the text of a scripture chronicling a Judeo-Christian civilization in pre-Columbian America—making it a truly *American* brand of Christianity—Joseph (scholars and devotees alike typically refer to the prophet by his first name) settled his growing flock first in Ohio where they raised their original temple in their new "Zion" and established a communal lifestyle called the United Order.[33] In Ohio, then in Missouri, in Illinois, and finally in Utah, the

faithful under Joseph and his successors, like Brigham Young, "sought to create a sociopolitical order that combined the virtues of government by God (theocracy) and by the people (democracy)."[34]

If these sound like clashing values, they are really the essence of republican theology or what Joseph himself called *theodemocracy*. A statement adopted by the church in 1835 taught that "governments were instituted of God for the benefit of man" in order to "secure to each individual the free exercise of conscience, the right and control of property, and the protection of life."[35] The second part of that quotation is standard language from the Declaration of Independence and the Constitution, typifying the republican-theological

Fig. 3 An 1893 engraving by Edward Stevenson of the Angel Moroni delivering the Golden Plates to Joseph Smith in 1827

---

[33] Nels Anderson, *Desert Saints: The Mormon Frontier in Utah* (Chicago and London: The University of Chicago Press, 1966 [1942]), xxxi.

[34] Patrick Q. Mason, "God and the People: Theodemocracy in Nineteenth-Century Mormonism," *Journal of Church and State* 53, no. 3 (2011), 350.

[35] Quoted in ibid., 352.

adoration of America's founding documents. For Mormons then and today, the Constitution is an "inspired document," semi-divine in origin, and America itself is "a special place ... populated by a chosen people for a singular destiny."[36] This destiny includes the instituting of God's kingdom on earth (specifically on American territory), a kingdom which naturally "was ultimately to assume sovereignty over all of the kingdoms of the world."[37]

While America was the vessel of their god's plan, the country around them was corrupt and fallen, in need of a restoration that the Saints could effect. The seed of this revival would be the Mormon "*imperio in imperium*—a religious sovereignty within the civil sovereignty of the United States of America."[38] In Nauvoo, Illinois between 1839 and 1844, the Mormons put theodemocracy into practice, chartering a city where they could construct their "own alternative civil and political institutions as the basis of theocracy."[39] Theodemocracy, in contrast to straight theocracy, supposedly means that God possesses sovereignty and citizens freely consent to and follow the voice of God as expressed through scripture and prophets—suspending divine and human will, theocracy and democracy, in a permanent tension. At Nauvoo, Joseph was chief priest, governor, and commander-in-chief of the militia; he even made a run for the U.S. presidency in 1844, until he was killed in June.

After Joseph's death and the ascent of Brigham Young, the Mormons thought they had achieved their dream of a new Jerusalem along the Salt Lake of Utah. The desert kingdom of Deseret was to be the theodemocratic Mormon state, and the High Council set about promulgating a legal code "for the government of the people in the valley," with statutes prohibiting immoral behavior like idleness, disorderly conduct, adultery and fornication, and drunkenness, cursing, and so forth.[40] In their theodemocratic philosophy, they believed that any just government comes from God and that authority rests with the priesthood; Young was head of the church and also governor (and de facto commissioner of Indian affairs). Even after the U.S. annexed Utah as an American territory, Young and the elders of the church acted as a "ghost government," meeting to ratify the decisions of the official government. But despite efforts to prevent immigration of non-Mormons, "Gentiles" came to Deseret too, creating the perpetual problem of

---

[36] Philip L. Barlow, "Chosen Land, Chosen People: Religious and American Exceptionalism Among the Mormons," *The Review of Faith and International Affairs* 10, no. 2 (2012), 51.

[37] Mason, "God and the People," 354–55.

[38] Alan P. Koenig, "'God is Near': American Theocracy and the Political Theology of Joseph Smith" (PhD diss., City University of New York, 2016): 18, https://academicworks.cuny.edu/gc_etds/1528.

[39] Ibid., 20.

[40] Mason, "God and the People," 84.

religious pluralism for all would-be theodemocracies; conflicts between believers and non-believers, not to mention disputes within the Mormon fold, eventually dashed the dream of an independent Deseret, and Utah (not Deseret) was granted statehood in 1896—oddly, a goal that the Saints had pursued since 1856 but which submerged their godly kingdom within the secular (and decidedly non-Mormon) U.S.A.

The Ku Klux Klan:
The Invisible Empire

According to Mason, the Mormons did not construe their theodemocracy "as competing with the principles of American constitutional democracy, but rather fulfilling them."[41] But as history repeatedly shows, there is more than one way to fulfill a principle, and the vilest and most violent philosophies can abscond with the mantle of democracy and national restoration. The Ku Klux Klan offers an example of a political theology that blends strident nationalism with Christianity, along with a noxious dose of white supremacy.

There have actually been three Klans over American history (or really, many more, as doctrinal and power schisms as well as local autonomy of groups bred multiple instantiations of the Klan), the first rising out of the ashes of the defeated Confederacy in the 1860s. The original Klan, which may have started as a social club for former Confederate soldiers in Tennessee, soon morphed into a vigilante squad bent on preventing freed African Americans from enjoying their new constitutional rights. This Klan, which was not especially religious (no more so than the ordinary Southerner at the time), pushed back against the policies of Reconstruction, eventually employing terrorism to preserve white privilege; it would be crushed by the federal government but would also run out of steam when its main objective was achieved—the end of Reconstruction and the resumption of Southern white rule (with the gradually hardening system of segregation and the "scientific racism" that justified it).

The second incarnation of the KKK grew out of early twentieth-century popular culture. A former Baptist minister turned lecturer and author named Thomas Dixon published a novel titled *The Clansman* in 1905 (subtitled *An Historic Romance of the Ku Klux Klan*). Its partisan portrayal of the Klan as defenders of true America against the forces of (Northern) injustice and barbarism was made into a pivotal feature film, *The Birth of a Nation*, by W. D. Griffith in 1915. Garnering praise and profit, it inspired another former preacher, William Simmons, to revive the Klan as a "benevolent fraternity" which "stressed 100 per cent Americanism and the supremacy of the Caucasian race. It was Protestant rather than anti-Catholic,

---

[41] Mason, "God and the People," 365.

and to favor 'keeping the Negro in his place' was little more than the meaning of the term, Caucasian."[42] Simmons it was who injected the tradition of cross burning to the new KKK during a ceremony on Thanksgiving 1915 (although a cross was burned a few months previously after the lynching of Leo Frank, a Jewish man falsely accused of murdering a young white girl); as Wyn Craig Wade reminds us, "Burning crosses had *never* been part of the Reconstruction Ku-Klux. They had come from the exotic imagination of Thomas Dixon."[43]

But this theatrical touch augured an equally unprecedented injection of religion too. For instance, among the questions posed to a Klan recruit were these:

- "Are you a native-born white, Gentile American citizen?"
- "Do you believe in the tenets of the Christian religion?"
- "Do you esteem the United States of America and its institutions above any other Government, civil, political, or ecclesiastical, in the whole world?"[44]

Indeed, one of the more successful recruiting tools for the renascent Klan was the "church visitation": "A group of gowned and hooded Klansmen would go unannounced into a local church, march solemnly down the aisle, and interrupt the sermon to present the pastor with a substantial donation of money."[45] Donald Chalmers, in his all-too-aptly named *Hooded Americanism*, adds that the pastor himself would be offered a free Klan membership and invited "to take office in the to-be-formed local, either as its chaplain (Kludd) or higher up in the leadership structure. Hundreds upon hundreds did join, and in some areas constituted a major portion of the local officialdom. Others left their flocks for wider Klan calling as either organizers or speakers. *Almost all of the national Klan lecturers were ministers*."[46]

The time was unusually ripe for a Klan marriage to Christianity. Fundamentalism was launched at virtually the same moment, with the series of essays known as "The Fundamentals" released between 1910 and 1915. The new KKK and the new Christian fundamentalism had much in common, particularly a struggle against modernity and its myriad threats to American identity and culture. In fact, Chalmers makes a compelling case that the

---

[42] David M. Chalmers, *Hooded Americanism: The History of the Ku Klux Klan* (Durham, NC: Duke University Press, 1981 [1965]), 30.

[43] Wyn Craig Wade, *The Fiery Cross: The Ku Klux Klan in America* (New York: Simon & Shuster, 1987): 146.

[44] Ibid., 421.

[45] Ibid., 176.

[46] Chalmers, *Hooded Americanism*, 34, emphasis added.

twentieth-century Klan was aggrieved equally or less by traditional black/white issues than by the perils of "alien enemies, slackers, idlers, strike leaders, and immoral women," especially in the shadow of World War I and the sudden advent of the Soviet Union.[47] To the provocations of "the Negro, Jew, Oriental, Roman Catholic and alien, were added dope, bootlegging, graft, night clubs and road houses, violation of the Sabbath, unfair business dealings, sex, marital 'goings-on,' and scandalous behavior as the proper concern of the one-hundred-percent American."[48]

One of the most interesting actions of the KKK was its process of burrowing into Christianity and sharing its legitimation. Burnt crosses and suborned ministers were the least of their tactics. Lynn Neal, for instance, describes how the books of Alma White (*The Ku Klux Klan in Prophecy*, *Klansmen: Guardians of Liberty*, and *Heroes of the Fiery Cross*), and still more so the accompanying illustrations by Branford Clarke, built bridges between Christ and Klan. White's writings insinuated that God "had 'raised up' the Klan to combat the enemies threatening Christian civilization (the United States),"[49] and Clarke's drawings gave visual testimony to the Klan in biblical scenes and to Jesus in contemporary American ones. The message was clear:

Fig. 4 Ku Klux Klan parade, September 13, 1926

Just as Klansmen peopled the landscape of ancient Palestine, they also appeared in the annals of American history. Samuel Adams, Paul Revere, and George Washington joined ranks with Gideon, Samson, and Jesus—they all belonged to the Klan. By merging the American past and the Klan's present, White and Clarke attempted to convince readers of the Klan's legitimacy through its historicity and sanctity. It also served as a call to action.[50]

[47] Chalmers, *Hooded Americanism*, 31.

[48] Ibid., 33.

[49] Lynn S. Neal, "Christianizing the Klan: Alma White, Branford Clarke, and the Art of Religious Intolerance," *Church History* 78, no. 2 (2009), 358.

[50] Ibid., 371.

This appeal was echoed throughout the Invisible Empire, as members fancied themselves, as in Reverend E. F. Stanton's sermon "Christ and Other Klansmen."

The Klan's theology was robust and imaginative, but there was probably more politics than theology in Klan political theology, and it was executed much more successfully than Mormon theodemocracy. Recognizing that the best way to defend the government was to penetrate that government, the KKK supported congenial candidates or ran its own. Many Klansmen or Klan sympathizers filled offices of mayor, councilman, or sheriff across the country; "The Klan also helped elect sixteen men to the U.S. Senate (nine Republicans and seven Democrats), eleven governors (six Republicans, five Democrats), and an unknown number of congressmen."[51] In Indiana it managed to elect the governor, both senators, and influenced both parties during the presidential election of 1924.

Deflated in the 1940s but reborn in the 1960s in outraged reaction to civil rights, liberalism, immigration, and all the normal complaints, the Ku Klux Klan with its virulent composite of nationalism, racism, and religion survives today, arguably stronger than in recent years. (A number of Klansmen in full costume marched in Virginia in July 2020 to protest the removal of a statue of Confederate general Robert E. Lee.) The Knights Party, the public and political face of the Klan congratulating itself as "the premier voice of America's white resistance," declares on its current website (www.kkk.com) that "America was founded as a Christian nation" and "America was founded as a White nation." Further, it encourages "love and appreciation of our unique European (White) culture … as the bedrock of American liberty and self-government." It would restrict immigration (demanding troops on the border to halt illegal immigration), withdraw from the United Nations and multilateral treaties like NAFTA, abolish the Federal Reserve, end affirmative action and gun laws, drug-test welfare recipients, outlaw abortion and homosexuality, "remove the humanist influence in our schools" and grant students the freedom "to practice their Christian faith in the classroom" or else attend private or home schools, and offer the generous gift of "voluntary repatriation of everyone not satisfied with living under White Christian rules of conduct back to the native lands of their people."

Christian Identity:
White American Israel

Taking the religious destiny of the United States to new, and more bellicose, heights is the Christian Identity movement, which seizes the status of God's people, of the true house of Israel, for the white race in general and for American whites in particular. The American version of white chosenness

---

[51] Wade, *The Fiery Cross*, 196.

grew out of Anglo-Israelism or British Israelism, a doctrine espoused as early as 1840, in the midst of Britain's imperial project (imperialism encouraging a strong sense of Western national and racial superiority). Sources like John Wilson's "Lectures on our Israelitish Origin" asserted that the Anglo-Saxon people were the biological descendants of the original ten tribes of Israel, bearing the blessing of that ancient people. The doctrine was transmitted to the U.S. by Howard Rand, who founded the Anglo-Saxon Federation of America in 1930 and is credited with inventing the term "Christian Identity." Part of his philosophy, and that of the movement he launched, was that contemporary Jews were not true Israelites but rather Canaanites; their lost birthright had been transferred to the Anglo-Saxon race.

This new, more elaborate form of religious Americanism attracted many religious leaders such as Gerald Smith and Wesley Swift. Smith established the Christian Nationalist Crusade in St. Louis in 1942 and the America First Party in 1943 (running for president under the latter banner in 1944) and published a magazine titled "The Cross and the Flag" that espoused principles central to the nascent movement—America as a Christian nation, anti-communism, anti-"mongrelization" (mixing of races), anti-world government (e.g., the United Nations), and pro-Constitution.[52] He also planted the notion of the "seed" of Abraham, which would become central to many in the Christian Identity movement, especially Wesley Swift.

Swift, a former promoter of the Ku Klux Klan, opened his Church of Jesus Christ Christian, originally called the Anglo-Saxon Christian Congregation, around the same time. He and his ilk escalated the diatribe against the Jews, demonizing and dehumanizing them as "imposter Israelites" and "a synagogue of Satan"; only "the white Adamic race" possessed "the bloodline of the righteous."[53] This notion grew into the *two-seedline theory* of Jewish and American/Christian/white identity:

In the Biblical story, Eve had had two sons, Cain and Abel. However, Swift declared, only Abel was the child of Adam. The boys were the products of two different seedlines. Israel descended from one of those lines, while Jews were the children of Cain's real father, Satan.[54]

Thus, Jews were more than bad, seeking to replace true Christians in America and globally; they were literally satanic.

---

[52] "The Cross and the Flag: In Memory of Gerald l. K. Smith," The Cross and the Flag, accessed May 22, 2020, http://thecrossandflag.com/articles.html.

[53] Martin Durham, "Christian Identity and the Politics of Religion," *Totalitarian Movements and Political Religions* 9, no. 1 (2008), 80.

[54] Ibid., 81.

Christian Identity has always been more a rallying idea than a centralized organization. Many leaders and groups have sprouted to further its mission, often with gleeful violence. One important figure is Pete Peters, a white supremacist and separatist who moved from the Christian Patriots Defense League to start his own congregation, the LaPorte Church of Christ, in Colorado. Other organizations that splintered from earlier ones include the Church of Israel, Aryan Nations, the Order, and the Covenant, the Sword, and the Arm of the Lord. As Martin Durham puts it, these subsequent groups represent

> Identity at its most apocalyptic. Writing at the beginning of the decade, [Dan] Gayman [head of the Church of Israel] prophesised [sic] a full blown revolutionary onslaught. Unleashed by Jewish "agents of Satan," mobs composed of "white trash, many minority ethnic groups, and millions of Negroes" would bring the country to its knees. An "anti-Christ dictatorship" would emerge, and among those who would perish would be many patriots who believed in God but did not understand His Kingdom. However, "the Saints of the Most High God" would survive, and "the beast system" would not. "The defenders of the faith will have been training and planning for the erection of a free and independent government under God which will assume control and will be the government which will be placed upon the shoulders of Christ when He returns to rule on Earth."[55]

Peters himself did not endorse the two-seedlines theory, viewing Jews more in terms of culture than of race; the real distinction between Jews and Anglo-Saxon Israel was that the true god "wrote his law" only on the hearts of the latter: "Other races do not have the law of God written on their hearts" and so do not participate in the biblical covenant and, contrary to Christianity's ordinary message of love, do not merit the Christian god's love.[56] Nevertheless, he was instrumental in uniting the disparate wings of the white nationalist movement and of propelling them into the armed militia movement with his 1992 "Rocky Mountain Rendezvous" in Estes Park, Colorado. Incensed by the recent attack on Randy Weaver's compound in Idaho, Peters invited 160 members of Aryan Nations, Gun Owners of America, Christian Crusade for Truth, CAUSE (an acronym composed of the first letters of the major white countries or regions—Canada, Australia, United States, South Africa, and Europe), and other organizations to plan a leaderless resistance against non-whites and non-Christians, including and

---

[55] Durham, "Christian Identity," 81.

[56] Ann Burlein, *Lift High the Cross: Where White Supremacy and the Christian Right Converge* (Durham, NC and London: Duke University Press, 2002), 56.

especially the "ZOG" or Zionist-occupied government. The attendees drafted a letter to the Weavers, which read in part:

> Impelled by the spirit of our Heavenly Father, We, 160 Christian men assembled for three days of prayer and counsel, at Estes Park, Colorado. At our gathering the sad events of Ruby Creek [sic] were recounted....
>
> We have not the power to restore to you the loved ones who were cruelly stolen from you! [Weaver's wife Vicki was killed in the FBI raid on Weaver's Ruby Ridge home]
>
> But as Christian men, led by the word of our Heavenly Father, we are determined to never rest while you are in peril and distress!
>
> We are determined to employ HIS strength and to work continually to insure that Vicki and Samuel's mortal sacrifices were not in vain!
>
> We call for Divine Judgment upon the wicked and the guilty who shed the blood of Vicki and Samuel![57]

Surely enough, the Militia of Montana appeared in 1994, whose leader, John Trochmann, had already declared his sovereignty and independence from the United States. This and other armed groups such as the Michigan Militia announced their intention to "stand against tyranny, globalism, moral relativism, humanism, and the New World Order threatening to undermine these United States of America"; Reverend Norman Olson of the Michigan Militia added that, "If this country doesn't change, armed conflict is inevitable ... Who is the enemy? Anyone who threatens us."[58]

Peters summarized the political theology of Christian Identity succinctly in his booklet *Remnant Resolves* which proclaims that his god made the United States "as a nation whose nature IS the Bible": "We recognize that our purpose on the earth is to worship God and enjoy Him forever, and that the highest form of worship is obedience to His Law." As Burlein further documents:

> The first section of Remnant Resolves delineates what, then, one must do to build this vision. The most fundamental building block, according to the pamphlet, is self-government. Yet self-government does not mean democracy. According to *Remnant Resolves*, any government in which men make law enshrines human hubris as a collective King George. Instead, *Remnant Resolves* promotes biblically correct government in which (white Christian) men *administer* laws given by God.[59]

---

[57] Quoted in Morris Dees, *Gathering Storm: America's Militia Threat* (New York: HarperCollins Publishers, 1996), 65–66.

[58] Quoted in Kenneth Stern, *A Force upon the Plain: The American Militia Movement and the Politics of Hate* (New York: Simon & Schuster, 1996), 97.

[59] Burlein, *Lift High the Cross*, 78.

Reconstructionism/Dominionism:
God's Sovereignty and Old Testament Law

> [W]e believe that the Bible should apply to all of life, including the
> state; and … we believe that the Christian state should enforce Biblical
> civil law; and finally … we believe that the responsibility of Christians
> is to exercise dominion in the earth for God's glory.[60]

With Christian Reconstructionism, we pierce to the heart of American
political theology. Shorn of the racism of the Klan and Christian Identity and
of the denominational exclusivism of Mormonism, it connects the two
essential pieces of the political-theological puzzle—law and religion.

Although it has roots in prior theologies, all the way back to
Calvinism (its official creed states that a Christian Reconstructionist is a
Calvinist), contemporary Christian Reconstructionism (CR) is largely the
brainchild of one man, Rousas John Rushdoony, whose 1965 Chalcedon
Foundation and 1973 book *The Institutes of Biblical Law* constitute the
touchstones of the philosophy and the movement. Rushdoony grasps the
political-theological point that "the fundamental question all humans must
face, the inescapable question, concerns authority: what is its source, and
how do we live appropriately according to it."[61] As he sees it, there are only
two options: either humans are the source of their own law and order, or the
biblical god is the source. But since the biblical god is the one absolute and
eternal source of law, then this god is the one source of authority. (He gives
no thought to other religions' gods, let alone other supernatural but non-
divine beings.) Hence, he writes in *The Institutes of Biblical Law*, "We must
conclude therefore that *authority is not only a religious concept but also a
total one*. It involves the recognition at every point of our lives of God's
absolute law-order."[62] In a word—a word that he himself uses—his political
theology is *theonomy*, god-law. The Bible is a book of law, of "case law" in
the formal sense, which leads to his political-religious theory of
dominionism. A Christian Reconstructionist, sometimes also called a
Dominionist,

> takes seriously the Bible's commands to the godly to take dominion in
> the earth. This is the goal of the gospel and the Great Commission. The
> Christian Reconstructionist believes the earth and all its fullness is the

---

[60] "What We Believe," Chalcedon Foundation, accessed May 22, 2020,
https://chalcedon.edu/credo.

[61] Julie Ingersoll, *Building God's Kingdom: Inside the World of Christian
Reconstructionism* (Oxford and New York: Oxford University Press, 2015), 40.

[62] Rousas J. Rushdoony, *The Institutes of Biblical Law* (Nutley, NJ: The Craig
Press, 1973), 218.

Lord's—that every area dominated by sin must be "reconstructed" in terms of the Bible. This includes, first, the individual; second, the family; third, the church; and fourth, the wider society, including the state. The Christian Reconstructionist therefore believes fervently in Christian civilization. He firmly believes in the separation of church and state, but not the separation of the state—or anything else—from God.[63]

To explicate his position more fully, Rushdoony borrows from Calvinist thinker Abraham Kuyper the concept of "sphere sovereignty." Rushdoony posits three distinct and autonomous spheres of authority, as mentioned above—the family, the church, and the state or what he often calls the civil government. The family, as decreed in the Bible, has authority over property and over children, particularly over the *education* of children. Understandably then, he became an influential figure in the struggle for private Christian schools and Christian homeschooling, providing expert testimony for court rulings such as *Ohio v. Whisner et al.* (1976), *State ex rel. Nagle v. Olin* (1980), and *Leeper et al. v. Arlington ISD et al.* (1987).[64]

The church obviously enjoys a separate sovereignty, but Rushdoony's view on the relation between the respective sovereignties of church and civil government is somewhat unusual. (We should note that he holds a fairly sophisticated understanding of "government" as applying far beyond the state to other sites and institutions including the workplace and community or society.) Despite his dominionist slant, in which government and society must be reconstructed on a biblical model, he does not support a theocracy in the ordinary sense. Indeed, he insists that CR is not a "political" initiative at all. The key to the Christian Reconstructionist theory of state is actually the standard political-theological idea of the "limited state" or the "minimal state." The role of the limited state is "the public suppression of evil," in the words of CR scholar Gary North, radical libertarian economist and son-in-law of Rushdoony, in his *Millennialism and Social Theory*:

> The State imposes negative sanctions against evil public acts. The civil magistrate is in fact a minister of God.... But the State is not an agency of salvation. It does not save man by making him positively good.... Christianity teaches that the reform of society must begin with the individual. To sustain a positive reform of society, God must initiate His

---

[63] "The Creed of Christian Reconstructionism," Chalcedon Foundation, accessed May 22, 2020, https://chalcedon.edu/creed-of-christian-reconstruction.

[64] "Christian Reconstructionism," Association of Religion Data Archives, accessed May 22, 2020, www.thearda.com/timeline/movements/movement_27.asp.

transforming grace among many people. He is the agent of positive transformation, not the State.[65]

The problem as Rushdoony formulates it is that "civil government" has expanded to usurp the powers of all the other sites and institutions of government, from family and church to community. A properly reconstructed and severely curtailed civil government would do much less than the modern state does, but the laws of the land—being biblical—would be harsher, featuring Old Testament death penalties for many crimes including homosexuality. Nevertheless, Rushdoony urges patriotism on Christian Reconstructionists in America, evincing the typical republican-theological reverence for the Constitution as a guarantee of equality and religious freedom and in fact a license to propagate Christian social order.

Conclusion:
Republic, Religion, and Trump

We are determined to take our country back.... We are going to fulfill the promises of Donald Trump. That's what we believed in. That's why we voted for Donald Trump, because he said he's going to take our country back.

—David Duke,
former Grand Dragon of the Ku Klux Klan[66]

This admittedly highly limited selection of American political theologies could be extended to include everything from pietistic separatists like the fundamentalists described by Nancy Ammerman in her *Bible Believers*, who simply want as little to do with the outside world as possible;[67] to Amish who live in their anachronistic bubbles; to the Christian Exodus movement (christianexodus.org) that has given up on America and seeks to create its own sovereign Christian society, apparently in South Carolina; to "new religions" such as Scientology or Unification Church; to doomsday cults like Jim Jones' Jonestown; to non-Christians like *shari'a*-practicing Muslims who desire their own laws and courts, just as Jews have the Beth Din of America to adjudicate matters like interpersonal disputes and divorces.

---

[65] Gary North, *Millennialism and Social Theory* (Tyler, TX: Institute for Christian Economics, 1990), 68. The book is available as a free digital volume at https://www.garynorth.com/freebooks/docs/pdf/millennialism_and_social_theory.pdf

[66] Quoted in Libby Nelson, "'Why We Voted For Donald Trump': David Duke Explains the White Supremacist Charlottesville Protests," Vox.com, August 12, 2017, https://www.vox.com/2017/8/12/16138358/charlottesville-protests-david-duke-kkk.

[67] Nancy J. Ammerman, *Bible Believers: Fundamentalists in the Modern World* (New Brunswick, NJ and London: Rutgers University Press, 1987).

Despite the very real differences between our four cases, they suffice to portray some of their common and enduring elements—elements that are shared with political theories that have no explicit theological content (e.g., the ultra-libertarian Free State Project [www.fsp.org], eyeing New Hampshire as the home for Second Amendment constitutionalism, business-friendly tax systems, homeschooling, decriminalization of marijuana, and nullification of odious federal laws like Obamacare and a national identity card). Mormonism, the Klan, Christian Identity, and Christian Reconstructionism all contain a strong dose of Lynerd's republican theology, mingling religion (Christianity) with government (state institutions and the underlying Constitution) and nation (often construed as race). All of them merge these ingredients to promote a vision of a good society—a Great America—that self-consciously grapples with the political-theological issue of authority and legitimation. All of them believe that they have the best intentions for the nation, however "best" and "nation" are defined.

Any astonishment at the ease with which the faithful fuse their religion with patriotism, constitutionalism, and racism can be attributed to two misunderstandings about religion. The first is the common and popular view, arguably inscribed into the Constitution and into Western scholarship, that religion is (or should be) a purely personal private affair and that it is a subject of (propositional) "belief." This view, which makes religious neutrality in the context of religious pluralism more attainable, speciously isolates religion from its many other dimensions, including the public and "political," if we appreciate politics in the political-theological sense as the most basic and pervasive questions of power, authority, legitimation, and social organization. Further, as we argued in the Introduction and as Rushdoony rightly chastises us, "politics" means much more than state or civil government, encompassing all of the ways and means by which we regulate ourselves and each other.

The second misunderstanding of religion is the failure to comprehend its thoroughly modular nature. Like every other aspect of society (and perhaps of reality as well), "religion" is not monolithic, and it most definitely is not merely theism or any one or a few propositional beliefs. A religion is composed of various bits or modules, none of which is essential and all of which are detachable and replaceable; familiar modules like "prayer" or "Bible-reading" or "church attendance" or "ritual" or beliefs in/about gods and heaven and hell, etc. may or may not be present, particularly if we think about religions other than Christianity. Then, since religion is so incredibly modular, "non-religious" modules can attach to "religion" too, among them popular culture, technology, and of course race and nationalism.

Finally, and extrapolating from these two points, "religion" never stays in its assigned religious "slot." Religion diffuses out into the wider society and culture, just as the wider society and culture diffuse into religion.

Religion achieves a sort of *colonization of collective culture and individual consciousness* which means that everyday vernacular concerns and aspirations inevitably shape and are shaped by religion. The most basic concerns and aspirations deal with how we live our lives, how we govern ourselves, and *why* we live and govern as we do—which is the province of political theology.

Where then does Trump belong in this landscape of republican theology? He is not a Mormon or a card-carrying member of the Ku Klux Klan or of any Christian Identity or Christian Reconstructionist group. By any measure, he is hardly a Christian at all. But that has not prevented characters like the KKK's David Duke and other Christian/white nationalist leaders from lyrically praising him and embracing him as one of their own.

As this chapter has illustrated, there is arguably more republic than theology in American republican theology (with ample doses of race, class, gender, and region, to be explored in subsequent chapters). Like Bellah's civil religion, Trump can make the most oblique references to a god or religion—or virtually no reference whatsoever—and still ring the bell of this uniquely American political theology. He can, likewise, emphasize the secular/political elements of republican theology (small government, "freedom," American exceptionalism, etc.) or subtly endorse its racist elements and thereby summon the entire frame of republican theology without uttering a word of theology. Again like civil religion, Trump's calls are sufficiently familiar yet empty that any American so inclined may hear in them almost anything she wants.

American republican theology is a stage, an ecosystem, on and into which Trump walked. For better or worse, it is part of our cultural inheritance. It preceded him, produced him, is perpetuated by him, and will persist after him. This raises the critical Schmittian question of whether and to what extent Trump is an exception in American political history, to which we turn in the next chapter.

2

Trump: Exception or Apotheosis?

[H]ave we now, eight years after Bush left office, elected our first Schmittian President?

—Quinta Jurecic[1]

Let me tell you, the one that matters is me. I'm the only one that matters, because when it comes to it, that's what the policy is going to be. You've seen that, you've seen it strongly.

—Donald Trump[2]

The one question on the minds of nearly everyone, scholar and layperson alike, is whether Donald Trump is really different, an exception, an aporia or break or disjunction in American history. If he is, some applaud his exceptionality, cheering as he topples rotten pillars in American politics and returns the country to the condition—and the people—to which it truly belongs. Detractors, on the other hand, agonize about the permanent damage he does to the republic and about the ruinous precedent he sets for future tyrants and demagogues; for Trump's opponents, he is the end of American democracy.

A recent book by Jon Herbert, Trevor McCrisken, and Andres Wroe assesses the Trump presidency as immanently ordinary.[3] Granting his unorthodox public persona and communication style, they refer primarily to his achievements in office, which they regard as unimpressive and commonplace and relatively consistent with long-time Republican goals (his one signature accomplishment, a tax cut, qualifies for all those judgments). At the same time, Wroe has stated that Trump

> is absolutely incompetent and ineffectual at being a president, with none of the skills required. He can't take advice, he doesn't trust experts and

---

[1] Quinta Jurecic, "Donald Trump's State of Exception," Lawfare, December 14, 2016, https://www.lawfareblog.com/donald-trumps-state-exception.

[2] "Trump: 'I'm the Only One That Matters'," CNN, accessed May 24, 2020, https://www.cnn.com/videos/politics/2017/11/03/trump-im-only-one-that-matters-fox-sot.cnn.

[3] Jon Herbert, Trevor McCrisken, and Andres Wroe, The Ordinary Presidency of Donald J. Trump (Cham, Switzerland: Palgrave Macmillan/Springer Nature, 2019).

he has no idea how to make the presidency work. He sees it as a gameshow where you need to be seen to be winning and everything is funneled through his focus on himself.[4]

Of course, competence or incompetence is not a measure of exceptionality; it is simply a position along the scale of qualification for the job. At the same time, other observers and critics have speculated that his unique interaction and governing style is symptomatic of true deviance, verging on pathology, alternately diagnosed as narcissistic personality disorder, Alzheimer's, or brain damage.

But neither of these points is the subject we are pursuing here: we are not concerned with either his personality or his legislative record. Our question is about power and sovereignty in a democratic republic, albeit one with a deep and often dark tradition of republican theology as explored in the previous chapter. In fact, the question of Trump as exception was the spark that lit the present book in the first place, since "the exception" is the foundational concept in Carl Schmitt's theory of political theology. To what extent does the exceptional Donald Trump fulfill—or aspire to fulfill—the status of a sovereign in Schmitt's sense? Without claiming that Trump has a self-consciously Schmittian political philosophy (or any political philosophy at all), Benjamin Schupmann opines that Trump exploits three of Schmitt's sovereignty factors that "create a serious constitutional danger": the legal discretion that attaches to the declaration of emergencies, the "presumed lawfulness of power holders" which affords an aura of legality on even dubiously legal acts, and the "direct enforceability of those decisions" by the executive, who by definition has the power and duty to enforce the very acts, declarations, and laws that he promulgates.[5]

This highly conspicuous situation has led some observers to sound a more ominous alarm, that Trump "is advancing a particularly self-serving version of that idea [i.e., sovereignty]—one in which he is the sovereign, free not so much from foreign interference, but from the internal institutions that exist to scrutinize and curb his executive power. This kind of sovereignty is an enemy of democracy, not its ally."[6] Yet here too, Trump is

---

[4] Quoted in Sandy Fleming, "Nothing More Than an 'Ordinary President'," University of Kent, March 11, 2019, https://www.kent.ac.uk/news/society/21528/new-book-reveals-donald-trump-is-nothing-more-than-an-ordinary-president.

[5] Benjamin A. Schupmann, "Emergency Powers and Trump: Lessons from Carl Schmitt," Public Seminar, March 22, 2019, https://publicseminar.org/2019/03/emergency-powers-and-trump-lessons-from-carl-schmitt.

[6] Alexis Papazoglou, "Trump Has a Peculiar Definition of Sovereignty," *The Atlantic*, September 28, 2019, https://www.theatlantic.com/ideas/archive/2019/09/trumps-undemocratic-obsession-with-sovereignty/598822.

not alone; he would hardly be the first executive to gather extraordinary powers to himself (from Julius Caesar to Napoleon to Stalin), and Jason Pack is not the only commentator to see that Britain's Boris Johnson displays some of the same tendency to create a "sovereign executive,"[7] not to mention Vladimir Putin and a coterie of demagogues and populists in the world today, as we will discuss further in the next chapter.

The mission of this chapter, then, is to weigh Trump's exceptionality in the light of Schmitt's analysis of the source and exercise of authority through decision-making. It should already be apparent that this is not a simple project. We must transcend the binary distinction between exceptional and unexceptional (just as social scientists must transcend other binaries like traditional/modern); exceptional and unexceptional are not mutually exclusive, and exceptional can be merely the far end of a spectrum. We will see that Trump's implicit—and sometimes explicit—arrogations of executive, even personal, sovereignty are both like and unlike previous presidential reaches and, more importantly and disturbingly, in line with general global political developments. Finally, many of the purposes for which he uses this sovereignty are rather standard conservative, indeed American, fare. He is most assuredly not a force that appeared *ex nihilo*.

Trump the Exception

In some fairly indisputable ways, Donald Trump is an exception as an American president. He is the oldest man ever to assume the office (seventy years old on inauguration day 2017) and probably the richest. He also never previously held elected public office, which is unheard of; we expect the holder of the highest office in the land to have some political experience. Neither has he any military experience, controversially avoiding the draft during the Vietnam War five times (which is *not* entirely unheard of for sons of wealthy families). Of course, he himself, and many of his supporters, proclaim that he is exactly what America needs in its leadership, someone who is not a "normal politician"—not a career politician but has had a career in "the real world" and not someone beholden to special interests (although he is arguably a walking special interest, magnate of a global corporation or multiple global corporations) and someone who is rich enough to fund his own presidential campaign (although he did not and amassed a vast war-chest of donations for his re-election bid, although less than Joe Biden).

Much of the focus in the evaluation of Trump's exceptionality naturally falls on his personality and his communicative practices. In terms of medium, no president has ever used Twitter as extensively as he does

---

[7] Jason Pack, "Johnson and Trump Are Trying to Create Sovereign," Al-Jazeera, October 11, 2019, https://www.aljazeera.com/indepth/opinion/johnson-trump-create-sovereign-executives-191010091924052.html.

(granted that it is a relatively new technology); Barack Obama and political movements like the "Arab spring" enlisted social media effectively too, but deploying Twitter to broadcast short bursts of what can only be considered policy is new (and ironic as well, given Trump's bashing of Hillary Clinton's use of non-secured personal accounts for official business). And much more significant than the medium is the message and the style in which it is delivered. Linguistic anthropologist Adam Hodges perceives a formula in Trump's Twitter tirades, which even before the election had mounted to almost three hundred insults. The basic four-step formula involves (1) selecting from a short list of condescending nouns such as "clown, disaster, dummy, joke, liar," and as we know too well, "hoax"; (2) adding on disparaging adjectives like "biased, boring, corrupt, crazy, crooked, disgraceful, disgusting, dumb, failed ... and, of course, sad, stupid, terrible, weak"; (3) dosing the language with "intensifiers—semantically vacuous adverbs" including "very, totally, so, really" and "100%," often in all caps; and then (4) repeating *ad infinitum*. Facetiously, Hodges anticipates Trump's response tweet to his analysis: "Biased and 100% irrelevant. Has zero credibility. Written by a failing dopey writer. Knows NOTHING! What a clown. Don't read #TrumpedUpWords."[8]

This commentary speaks to the more overarching way in which Trump uses language. He is foul-mouthed and abusive, delighting in sophomoric nicknames for his rivals (crooked Hillary, sleepy Joe [Biden], lying Ted [Cruz], Jeff Flakey [for Jeff Flake], Nervous Nancy [Pelosi], Little Adam Schitt or Pencil Neck [Adam Schiff], Morning Psycho [for Joe Scarborough], and many more.[9] His speech and writing, which he boasts exhibit the eloquence of Lincoln, are closer to the taunts of a badly-behaved seven-year-old. His remarks about women are especially egregious: he has directly or indirectly called women ugly (of Carly Fiorina: "Look at that face, would anyone vote for that?"; Stormy Daniels was "Horseface") or in other instances made crude inappropriate comments like calling Omarosa Manigault Newman, a former White House aide and contestant on his TV game show, a "dog" and a "crazed, crying lowlife" and accusing Democratic congresswoman Maxine Waters of being an "extraordinarily low-IQ person" (not to mention his repeated ethnic slur for Elizabeth Warren, i.e., Pocahontas). Most recently, he recirculated someone else's tweet (a way of delivering an insult without owning it himself) calling Hillary Clinton a "skank."

---

[8] Adam Hodges, "Trump's Formulaic Twitter Insults," *Anthropology News* 58, no. 1 (2017).

[9] See en.wikipedia.org/wiki/List_of_nicknames_used_by_Donald_Trump for an extensive list of nicknames that Trump has spouted at individuals and organizations he does not like.

His narcissism and egoism are well documented. Everything about him and his work is "the best ever," whether it is the attendance at his inauguration, his Electoral College majority, his tax cut, or the medical efficacy of hydroxychloroquine (none of which, empirically, was the biggest or best of its kind). He applies equal and opposite overstatement to the failings and evils of his opponents: Bill Clinton was "the WORST abuser of woman [sic] in U.S. political history," the investigation into his Russia connections was the biggest hoax ever, etc., etc., etc.

Some question his basic intelligence and literacy. Windsor Mann details what he calls Trump's "lethal aversion to reading." Citing Tony Schwartz, Trump's ghostwriter for his acclaimed *The Art of the Deal* who alleged that Trump has not read one book in his entire adult life, Mann goes on to tell us that the president will not even read a daily briefing memo, partly because he gets easily bored and partly because he only wants to hear about himself, another example of his vanity and hubris (and which exploded in the summer of 2020 into another scandal surrounding alleged Russian bounties for American soldiers).[10] And people in the modern world who do not read cannot be well-informed, a prerequisite, one would think, to making good decisions. Accordingly, Kayla Jordan and James Pennebaker measure the quality of analytic thinking in the speeches and writings of all of the presidents, placing Trump dead last with half the analytic score of heroes like Washington, Jefferson, and Lincoln (while, admittedly, noticing an overall downward trend over the past century).[11]

Also well-documented and prominently on display is his penchant for chaos and conflict. Prior to his election, he was frequently dubbed a chaos candidate, someone who likes to stir up controversy if not rancor. He seems to relish being in multiple feuds at the same time, with rivals and allies alike, and may actually indulge in enmity and quarrelsomeness as a governing strategy—not only, as is widely believed, to distract from real problems but more generally to keep his audiences off-balance. Whether it is a cause or an effect, he further seems to make or take everything personally, illustrated by his rejection of a sober study by the National Institutes of Health of the risks of his loudly-praised anti-coronavirus drug of choice, hydroxychloroquine, as "a Trump enemy statement." Similarly, he dismissed research from Columbia University on the grounds that it is "an institution that's very liberal" and that therefore the report is "just a political hit job."

---

[10] Windsor Mann, "Trump's Lethal Aversion to Reading," The Week, May 21, 2020, https://theweek.com/articles/915606/trumps-lethal-aversion-reading.

[11] Kayla N. Jordan and James W. Pennebaker, "The Exception or the Rule: Using Words to Assess Analytic Thinking, Donald Trump, and the American Presidency," *Translational Issues in Psychological Science* 3, no. 3 (2017), 314.

And he lies like no president—maybe no person—in recent memory. His lying is so prolific and gratuitous that it merits a separate chapter of the present book.

As if these traits are not worrisome enough, his approach to governing and to the competencies on which good governance depends are likewise exceptional, which begins to take us to the crux of the Schmittian question of power and sovereignty. Like many scholars and pundits, Quinta Jurecic marvels at his "apparent lack of understanding of the [Constitution's] significance and power as the bedrock of democracy and the rule of law—an understanding that normally commits the President to behaving in a constitutional fashion by heeding the good-faith advice of legal counsel."[12] She explains that observers fretted that George W. Bush demonstrated Schmittian tendencies of operating outside the law but was nonetheless eager to acquire a veneer of legality for his administration's actions (e.g., getting a United Nations resolution to condemn Iraq and launch a war or trying to craft a legally-acceptable definition of torture) and willing to accept judicial rulings against them. Trump comes across as comparatively indifferent to legality and judicial rulings and to the very Constitution itself—which is odd given the reverence with which the charter is held in most republican theologies, as we witnessed in the previous chapter—particularly in regard to the checks-and-balances of three-branch government. Benjamin Schupmann contends that Trump exudes "hostility to the U.S. Constitution with his systematic use of executive powers"—powers, by the way, that he decried when Obama used them—"and privileges in the pursuit of goals antithetical to its basic commitments to liberalism and democracy."[13] Part of this antagonism may flow from a profound lack of knowledge about the Constitution and constitutional government, as when he flippantly pledged fidelity to all of the articles of the document including Article XII *when it only has seven articles*, or when he assumed at the height of the COVID-19 crisis that he had total authority over states, which he does not.

His exceptional disdain for constitutional government results not only or perhaps primarily from ignorance about it as from refusal to accept the limitations to executive sovereignty that it imposes. Jurecic emphasizes, for instance, his "bizarre disregard for the legal protections of criminal procedure," including demeaning judges who rule against him, which is bizarre only if we fail to see the tactical value of such disregard. More troubling, if that is possible, is his insistence that he is above the law, as in his absurd assertion that a president cannot have a conflict of interest and therefore cannot violate the emoluments clause of the Constitution (which

---

[12] Jurecic, "Donald Trump's State of Exception."
[13] Schupmann, "Emergency Powers and Trump."

makes us wonder why the framers put it there), which, Jurecic reminds us, is reminiscent of Richard Nixon's equally ludicrous and self-serving insistence that "When the President does it, that means it is not illegal." A Schmittian sentiment if there ever was one.

In a word, Trump appears to operate, and/or to think he can operate, in an *extraconstitutional* manner unfettered by law, which is the essence of Schmitt's sovereign. He shows a similar disregard for more informal norms and traditions of presidential conduct. Until the coronavirus outbreak in early 2020, he basically eschewed the convention of presidential press conferences or prime-time speeches in favor of his ubiquitous tweets. He has ceased attending the annual White House Correspondents' Dinner because he might hear something that would hurt his feelings. And in a typically petty gesture, he refused to host the customary ceremony for the unveiling of the official White House portrait of his arch-enemy and predecessor; in the last few days, he moved portraits of Clinton and Bush II to an obscure room.

Trump's extraconstitutional and anti-traditional conduct as a refutation of limits to his executive power extends to, and is portrayed most sharply by, his *extra-empirical* conduct, that is, his contempt for facts. Of a piece with his lying, to which we will return later, inconvenient facts—in other words, facts that impede or contradict his policy intentions (in other words, *facts*)—are ignored, contested, denied, or replaced with "alternative facts." Occasionally these antics are mildly amusing, sometimes vexing, and other times potentially deadly, as when he suggested that Americans concerned for their health might ingest chlorine bleach or Lysol (and then attempted to wriggle away from by excusing his words, not for the first time, as a "prank"; perhaps one should not prank one's own country in a time of plague—or ever). This scorn for truth manifests most dramatically in attacks on science, from medical science to climate science—any science that gets in the way of his agenda, power, and profit.

Finally, just as his enemies list teaches us much about his dreams of executive sovereignty, so does his friends list. Without even mentioning the company he keeps in the likes of Steve Bannon or Roger Stone (whose prison sentence Trump lately commuted), he only slightly less-than-openly courts white nationalists, who welcome him as their own, and cozies up to other leaders who are further along the path to executive sovereignty (like Putin, Kim Jong-Un, Rodrigo Duterte of the Philippines, and Jair Bolsonaro of Brazil) while alienating long-time allies in Canada, France, and Germany. Trump said in mid-2018 that he wished that "my people," the American people, would "sit up at attention" the way North Koreans straighten up for Kim. That is every Schmittian sovereign's fondest wish. In the same breath, he unilaterally shreds long-standing international agreements, not only the hated Paris climate accord, Trans-Pacific Partnership (TPP), and North American Free Trade Agreement (NAFTA), but the Intermediate-Range

Nuclear Forces Treaty which helped prevent nuclear war with Russia, the South Korea trade pact KORUS, the UN Human Rights Council (after the United Nations dared to criticize his separation policies for immigrant children), most recently the Open Skies treaty, and other innocuous agreements like the Optional Protocol to the 1961 Vienna Convention on Diplomatic Relations, the UN Educational, Scientific, and Cultural Organization (UNESCO), and the Universal Postal Union. Naturally, he threatened to withhold funding to the World Health Organization for botching COVID-19 and then exited the organization.

Based on the whole body of evidence, Quinta Jurecic and Benjamin Wittes conclude of Trump:

> His approach to governing continues to be authoritarian in character: He lacks any appreciation for the importance of democracy and the necessity of checks on his power. He admires strongmen around the world, as he's expressed again and again in his declarations of affection for leaders such as Russia's Vladimir Putin and Saudi Crown Prince Mohammed bin Salman. The powers of the presidency that he seems to take the most pleasure in exercising are those best suited to aggressive, unilateral wielding and entirely free from constraint—most notably, the pardon power.[14]

However, they wickedly reckon that Trump is prevented from becoming a true Schmittian sovereign by his laziness and lack of concentration and by his evasion of actual responsibility for the consequences of his decisions, best illustrated by his waffling on the coronavirus and related efforts to shove the burden back on the states and their governors, who can then be summarily blamed. This is all consistent, they say, with his "larger management of the executive branch itself, which involves boldly asserting his power but also allowing underlings to contradict him or run their own independent policies much of the time"; what we see in the end "isn't a Schmittian executive. It's an executive that eyes the Schmittian executive enviously before ducking and taking cover."[15]

Trump the Apotheosis

I will suggest that Trump stands firmly within trends in recent American politics and culture. Trump is not the sudden and unexpected eclipse of Obama's sun. Even his most noxious policy moves do not mark a

---

[14] Quinta Jurecic and Benjamin Wittes, "Being an Actual Authoritarian Is Too Much Work for Trump," *The Atlantic*, April 14, 2020, https://www.theatlantic.com/ideas/archive/2020/04/lazy-authoritarian/609937.
[15] Ibid.

fundamental, apocalyptic aporia in American politics. No aberration, Trump is but a representative of American character and culture in the early 21st century.

—Daniel M. Bell, Jr.[16]

In many ways—few of them good—Donald Trump is an exception to our experience and expectation of an American president. That is precisely what many of his advocates like about him. He promised, and they desired, that he would disrupt business as usual in Washington, shake things up, maybe break a few things. By that means, he would return the country to its rightful owners and "make America great again."

Yet, no matter how exceptional they seem, the policies and practices of Trump—including the most Schmittian ones, the ones that tend most strongly toward the sovereign executive—are not a radical break from American political trajectories. Most of Trumpism is, on cool-headed inspection, a furtherance of long-term Republican and conservative activism; much of it is consistent with republican theology. Indeed, we could rightfully apply the theologically relevant term *apotheosis* to much of Trumpism, he and his policies and his personal style representing a culmination or perfection, almost (and in some supporters' minds apparently, literally) a deification, of decades-long trends. And Trumpism could not have taken root unless the soil was fertile for him, which says more about American society and character than about Trump the person and politician. In a serious way, Trump is an effect or symptom more than a cause, and his like (or worse) could follow him now that he has shown the way.

The Ultimate Outsider

As noted, Trump was never an elected official or public servant (or did any kind of public service) before his ascent to the presidency, which is exceedingly unusual. In another way, though, it is consistent with America's odd obsession with the "outsider" as leader. There is something noble about the outsider who has not made a self-serving career out of politics (or at least out of Washington), and many a candidate for public office tries to claim the status of the outsider. An outsider could theoretically also bring fresh ideas to a stuffy and cynical government. So Trump's outsider status is not exceptional in concept, only in breadth: he is the ultimate outsider, never previously sullied by "normal politics."

But there is more than one way to be cynical. Trump in actuality is very far from an outsider: although never an elected officeholder, he is no

---

[16] Daniel M. Bell, Jr., "Trump as Mirror for the Church: Death and Despair, Hope and Resurrection of the Church," *Religions* 11, no. 3 (2020), 2.

stranger to the halls of power, having rubbed shoulders with government and business leaders in New York, the United States, and the world for his entire adult life. He is also, ironically, by any standard a member of the "East Coast elite" that he and his minions belittle, born and raised in New York City, educated at a private boarding school and the Ivy-League Wharton Business School, and ostentatiously rich. So "outsider" is a relative term. (He also likes to tout that he won the highest office on his first foray in politics—making him the most successful candidate ever—but that is not true: he explored running for president on the Reform Party ticket in 2000 but dropped out after polls showed his popularity at seven percent. If you never finish competing, you never lose!)

The Christian Connection

The marriage between American Christians, especially fundamentalists and evangelicals, and the Republican Party has been so unbreakable that we forget it has not always been so. For a long time before and after the Civil War, it was the Democratic Party that reigned in the South and in rural areas (more than a few partisans today still admire the Confederacy as the righteous Christian side in the War Between the States). Even so, Lynerd insists that evangelicals "had never before coalesced behind a national political party" prior to the mid-twentieth century.[17] Only gradually, as the Democratic Party shifted first to support for labor and then, by the 1950s and 1960s, for civil rights, Hispanic rights, women's rights, and most unforgivably gay and abortion rights, did Christians begin to unite around the Republicans. The transition was accelerated by Richard Nixon's "southern strategy" and fulfilled by Ronald Reagan's alliance with the newly-energized Christian Right. So-called republican theology duly became Republican theology.

While it is noteworthy that Trump commanded eighty percent of the evangelical vote in 2016, this result is totally consistent with recent electoral history. Among white evangelicals, Mitt Romney polled seventy-nine percent in 2012, the same proportion as born-again George W. Bush, and just slightly more than John McCain's seventy-three percent in 2008. What *is* fascinating is that, given the choice in 1980 between evangelical Democrat Jimmy Carter and not-especially-religious Republican Ronald Reagan, evangelicals shunned one of their own in favor of someone who, they decided, represented their *interests* rather than their *beliefs*.

Meanwhile, Christianity has stalked the halls of power in America's capitol city. Billy Graham's revivalist saving-America-one-soul-at-a-time approach began to yield to evangelical and fundamentalist activism in the

---

[17] Benjamin T. Lynerd, *Republican Theology: The Civil Religion of American Evangelicals* (Oxford and New York: Oxford University Press, 2014), 160.

1970s, in which Bill Bright of Campus Crusade for Christ was instrumental. Bright "added to his revivalist nationalism a concern for party politics and the political process and the Christian injunction to 'help elect men and women of God in every position of influence.'"[18] Other organizations like James Dobson's Focus on the Family and Jerry Falwell's Moral Majority gave further political clout to evangelical Christians. Less well-known, even shadowy, but more directly oriented toward influencing government are the Faith and Freedom Forum (headed by Ralph Reed, a former leader of Pat Robertson's Christian Coalition) which showers "resources on state legislative races and local initiatives in addition to congressional campaigns and the Republican presidential primary"[19] and two groups committed to not just reaching political leaders but training them in a Christian spirit— Christian Embassy (a project of Bright's old organization, known obliquely today as Cru) and The Family, which launched the National Prayer Breakfast for political and other leaders in 1953 and which Jeff Sharlett characterizes as a movement of "elite fundamentalism, bent not on salvation for all but on the cultivation of the powerful, 'key men' chosen by God to direct the affairs of the nation" and ultimately of the world.[20]

Conservatism Triumphant

Much has been made of the vicissitudes of Trump's personal politics. He was a registered Democrat in 2001 and only switched to the Republican Party in 2009 (after Obama was elected president). Nor has he always held conservative opinions: in a 1999 interview, he expressed no objection to same-sex marriage or gays serving in the military and identified himself as "very pro-choice" on abortion (and openly attributed his liberal positions to being a New Yorker and not from "Iowa").[21] For whatever reason, he came to abandon those positions, and now most of his rhetoric and his administration's policies are well within the realm of contemporary conservatism.

His record of legislation and executive orders reads like a standard conservative wish list, the sorts of changes that conservatives have demanded since the 1980s, if not the 1930s. His every action has been pro-business, anti-tax (with tax cuts particularly for the rich and for

---

[18] Daniel Hummel, "Revivalist Nationalism Since World War II: From 'Wake Up, America!' to 'Make America Great Again'," *Religions* 7, no. 11 (2016), 3.

[19] Lynerd, *Republican Theology*, 190.

[20] Jeff Sharlett, *The Family: The Secret Fundamentalism at the Heart of American Power* (New York and London: Harper Perennial, 2008). 7.

[21] "Trump in 1999," NBC News, July 8, 2015, https://www.nbcnews.com/meet-the-press/video/trump-in-1999-i-am-very-pro-choice-480297539914.

corporations), and anti-regulation. More, this program is in concert with republican theological calls for "limited government." American conservatism has opposed the regulatory state and the welfare state since both were instigated in the mid-twentieth century, and conservatives, mostly through the Republican Party and its auxiliary apparatus of think tanks and well-funded foundations, have been chipping away at those institutions and policies ever since they were introduced.

On the social and "moral" front, the Trump agenda is also an extension and acceleration of established conservative interests and of the "culture war" that has been raging since the 1980s or earlier. Restrictions on abortion and gay rights are weathered planks in the conservative/Republican platform, as are reductions in the social safety net, most recently including concerted efforts to destroy the Affordable Care Act (a.k.a. Obamacare). ("Welfare" as we used to know it was ended in 1996 with the Personal Responsibility and Work Opportunity Act, signed by Democrat Bill Clinton but pushed by congressional Republicans after winning majorities in the House and Senate during the 1994 mid-term elections and Newt Gingrich's "Contract with America," promising tax cuts and welfare reform.)

Although Trump's attacks on neoliberalism and globalization break with recent Republican discourse (conservatives were the first and boldest champions of international market freedom—so long as that freedom benefited America), his undeterred assault on global institutions and trade deals is not foreign to conservative thinking. As soon as the United Nations was formed, conservatives began to demand America's departure (just as America refused to join the post-World War I League of Nations altogether). Despite George H. W. Bush's flirtation with the "new world order" after the fall of the Soviet Union, American conservatives have typically been furiously opposed to multilateralism and the mirage of "world government," both perceived as threats to American sovereignty. And even Trump's treaty-breaking is not unprecedented: besides violating every treaty ever signed with Native Americans, the United States has broken treaties, or failed to ratify or even approve them in the first place, on many occasions, including the 1949 International Labor Convention, the 1954 Geneva Agreement (ending the Korean War), the 1979 Convention on the Elimination of All Forms of Discrimination against Women, the 1982 Law of the Sea, the 1989 Convention on the Rights of the Child (the U.S. being the only country on the planet not to ratify it), the 1996 Comprehensive Nuclear Test Ban Treaty, the 1997 Kyoto Protocol (limiting carbon emissions), and many others. Sometimes the objection is that the agreement restrains American trade and thus wealth; always the objection is that it restrains American external sovereignty.

Corey Robin, author of a historical synopsis of the conservative tradition, goes so far as to reason that Trump is the inevitable outcome of that tradition, its apotheosis (so far). In an interview with Sean Illing of Vox, Robin argues that Trump is the "most successful practitioner of the mass politics of privilege in contemporary America."[22] Robin's book, published in 2011 before the rise of Trump, nevertheless spells out the logic of his success, with profound political-theological implications. In a scathing historical survey looking back as far as Edmund Burke (1729–97), who is commonly credited with siring the modern conservative movement out of horror at the French Revolution, Robin posits that the core of conservatism is not capitalism or some inventory of cultural demands but *power*, more specifically "the felt experience of having power, seeing it threatened, and trying to win it back."[23] And the most elemental aspect of this loss of power is *loss of power to the lower classes*. Conservatism "is the theoretical voice of this animus against the agency of the subordinate classes. It provides the most consistent and profound argument as to why the lower orders should not be allowed to exercise their independent will."[24] In other words, it denies sovereignty to "the people," who are viewed as subordinates and inferiors. Burke himself, according to Robin, accepted that average working-class citizens had "a great many rights….But the one right he refused to concede to all men was that 'share of power, authority, and direction' they might think they ought to have 'in the management of the state.'"[25]

Burke thus offers an answer to the driving question of political theology, albeit a negative answer, that is, where sovereignty and the power of decision are *not* to be located. Conservatives do not so much fear and despise change as *equality* and the political and social *freedom* that such equality would bestow; the consequence of true liberty would be *competition*, the very real possibility of having to share—or worse, temporarily or permanently surrender—power and privilege. Conservatism values hierarchy and opposes "the liberation of men and women from the fetters of their superiors, particularly in the private sphere."[26] Worse, as a movement it believes that the first battle has already been lost: whether it is the Bolshevik proletariat, the Paris mob, the labor union, or the secular humanists, the conservative feels "that the left has been in the driver's seat" for too long; therefore, "if he is to preserve what he values, the conservative must declare war against the culture as it is."[27]

---

[22] Sean Illing, "The Conservative Movement Was Destined to Produce Trump," Vox.com, March 9, 2019, https://www.vox.com/policy-and-politics/2019/3/8/18250087/the-reactionary-mind-trump-conservatism-corey-robin.

[23] Corey Robin, *The Reactionary Mind: Conservatism from Edmund Burke to Sarah Palin* (Oxford and New York: Oxford University Press, 2011), 4.

[24] Ibid., 7.

[25] Ibid., 8.

[26] Ibid., 16.

[27] Ibid., 25.

Accordingly, in Robin's estimation, conservatives have no alternative but to fight. They believe that they are locked "in the arduous struggle for supremacy" where "nothing matters, not inheritance, social connections, or economic resources, but one's native intelligence and innate strength. Genuine excellence is revealed and rewarded, true nobility is secured"; accordingly Burke proclaimed, *"Nitor in adversum* [I strive against adversity] is the motto for a man like me."[28] This accounts for not only the martial character of conservatism but its two main battlefields—military combat and economic competition. The modern conservative hero in times of peace is the captain of industry, the rich entrepreneur, the prosperous businessman. Such conservative paladins are not born with wealth and privilege:

> They seize it for themselves, without let or permission. "Liberty is a conquest," wrote William Graham Sumner. The primal act of transgression—requiring daring, vision, and an aptitude for violence and violation—is what makes the capitalist a warrior, entitling him not only to great wealth but also, ultimately, to command. For that is what the capitalist is: not a Midas of riches but a ruler of men.[29]

The difficulty is that no industrial or post-industrial brahmin can rule by himself; he is always outnumbered by the masses and inevitably needs their acquiescence, if not their cooperation and support (these days, in the form of the vote, the final secular solution to the problem of political theology). The conservative dreamworld "must incorporate the lower orders in some capacity other than underlings or starstruck fans"—although a mass of starstruck fans can carry a political leader very far—so the people "must either be able to locate themselves symbolically in the ruling class" (perhaps by race or religion) "or be provided with real opportunities to become faux aristocrats themselves in the family, the factory, and the field" (which appeals to, and is addressed to, males in particular).[30]

We should easily recognize in this analysis the Trump presidency and the specter of Schmitt. If William Scheuerman is correct in his interpretation, the greatest menace but also asset to Schmitt's sovereign executive is the citizenry, "the people," which "represents an ever-looming presence—if necessary, one that can be mobilized against existing institutions and ordinary political procedures."[31] Now the purported "populism" of Trump (and other global right-wing politicians, to whom we

---

[28] Robin, *The Reactionary Mind*, 29.

[29] Ibid., 30.

[30] Ibid., 35.

[31] William E. Scheuerman, "Donald Trump Meets Carl Schmitt," *Philosophy and Social Criticism* 45, no. 9/10 (2019), 1173.

turn in the next chapter) makes more sense. "The people" must be carefully mobilized and managed, after they have been still more carefully defined; as Trump himself exhorted during a rally in May 2016, the "only important thing is the unification of the people, because the other people don't mean anything."[32] This is why, evidently in America and around the world, present-day right-wing populism "is profoundly anti-liberal":

> As soon as basic rights or the separation of powers impede the unified popular will's (supposed) embodiment in the single person of the leader, they can be pushed aside. When in power, populists remodel legal and constitutional practice according to the adage "for my friends everything, for my enemies, the law." They transform law and courts into discriminatory weapons against their political "enemies," while looking the other way when "friends" skirt the law's boundaries.[33]

By so crippling and weaponizing the law, a huge step is taken toward Schmittian sovereignty. In his at-first-glance exceptional agenda and record, Trump is merely doing what a generation of American conservatives has fantasized about but lacked the will, indiscretion, or hubris to perpetrate.

The Narrative of Loss

Some detractors of Trump have castigated him and his vision of America as nostalgic, but Trump's nostalgia, like that of the wider conservative movement, is no trivial thing. As the very word denotes, what many Americans feel today is a pain for their lost "home" (*nostos* = return home, *algos* = pain). Robin alludes to this quintessential "narrative of loss" and its associated "program of recovery,"[34] but it is not unique to the conservative mind. Rather, the experience of something lost, of something out of joint, of something broken, is at the beating heart of most if not all social movements. Why else move, and in what direction? Irredentist social movements explicitly aim at returning to a lost homeland, of "redeeming" that land, such as Zionism or "greater Serbia." Ethnicity in general can be construed in many instances as a similarly displaced and nostalgic movement; write Remo Guidieri and Francesco Pellizi, "Exile creates 'ethnicities.' No people truly is, *chez soi* [in its own house/place], an ethnic group, because that which defined ethnicity is Difference."[35]

---

[32] Scheuerman, "Donald Trump," 1172.

[33] Ibid.

[34] Robin, *The Reactionary Mind*, 23.

[35] Remo Guidieri and Francesco Pellizi, "Introduction: 'Smoking Mirrors'— Modern Polity and Ethnicity," in *Ethnicities and Nations: Processes of Interethnic*

The United States has been poignantly and peculiarly vulnerable to the power of nostalgia almost from its inception and unmistakably since the late 1800s. The country really did rip apart during the Civil War, inflicting a psychic scar that has not completely healed. Memories of that trauma transformed an antebellum society rather indifferent if not hostile to the past into one comparatively obsessed with its history and its identity. In the years after the 1860s, America was buffeted repeatedly and mercilessly by disorienting and threatening forces, not the least of which was mass immigration. Other changes included urbanization, industrialization, and the first rumblings of a modern labor movement, which would soon crystallize as socialism and Soviet communism. In this environment, as Michael Kammen maintains in his *Mystic Chords of Memory: The Transformations of Tradition in American Culture*, the driving imperative for many Americans in the face of these restless foreign and/or urban and/or working-class multitudes was loyalty, which explains the explosion of new "traditions" in the decades from 1870 to 1920. Kammen writes, "When we look more closely at the passion for tradition on the part of most nativists during the later nineteenth century, we discover a deep-seated resistance to (often resulting from a genuine fear of) change."[36]

It is easy to see—and hard not to see—a nervous and self-conscious invention of tradition, and of the American self and state, in the founding of organizations like Sons of the American Revolution (1889), Daughters of the American Revolution (1890), Mayflower Descendants (1897), and the forgotten but once-influential Grand Army of the Republic (1866) which played an outsized role in the introduction of many familiar patriotic traditions including the Pledge of Allegiance (first performed in 1892), Memorial Day (originally intended to honor the dead of the Civil War *and probably first celebrated in the former Confederacy*), and flag ceremonies of various kinds. These and many more such initiatives were part of a sustained Americanization and assimilation campaign (including innocuous traditions like Mother's and Father's Day) to assuage the anxieties about the imminent loss of the country to "others," non-Americans of various stripes.

Little wonder then, as Richard Hofstadter instructs in a classic essay like Bellah's description of American civil religion but darker, that "American politics has often been an arena for angry minds."[37] Already nearly six decades ago he could say that "we have seen angry minds at work mainly among extreme right-wingers, who have now demonstrated ... how

---

Relations in Latin America, Southeast Asia, and the Pacific, ed. Remo Guidieri, Francesco Pellizi, and Stanley J. Tambiah (Austin: University of Texas Press, 1988), 155.

[36] Michael Kammen, *Mystic Chords of Memory: The Transformation of Tradition in American Culture* (New York: Knopf, 1993 [1991]), 248.

[37] Richard Hofstadter, "The Paranoid Style in American Politics," *Harper's Magazine* (November 1964), 77.

much political leverage can be got out of the animosities and passions of a small minority."[38] This paranoia presents as "exaggeration, suspiciousness, and conspiratorial fantasy" about ominous others, although the specific objects of the conspiracy fears and fantasies have altered over time—Masons, Catholics, African Americans, Communists, Hispanics, Muslims, liberals and secularists, *ad nauseum*. In every case, Hofstadter opines, the paranoid right-wing "feels dispossessed: America has been largely taken away from them and their kind, though they are determined to try to repossess it and to prevent the final destructive act of subversion."[39] Frequently, the government itself is believed to have been infiltrated by the Other and the Enemy, whether communist, Jew, or homosexual. This sense of existential menace and betrayal naturally encourages the suspicious political actor to think that s/he is living on "the barricades of civilization," in a life-and-death struggle with anti-civilization. "The enemy is clearly delineated: he is a perfect model of malice, a kind of amoral superman—sinister, ubiquitous, powerful, cruel, sensual, luxury-loving."[40] Therefore, violence in the defense of America and Americanism is more than merited:

> The paranoid is a militant leader. He does not see social conflict as something to be mediated and compromised, in the manner of the working politician. Since what is at stake is always a conflict between absolute good and absolute evil, what is necessary is not compromise but the will to fight things out to a finish.[41]

Only two years ago, philosopher Martha Nussbaum put the same sentiment in different words, associating America's fear and paranoia with "aggressive 'othering.'" Americans have long feared the foreigner—the Native American, the African slave, the dark-skinned immigrant, the non-English speaker, the non-Christian—but she senses that Americans have new and more amorphous fears today:

> What is today's fear about? Many Americans feel themselves powerless, out of control of their own lives. They fear for their own future and that of their loved ones. They fear that the American Dream—that hope that your children will flourish and do even better than you have done—has died, and everything has slipped away from them. These feelings have their basis in real problems: among others, income stagnation in the lower middle class, alarming declines in the health and longevity of members of this group, especially men, and the escalating costs of

---

[38] Hofstadter, "The Paranoid Style," 77.
[39] Ibid., 81.
[40] Ibid., 85.
[41] Ibid., 84.

higher education at the very time that a college degree is increasingly required for employment. But real problems are difficult to solve, and their solution takes long, hard study and cooperative work toward an uncertain future. It can consequently seem all too attractive to convert that sense of panic and impotence into blame and the "othering" of outsider groups such as immigrants, racial minorities, and women. "They" have taken our jobs. Or: wealthy elites have stolen our country.[42]

America, a historically beleaguered nation, feels unusually beleaguered now, as the ever-resilient American Dream itself seems to be imperiled by forces visible (Mexican immigrants and Chinese corporations) and invisible (neoliberalism, globalization, and Chinese viruses). Add to that the demographic alarm at the perceived ebb of the white race and white/Western culture, in the U.S. and other white/Western countries, and the panic grows in intensity.

In this light, Trump's nativism is understandable but far from original. He and his followers single out many of the usual suspects, including the ever-blamable Jews (Trump himself seldom says a bad word about Jews, other than that they are self-destructive in their attachment to the Democratic Party, but white nationalists in Charlottesville, with Trump's approval, intoned the familiar paranoia when they chanted, "Jews will not replace us.") Trump's very signature rallying cries and

Fig. 5 A button from Ronald Reagan's 1980 U.S. presidential campaign.

slogans are old hat in American politics. "Make America Great Again" is a retread of Ronald Reagan's 1980 campaign slogan, "Let's Make America Great Again" (which is at least an invitation to participation rather than a Trumpian imperative).

"America First" has a yet older and more portentous pedigree. Sarah Churchwell discovers that "America First" has been a political motto for more than a century. Woodrow Wilson used it in 1915 for assigning duties to Americans, with many of its contemporary connotations. For one, newly-arrived immigrants were to relinquish their former identities and place America first in their hearts and minds; for another, American citizens were to put the good of their country ahead of those of the outside world.

---

[42] Martha C. Nussbaum, *The Monarchy of Fear: A Philosopher Looks at Our Political Crisis* (Oxford and New York: Oxford University Press, 2018), 1–2.

(Churchwell even reports that 1915 saw a reference to "fake news."[43]) At its worst, thus, "America First" is not only anti-pluralist and anti-immigrant but isolationist, shading into "America Alone" and, for the world's only superpower, an abdication of global leadership.

Finally, some scholars trace Trump's politics to a very much older tradition in the United States, fully two hundred years past to the worldview of Andrew Jackson. Long before Trump came along, Walter Russell Mead surmised that four streams of political thought pervade American history, one of which is Jacksonian. Its distinguishing traits are populism, a glorification of the "folk" in their rural embodiment, and a preoccupation with honor.[44] In another essay, Mead reckons that Jacksonians "believe that government should do everything in its power to promote the well-being— political, economic, and moral—of the folk community. *Any* means are permissible in the services of this end, as long as they do not violate the moral feelings or infringe on the freedoms that Jacksonians believe are essential."[45] As Taesuh Cha warns in his 2016 study of the return of Jacksonianism (which, of course, never actually went away), this folk politics easily slides into nativism which "imagines the United States as an exclusive ethno-religious community of white Christians."[46]

Sadly, that is the same message that American republican theologies like the Klan and Christian Identity have been selling for decades, with all the predictable negative effects. In its twenty-first century iteration, Jacksonianism manifests as "an illiberal, populist ideological system" escorted to the present via the Tea Party, and "the culmination of this populist, anti-intellectual trend is the victory of Donald Trump," distinguished by "both attacking the U.S. elites and scapegoating a variety of 'others' … as solutions to various present ills, domestic and international."[47] In regard to international relations, Jacksonianism also foreshadows Trump's foreign policy, advocating minimal engagement in global affairs unless America's "national honor" is at stake. Forsaking idealistic projects like spreading democracy or promoting human rights (incidentally, in July 2020, Secretary of State Mike Pompeo actually said that some rights are worth defending and some are not!), Jacksonians like Trump demand respect but are uninterested in, or opposed to, the restrictions of grand multilateral

---

[43] Sarah Churchwell, *Behold, America: The Entangled History of "America First" and "The American Dream"* (New York: Basic Books, 2018), 42.

[44] Walter Russell Mead, *A Special Providence: American Foreign Policy and How It Changed the World* (New York: Routledge, 2000).

[45] Walter Russell Mead, "The Jacksonian Tradition and American Foreign Policy," *The National Interest*, no. 58 (Winter 1999/2000), 8.

[46] Taesuh Cha, "The Return of Jacksonianism: The International Implications of the Trump Phenomenon," *The Washington Quarterly* 39, no. 4 (2016), 83–84.

[47] Ibid., 84, 86, 87.

agreements and grandiose moral principles or international governance structures. Trump talks Jackson's language when he implies that

> the whole architecture of economic multilateralism can be either redesigned or abandoned to initiate an era of bilateralism and protectionism against the long-cherished principle of free trade. In order to turn the United States' "bad" trade agreements that kill U.S. jobs and destroy the middle class into "great" trade agreements, he declared, "I will make individual deals with individual countries. No longer will we enter into these massive transactions, with many countries."[48]

And as time has proven, he will unilaterally abrogate or violate international treaties if he calculates that such behavior will contribute to America's (or his own) "winning."

Conspiracy Theories and Alternate Realities

One of the most disheartening aspects of Trump is his indulgence in conspiracy theories and science (and other fact) denial. For instance, in late 2015 before the presidential campaign heated up, he claimed that he had witnessed "thousands and thousands of people" cheering in the streets as the World Trade Center fell in 2001, even repeating the next day that he had seen it on television, whereas no such thing happened. In spring 2020, he repeated such ugly and patently false rumors as that Speaker of the House Nancy Pelosi, whom he called a "sick puppy" in a March 30 tweet, was "dancing in the streets" over COVID-19 (Trump has a bit of a bug about people celebrating in the streets) and inviting Chinese travelers to enter the country and bring their infection with them; he has blamed rival Joe Biden for wanting to destroy the suburbs and accused "psycho Joe" Scarborough of murdering an assistant in 2001, a woman who fainted from a heart condition and died after hitting her head.

Indeed, Trump made much of his fame peddling conspiracy theories, primarily the "birther" allegation that Barack Obama was born in Kenya and therefore disqualified to run for president. He continuously hypes widespread voter fraud and has echoed disproven connections between vaccines and autism (while ironically taking credit for an elusive COVID-19 vaccine). On the other hand, he regularly reproaches others for promoting conspiracies, not the least of which are the global warming conspiracy, the coronavirus conspiracy (e.g., that the Chinese manufactured the virus in a lab), and the Russian collusion and impeachment "hoaxes." He once said that the noise from windmills causes cancer.

---

[48] Cha, "The Return of Jacksonianism," 89.

It would be some consolation, or we could dismiss Trump as a kook, if conspiracy theories were rare before him, but Americans have been prone to conspiracy thinking for a very long time. Recall that Hofstadter pinpoints conspiracies as of a piece with the paranoid political style: some cabal, often international in scope but frequently having already penetrated and subverted American society—and especially American government—is afoot, whether the Catholic Church, global Jewry, Marxist Communism, or the Illuminati. Remember, in the more feverish conservative mind, *we have already lost or are in the process of losing.*

But conspiracies in America, big and small, multiply and are stubborn to extinguish because they are difficult to refute and because, like any good delusion, they can absorb almost any attempt at disproof (the lack of evidence for the conspiracy is *part of* the conspiracy). And Americans have been spinning out, and falling for, conspiracies for a long time, from communists in the government and behind the Kennedy assassination to fake moon landings, real alien invasions, and insider 9/11 attacks. Despite all experience, a frightening number of Americans believe the earth is flat. The perplexing question is why Americans are so susceptible to unlikely if not preposterous conspiracies, especially when the facts so clearly speak against them. One not-negligible answer is because they are fun; it is entertaining to imagine that aliens walk among us. At the same time, they are scary, which keeps us highly mobilized and attentive. Again, almost any evidence or absence of evidence can be integrated into the theory; conspiracies are wonderfully self-repairing and self-replicating.

But there are much more momentous messages from the political front. Americans, at least since the 1960s, have become intensely distrustful of their government (which is often party to the conspiracy) and of experts of all sorts. This relates to America's extreme individualism and general diffidence toward authority: Americans do not like others telling them what to do, even if it is a doctor advising them to take their medicine (or wear a mask). Facts, in a word, can get in the way of our liberty, including our liberty to believe whatever we want. And politicians and influencers, not exclusively but predominantly on the conservative side, have realized the value of conspiracies—of promoting fear of conspiracies while inventing conspiracies of their own. Kurt Andersen draws our attention to the power of right-wing talk radio and "splenetic" personalities like Rush Limbaugh who serve up daily doses of "sociopolitical alternate reality," only escalated when Fox News began "offering viewers an unending and immersive propaganda experience of a kind that had never existed before."[49] Andersen also uncomfortably attributes a good deal of America's gullibility to religion,

---

[49] Kurt Andersen, "How America Lost Its Mind," *The Atlantic*, December 28, 2017, https://www.theatlantic.com/magazine/archive/2017/09/how-america-lost-its-mind/534231.

since the Republican Party "is now quite explicitly Christian. The party is *the* American coalition of white Christians." But religion notwithstanding, "America simply has many more fervid conspiracists on the right, as research about belief conspiracies confirms again and again. Only the American right has had a large and organized faction *based on* paranoid conspiracism for the past six decades."

Fig. 6 A Trump supporter promoting the QAnon conspiracy known as Pizzagate. The triple parentheses around the name 'Epstein' are an anti-Semitic symbol identifying Epstein as Jewish.

For all these reasons, as Andersen titles his book-length study of American irrationalism, the country and especially its political landscape has become a "fantasyland."[50] The sustenance and political advancement of this collective fantasy is no accident. He sees a "fantasy-industrial complex" at work, spewing alternate realities and bathing vulnerable brains in their corrosive fluid. And Andersen is not alone in despairing of the toxic effects. Philosopher Julian Baggini, among many others, judges that Americans, and Western societies on the whole, "have lost our reason, and our loss is no accident.... We have become suspicious of its claims, unwilling to believe that it can lead us to anything worthy of the name 'truth.'"[51] He further cautions us that "when we give up on reason, the only tool we have left is coercion"[52]—which is probably true if we widen the term to include physical force, psychological force, and force of will.

Andersen thus admonishes us that Trump is no exception to American conspiracism but living proof of it: "People see our shocking Trump moment—this post-truth, 'alternative facts' moment—as some inexplicable and crazy new American phenomenon. But what's happening is just the ultimate extrapolation and expression of mind-sets that have made America exceptional for its entire history."[53] Indeed, Trump "is, first and last, a creature of the fantasy-industrial complex. 'He is P. T. Barnum,' his

[50] Kurt Andersen, *Fantasyland: How America Went Haywire—A 500-Year History* (New York: Random House, 2017).

[51] Julian Baggini, *The Edge of Reason: A Rational Skeptic in an Irrational World* (New Haven, CT: Yale University Press, 2016), 1.

[52] Ibid., 3.

[53] Andersen, "How America Lost Its Mind."

sister, a federal judge, told his biographer Timothy O'Brien in 2005." One appalling point of contact between Trump and the fantasy-industrial complex is the mysterious person/organization/movement known as QAnon. QAnon, which materialized from the murky depths of internet spaces like 4chan, was complicit in the infamous "Pizzagate" conspiracy, which bellowed that Democrats were operating a child-sex ring out of a Washington, D.C. pizza joint called Comet Ping Pong—and actually enflamed one supporter to tote his gun to the location to liberate the children. QAnon and its followers are enthusiastically pro-Trump (some convinced that Q, the anonymous online voice, *is* Trump); they say things like Trump "really opened our eyes to what's happening" or that "the reason I feel like I can trust Trump more is, he's not part of the establishment."[54] And Trump returns the favor: as of late 2019, he had retweeted at least 145 QAnon (and other) conspiracy messages.[55] What do these messages amount to? A vast "deep state" (and anti-Trump) plot that will inspire an unstoppable, worldwide Great Awakening.

The Imperial Presidency

This entire discussion has been circling around the nucleus of Schmitt's political theology, that is, the relationship between the leader and the law. We learned in the introductory chapter that Schmitt's sovereign obeys the law in normal times but also surpasses the law by (1) making the law in the first place and (2) nullifying the law via his/her "monopoly over the last decision" as to when and how the law is applied. This is Schmitt's "state of exception," and the real question for us is not whether Trump is exceptional but whether his presidential actions constitute, sporadically or systematically, a Schmittian ascension over the law.

Like a Schmittian sovereign, Trump regularly asserts extraordinary powers for himself. His use of the executive order has been extensive. He has consistently asserted his authority over the Justice Department, demanding personal loyalty from its staff and treating a willing Attorney General like his personal lawyer. He defies congressional requests and subpoenas and openly criticizes judges who rule against him. Most recently during the coronavirus crisis, he declared that he had "absolute authority" to command the reopening of businesses and schools in the states, actually (and falsely) saying that, "When somebody's the president of the United States,

---

[54] Adrienne LaFrance, "Nothing Can Stop What is Coming," *The Atlantic* 325, no. 5 (June 2020), 33–34.

[55] Ibid., 30.

the authority is total."[56] In the restless summer of 2020 he ordered federal "agents" (un-badged paramilitaries) into cities still tolerating protests and displayed a taste for more such militarization. He alleges his right to keep his tax records from public view before the Supreme Court, which in July 2020 at least partially denied his immunity from investigation. Then, in his battle with Twitter in May 2020, he assumed for himself the power, through executive order, to undo statutory law concerning social media platforms; he said that he would, if he could, shut Twitter down altogether (another irony, as Twitter is his main megaphone).

Under "any reasonable reading of the Constitution or federalism," argues political historian Matthew Dallek, Trump does not have many of the powers he presumes for himself and the presidency, but Dallek puts his finger on the key question when he asks, "What has limited Trump previously? Not very much."[57] If an executive seizes ungranted powers, or exempts him/herself from the limitations placed by law, can the law stop it?

As egregious as Trump's aggrandizement of his powers is, even here we are seeing behavior with historical precedent. The office of president in the United States possesses awesome power in its constitutional construction. It combines all three of Schmitt's sovereignty variables—constitutional authority, the discretion to declare emergencies and assume additional emergency powers, and the role of executing and enforcing its own decisions—in addition to its prerogatives as commander-in-chief of the armed forces and chief diplomat. The president nominates federal judges (including Supreme Court judges), ambassadors, and other office-holders like the head of the Federal Reserve. The president also has the power to veto congressional legislation, which is difficult to override, and is almost impossible to remove from office, requiring a two-thirds majority of the Senate to convict after impeachment (a level that has never been reached in American history). The tradition (untested to this day) that a sitting president cannot be criminally charged places the office virtually beyond the reach of the law. The president's control over a sprawling executive apparatus, including Cabinet officials and an immense bureaucracy and multiple regulatory agencies, enhances the office's reach. The principle of "executive privilege" shields many of the president's actions and decisions—and by extension those of staff members—from public scrutiny. Finally, as the personification of the country, the president enjoys the Theodore Roosevelt's "bully pulpit," from which Trump can act the bully.

Over time, the prerogatives of the presidency have only grown, closely related to America's emergence as a great power and then a

---

[56] Jill Colvin, "Trump Claims Broad Powers He Does Not Have," Courthouse News Service, May 28, 2020, https://www.courthousenews.com/trump-claims-broad-powers-he-does-not-have.

[57] Quoted in ibid.

superpower. Social scientists have long noted that war has a profound centralizing effect, and presidents have gathered more power as war or "national defense" has become a permanent aspect of American politics. For instance, Abraham Lincoln, as commander-in-chief during the utmost national emergency, expanded the army and made exceptions from the law (suspension of habeas corpus, censorship, arrests, martial law) without attempting to base those actions on the Constitution. Instead, he insisted that his extraconstitutional powers were temporary but necessary—the perfect Schmittian exception. Since then, presidents have deployed troops and fought wars (or police actions or whatever you choose to call them) unilaterally. William McKinley ordered American soldiers to participate in the suppression of the Chinese Boxer Rebellion in 1900 without authorization by Congress. Theodore Roosevelt invaded several Latin American countries, and Calvin Coolidge again sent the army into Nicaragua in 1927. Better known are America's two undeclared late-century wars, in Korea and Vietnam; Richard Nixon extended the Vietnam War to Laos and Cambodia not just without congressional approval but without their knowledge, and when Congress ordered an end to American military activity in Southeast Asia, Nixon ignored them, holding that military affairs were the sole prerogative of the president.

Between Nixon's monopoly of war powers, his use of the Justice and Treasury Departments in his own interests (for example, to punish political enemies), and his moves to fire or force the resignation of duly-deputized officials who threatened or defied him (e.g., Special Prosecutor Archibald Cox, Attorney General Elliot Richardson), by 1973 Arthur Schlesinger decided that he was witnessing the birth of an "imperial presidency." In a book by that title, Schlesinger charges Nixon, at the culmination of decades of presidential enlargement, with fomenting

> a new balance of constitutional powers, an audacious and imaginative reconstruction of the American Constitution. He did indeed contemplate, as he said in his 1971 State of the Union message, a New American Revolution. But the essence of this revolution was not, as he said at the time, power to the people. The essence was power to the presidency.[58]

Nixon's wanton ordering of a crime (the Watergate break-in) and subsequent cover-up finally drove him from office, and in 1973, Congress passed the War Powers Act to restrain presidents from engaging the military without congressional approval. Yet a resignation and a congressional act could not deter the steady march toward presidential supremacy.

---

[58] Arthur M. Schlesinger, Jr., *The Imperial Presidency* (Boston: Houghton Mifflin Company, 1973), 252.

Executive orders and secret (if not criminal) behavior can get a president far. But William Howell describes how many other tactics presidents have discovered or invented of late. Remarking first that a president's power extends far beyond mere "persuasion," he adds *executive agreements* (promises with other countries, which unlike treaties do not require ratification) to the presidential tool-kit. Then there are *executive memoranda, determinations, findings, administrative directives,* and *proclamations* as well as (secret) *national security directives.* Stunningly,

> The U.S. Constitution does not explicitly recognize any of these policy vehicles. Over the years, presidents have invented them, citing national security or expediency as justification. Taken as a whole, though, they represent one of the most striking, and underappreciated, aspects of presidential power in the modern era. Born from a truly expansive reading of Article II power, these policy mechanisms have radically impacted how public policy is made in America today. The president's powers of unilateral action exert just as much influence over public policy, and in some cases more, than the formal powers that presidency scholars have examined so carefully over the past several years.[59]

Not mentioned in this analysis are the powers to create or abolish executive branch agencies, to reorganize administrative and regulatory processes, and to determine how legislation is implemented, if at all. As presidents since Reagan have recognized, there are many ways to monopolize power besides undeclared/secret wars or explicit orders. One of Reagan's artifices was "to reduce sharply the role of the federal government in gathering, processing, and disseminating a wide variety of social, economic, and other data"; the banner of cutting the federal budget and limiting the size and role of government (a cherished goal of republican theology) served "as a justification for cutting the budgets of statistical agencies" such as "the Bureau of the Census, Bureau of Economic Analysis, Bureau of Justice Statistics, Bureau of Labor Statistics, Energy Information Administration, National Agricultural Statistics Service, National Center for Education Statistics, and National Center for Health Statistics."[60] Without the data, such agencies could not effectively critique presidential decisions. George W. Bush perpetuated some of the Reaganite tactics of hobbling regulatory and watchdog agencies with budget and staff cuts, going an extra mile by appointing partisan or unqualified heads of such agencies, for

---

[59] William G. Howell, *Power Without Persuasion: The Politics of Direct Presidential Action* (Princeton, NJ and Oxford: Princeton University Press, 2003), 7.

[60] Jarol B. Manheim, *Strategy in Information and Influence Campaigns: How Policy Advocates, Social Movements, Insurgent Groups, Corporations, Governments, and Others Get What They Want* (New York and London: Routledge, 2011), 60.

instance putting industry leaders in important public positions in the Environmental Protection Agency and the like. In other instances, corporations were given oversight over the very agencies that were designed to oversee those corporations. Or, when a finding or ruling went against an industry, the administration would delay the publication of the report or the implementation of any response.

So the presidency is an incredibly powerful office, one that has been accruing power for generations. Trump is the inheritor of that legacy. But Trump is singular in the breath-taking *hubris*, the cavalier disrespect, with which he marshals presidential power and reaches for more. It would be tempting to ascribe his heedlessness of law, tradition, and norm to sheer ignorance, and there is undoubtedly some of that in play, but he has enough advisors (and critics) that he cannot hide behind obliviousness alone. Besides, *why* he flaunts the law is less consequential than *how* he does it, that is, how he manages, in a supposed constitutional republic, to get away with so much lawlessness—if not actually having his way legally, then at least paying so little political price for trying.

The case of Trump's spastic power grabs demonstrates two crucial political-theological truths, which Trump, for all his illiteracy, surely intuits instinctively. The first is that *power exists when and insofar as a will can call it into existence.* For religionists, that will is divine, but it clearly need not be. If a willing agent asserts a power—and even more, successfully exercises a power—then that power is real. Note that we say "successfully exercises," which raises the second truth: *the only force that can block a willing agent is another stronger willing agent.* Here we come to the matter (a) of the Constitution and the constitutional balance of powers and (b) of public opinion, both purported checks on the ambitions of the executive. Two interrelated correlates to the political theology of will and power are, first, that *the law is not an agent and cannot defend itself* and, second, that *the institutions of law are fragile, easily trampled and easily damaged.*

Law exists in books and in minds, but it only acts when people act as the embodiment of law and perform the law (as political office-holders, police, judges, prosecutors, etc.), thereby reproducing and defending it. Schlesinger rightly reckons that the crisis of the imperial presidency follows from the shift in balance of power between the three branches of government. In this sense, there are only two ways that a president can increase power—by decreasing the power of Congress and the courts and/or by co-opting those institutions. Trump, like presidents before him, has actively pursued both. He has stacked federal courts with loyalists and presidential supremacists. In fact, Scheuerman surmises that Trump selected Neil Gorsuch and Brett Kavanaugh for the Supreme Court "as much for their deep hostility to the modern regulatory and administrative states as their conservative views on 'social' issues such as abortion and same-sex marriage."[61] An example of judicial license to swell presidential prerogatives is Kavanaugh's defense of "signing statements"—a tool used prodigiously by George W. Bush at the time when Kavanaugh served as White House staff secretary—which are pronouncements that the executive branch will not honor or enforce rightfully-passed legislation, although the president has signed it, on the basis that the president considers the law unconstitutional. The voice of Schmitt resounds in that sentiment: *the president can decide what is constitutional or not constitutional, which renders the president extra-constitutional or super-constitutional.*

This takes us to the second issue, the fragility and defenseless of institutions. Obviously the Constitution cannot cry out in pain over its mistreatment. As Schupmann understands, "The actual limit of the constitutionally-granted powers of the President and the real guarantee against the abuse of power comes from the willingness of Congress to resist such abuses actively, using whatever legal and political tools it has."[62] But when Congress fails or refuses to exercise its countervailing power—or worse, tacitly or openly *approves* of his (ab)use of power, as the Republican-led Senate currently does—the president is free to act as wildly as he likes: "Through hand-wringing, equivocation, and other forms of inaction, a counter-power surrenders its ability to defend the Constitution." This inaction may, as in the current House of Representatives, result from political calculation (e.g., that standing up to Trump may cost them in the next election), cowardice, ambivalence, or genuine fear of a constitutional crisis of untold proportions (what if the House sent members to arrest the president?!). Recall that the House did muster the courage to impeach Trump, although only on two minor charges. That takes us to the current Senate, which, although part of the legislative check on the presidency, is complicit with this president, down to plotting impeachment trial strategy (basically, hold no hearings) with him.

Schupmann justifiably places much of the onus on the legislative branch, but he is wrong to think that the *only* limit to presidential overreach lies in Congress. The federal courts can countermand, and on occasion have countermanded, Trump's orders, but he has largely filled those courts with sympathizers and partisans. State courts and state governments also constrain a president, constitutionally reserving powers against federal supremacy. And, in a twist of institutions, the sprawl of the executive branch itself poses an obstacle for a grasping presidency. Although Trump often treats it like his private property, the executive branch is full of offices and agencies that monitor and constrict a president, not the least of which is the FBI. Accordingly, Trump has been at war with his own executive branch as much as with the other branches, firing people (first, James Comey, director

---

[61] Scheuerman, "Donald Trump Meets Carl Schmitt," 1176.
[62] Schupmann, "Emergency Powers and Trump."

of the FBI and most recently a series of Inspectors General, whose duty is to monitor functions of government) and intimidating others, motivating them to resign. In an article gloomily titled "The President is Winning His War on American Institutions," George Packer reports the fear, low morale, and attrition in various federal agencies. "In Trump's first year," he writes, "an exodus from the Justice Department began.... Some left in the honest belief that they could no longer represent their client [i.e., Trump], whose impulsive tweets on matters such as banning transgender people from the military became the office's business to justify."[63] Over time, conditions worsened. "The atmosphere of open discussion dissipated.... People began to shut up" and to worry for their jobs. Meanwhile Trump gutted whole departments like the State Department, disbanded teams like the pandemic readiness team, and cut funding for other organizations like the Centers for Disease Control. A hollowed-out executive branch, staffed at the top with cronies and true believers like William Barr and Mike Pompeo, succumbed to Trump's will.

Finally, the last line of defense against presidential misconduct is public opinion, but there too Trump has had little to care about and less inclination to care. He has never been popular—never achieving fifty percent approval during his term—but he seems untroubled. He has a solid forty-something percent base with an almost religious (and in some cases, an actual religious) devotion to him, many of whom are caught in webs of conspiracy thinking themselves. For them, criticism of Trump is essentially proof that the "deep state," the "fake news," and the liberal elites are out to get him. And at the end of the day, anyone who believes (or knows?) that he could shoot someone in broad daylight and not lose any support, as Trump bragged in January 2016, has no reason to fear public opinion.

Trump the Resonant Rupture

Love him or hate him, Donald Trump is a force of nature, a walking Nietzschean will to power. But is he an anomaly, an aporia, an exception? The evidence of history says no. Like John before Jesus, past presidents have made straight the path that Trump walks, and the other institutions of American government and society have displayed little will, and less ability, to stop them and him. Trump's so-called exceptionalism is more rightly extremity, discovering or devising presidential powers that no predecessor dared. He shows how a constitutional republic remains vulnerable to Schmittian aspirations of unfettered sovereignty.

---

[63] George Packer, "The President is Winning His War on American Institutions," *The Atlantic*, April 2020, https://www.theatlantic.com/magazine/archive/2020/04/how-to-destroy-a-government/606793.

In conclusion, to think in new ways about political theology, about continuity and discontinuity, about exception and apotheosis, I suggest a theological concept from a radically different context. In her study of Christianity, specifically Pentecostalism, among contemporary Navajos, Kimberly Marshall introduces the term "resonant rupture." Resonant rupture looks "beyond theologies and doctrines to see how continuity and rupture are navigated ... in performance," resulting in a form of behavior or organization that "is neither wholly assimilative nor wholly traditional but is a type of rupture enriched by 'feelingfully' familiar aesthetic forms."[64] It is perhaps distasteful to dignify Trump's power-hunger with the label "aesthetic," but in the sense of the "feel" of the office and his performance in it, the term is apt. To all Americans, the imperial presidency is a familiar and desirable aesthetic form, and to many Americans, Trump's personal brand of chest-thumping and grievance-moaning bravado feels good—honest, authentic, tough, and sticking-it-to-the-system.

Just as resonant rupture permits Navajos to practice Christian Pentecostalism without a complete loss of either Navajo-ness or Pentecostal-ness—to practice a Navajo Pentecostalism that blends novelty with tradition rather than opposes novelty against tradition—so interpreting Trumpism as resonant rupture enables us to see how he can practice a Trumpian presidency without a complete loss of either the novelty of Trump or the tradition of the presidency. The Trumpian presidency resonates with Americans just as Navajo Pentecostalism resonates with Navajos because "the idea that the ambiguity of expressive forms and the ability of performers to communicate conflicting meanings through them makes expressive forms the ideal foci understanding how [Americans and Navajos] reconcile multiple and contested subjectivities."[65]

In the coming chapters, we will add other neglected, and often non-Christian, theological concepts to our political theology of Donald Trump.

---

[64] Kimberly Jenkins Marshall, *Upward, Not Sunwise: Resonant Rupture in Navajo Neo-Pentecostalism* (Lincoln and London: University of Nebraska Press, 2016), 15.

[65] Ibid., 14.

3

Right around the World: Right-Wing Populism and the Sacred Nation in Global Perspective

[T]he real nature of the threat Trump poses can only be understood in a much wider context: that of the far-right populists who have been gaining strength in every major democracy, from Athens to Ankara, from Sydney to Stockholm, and from Warsaw to Wellington. Despite the obvious differences between the populists who are on the rise in all these countries, their commonalities go deep—and render each of them a danger to the political system in surprisingly similar ways.[1]

The questions of the exceptionality of Donald Trump and of his relevance to political theology do not end at America's shores. The twentieth century, if not all of recorded human history, is a parade of overweening executives—dictators, totalitarians, party chairmen, *duces*, and *führers*—all committed to bending society by and to their will. They showed little regard for the rule of law, indeed regarded themselves as the source and embodiment of law insofar as law concerned them at all. Autocracy (literally, the rule of/by one self) in the seat of power proves hard to resist.

Since the second half of the twentieth century, and incredibly and distressingly *more* frequently in the twenty-first, which was supposed to be the era of liberal democracy triumphant, many of these leaders and the movements that carried them to power have been labeled, or have proudly labeled themselves, "populist." Claiming to govern in the interest and the name of "the people," such populist regimes offer a solution to the first problem of political theology, the problem of the source of political authority, without necessarily any religious or supernatural appeal whatsoever. Yet, while modern secular populism provides a perfectly god-free ground for sovereignty, it can also acquire a religious tinge, with a spiritualization or sacralization, perhaps of "the people" or "the nation" and its land and culture, that compels us to reconsider the nature of both politics and religion.

---

[1] Yascha Mounk, *The People vs. Democracy: Why Our Freedom is in Danger and How to Save It* (Cambridge, MA and London: Harvard University Press, 2018), 7.

This chapter explores the contemporary prevalence of right-wing populism, especially, although not exclusively, in traditionally democratic countries. The analysis demonstrates that even secular liberal democracies are not immune to populism or to self-sacralization and that democratic politics has not and cannot shed its emotional, embodied, identitarian, and even religious qualities. It suggests new ways to understand, and on some occasions invert, Schmittian concepts of religion and sovereignty. And it illustrates that Trump is one instance of a much wider political-cultural phenomenon.

What is Populism?

"A spectre is haunting the world—populism," write Ghita Ionescu and Ernest Gellner in the opening line of the introduction to their precocious 1969 volume *Populism: Its Meaning and National Characteristics*.[2] Nor are they the first to detect a shift in global politics; more than a dozen years earlier, the eminent Edward Shils recognized a movement called populism which "proclaims that the will of the people as such is supreme over every other standard."[3]

Like most important political and cultural terms, populism has been defined in many different ways, acquiring connotations and associations over time, so that, for instance, populism in the early twenty-first century tends to conjure images of *right-wing* and *authoritarian or illiberal* populism. Arguably, that is the predominant form of populism in the current moment. Populism can mean and has meant many things over time, though, and has assumed many forms.

In his seminal study *On Populist Reason*, Ernest Laclau reminds us that the word "populism" originated in late nineteenth-century America, where it was a comparatively "leftist" movement. Mobilizing farmers, workers, and other "little people" against the ravages of modernization and capitalist accumulation, the People's Party of America was founded in 1892 in St. Louis with a platform dedicated to saving the country from "moral, political and material ruin" caused by corruption of government, silencing of the press, concentration of land and wealth in the hands of the few, repression (often violently) of labor, and a "vast conspiracy against mankind" that threatened "the establishment of an absolute despotism."[4] In

---

[2] Ghita Ionescu and Ernest Gellner, "Introduction," in *Populism: Its Meaning and National Characteristics*, ed. Ghita Ionescu and Ernest Gellner (London: Weidenfeld & Nicolson, 1969), 1–5.

[3] Edward Shils, *The Torment of Secrecy: The Background and Consequences of American Security Policies* (Glencoe, IL: The Free Press, 1956), 98.

[4] Quoted in Ernesto Laclau, *On Populist Reason* (New York: Verso, 2005), 201–2.

fact, Dwayne Woods, among others, contends that the past century has witnessed three waves of populism, the initial two of which we could rightly call left-wing. The first wave, represented by the American People's Party as well as peasant-friendly programs like the *narodniki* movement in Russia, was agrarian in nature. (In the context of urbanization and industrialization, peasants and rural populations often were, and still are, valorized or romanticized as the "true people" of rapidly changing societies.) The second or Latin American wave commenced in the 1940s and 1950s with such figures as Juan Péron in Argentina and Getúlio Vargas in Brazil; this brand of populism was typically class-oriented, vowing to defend the working class and poor (Vargas was nicknamed "the father of the poor") and to promote social reforms and national independence from American domination. For instance, Péron oversaw sharp increases in wages and health coverage while nationalizing banks and essential sectors like railways and universities, inevitably irritating powerful interests both domestic and foreign. Left-wing populism survived into the late-twentieth and early-twenty-first centuries in such characters as Venezuela's Hugo Chavez.[5]

Obviously, then, populism is not synonymous with right-wing populism, nor, except for the word itself, does it pertain only to the nineteenth century and beyond. In a very real way, the French Revolution was populist (and leftist), drawing its authority from and governing on behalf of "the people" of France and overthrowing the privileges of class and nobility. The United States, with its constitutional appeal to "We the people" and Lincoln's Gettysburg invocation of "of the people, by the people, and for the people," is inherently populist after a fashion. Nor, surprisingly, are references to "the people" exclusive to democracies: a benevolent monarch might reign for the benefit of (but never by the will of) the people, and Russian Bolshevism insisted that it dictated on behalf of and in the name of the people (very narrowly conceived, as the laboring class).

The third wave of right-wing populism inherits from its leftist predecessors but branches off in new directions. Its elected executives are legion, from Andreas Papandreou (Greece, 1981) and Alberto Fujimori (Peru, 1990) to Silvio Berlusconi (Italy, 1994), Viktor Orbán (Hungary, 1998 and 2010), Recep Tayyip Erdoğan (Turkey, premier 2003, president 2014), Lech Kaczyński (Poland, 2005) and Andrzej Duda (Poland, 2015), Vladimir Putin (Russia, president 2000, prime minister 2008, president again 2012), and Jair Bolsonaro (Brazil, 2019), not to mention the long list of parties and partisans who have not attained executive power such as Marine Le Pen of France's National Front (lately the National Rally) and Geert

---

[5] Dwayne Woods, "The Many Faces of Populism: Diverse but Not Disparate," in Woods, Dwayne and Barbara Wejnert, eds. *The Many Faces of Populism: Current Perspectives* (Bingley, UK: Emerald Publishing, 2014), 1–25.

Wilders of the Netherlands People's Party for Freedom. It is this wing of populism that will concern us here, and which concerns many anxious observers, as it appears to be a dominant force in politics worldwide and shares the most with America's right-wing populist, Trump.

Because populism is such a nebulous phenomenon, Margaret Canovan, in her classic and simply titled *Populism*, proposes a typology instead of a definition. Her basic distinction is between agrarian populisms and political populisms. Among agrarian types, she includes "farmers' radicalism" of the American People's Party sort, "peasant movements" (of which there are examples dating back centuries), and "intellectual agrarian socialism" like the aforementioned Russian *narodniki*. Four subtypes fall under the political heading—"populist dictatorship" (á la Péron), "populist democracy" (which is identifiable by its calls for "participation" by the people, often in the form of plebiscites and referenda), "reactionary populisms" (among which she counts American ultra-conservative, racial segregationist, and presidential candidate George Wallace), and "politicians' populism" (in her thinking, "broad, nonideological coalition-building that draws on the unificatory appeal of 'the people'").[6] As others before me have complained, these types are hardly mutually exclusive, and farmers' radicalism and peasant movements can be and often are "political," for instance by creating parties or potentially achieving power. Further, her political populisms are obviously not committed to either rightist or leftist politics in particular.

Since it is clear that populism can tilt left or right, it is equally clear that populism is not a specific ideology or agenda; it is compatible with different, even opposite, social projects. It is more accurately understood, in Laclau's words, as "a political logic," a way of thinking about and organizing power and then, once winning power, of governing.[7] In Laclau's analysis, populism consists principally of three elements—"the people," a practice of naming and an affective relationship to the named, and the leader. Again, not all governments, parties, and movements that refer to "the people" are populist, but there is no populism without a reference to, verging on a fetishizing of, "the people." Takis Pappas, in his study of populism and liberal democracy, refines this notion when he opines that

> populism could well be defined as the idea that political sovereignty belongs to and should be exercised by "the people" without regard to institutions. Obviously, the key term in the foregoing definition is "the people"—the meaning of which may differ from one place to another, and thus can only become clear after empirical and comparative

---

[6] Margaret Canovan, *Populism* (New York: Harcourt Brace Jovanovich, 1981), 13.

[7] Laclau, *On Populist Reason*, 113.

research. Whatever the case, the foregoing conceptualization of populism entails four essential attributes of "the people": (a) its potential to form a political majority; (b) its allegedly homogeneous, oversoul nature; (c) its subservience to impersonal institutions; and (d) its belief of holding the moral right.[8]

Much that we need for this chapter, this book, and this subject is contained in those remarks.

To start, although there is general consensus that populism necessarily invokes "the people," exactly what is being invoked in particular populisms varies extensively. Sometimes, as in Bolshevik Russia, "the people" may refer to a specific class, the workers or proletarians. In revolutionary France, it may designate simultaneously a nationality ("the French nation") and a class (the commoners) or some collective still more specific (the Paris mob). For the People's Party, "the people" were farmers and laborers, and, as we discovered in the previous chapter, for American republican theology, "the people" has tended to mean the overlap of a race and a religion (white Christians). In contemporary European and American nativism, "the people" means the native-born and therefore rightful (in both senses of the term: proper and fully rights-bearing) citizens of the country, that is, native-born (white?) Americans in the United States, native-born Hungarians in Hungary, etc.

The import of this populist summoning of "the people" is not difficult to grasp. Laclau expresses it when he explains that "the people" is not a given but "an act of an institution that creates a new agency out of a plurality of heterogeneous elements"—sundry classes, races, religions, and so forth—such that he advises that the real unit of analysis in populism is not the alleged group but instead "the socio-political *demand*" that interpellates the group "the people."[9] Hence, Laclau's emphasis on naming. It is almost inevitable too that the designated and desired "people" will exclude some segments of the actually-existing society—which may be the whole point. Jeff Maskovsky and Sophie Bjork-James, in a volume on contemporary "angry politics," justifiably assert that "'the people' is almost always constituted as a raced, classed, and gendered political subject."[10] To that short list, we must add ethnicized, regioned/geographized (e.g., a rural or small-town resident), nationalized, and culturized or civilizationized (e.g., a member of Western/Christian civilization).

---

[8] Takis S. Pappas, *Populism and Liberal Democracy: A Comparative and Theoretical Analysis* (Oxford and New York: Oxford University Press, 2019), 33.

[9] Laclau, *On Populist Reason*, 224.

[10] Jeff Maskovsky and Sophie Bjork-James, "Introduction," in *Beyond Populism: Angry Politics and the Twilight of Neoliberalism,* ed. Jeff Maskovsky and Sophie Bjork-James (Morgantown: West Virginia University Press, 2020), 7.

In other words—and this is critically important—"the people" not only names who the movement or the government is for but who it is *against*. A populism may be against certain classes (the upper classes, the nobility, etc.), races (non-whites), ethnicities (immigrants from other countries and language groups), religions (Jews, Muslims), regions (urbanites, East Coasters), civilizations (non-Western civilizations), and any combination thereof. Meanwhile, however "the people" is bounded, it also tends or works to obscure or deny differences *within* the group, to present them as "a homogeneous unity" with one identity and one set of interests.[11] Erasing fault lines within the in-group makes the line between in-group and out-group sharper and more impenetrable.

These outsiders, these Others, are regularly portrayed as a threat to "the people"—to "our" power, prosperity, culture, identity, and very survival. They are the ones who take our jobs, consume our wealth, occupy our land, change our society, and endanger our lives, who want to "replace us." This not-us is consequently a group "whose interests can rightfully be disregarded."[12] But equally, if not more perturbing for populists, are the in-group "elites" who at best stand by feebly as this menace unfolds and at worst facilitate it with their talk of multiculturalism and human rights. The "elites" are the internal other, including liberals, intellectuals, city-dwellers, secularists, rich special interests, and often enough practitioners of "normal" politics such as party loyalists and elected officials. In its most radical form, populism judges the entire existing political system as fraudulent, decadent, even traitorous. For this reason, Jan-Werner Müller, in another key text, characterizes populism as "a particular *moralistic imagination of politics*, a way of perceiving the political world that sets a morally pure and fully unified—but, I shall argue, ultimately fictional—people against elites who are deemed corrupt or in some other way morally inferior."[13]

These considerations lead us to another fundamental point that Schmitt makes about politics. In his 1927 *The Concept of the Political*, he ponders the essence of politics and resolves that politics can be reduced in the end to the distinction "between friend and enemy."[14] Straddling the border of rationality and symbolism, Schmitt holds that at its core politics "is the most intense and extreme antagonism, and every concrete antagonism becomes that much more political the closer it approaches the most extreme

---

[11] Paula Diehl, "Twisting Representation," in *Routledge Handbook of Global Populism*, ed. Carlos de la Torre (London and New York: Routledge, 2019), 134.

[12] Mounk, *The People vs. Democracy*, 42.

[13] Jan-Werner Müller, *What Is Populism?* (Philadelphia: University of Pennsylvania Press, 2016), 19–20, emphasis in the original.

[14] Carl Schmitt, *The Concept of the Political*, trans. George Schwab (Chicago, IL and London: The University of Chicago Press, 2007 [1927]), 26.

point, that of the friend-enemy grouping."[15] Populism then might approximate the purest case of politics for Schmitt, apart from actual war. Cultural and racial others are not merely others but enemies, as are their in-group enablers and collaborators:

> Most populists, however, take the accusation that the leaders of the old parties are traitors one step further. They don't just claim that members of the political caste are in it for themselves, or that they are in the pocket of special interests. Rather, they claim that they harbor a special loyalty to the enemies of the people, making them more interested in advancing the interests of unpopular ethnic or religious minorities than in the fate of the majority.[16]

We arrive, finally, at probably the most influential definition of populism in the recent literature. Drafted by Cas Mudde and Cristóbal Kaltwasser in their edited volume on populism in Europe and the Western Hemisphere, populism is

> a thin-centred ideology that considers society to be ultimately separated into two homogeneous and antagonistic groups, "the pure people" and "the corrupt elite," and which argues that politics should be an expression of the *volonté générale* (general will) of the people....This means that populism is in essence a form of moral politics, as the distinction between "the elite" and "the people" is first and foremost moral (i.e. pure vs. corrupt), not situational (e.g. position of power), socio-cultural (e.g. ethnicity, religion), or socio- economic (e.g. class). Moreover, both categories are to a certain extent "empty signifiers"..., as it is the populists who construct the exact meanings of "the elite" and "the people."[17]

By "thin-centred," they mean specifically that populism is an ideology that can readily be attached to many other ideologies and identities, both right-wing and left-wing, whether nation-, class-, race-, ethnic-, or religion-based or some mixture of these variables.

---

[15] Schmitt, *The Concept of the Political*, 29.

[16] Mounk, *The People vs. Democracy*, 42.

[17] Cas Mudde and Cristóbal Kaltwasser, "Populism and (Liberal) Democracy: A Framework for Analysis," in *Populism in Europe and the Americas: Threat or Corrective for Democracy?* ed. Cas Mudde and Cristóbal Kaltwassser (Cambridge and New York: Cambridge University Press, 2012), 8–9.

Populist Leadership and Governance

Another requisite ingredient for a populist movement according to Laclau and all observers is the leader. Of course, every party, movement, and administration needs a leader, but populism is a uniquely leader-driven brand of politics. If populism is a singularly intense practice of political theology, it only stands to reason that it would recruit a savior.

Because of the deep distrust of and antagonism toward the political class and established parties, there is a premium for the would-be populist leader to erupt from outside of government. As we will see below, most but not all contemporary populist leaders have not held previous elected office. Lacking political experience and free of party affiliation, they may construct their own parties or political machinery. Pappas stresses that the other path to populist power besides creating a political apparatus is to break through "as maverick politicians within already established parties, i.e. against ordinary intraparty procedure and often bypassing time-honored practices of those parties' official rank and file, or both. In such cases of party seizure, populist leaders are able to transform erstwhile liberal parties into populist ones."[18]

The insurgent quality of populist leadership is only a symptom of a more profound and exceptional political reality. A party or political machine is

Fig. 7 Meeting of Marine le Pen on Sunday, March 26, 2017 for the French presidential election.

useful, both for acquiring power and governing, but populism remains a deeply personalistic political style. Populist leaders seek a more direct and intimate connection with their followers, and populist followers want the same from their bond with their leader. As Paula Diehl reasons, the anti-elite attitude intrinsic to populism extends to institutions like parties themselves, which only get in the way of the preferred "direct and unmediated relationship to the leader."[19] Portraying himself (for populist leaders are disproportionately male, France's Marine Le Pen of the National Front, recently renamed the *Rassemblement national* or National Rally, posing one exception) as a "man of the people," he aims to speak directly to the people. But much more, the populist leader professes to speak *for* the people, to

---

[18] Pappas, *Populism and Liberal Democracy*, 103.
[19] Diehl, "Twisting Representation," 134.

represent the people against the discredited elite and government, and, in the ultimate case, to *embody* or *personify* the people.

This dynamic between the people and the leader clarifies a number of other features of populism. Populist leaders are often said to be charismatic; charisma is a definite advantage for populists, although charisma is not exclusive to populists. However, the charisma of the populist serves a greater function—in the words of Pappas above, to free the people from "the subservience to impersonal institutions." So central to the populist project is the person of the leader, versus any party or movement s/he might head, that Kurt Weyland defines populism precisely as a "political strategy through which a personalistic leader seeks or exercises power based on direct, unmediated, uninstitutionalized support from large numbers of mostly unorganized followers."[20]

Because they speak *to* and *for* the people, they must also speak *like* the people, so populist rhetoric typically displays a style or mood that is "popular" (some have condemned it as "tabloid") or, in Canovan's estimation, "'democratic' in the sense of being aimed at ordinary people":

> Capitalizing on popular distrust of politicians' evasive and bureaucratic jargon, they pride themselves on simplicity and directness. When members of the political establishment are accused of adopting "populist" tactics, one of the relevant pieces of evidence is their willingness and ability to communicate in this tabloid style. But simple, direct language is not enough to mark a politician as populist unless he or she is prepared also to offer political analyses and proposed solutions that are also simple and direct.[21]

Populist communication style is usually simple if not folksy or downright vulgar. Benjamin Moffitt contends that populist leaders, intentionally or instinctively, show "bad manners" in their speech and conduct:

> A function of the appeal to "the people" as the arbiters of "common sense" and of the urgency of the matters that populist actors present is a coarsening of political rhetoric, and a disregard for "appropriate" modes of acting in the political realm.... Ostiguy (2009) has identified this as the "low" of a high-low axis that runs orthogonal to the traditional left-right axis. Such elements of this "low" include the use of slang, swearing, political incorrectness, and being overly demonstrative and

---

[20] Kurt Weyland, "Clarifying a Contested Concept: Populism in the Study of Latin American Politics," *Comparative Politics* 34, no. 1 (2001), 14.

[21] Margaret Canovan, "Trust the People! Populism and the Two Faces of Democracy," *Political Studies* 47, no. 1 (1999), 5–6.

"colourful," as opposed to the "high" behaviors of rigidness, rationality, composure, and the use of technocratic language.[22]

Moffitt's wider work takes Laclau's suggestion about the *logic* of populism and expands it into a study of the *performance* of populism.[23] Other elements of the populist performance include echoing (and perhaps actually sharing) the people's anger over their perceived predicament and feeding it back to them with incendiary and insulting words and gestures. Violence is never far behind the scene, and a crisis or breakdown is always imminent if not underway. As for confronting the problems and threats that plague the people, Mounk insists that

> glib, facile solutions stand at the very heart of the populist appeal. Voters do not like to think that the world is complicated. They certainly do not like to be told that there is no immediate answer to their problems. Faced with politicians who seem to be less and less able to govern an increasingly complex world, many are increasingly willing to vote for anybody who promises a simple solution. This is why populists from India's Narendra Modi to Turkey's Recep Tayyip Erdoğan, from Hungary's Viktor Orbán to Poland's Jarosław Kaczynski, and from France's Marine Le Pen to Italy's Beppe Grillo sound surprisingly similar to each other despite their considerable ideological differences.[24]

So standardized indeed is the style and mood of populism that with minor cultural variations, a "recipe" for populism was formulated by one Venezuelan citizen, as reported by Pappas:

> Find a wound common to many, find someone to blame for it, and make up a good story to tell. Mix it all together. Tell the wounded you know how they feel. That you found the bad guys. Label them: the minorities, the politicians, the businessmen. Caricature them. As vermin, evil masterminds, haters and losers, you name it. Then paint yourself as a savior. Capture the people's imagination. Forget about policies and plans, just enrapture them with a tale. One that starts with anger and ends in vengeance. A vengeance they can participate in. That's how it becomes a movement. There's something soothing in all that anger.[25]

---

[22] Benjamin Moffitt, "The Performative Turn in the Comparative Study of Populism," *Comparative Politics Newsletter* 26, no. 2 (2016), 55.

[23] See, for instance, Benjamin Moffitt, *The Global Rise of Populism: Performance, Political Style, and Representation* (Stanford, CA: Stanford University Press, 2016).

[24] Mounk, *The People vs. Democracy*, 38.

[25] Quoted in Pappas, *Populism and Liberal Democracy*, 114.

The main recurring ingredients of this populist script are victimhood, resentment, and redemption, or what Diehl calls the "narrative of the betrayed people."[26]

It is easy to see why Canovan asserts that populism is politics but "not ordinary, routine politics."[27] Many decent members of society react with embarrassment or horror as populists malign rivals, abuse allies, betray former friends, demean minorities, ignore traditions, violate norms, and literally break laws, but it is incumbent upon us to comprehend such behaviors as populist performance *par excellence*. What shocks and dismays some, excites and satisfies others. A populist leader who followed the rules and tiptoed around norms and traditions would not be a populist leader at all; breaking things, even the most hallowed rules of the society and the institutions that construct and protect them, is what populism—especially contemporary right-wing populism—is all about. It is authenticity to the audience, proof that the leader is not just talking but means and lives what he says. He is a political shock jock. But more significantly, he is a Schmittian actor, performing in his words and deeds his freedom from and transcendence of the normal legal order.

Yet this "redemptive face," as Canovan dubs it, of what is indisputably a version of democratic politics (in contrast to the "pragmatic face" or rational, rule-abiding politics as usual)—distinguished by its ambition to be the *vox populi, vox dei*, by its promise of "salvation through politics," by its faith in the sovereignty of the people as more than "simply a form of government" or legal procedure, and by its well-documented "strong anti-institutional impulse: the romantic impulse to directness, spontaneity, and the overcoming of alienation"[28]—still reveals familiar political limitations and contradictions that inform on the fundamental issues of political theology. One of these inescapable factors is representation. Some critics hold that the populist leader solves or eliminates the problem of representation, either by disregarding those whom he allegedly represents or by so collapsing the distance between himself and his constituency that there is no "representation" happening at all. Usually still operating in a democratic-electoral context, though, his authority can, theoretically at least, be wrested from him; populists have been voted out of office, or they have succumbed to other political forces like the military (through coups) or the courts (through criminal convictions). They are not truly sovereign in the final analysis.

Furthermore, always acting as the representative of the people, the populist leader's power is secure only as long as he plays that role

---

[26] Diehl, "Twisting Representation," 137.
[27] Canovan, "Trust the People," 6.
[28] Ibid., 10.

successfully. Indeed, populism may flourish where there is a so-called "crisis of representation," that is, where citizens feel that their representatives (the elected government, the party system, mainstream institutions, even laws and constitutions) do not hear them or work on their behalf. But contrary to some assertions, populists do not rule with impunity from representation; rather, they depend on representation and especially on *a monopoly of representation*. Müller holds that a representative political system is a prerequisite for contemporary populism: it is just that the populist leader declares that he (and his party, if there is one) is the sole legitimate representative of the people. This is why Müller calls populism "the shadow of representative democracy."[29] He even remarks that populists are comfortable with elites so long as *they* are those elites.

The relation between populism and representation puts the populist leader in an awkward position. "If populism produces a cult of immediacy," warns William Mazzarella in his pertinently titled lecture "Populism as Political Theology," "then that can only be because it's so thoroughly mediated."[30] In other words, the direct contact that followers think they enjoy with the leader is achieved through heavily and deliberately constructed effort (for example, mass rallies, posters, television appearances, tweet storms, and so forth). Beyond this valid point lies a more inescapable contradiction, a "twist" on representation as Diehl sees it. The contradiction is between what she calls accountability versus authorization. That is, the populist leader's authority hypothetically flows from the people, rendering him hypothetically accountable to the people (i.e., as we previously noted, the people can rescind the leader's authority). But in actual populist practice, "democratic accountability has been suppressed" if only because the people are asked to place "unquestioned trust in the leader."[31] Worse, the populist leader transforms the people's power into powerlessness: if the people were so powerful, they would not need a populist leader to enforce their will. Instead, the pre-existing situation of "bad representation by established politicians, parties, and elites" indicates that the people are relatively weak and ineffectual, even dupes, who can only be saved by a commanding leader. As she judges it, populist leaders pay lip service to "popular sovereignty," but they "simultaneously insist on their own leadership role and stress the verticality of their relationship with the people" (that is, the leader and the people are not as much on the same level as populism would have them believe); "in so doing, they neglect their original demand for

---

[29] Müller, *What is Populism?*
[30] William Mazzarella, "Populism as Political Theology" (lecture, Columbia University, New York, NY, April 23, 2019), https://www.academia.edu/42286798/Populism_as_Political_Theology.
[31] Diehl, "Twisting Representation," 130.

greater popular power and democratic accountability."[32] We might say that a populist leader flatters the power of the people and then asks that the people surrender all of that power to him.

This dynamic between the leader and the people, added to the thoroughgoing anti-institutionalism that lifts the populist leader to power in the first place and characterizes his governance, results in a clash between decentralized rhetoric and centralized reality. Within their party or movement, and their government if they seize office, populist leaders tend to brook no debate or disagreement. Consequently, populism is "particularly prone to internal authoritarianism":

> If there is only one common good and only one way to represent it faithfully (as opposed to a self-consciously partisan but also self-consciously fallible interpretation of what the common good might be), then disagreement within the party that claims to be the sole legitimate representative of the common good obviously cannot be permissible.[33]

The apotheosis of monolithic populism is Dutch populist Geert Wilders and his Party for Freedom (*Partij voor de Vrijheid* or PVV), which is

> not just metaphorically a one-man-party; Wilders controls everything and everyone. Initially, Wilders and his chief intellectual Martin Bosma did not even want to establish a political party but a foundation. This proved legally impossible, but the PVV today operates as a party with exactly two members: Wilders himself and a foundation, *Stichting Groep Wilders*, with (one might have guessed it) once again Wilders as the only member. The members of the PVV in parliament are merely delegates (and are extensively coached by Wilders every Saturday on how to present themselves and how to do their legislative work).[34]

Logically what applies inside the party/movement applies outside as well. From a governance perspective, the populist in power "needs to abolish the institutional roadblocks that might stop him from carrying out the will of the people."[35] Consistent with their path to office, once they have ridden the wave of putative popular sovereignty to the seat of power, populist leaders "increasingly direct their ire against a second target: all institutions, formal or informal, that dare to contest their claim to a moral monopoly of representation."[36] This comes natural to them, since it was institutions

---

[32] Diehl, "Twisting Representation," 134.
[33] Müller, *What is Populism?*, 36.
[34] Ibid., 37.
[35] Mounk, *The People vs. Democracy*, 8.
[36] Ibid., 43.

(legislatures, courts, parties, media, universities, and the rest) that were the prime suspects in deceiving the people in the first place and preventing the people's will from being heard and respected. As Mounk memorably summarizes the situation, populist leaders instinctively understand

> how dangerous intermediary institutions with a real claim to representing the views and interests of large segments of society are to the fiction that they, and they alone, speak for the people. They therefore work hard to discredit such institutions as tools of old elites or outside interests. Where this doesn't suffice, they introduce laws limiting foreign funding to weaken them financially, or use their control over the regulatory state to impede their operation.[37]

In following such a program, they are, sometimes unwittingly, enacting the Schmittian sovereign.

One last observation is worth making about the populist leader. Despite its arguable modernity, populism manifests an ancient dimension of politics and of theology—the very materialization of the people and the people's will in the person of the leader. In our introductory chapter, we mentioned the cross-cultural phenomenon of sacred kingship, in which the leader not only symbolizes but incarnates political society and sometimes nature itself. In sacred kingship, there are literally two bodies at play, which mirror or inter-represent each other, as Ernst Kantorowicz theorizes in his classic *The King's Two Bodies*, a self-identified study of political theology.[38] The twin bodies include the "body natural," the physical person of the sovereign, and the "body politic," the monarch's society, his subjects, or "the people." More importantly, there is a fundamental and mystical identity between the two: the king is immediately present in the society, and the society is equally immediately present in the king.

Twenty-first century populism may not advance the explicit claim that the populist leader is the mystical embodiment of the nation or people (although sometimes it may), but we can recognize the sway of such pre-modern thinking in this ostensibly modern politics. The desire for an unmediated bond between (representative) populist leader and (represented) people resembles the ancient longing for a leader who instantiates and thereby focuses into one person the mind and will of the people. Mazzarella calls this "a direct and immediate presencing of the substance of the people and, as such, a reassertion, a mattering forth of the collective flesh."[39]

---

[37] Mounk, *The People vs. Democracy*, 45.

[38] Ernst H. Kantorowicz, *The King's Two Bodies: A Study in Medieval Political Theology* (Princeton, NJ: Princeton University Press, 1957).

[39] William Mazzarella, "The Anthropology of Populism: Beyond the Liberal Settlement," *Annual Review of Anthropology* 48 (2019), 49.

Admittedly, liberal democracy, and modernity in general, is uncomfortable with and suspicious of such a non-rational, magical notion, but Mazzarella justifiably insists that "there is something affect-intensive and corporeal about populism," as demonstrated in the "lusty disinhibition of populist style."[40] One veritable aspect of the alleged charisma of the populist champion is "the radical fullness of the body of a leader in which the people may find a palpable image of their own substance."[41]

Without pushing the idea too far (and honestly, some followers of the populist leader may well experience a semi-mystical or religious attachment to him), this "politics of immediation" in which the people take fleshly form before their very eyes might make sense of some of the more otherwise anomalous features of contemporary populism. The highly emotional (even "effervescent" in Durkheim's terms; see Chapter 7) nature of populism approaches religious fervor in some instances, molding a nearly Durkheimian unity of individuals. Populist leaders encourage visceral reactions (more so than intellectual ones, to the consternation of cooler-headed political pragmatists), offering redemption through submission and often through (at least the discourse of) violence. The leader's pompous denunciation of enemies and institutions (and of institutions as enemies) radiates his power and his conviction. Even traits that would be deficits in other contexts—being bellicose and pugilistic, vulgar, misogynistic, or hypersexual, even overweight—are signs of his larger-than-life persona, one that transcends norms and promises victory over all comers.

As we will see in the remaining sections of this chapter and in future chapters, analysts of populism are unwise to scoff at these non-rational and pre-modern dimensions of politics. Like Bruno Latour once said, we have never been modern,[42] and we remain easily seduced by our instincts, by our guts and groins, to follow leaders who can arouse our emotions and bodies, even as they themselves perform for us those same emotions and bodies. Victoria Kahn may be onto something when she pronounces, as we noted in our introduction, that political theology, of which we now recognize populism as one type, is a kind of haunting of the law by the body.

---

[40] Mazzarella, "The Anthropology of Populism," 49.

[41] Ibid., 52.

[42] Bruno Latour, *We Have Never Been Modern*, trans. Catherine Porter (Cambridge, MA: Harvard University Press, 1993 [1991]).

Right-Wing Populist Regimes,
Illiberal Democracy, and the Sacred Nation

Wir sind das Volk (We are the people)—a German populist slogan

In the early days of serious academic attention to populism (the 1960s and 1970s), the assumption was that populism was a primarily non-Western phenomenon (and problem). It seemed to spring up in newly-decolonized countries in Africa, Asia, or the Middle East or in immature democracies in Latin America. It was the very antithesis of Clifford Geertz's prognosis of an "integrative revolution" that foresaw the transfer of identity from local and pre-modern (tribal, ethnic, religious) entities to higher and modern ones, specifically the nation-state; as the title of his edited volume predicts, independent peoples would swap their old societies for new states.[43] Events did not go as planned.

Those previous variations of populism, as we have discussed already, were often more leftist in orientation, positing wealthy elites, multinational corporations, and Western governments (especially in Europe and the United States) as the enemy. Some mobilized one tribe, class, ethnic group, or religion, while others were more hopefully trans-local, calling on "the people" of some new state to unite under the banner of (some elements of) their traditional culture to expel foreign influence and attain true independence if not greatness. (An example is Julius Nyerere's "African socialism," based on the native concept of *ujamaa* or community/family.)

To the surprise of many, recent populism of right-wing orientation has appeared in places presumed to be immune to such movements, having only recently survived fascist regimes in Germany, Italy, Spain, and elsewhere. Much of the focus presently falls on Europe (both Western and former communist Eastern) in the form of right-wing populist parties in France (National Front/Rally), the Netherlands (Party for Freedom), Denmark (People's Party), Switzerland (Swiss People's Party), the United Kingdom (UK Independence Party), Poland (*Prawo i Sprawiedliwość*, Law and Justice), Germany (Alternative for Germany), Greece (Golden Dawn), and Hungary (Fidesz). In fact, every country in Europe seems to have one or more right-wing populist parties, but they are also to be found in Turkey, Brazil, India, the Philippines, and (if we count Trump's Republican party) the United States. In some countries, right-wing populists have acceded to the highest office; in others, right-wing populist parties are competitive but have not yet broken through to victory.

In this section we will examine just a few of these parties and leaders to discover what is consistent and what is different between them.

---

[43] Clifford Geertz, ed., *Old Societies and New States: The Quest for Modernity in Asia and Africa* (New York: The Free Press, 1963).

We cannot hope to cover every possible case or to cover any case in great depth, but our brief survey will show that there is indeed a wave of right-wing populism crashing around the globe.

Illustrating the kinship between populisms right and left, Andreas Papandreou of Greece led the leftist Panhellenistic Socialist Movement (PASOK) in Greece from 1974 to 1996, winning three terms as prime minister of the country (1981, 1985, and 1993). Although his policies contrasted diametrically with most later right-wing parties and executives, he is reported to have uttered the quintessential populist motto, "There are no institutions—there's only the people."[44]

A transitional figure in international populism is Peru's Alberto Fujimori (1990-2000), who combined elements of left- and right-wing politics in a textbook case of the populist trajectory. A Peruvian of Japanese descent without prior political experience or an organized party, he stepped onto the stage amid an economic crisis and a Marxist/Maoist insurgence in the form of the Shining Path. Running as a consummate ethnic and political outsider, he succeeded in mobilizing traditionally disempowered segments of society; a campaign slogan sold him to the masses as "A President Like You," and his rhetoric divided society into the "pure people" and "the corrupt elite," associating the latter with whites and the former with the country's *cholos* or dark-skinned people. "Fujimori claimed to represent the 'real Peru, *cholo* Peru,' declaring at one campaign rally: 'We may be *chinitos* [Chinese/Asian] and *cholitos*, but we are the real people.'"[45]

Once in office, though, he leavened his left-wing populism with many of the standard reforms of neoliberalism, which typically have not served the little people of a country, such as reducing government spending, easing regulations, and opening markets, while also instituting liberal changes like an increase in the minimum wage and the creation of a poverty relief fund. Although adopting much of the program of elites and multilateral organizations like the International Monetary Fund, he continued and escalated his criticism of "the political class," chastising "the political parties, Congress, and the judiciary," branding legislators "as 'unproductive charlatans' and judges as 'jackals'" who advanced their own interests over those of the people.[46] When he began to rule by executive order, the legislature responded to contain his executive powers and potentially impeach him. After less than two years in office, he conducted

---

[44] Quoted in Pappas, *Populism and Liberal* Democracy, 107.

[45]   Steven Levitsky and James Loxton, "Populism and Competitive Authoritarianism: The Case of Fujimori's Peru," in *Populism in Europe and the Americas: Threat or Corrective for Democracy?* ed. Cas Mudde and Cristóbal Kaltwassser (Cambridge and New York: Cambridge University Press, 2012), 168–69.

[46] Ibid., 170.

his *autogolpe* or "self-coup," a presidential assault on all other political institutions, including

> closing the congress, dissolving the constitution, and purging the judiciary and other state institutions. Most major media outlets were occupied by the armed forces, several leading journalists and members of congress were arrested, and ex-president Alan García was forced into exile. Fujimori defended the coup as a step towards what he called a "true" and "sui generis" democracy.[47]

Remarkably, his actions increased his popularity, simultaneously eroding public support for the legislature, the courts, and the party system.

Although he was forced to abandon plans to govern as dictator, he managed to compel elections for a new legislative assembly vested to write a new constitution. In the interim, Fujimori used his expansive executive authority to further enhance his power while undermining that of competing government institutions, including the creation a new presidential "superministry" that increased the executive's ability to distribute patronage.[48]

With a decisive victory in his re-election bid, he was freed to continue packing the courts with loyalists, which in turn were used to protect his supporters from prosecution and to harass and punish his enemies. Courts and tax-collecting agencies were aimed at "opposition politicians, businesspeople, journalists, and media owners, forcing some of them into exile."[49] The media was rendered subservient and compliant, and rivals were sometimes subjected to actual physical violence. Against the complaints of legal experts, he managed to push through a rule change that allowed him to run for—and win—an unconstitutional third term in office. A few weeks later, however, he bowed to mounting pressure to call another election in which he did not run, instead fleeing to Japan in November 2000; in absentia, he was removed from office and, in 2009, convicted of embezzlement, kidnapping, and murder and, having been extradited back to Peru, sentenced to prison for twenty-five years.

Fujimori's case, in many ways a model populist tale, raises the interesting point that not all populist movements or leaders are wholly leftist or rightist. Indeed, in eastern Europe, to which much of the right-wing populist activity shifted in recent decades, Lenka Bustikova finds that right-wing parties and governments often adopt "left-leaning" economic policies, for instance, strengthening government control over the economy and implementing social programs (albeit programs for "the people" and not for

---

[47] Levitsky and Loxton, "Populism and Competitive Authoritarianism," 171.

[48] Ibid., 174.

[49] Ibid., 175.

those who disqualify as "the people" such as immigrants).[50] Where they do not stray from the right-wing populist script is in their "linkages between identity and democratization"—that is, associating native-born and/or culturally pure citizens of the state with "the people" and ascribing democratic sovereignty to them—and in their resentment toward the European Union (and often the United States) "which is associated with rights for ethnic, social, and sexual minorities, along with restrictions on national sovereignty."[51] The exclusionary and anti-pluralist nature of right-wing populism has frequently been reproved as racist or nativist, but it is sometimes presented within populist movements as culturist or civilizational—not exactly disparaging outsiders for their racial differences but fencing them from the authentic people of the society and state for their cultural differences.

On the far eastern edge of Europe sits the right-wing and increasingly autocratic regime of Turkey. Recep Tayyip Erdoğan of the Justice and Development Party (AKP) served for a dozen years as Turkish prime minister (2003–2014) before being elected president in 2014, an office he continues to hold. His initial populist appeal, a not unreasonable one, targeted the unusual "legal-institutional role" of Turkey's military, which "amounted to a virtual veto power over elected officials."[52] However, after reasonably curbing the extra-legal powers of the armed forces, Erdoğan's and the AKP's populist "moral valorization of the ordinary people" has inexorably "evolved into a more exclusionary type to legitimize authoritarian power grab."[53] Like Fujimori before him and others since, Erdoğan uses his popular mandate "to dominate political institutions and exploit state resources in a partisan manner" to crush resistance and trample opposition.[54] Consistent with populism's playbook, the AKP began weakening democratic institutions, criminalizing dissent, and attacking, censoring, and politicizing the media (e.g., fining pro-opposition outlets and blocking Twitter and YouTube) even before an attempted military coup in mid-2016, after which the country's parliamentary government system was replaced with an executive-style presidency premised on what some have labeled "Erdoğanism."

Ihsan Yilmaz and Galib Bashirov describe Erdoğanism as a typically personalistic brand of populism—verging on a cult of

[50] Lenka Bustikova, "Populism in Eastern Europe," *Comparative Politics Newsletter* 26, no. 2 (2016), 16.

[51] Ibid., 17.

[52] Berk Esen and Sebnem Gumuscu, "Rising Competitive Authoritarianism in Turkey," *Third World Quarterly* 37, no. 9 (2016), 1584.

[53] Bilge Yabanci, "Fuzzy Borders between Populism and Sacralized Politics: Mission, Leader, Community and Performance in 'New' Turkey," *Politics, Religion & Ideology* 21, no. 1 (2020), 101.

[54] Esen and Gumuscu, "Rising Competitive Authoritarianism in Turkey," 1584.

personality—that features electoral authoritarianism, "neopatrimonialism" in economics, and Islamism. Electoral authoritarianism (called competitive authoritarianism by some scholars; see the next chapter) is recognizable for its "uneven playing field for the opposition, elections that are neither fair nor free, and a widespread crackdown on fundamental freedoms."[55] As we have chronicled all too clearly, populist regimes do not want to share or lose power. Neopatrimonialism names a blend of old-fashioned patrimonialism in which "all power relations between ruler and ruled, and political as well as administrative relations, are personal relations; there is no differentiation between the private and the public realm" with "legal-rational bureaucratic domination" whereby a political patron "transfers public goods and services to his client" in exchange for loyalty.[56] Islamism here refers to instrumentalizing the religion of Islam as an ideology to legitimize the government and to shape and achieve specific political goals; this is particularly momentous in a country founded on secular (Kemalist) principles.

Erdoğan's populism takes on a specifically Turkish flavor by making the distinction between "White" and "Black" Turks, the former—although Turkish—not quite deserving inclusion in "the people." As Sedef Arat-Koç instructs, "White Turk" is a pejorative term for the "new middle classes" in the country, perceived as secular, urban, and largely Westernized elites who look down on their pious, rural or poor urban, conservative and non-Westernized cousins. Although the distinction predated the AKP, Arat-Koç argues that the party engages in a campaign of "polarizing and hyper-politicizing supposedly 'cultural' differences."[57] AKP rhetoric increasingly denigrates the liberal secular Turks, asserting that "conservative (Sunni) Muslims are the real, authentic Turkish subjects," thus banishing the former from "the people."[58] White Turks, in a word, are rebuked as "anti-nationals," "as outsiders, missionaries of a foreign culture, colonizing the authentic Muslim-Turkish nation" and guilty, implicitly or explicitly, of "illegitimate thoughts and acts of treason against the state."[59] As in other populist regimes, in Erdoğan's Turkey "there could be no legitimate place for opposition in Turkish politics"; anyone who disagrees with him, and

---

[55] Ihsan Yilmaz and Galib Bashirov, "The AKP after 15 Years: Emergence of Erdoganism in Turkey," *Third World Quarterly*, 39, no. 9 (2018), 1817, DOI: 10.1080/01436597.2018.1447371

[56] Ibid., 1819.

[57] Sedef Arat-Koç, "Culturalizing Politics, Hyper-Politicizing 'Culture': 'White' vs. 'Black Turks' and the Making of Authoritarian Populism in Turkey," *Dialectical Anthropology* 42, no. 4 (2018), 392.

[58] Ibid. 397.

[59] Ibid., 405.

therefore with "the people," "can only be 'terrorists,' 'traitors,' 'puppets,' or 'collaborators' of Turkey's enemies."[60]

One final example is also, fascinatingly, the most theoretically sophisticated case of right-wing populism. Hungary is one of Europe's fledgling democracies, the former People's Republic of Hungary being liberated from communist rule in 1989. The first post-socialist government was a center-right coalition, and Hungary moved politically toward the West by joining NATO (1999) and then the European Union (2004). In the interim, a group of radical students founded the Right-Wing Youth Association (*Jobboldali Ifjúsági Közösség* or JOBBIK), which evolved into a political party in 2003. (András Kovács tells us that "Jobbik" is a pun in Hungarian, as the word *jobb* means both "right(wing)" and "better."[61]) JOBBIK harbored a deep suspicion about the economic and political transformation after communism, believing that the same institutions, practices, and politicians ran the new Hungary as the old; both the left and the right, as JOBBIK supporters found them, were elites blocking the realization of true democracy. Bizarrely maybe, but in a preview of global political thinking to come, JOBBIK's rhetoric was highly "anti-American, anti-Israel, pro-Russian, pro-Palestinian, and pro-Iran."[62]

JOBBIK never rose to power, but another similar party, the Alliance of Young Democrats (*Fiatal Demokraták Szövetségeo* or Fidesz), eventually did. Tracing back to an anti-communist party from the late 1980s, Fidesz

won six percent of the vote in 1990, earning seats in the new legislature. The party's leader, almost continuously since 1993, is Viktor Orbán, who, unlike most right-wing populist executives, was no stranger to public office when he first became prime minister in 1998, having served in the National

Fig. 8 Viktor Orbán speaking at the European People's Party, March 7, 2014

Assembly since 1990. After falling short in two plebiscites (2002 and 2006), Orbán and Fidesz won a supermajority in the 2010 election, and he has reigned as prime minister again since 2010. Along the way, both the man and the party turned sharply in the right-wing populist direction.

---

[60] Arat-Koç, "Culturalizing Politics," 406.

[61] András Kovács, "The Post-Communist Extreme Right: The Jobbik Party in Hungary," in *Right Wing Populism in Europe: Politics and Discourse*, ed. Ruth Wodak, Majid KhosraviNik, and Brigitte Mral (London and New York: Bloomsbury, 2013), 224.

[62] Ibid., 227.

According to Pappas, Orbán's Hungarian populism conceives of "the people" as a "fusion of the average, hard-working Hungarian citizens and the entire Hungarian nation, both forming a civic community (*emberek*) distinguished by its Christian and conservative principles and with its own distinct interests."[63] As if reading from the right-wing populist recipe, Orbán accuses "lying millionaire swindlers" and "conmen protected by the state" of taking what rightfully belongs to the people—although he seems to understand the scholarly point that "the people" is a relative and potential unit by stating "the Hungarian nation is not simply a group of individuals but a community that must be organized, reinforced and in fact constructed."[64] Most ominously, Orbán overtly views normal democratic institutions and practices as not the best means to consolidate the people and serve their interests, indeed as a positive hindrance to that identity and interest. Speaking against the "open society" so valorized by liberal democrats, he cautions that the path of the open society leads to a Hungary

weakened, bled, shaken in its morals, confused in its self-awareness, tormented by guilt feeling, and deprived of self-confidence. An "open society" where there is no country any more, only habitat, there is no homeland anymore, only an investment site. Where no nation, only population exists. Where progress equals assimilation into worldwide processes. Where progress does not serve the interests of the nation but simply satisfies the ambition of the narrow power elite to become world citizens.[65]

A power grab, a Fujimori-like executive coup, in the ostensible name of the people follows almost logically from this sentiment. Immediately, he "systematically consolidated his rule. He appointed loyal followers to lead state-run television stations, to head the electoral commission, and to dominate the country's constitutional court. He changed the elector system to benefit himself, pushed out foreign corporations to channel money to his cronies, instituted highly restrictive rules on NGOs, and attempted to shutter Central European University," an academic institution founded by his former teacher and arch-nemesis, George Soros.[66] Predictably (drearily so), he rails against immigrants for not only consuming Hungarian wealth but threatening Hungarian culture. Then, less than two years into office, Orbán orchestrated the passage of the New Fundamental Law, which went into effect on January 1, 2012. According to András Bíró-

---

[63] Pappas, *Populism and Liberal Democracy*, 119.
[64] Ibid.
[65] Quoted in ibid., 120.
[66] Mounk, *People vs. Democracy*, 10.

Nagy of the Hungarian Academy of Sciences, the New Fundamental Law contains the following provisions:

- It limits constitutional review by the courts, allowing the government to make laws that are otherwise unconstitutional; it also grants the majority party the power to select judges.
- Major offices such as chief prosecutor, state audit officers, and the Fiscal Council could be staffed with Fidesz members or other pro-regime experts; the office of ombudsman was eliminated altogether.
- An electoral system that "compensated the winner" was introduced, guaranteeing the party's majority in future elections. (Fidesz had originally taken sixty-eight percent of the legislative seats after winning only fifty-three percent of the popular vote.)
- "A self-censoring, biased, and overly pro-government centralized media was built up....News anchors with expertise were fired and replaced by inexperienced amateurs often giving near comical onscreen performances."
- Civil liberties and civil society institutions outside of the ruling populist party were constricted and disempowered.[67]

These maneuvers would be joined in 2015 by a repellent anti-refugee campaign that painted refugees, mostly from the Middle East and Africa, as infectious invaders, almost subhumans, bent on destroying Hungary and Western civilization in general.

Attila Antal, a law scholar at Budapest's Eötvös Loránd University, reacts powerfully to Orbán's project for Hungary, christening it not only populism but "biopopulism," which "starts to use the concept of nationalist-populism to regulate the human life, create a permanent state of exception."[68] The idea of a permanent state of exception, a troubling twist on Schmitt's theory of sovereignty, leads Antal to recognize Schmitt in the Hungarian case, arguing that Schmitt's thinking "has fundamentally influenced the political advisers around Orbán's government."[69] Recall that Schmitt's central complaint was that liberal democracy cannot provide the justification for its own powers and, slave to law and bureaucracy, cannot deal with exceptions to law and bureaucracy; at those moments of

---

[67] András Bíró-Nagy, "Illiberal Democracy in Hungary: The Social Background and Practical Steps in Building an Illiberal State." *Illiberal Democracies in the EU: the Visegrad Group and the Risk of Disintegration. Barcelona: CIDOB Editions* (2017), 37.

[68] Attila Antal, "Nationalist Populism and Illiberalism in Hungary: Historical Origins, Current Trajectories" (lecture, Carleton University, Ottawa, Canada, May 9, 2018), 19.

[69] Ibid., 8.

breakdown, the fact of the decision and the decider becomes manifest. Now, Orbán does not use the term "biopopulism," referring initially to his political philosophy as "national cooperation" (the nation, of course, biologically and culturally circumscribed). However, increasingly pressed to clarify his administration and his philosophy of government, he has slid toward Schmittian disdain for liberal democracy. Today, "he states his opposition to liberal democracy loud and clear. Democracy, he vows, should be hierarchical rather than liberal. Under his leadership, Hungary will become an '*illiberal new state based on national foundations*.'"[70]

What is this thing, illiberal democracy? Mounk summarizes it tersely as "democracy without rights" (and contrasts it not only to liberal democracy but to *undemocratic liberalism* or "rights without democracy").[71] While many pundits and ordinary citizens view illiberal democracy as an oxymoron, this short-sightedness depends on a failure to distinguish liberalism from democracy. In a prescient 1997 essay, Fareed Zakaria emphasizes that "democracy" in common parlance means *liberal democracy*, a democratic system "marked not only by free and fair elections, but also by the rule of law, separation of powers, and the protection of basic liberties of speech, assembly, religion, and property" (i.e., Mounk's "rights").[72] Democracy, strictly speaking, implies nothing other than "the rule of the people"; *how* they rule, or even *who* the people are, is underdetermined. As mentioned previously, the French revolutionaries leading the reign of terror claimed to be acting in the name of the people, and Soviet communism governed in the name of the people, represented by the monopolistic Communist Party; consider also the People's Republic of China or the Democratic People's Republic of Korea (North Korea), whose official webpage (www.korea-dpr.com) promotes the country as a society where "the workers, peasants, soldiers, and intellectuals are the true master of their destiny"—*democratic but far from liberal.*

"The tension between constitutional liberalism and democracy," Zakaria maintains, "centers on the scope of governmental authority," the vital Schmittian question.[73] Zakaria is not the first to sense that the "tendency for a democratic government to believe it has absolute sovereignty (that is, power) can result in the centralization of authority, often by extraconstitutional means and with grim results."[74] In ancient times, philosophers already dreaded the "tyranny of the majority," which we might reformulate for the modern age as *the tyranny of "the people."* From a

---

[70] Mounk, *The People vs. Democracy*, 10, emphasis added.

[71] Ibid., 14.

[72] Fareed Zakaria, "The Rise of Illiberal Democracy," *Foreign Affairs* 76, no. 6 (1997), 22.

[73] Ibid., 30.

[74] Ibid.

populist perspective, only "the people"—almost always narrowly defined, by nationality, ethnicity, race, religion, etc.—have a right to rule and, moreover, have a right to have rights. And, as we have detailed in various cases, populist-style democracy too often permits no competition with and no alternative to the will or voice of the people. Hence, Zakaria could conclude over thirty years ago that

> elected governments claiming to represent the people have steadily encroached on the powers and rights of other elements in society, a usurpation that is both horizontal (from other branches of the national government) and vertical (from regional and local authorities as well as private businesses and other nongovernmental groups). Lukashenko [Alexander Lukashenko, president of Belarus since 1994] and Peru's Alberto Fujimori are only the worst examples of this practice.[75]

Zakaria also observes that Russia's Boris Yeltsin used military force against the country's parliament and subsequently "suspended the constitutional court, dismantled the system of local governments, and fired several provincial governors," creating "a Russian super-presidency"; he adds that history "can only hope his successor will not abuse it"—a wish not granted.[76]

The pattern that Pappas identifies as the "populist blueprint" is also an illiberal blueprint. When populists (and not only right-wing populists, unfortunately) gain power by constitutional or unconstitutional means, they tend to follow a program that includes "(a) colonizing the state with loyalists, (b) reinforcing the party and state leader's executive capacity, (c) assaulting liberal democratic institutions [which he labels the "institutional blitz"], and (d) utilizing various forms of state patronage to the benefit of their supporters," not only wealth transfers but immunity from penalties for breaking the law.[77]

It is fair to say—which Schmitt also realizes but bemoans—that liberalism and constitutionalism exist precisely to *limit* power, both the government's power and the people's power. Notwithstanding Schmittian exceptions, which a constitution also seeks to contain, liberalism compels the government and the people to work within the boundaries of law and institutions (granted that these laws and institutions are subject to change). It also prevents the majority from crushing the minority, and it tends toward universalism in assigning equal rights ("human rights," not citizens' rights or "peoples' rights") to all members of the society and ideally to all humans regardless of society. Liberalism subordinates "the people" to the law and

---

[75] Zakaria, "The Rise of Illiberal Democracy," 30.

[76] Ibid., 34.

[77] Pappas, *Populism and Liberal Democracy*, 201.

denies them their specialness and their infinite sovereignty. And, as some students have commented and complained, it "depoliticizes" various aspects of society, of government itself, by ideally removing them from partisan debate and manipulation, particularly the constitution and the instruments of government.

No wonder that dedicated populists struggle *against liberalism in pursuit of democracy*, repoliticizing what liberalism depoliticizes. Not only are laws and institutions a barrier to perfect popular sovereignty (not to mention the ambitions of the leader), but those laws and institutions are often interpreted as the cause of the people's problems, the product and perpetuator of corruption and oppression and an unwelcome mediation between the people and their government, personified by the populist leader. To the objections against laws and institutions as such must be added the perceived empirical failures of both, aggravated by declining standards of living, disorienting cultural diversity and the often scorched-earth effects of neoliberalism and globalization. People might not even mind liberalism, laws, and institutions *if they worked*, but the association between liberal democracy and the experience of "losing" in the contemporary global economy stains liberalism. This understanding explains the otherwise incomprehensible glorification by Orbán of other countries that have "abandoned the liberal principles of societal organization" like China, Russia, and Turkey. In his mindset, "only an illiberal democracy can devotedly serve the general interest of the whole nation."[78] There is plainly an affinity between populists across international lines—an affinity blind to the fact that the interests of *our* whole nation are necessarily at odds with the interests of *their* whole nations.

Beyond populism as a political project, yet often bundled with it—and adding another and higher dimension of illiberalism to "the people" that secular politics alone cannot confer—is the notion of the *sacred nation*. Most peoples throughout history have probably regarded themselves as special, even elect or chosen, sometimes the center of the world, sometimes the only real people in the world. But in the putatively secular politics of the twentieth century, national sacredness reappeared in unexpected ways. One of the first modern political philosophers to take notice was Eric Voegelin, in his 1938 essay "The Political Religions." A century earlier, Hegel had mystified the state as an expression of spirit, a world-historical leader like Caesar or Napoleon embodying the *Zeitgeist*, the spirit at the times. Voegelin argues, however, that the standard twentieth-century concept of the

---

[78] Bíró-Nagy, "Illiberal Democracy in Hungary," 36.

state lacks an appreciation of its "religious pretensions."[79] The state does not inhabit the "profane realm" alone; the state or the political community is

> also a realm of religious order, and the knowledge of a political condition will be incomplete with respect to a decisive point, firstly if it does not take into account the religious forces inherent in a society and the symbols through which these are expressed or, secondly, if it does include the religious forces but does not recognize them as such and translates them into areligious categories.[80]

"The language of politics is always interspersed with the ecstasies of religiosity," he reasons, "and, thus, becomes a symbol in the concise sense of letting experiences concerned with the contents of the world be permeated with transcendental-divine experiences."[81]

These words echo Schmitt, who could almost have uttered them himself. For Schmitt, though, political theology runs in only one direction, from theology to politics: in his estimation, political concepts are secularized religious concepts. Emilio Gentile guides us in exactly the opposite direction. In an essay on sacralized politics, he contends that the sacralization of politics "means the formation of a *religious dimension in politics that is distinct from, and autonomous of, traditional religious institutions*":

> The sacralization of politics takes place when politics is conceived, lived and represented through myths, rituals and symbols that demand faith in the sacralized secular entity, dedication among the community of believers, enthusiasm for action, a warlike spirit and sacrifice in order to secure its defense and its triumph. In such cases, it is possible to speak of religions of politics in that politics itself assumes religious characteristics.[82]

He elaborates on the idea of sacralization of politics, positing that it manifests when a political party or movement

---

[79] Eric Voegelin, *The Collected Works of Eric Voegelin: Volume 5, Modernity without Restraint*, ed. Manfred Henningsen (Columbia and London: University of Missouri Press, 2000), 28.

[80] Ibid., 70.

[81] Ibid.

[82] Emilio Gentile, "The Sacralisation of Politics: Definitions, Interpretations and Reflections on the Question of Secular Religion and Totalitarianism," *Totalitarian Movements and Political Religions* 1, no. 1 (2000), 21–22, emphasis in the original. DOI: 10.1080/14690760008406923

(a) consecrates the primacy of a *collective secular entity*, placing it at the center of a system of beliefs and myths that define the meaning and ultimate goals of social existence, and proscribe the principles that define good and evil.

(b) incorporates this conception into a code of ethical and social commandments which bind the individual to the sacralized entity, compelling the same individual to loyalty and dedication to it.

(c) considers its members an *elect community* and interprets political action as a *messianic function* aiming toward the fulfilment of a mission.

(d) develops a *political liturgy* in order to worship the sacralized collective entity by way of an institutionalized cult and figures representing it, and through the mystical and symbolic portrayal of a *sacred history*, periodically relived through the ritual evocations performed by the community of the elect.[83]

In the case of right-wing populism, the collective secular entity at the center of sacred politics is obviously "the people," to which the individual is bound and subordinated, and the messiah is the populist leader.

But while this analysis at first glance restates and fulfills Schmitt's theory, it is actually a perfect *inversion* of his thinking. It is not politics that is secularized religion but *religion that is spiritualized politics*. The politics is primary and real (if constructed), and the theology is secondary and residual. It elevates politics to a sacred level rather than reducing religion to a profane level. It is a means of instilling specialness, the ultimate specialness, to an otherwise mundane enterprise and, like any taboo, of putting that enterprise (here, the people's sovereignty) beyond approach and beyond reproach.

There are relatively trivial instances of the sacralization of politics. Bellah's civil religion is one, which, as we saw, provides a sheen of divine meaning and mission to everyday political business. Another is the American habit of referring to the flag or the Constitution as sacred, when (almost) no one believes that either was ordained by a deity (some men wrote the latter, and traditional political myth has it that a woman sewed the former). What Americans want to say when they call worldly social artifacts "sacred" is that those artifacts are very, very important, and Americans have no other word for that besides "sacred," which they borrow from religion.

Then there are decidedly non-trivial political sacralizations. Bilge Yabanci documents one in Turkey, where Erdoğan's populists "sacralize the political arena by attributing nominally secular entities such as the nation, the state and the leader 'religious' traits as objects of loyalty and faith."[84] Citing Gentile, Yabanci interprets Erdoğanism as "missionary politics"

---

[83] Gentile, "The Sacralisation of Politics," 22, emphasis in the original.

[84] Yabanci, "Fuzzy Borders Between Populism and Sacralized Politics," 92.

mobilized to save or redeem the nation from an "existential crisis" (*bekâ sorunu*) "inflicted by a group of vaguely defined internal and external 'enemies.'"[85] This soteriological narrative has all the elements of Christian *heilsgeschichte*, including devils (i.e., secularists and modernists as well as foreigners), ancient paradigms of heroism, virtue, and martyrdom (in the Turkish case, Ottoman Turks like Mehmet the Conqueror and Selim II, as well as the father of the modern state, Mustafa Kemal), and an apocalyptic setting that "invites the promise of 'resurrection,' the other component of missionary politics."[86]

"At the center of the AKP's missionary politics stands the venerated leader," the salvific figure, and the incarnation of the highest will (the people), namely Erdoğan.[87] Like any messiah, the people owe their allegiance, their "faith," to this man. Institutions and parties cannot save them; in fact, the "mission (*dava*) is beyond party politics."[88] Together, the leader and the people comprise a virtual church, "an exclusive and idealized 'brotherhood' of selfless individuals brought together around the mission."[89] The leader, people, and mission are unified not only through identity and ideology but what Yabanci calls "performance politics," which displaces and replaces ordinary politics and "democratic participation." Performance politics draws upon the reservoir of cultural symbols, myths, and rituals to orient the movement, to endow it with import and sacredness and the certainty of victory, and to permanently and energetically fuse the people to it (see Chapter 7). "In practice," Yabanci summarizes, performance politics "aims to turn political participation," ordinarily practiced through calm, rational means like voting and legal deliberation, "into outbursts of 'mass spectacle' performed jointly by the community of the elect that shall remain devotedly behind the mission."[90] And although Yabanci does not mention it, performance politics and the general sacralization of politics also spell out the cost of failure and of apostasy.

A second and arguably yet clearer example of sacralized politics introduces a right-wing populist not yet mentioned in this chapter, namely, India's Narendra Modi. In the assessment of Preeti Sampat, contemporary India is witnessing the "dismantling of the liberal secular democratic political order" in favor of "a strong Hindu nationalist state."[91] Modi and his

---

[85] Yabanci, "Fuzzy Borders," 100–1.

[86] Ibid., 102.

[87] Ibid., 103.

[88] Ibid., 102.

[89] Ibid., 105.

[90] Ibid., 109.

[91] Preeti Sampat, "Make in India: Hindu Nationalism, Global Capital, and Jobless Growth," in *Beyond Populism: Angry Politics and the Twilight of Neoliberalism*, ed. Jeff Maskovsky and Sophie Bjork-James (Morgantown: West Virginia University Press, 2020), 63.

Bharatiya Janata Party (BJP) rose to power in 2014, winning re-election in 2019, on a program of Hindutva. Hindutva, a term meaning "Hindu-ness" or "Hindu nationalism" and often equated to Hindu fundamentalism, was coined in the 1920s by Vinayak Damadar Savarkar, who counseled that Hindus were not only a single nation (*rashtra*) but the authentic indigenous nation of the Indian subcontinent. All true natives of the land, regardless of their caste, sect, or language, were Hindus, and the essence of Hindu identity was literally in their blood. Therefore, all of India was not only a home but a *sacred* home for Hindus. As for non-Hindus in the motherland, Madhav Sadashir Golwalkar admonished in his 1938 *We, or Our Nationhood Defined*:

> The foreign races in Hindustan must either adopt the Hindu culture and language, must learn to respect and hold in reverence Hindu religion, must entertain no idea but those of the glorification of the Hindu race and culture, i.e., of the Hindu nation and must lose their separate existence to merge in the Hindu race, or may stay in the country, wholly subordinated to the Hindu nation, claiming nothing, deserving no privileges, far less any preferential treatment not even citizen's rights.[92]

Meanwhile, a sacred-political ideology was translated into a political movement in the 1920s with the founding of the *Rashtriya Swayamsevak Sangh* (RSS, or National Volunteer Corps). It was not long before the RSS was a Hindu-nationalist organization more than half a million strong, with an increasingly paramilitary nature. Militant and anti-pluralist, the RSS scorned the partition of independent India as a capitulation to Muslims; it also condemned the secular constitution of the new country for omitting the ancient Sanskrit Laws of Manu. A political party and precursor to the BJP, the Bharatiya Jana Sangh, was formed in 1951, with the BJP itself following in 1980. Modi is described by Sampat as "a dedicated activist of the RSS before he was moved to the BJP," and his government is filled with "RSS activists."[93] Yet despite Modi's "charismatic, authoritarian, and [Schmittian] decisionist personality," Sampat judges that India's right-wing Hindutva populism is not a one-man outsider phenomenon as in some countries but "a historically emergent protofascist movement committed to creating a profoundly exclusionary *Hindu Rashtra*."[94]

Hindutva politicians and practitioners have self-consciously if not cynically pushed religious buttons, including the dispute over a holy site in the city of Ayodhya. A Muslim mosque, the Babri Masjid, had been built on the site of what was believed by Hindus to be the birthplace of the Hindu

---

[92] Quoted in Sampat, "Make in India," 63–64.
[93] Ibid., 66.
[94] Ibid.

god Ram. In 1992, a political rally organized in part by the BJP turned into a riot, culminating in the demolition of the mosque. Meanwhile, political discourse commonly associates the country with the Hindu goddess Durga; since colonialism, *Bharat Mata* or Mother India has been portrayed as a female deity but one "enslaved, bruised, and all-suffering in chains," occupied then by the British and today by non-Hindus of various sorts.[95] Among the persecutors of Mother India are Muslim men who have been accused of everything from seducing Hindu women for the purpose of birthing more Muslim babies to slaughtering sacred cows for their meat, resulting in several "cow protection" lynchings in BJP-governed districts.

Sordid events like the Ayodhya riots or lynchings over beef raise the menace of theologically-meaningful and politically-useful violence. In a discussion of the "political theology of violence" in contemporary India, which again invokes Schmitt, Thomas Blom Hansen reckons that acts of political and intercommunal violence "are interpreted and understood as signs of something else standing behind it; a sovereign will, a collective force of outrage and anger, a historical revenge, or even the 'hand of God.'"[96] Political-religious violence is sometimes welcomed as revelatory, as "opening Shiva's third eye" and transforming the leader "into a tool of the divine, the absolute, turning himself into God's hand," as in an uprising in Gujarat a decade after Ayodhya, when the BJP state government held back police and prevented news coverage of the violence, "allowing the local units of the RSS and the VHP [another right-wing Hindu organization, with a women's group named *Durga Vahini* or Carriers of Durga] and their many local supporters to wreak deadly revenge on Muslims all over the state."[97]

Lastly, Indian right-wing populism uses standard social-religious methods to inculcate their political-religious ideology in children. Jessica Marie Falcone reports on the Shantiniketan Summer Camp in Washington, D.C., a Hindutva version of Christian American "Jesus camps" for diaspora Indian families in the United States. During the four days and nights of the camp, children and parents participate in games as well as military-style drills and lectures in which they learn that they must fight "against the so-called Muslims and Christian onslaught: 'the battle is on. The Christian missionaries are trying to destroy us....Stand up!'"[98] Some of these families

---

[95] Atreyee Sen, "The Hindu Goddess in Indian Politics," Political Theology Network, May 29, 2015, https://politicaltheology.com/the-hindu-goddess-in-indian-politics-atreyee-sen.

[96] Thomas Blom Hansen, "The Political Theology of Violence in Contemporary India," *South Asia Multidisciplinary Academic Journal* special issue 2 (2008), 1.

[97] Ibid., 7–10.

[98] Jessica Marie Falcone, "Putting the 'Fun' in Fundamentalism: Religious Nationalism and the Split Self at Hindutva Summer Camps in the United States," *Ethos* 40, no. 2 (2012), 172.

are no doubt Hindutva supporters, but Falcone opines that, far from home and in a "white supremacist" America, others are merely hungry "for the romanticized narrative of belonging, acceptance, and Hindu unity that Hindutva stories have constructed."[99]

Moving on from India, and from the center of power to the fringe of society, many countries have developed small but sometimes influential sacred nation movements in the shape of (neo-)pagan and "native faith" religions. The phenomenon is especially prominent in Eastern Europe and the former Soviet Union, where religion mingles with or transforms into a "new nationalism." Fascinatingly, Hungary is a prime location for such thinking, which blends Hungarian biological and ethnic identity with religion and some pretty far-out national history. In this mentality, each nation or people need its own religion, its native faith, and in many local native faiths Hungarians are presented "as a pure and primordial people, as the continuation of great ancient civilizations."[100]

Réka Szilárdi asserts that in the process, "the linguistic, national, and political categories are sacralized. Being a chosen people plays an important role in their philosophy and causes exclusiveness and intolerance of other religions and sexual orientations, as well as of different national or political affiliations." If this sounds like a formula for right-wing populism, then we can anticipate Szilárdi's conclusion that these national-religious beliefs "result in political commitment, which means support for the radical right in the Hungarian case."[101]

In such native faiths, it is often not enough to be a proud people with a unique culture and religion; some Hungarian religions, like the Ancient Hungarian Church, declare that theirs is the first and all-inclusive religion and that all other religions—Christianity as well as eastern traditions such as Buddhism, Confucianism, and Taoism—sprouted from primordial Hungarian beliefs.[102] At the extreme edge of Hungarian national mythology is the Church of the Universe, which teaches that the ancestors of the Hungarians arrived from the star Sirius over six thousand years ago and settled on an island in the Pacific.[103] Even the somewhat milder claim that Hungarians are descended directly from ancient Sumer demands a conviction that "mainstream history" is false, a conspiracy foisted by

---

[99] Falcone, "Putting the 'Fun' in Fundamentalism," 169.

[100] Réka Szilárdi, "Neopaganism in Hungary: Under the Spell of Roots," in *Modern Pagan and Native Faith Movements in Central and Eastern Europe*, ed. Kaarina Aitamurto and Scott Simpson (Durham, UK and Bristol, CT: Acumen, 2013), 244–45.

[101] Ibid., 245.

[102] Ibid., 240.

[103] Ibid., 236.

secularists, modernists, and non-Hungarians to deny the nation its rightful place in human history and destiny.[104]

If various Hungarian native faiths are way out there, they are still more benign than the Russian native faiths documented by Victor Shnirelman, which feature both "a less politicized folklorist wing and a highly politicized national-patriotic wing."[105] As in Hungary and elsewhere, Russian Neopaganism typically aspires to recover the greatness of the Russian nation, but, as populist/nationalist movements are wont to do, it has coincided with cultural and biological visions of the nation. The "Russian identity" that is endangered by other ethnicities, by Westernization, and in some views by Christianity too, is a matter of blood, an idea attractive to many far-right and skinhead groups that have moved *Rodnovery* (Slavic native faith) in a more "xenophobic, racist, and chauvinistic" direction, merging "an ideology (ethnic nationalism and racism) and ... a fighting practice ('Slavic-Goritsa wrestling')" in a manner that can spill out as street violence.[106] (See Chapter 7 for more Russian and other political myths.)

Trump the Populist

[T]oday we are not merely transferring power from one Administration to another, or from one party to another—but we are transferring power from Washington, D.C. and giving it back to you, the American People. For too long, a small group in our nation's Capital has reaped the rewards of government while the people have borne the cost. Washington flourished—but the people did not share in its wealth. Politicians prospered—but the jobs left, and the factories closed. The establishment protected itself, but not the citizens of our country....January 20th 2017 will be remembered as the day the people became the rulers of this nation again.

—Trump's 2017 inauguration speech[107]

After everything discussed in this chapter, these words are familiar as the words of a populist. In the official act of assuming the presidency, Trump lambasted "the establishment" and lionized "the people." In power, he has

---

[104] Szilárdi, "Neopaganism in Hungary," 238.
[105] Victor A. Shnirelman, "Russian Neopaganism: From Ethnic Religion to Racial Violence," in *Modern Pagan and Native Faith Movements in Central and Eastern Europe*, ed. Kaarina Aitamurto and Scott Simpson (Durham, UK and Bristol, CT: Acumen, 2013), 63.
[106] Ibid., 73.
[107] Donald J. Trump, "The Inauguration Speech," Whitehouse.gov, January 20, 2017, https://www.whitehouse.gov/briefings-statements/the-inaugural-address.

faithfully followed the populist script summarized by Pappas: he has found or fashioned (and pressed on) wounds; blamed, caricatured, and ridiculed rivals and enemies; portrayed himself as the only solution and salvation; traded policies and plans for unsystematic tales and tirades; and offered his base vengeance and anger.

So in considering the fundamental question of Trump's exceptionalism addressed in the previous chapter, if he is a populist—and opinions vary on the subject, some branding him a plutocrat in populist's clothing—then he is not exceptional. He is indisputably not the first populist, not in the world and not in the United States; indeed, he is a relative late-comer to the populist party, just as Reagan was not the first neoliberal to lead a country (England's Margaret Thatcher took office almost two years earlier, and Chile's dictator Augusto Pinochet implemented neoliberal policies, spurred by Milton Friedman and his "Chicago Boys," as far back as 1973).

To be sure, Trump possesses the intuitions and performs the role of a populist, starting with the manners of an iconoclastic political outsider—"directness, playfulness, bullying, coarse language, a disregard for hierarchy and tradition, ready resort to anecdotes as evidence, and a studied ignorance of that which does not interest him."[108] He also, instinctively more than consciously, hews to the populist blueprint of power seizure, institutional blitz, and personal patronage:

> He sought to colonize top state administrative positions with his own people, although initially with no great success....Trump increasingly entrusted extensive government responsibilities to members of his family, like his daughter and her husband. He also made use of discretionary power through, for instance, a large number of executive orders.... [H]e attacked judges personally for rulings he was not in agreement with and questioned the constitutional authority of the courts.... Trump became particularly active in attacking the liberal media claiming that they produced "fake news," which, as he tweeted, "is not my enemy, it is the enemy of the American people!" ... Aiming to build a "political empire," Trump offered high-ranking administrative jobs especially to large campaign donors and business people in the expectation of their political support.[109]

In these and other ways, including his gleeful disregard of traditions of the office and his accumulation of executive powers in defiance of constitutional checks and balances (like ignoring congressional subpoenas and forbidding

---

[108] Moffitt, "The Performative Turn in the Comparative Study of Populism," 55.

[109] Pappas, *Populism vs. Liberal Democracy*, 189–90.

his staff and former staff from testifying at congressional hearings), he shows himself to be a standard if not tiresomely ordinary and ultimately petty populist. Indeed, although the sensibilities of most Americans are offended by such antics and power grabs, former and current populists around the world have done much worse than him. He has not dissolved the legislature, rewritten the Constitution, or illegally extended his term in office (although he has "joked" about the latter). Plus, as moribund and supine as legislative and judicial office-holders have been, there is still popular and institutional pushback against his worst behaviors, including at the time of this writing a remarkable denunciation by high-ranking military leaders of his conduct in regard to the Black Lives Matters protests, some stinging defeats in the Supreme Court, and a precipitous drop in approval rating over his handling of the COVID-19 virus. Populism in America has its limits, as it reached its limits in Peru and may some day in Hungary, Turkey, India, and elsewhere.

Apparently, all populist leaders have an authoritarian streak in them, if only because they feel that they do the people's, if not the deity's, work. The next chapter will place this authoritarian tendency in longer historical perspective.

4

1950s Wisdom for a 1950s President: On Agitators, Authoritarians, Totalitarians, and True Believers

The previous chapter judged that Trump fits the profile of a populist, a right-wing populist specifically, fairly closely. He has been branded as a populist, mostly by his opponents, since "populist" has acquired something of a derogatory if not alarmist ring. Among the other epithets that Trump has been called are autocratic, fascist, despotic, and authoritarian. He has also been accused of having a 1950s imaginary for his vision of America, imaginary especially because the image he paints of a blissful, stable, peaceful 1950s America is an illusion. The decade of the 1950s was in reality a time of great unrest and upheaval, despite the picture in many heads of "organization men" shuffling to work in gray flannel suits and wives doing housework in vintage dresses. Those were also the years of the nascent civil rights movement (the *Brown vs. Board of Education* ruling against racial segregation in public schools was handed down in 1954), the first stirrings of the feminist movement (Betty Friedan's *The Feminine Mystique* would introduce "the problem that has no name" in 1963), and the rise of youth culture with its associated moral panics over rock 'n' roll music and such (the films *Rebel Without a Cause* and *Blackboard Jungle* were both released in 1955, and Elvis Presley was giving society the vapors with his hip motion by 1956). Further, the 1950s were a time of social and political fear, as the United States entered another war (the Korean War, in 1950) and faced the prospect of nuclear annihilation at the hands of the evil Soviet Union. Finally, the 1950s were hardly idyllic if you were a non-white, non-straight, non-Christian, non-capitalist, non-male American.

At the same time, the 1950s were years of great productivity in political science, the world having only recently emerged from a period of real fascism in Germany, Italy, and their conquered territories and now facing the advancing enemy of communist totalitarianism in Russia and China. Because these anti-democratic systems and the destruction they wrought were such fresh and imminent menaces, great energy was invested in understanding why fascist/totalitarian/authoritarian leaders and regimes arise, why ordinary people follow them, and how democracies could best resist them. The traumas of the 1930s and 1940s gave scholars a perspective on anti-democratic forces that we largely lack today, those experiences being relatively remote for citizens of the twenty-first century.

It is interesting and profitable, then, to consider the Trump phenomenon through the lens of this body of 1950s literature and to assess how he does and does not conform to mid-twentieth century autocrats and authoritarians. The period that we are examining begins roughly in 1941, when the United States entered World War II and when Erich Fromm published his classic *Escape from Freedom*; it ends around 1963, when Stanley Milgram announced his famous "obedience" or electric-shock experiment findings. In between, a cascade of studies appeared, including Karl Popper's 1945 two-volume *The Open Society and Its Enemies*, Carl Friedrich and Zbigniew Brzezinski's 1956 *Totalitarian Dictatorship and Autocracy*, and the four books that we will feature in this chapter—Leo Lowenthal and Norbert Guterman's *Prophets of Deceit: A Study of the Techniques of the American Agitator* (1949), Theodor Adorno et al.'s *The Authoritarian Personality* (1950), Hannah Arendt's *The Origins of Totalitarianism* (1951), and Eric Hoffer's *The True Believer: Thoughts on the Nature of Mass Movements* (1951).

The key subject of the present chapter is authoritarianism. Of the various pejoratives applied to Trump, it is probably the most appropriate. He is not really a fascist, nor can he seriously hope to be an autocrat or a totalitarian. Authoritarianism, however, is within the reach of a dedicated populist; in fact, while not all authoritarians are populists by any means, the last chapter indicated that authoritarianism is an ever-present threat in populism—and an acceptable, even a popular threat, if "the people" believe that their will (in the person of the populist) should reign supreme. A basic definition of authoritarianism, as it is currently understood, implies its close relationship with populism:

blind submission to authority, as opposed to individual freedom of thought and action. In government, authoritarianism denotes any political system that concentrates power in the hands of a leader or a small elite that is not constitutionally responsible to the body of the people. Authoritarian leaders often exercise power arbitrarily and without regard to existing bodies of law, and they usually cannot be replaced by citizens choosing freely among various competitors in elections. The freedom to create opposition political parties or other alternative political groupings with which to compete for power with the ruling group is either limited or nonexistent in authoritarian regimes.[1]

---

[1] Britannica Academic, "Authoritarianism," *Encyclopedia Britannica*, November 2, 2017, academic-eb-com.aurarialibrary.idm.oclc.org/levels/collegiate/article/authoritarianism/3154.

Populism likewise tends to concentrate power in the hands of a leader whose authority is not bound by constitutions, institutions, norms and traditions, or the rule of law; all of those political forces, we learned, are precisely the corrupted obstacles to the unrestrained public will. Populists also tend to limit or eliminate competition, as no one other than the people personified by the leader has a legitimate right to rule; they accordingly often contort elections, media, and courts to guarantee their retention of power, if not intimidate and harass rivals and enemies. The quoted source further contends that authoritarianism contrasts essentially with democracy, but this is not entirely true: populists and their constituents typically think that they are acting democratically, in the sense that the *demos* is having its way politically. It would be more accurate to say, from the lessons of the last chapter, that authoritarianism contrasts with *liberal* democracy; it is completely consistent with, and in practice often synonymous with, *illiberal* democracy.

Elsewhere, Lowell Barrington attributes four traits to authoritarianism, which distinguish it from both democracy and totalitarianism. These include depoliticization or demobilization of the

population (i.e., the citizenry is not asked to be or remain politically active), lack of an official ideology (as opposed to totalitarianism, which promotes a state ideology like Nazism or communism), "legitimacy based on performance" (i.e., as long as the leader or regime is delivering the goods, the people are willing to accept his/its authority), and weak or absent limitations on government power.[2] As often eventuates in populist regimes, "the official rules of the game are subordinate to the will of the authoritarian ruler or rulers. Checks and balances (including judicial review) and the rule of law, both of which are familiar to citizens of many democratic countries, are unusual in authoritarian states."[3] He adds that the authoritarian may be an individual or party, a bureaucracy, or the military.

Fig. 9 Collage of totalitarian leaders (each row-left to right) Joseph Stalin, Adolf Hitler, Mao Zedong, Benito Mussolini, and Kim Il-Sung

---

[2] Lowell J. Barrington, "Authoritarianism," in *Ethics, Science, Technology and Engineering: A Global Resource*, 2nd ed., ed. J. Britt Holbrook (Boston, MA: Cengage, 2014), 155.

[3] Ibid., 156.

The two studies (Fromm and Milgram) that book-end the era highlight that much of the 1950s investigation into authoritarianism is psychological in orientation. A pair of underlying questions informs the research: what is the psychological nature (that is, the personality) of the authoritarian leader, and why do individuals submit to, indeed more commonly than we would expect *choose*, authoritarian leaders? Plenty of studies attempt to analyze (often psychoanalyze) characters like Hitler or Stalin, while other work asks the more perplexing question about followers. Fromm is fairly typical in pinpointing a desire *not* to be free; in his opinion, the freedom that comes to the individual with modern society, "though it has brought him independence and rationality, has made him isolated and, thereby, anxious and powerless. This isolation is unbearable and the alternatives he is confronted with are either escape from the burden of this freedom into a new dependence and submission, or to advance to the full realization of positive freedom which is based upon the uniqueness and individuality of man."[4] Authoritarianism specifically, or populism generally, is thus construed as a solution to a painful psychological affliction. Karl Popper, whose discussion starts with Plato (who was no democrat) and ends with Marx, likewise perceives the mass of humans as striving to abdicate responsibility and rationality, leaving their fate to the supposedly ineluctable machinery of history.[5] Milgram of course exposes the readiness of people to submit to authority, asking subjects to administer (supposedly) painful and potentially deadly shocks to others, which they reliably did through no malice of their own but because a white-coated expert ordered them to do so.

To take one more, small step back before we proceed, long before World War II and unrelated to fascism, numerous scholars evaluated the conditions of modernity as deleterious to the physical and mental health of human beings. Marx condemned English life in the mid-1800s, and Max Weber pronounced modernity an iron cage. For Louis Wirth, urban life was at the root of modern pathology. In 1938, he declared that the "superficiality, the anonymity, and the transitory character of urban-social relations," the diversity of the city's population, the poverty, not to mention the bright lights, the noise, and the dirt of the city, lead to confusion, isolation, and anomie (a concept also dear to Durkheim).[6] This is a possible example of a twist on our comment about authoritarianism: both were so new to 1950s scholars that they merited anxious consideration, whereas for us today

---

[4] Erich Fromm, *Escape from Freedom* (New York: Farrar & Rinehart, 1941), viii.

[5] Karl R. Popper, *The Open Society and Its Enemies, Volume 2 The High Tide of Prophecy: Hegel, Marx, and the Aftermath* (New York and Evanston, IL: Harper Torchbooks, 1945), 269.

[6] Louis Wirth, "Urbanism as a Way of Life," *The American Journal of Sociology* 44, no.1 (1938), 12.

authoritarianism is too remote and urbanism/modernity is too familiar. As a result, we are too sensitive to the former and not sensitive enough to the latter.

An Authoritarian Character:
The Agitator

Prophets of Deceit is a qualitative study of authoritarian/populist leadership. Part of the "Studies in Prejudice Series" steered by Max Horkheimer and Theodor Adorno (Horkheimer provides the introduction to the book), it describes the leader (without using the as-yet-unavailable term "populist") as a propagandist and a play-actor, someone who gives the impression of being a leader and one of the common people, and who borrows from "certain forms of religious revivalism, without regard to content, forms which exploit such rigid stereotypes as the distinction between the 'damned' and the 'saved.'"[7] Indeed, one of the agitator's key qualities is his ambiguity: he deliberately makes it difficult to discern if and when he is acting or being serious, preferring not to "commit himself for he is willing, temporarily at least, to juggle his notions and test his powers" and to tread the gray zone "between the respectable and the forbidden, … to use any device, from jokes to doubletalk to wild extravagances."[8]

Predictably, the agitator arises in times of social turbulence and frustration, offering to "defeat the social groups held responsible for perpetuating the social condition that gives rise to discontent."[9] Like the populists in the last chapter, those groups usually include foreigners and immigrants, almost always Jews, as well as the rich and the established political classes. Whomever he targets, the solution typically involves "the elimination of people rather than a change in political structure. Whatever political changes may be involved in the process of getting rid of the enemy he sees as a means rather than an end."[10]

The agitator seldom depends on rational argument alone, if at all. He prefers to enflame passions, activate unconscious forces, and "intensify the irrational elements in the original complaint," which entails outsiders and the non-deserving taking what rightfully belongs to the real people of the country and which not only makes the audience more amenable to his message but renders them "passively receptive to his personal influence." One of his tactics is to discredit the opposition with (to us in 2020, disappointingly familiar) words like "hoax, corrupt, insincere, duped,

---

[7] Leo Lowenthal and Norbert Guterman, *Prophets of Deceit: A Study of the Techniques of the American Agitator* (New York: Harper & Brothers, 1949), xii.

[8] Ibid., 5.

[9] Ibid., 6.

[10] Ibid., 7.

manipulate."[11] He cautions his listeners that they inhabit a dark, oppressive, and hostile world—sometimes "the darkest hour in American history"— from which only he can deliver them.

Echoing the contemporary populist who walks the thin line between authority and accountability and empowers the people while simultaneously weakening them, the agitator accuses them of being "eternal dupes" who have been fooled by sinister agents for too long. He attunes them to the conspiracies that undermine their interests and their sovereignty and offers himself as a defender of Americanism and Christianity. Yet he disparages the existing two-party system, rejecting even democracy itself as a "trick world": he is more likely to say things like "justice matters more than democracy" and "liberalism—in politics—leads to Anarchy."[12] As any good populist would, the agitator

> transforms democracy from a system that guarantees minority rights into one that merely affirms the privileged status of the majority. Persecution of minorities is thus within the rights of the majority and any attempt to limit the exercise of this "right" is interpreted as persecution of the majority by the minority.[13]

He is, in short, an anti-pluralist and an anti-universalist. Rights only apply to "the people," not to the Other.

It goes without saying that the Other is not just different but diabolical, a "ruthless enemy." Lowenthal and Guterman name, more than seventy years ago, basically the same cast of enemy characters as today—the rich, the self-serving and corrupt government officials, the socialists and communists, the foreigners, and, most strikingly of all from today's perspective, the refugees.

> For the agitator, the refugee is the most fearsome version of the foreigner. The very weakness, the very plight of the refugees is an argument against them, since "they fled from the wrath of the treacherously outraged peoples of those nations, as they may one day flee as well from the wrath of a finally aroused populace in America." The refugee becomes identified with the parasite who seeks dupes to do his dirty work.[14]

Paradoxically, he at once depicts the enemy as "helpless," as a group that can and surely will be defeated through a concerted effort of the people

---

[11] Lowenthal and Guterman, *Prophets of Deceit*, 13.
[12] Ibid., 29.
[13] Ibid., 32.
[14] Ibid., 50.

(behind his leadership, naturally), and as ominously powerful, as a group that poses a mortal threat. They are criminals, degenerates, "low animals," and the good people of the nation are called to root them out and hunt them down.

Still, for all the perils pitted against the people, the agitator is noticeably short on specific recommendations. His platform is mostly platitudes. Lowenthal and Guterman surmise that his audiences

> find the agitator's statements attractive not because he occasionally promises to "maintain the American standards of living" or to provide a job for everyone, but because he intimates that he will give them the emotional satisfactions that are denied them in the contemporary social and economic set-up. *He offers attitudes, not bread.*[15]

Equally, the agitator himself is more destructive than creative: his message and his manner allow him to "reject current values while avoiding the task of formulating a new set of values," and he certainly never offers any "universal standards or criteria that could take the place of discarded ideals and form the nucleus of a new moral, philosophical, religious, and political outlook."[16] Any such program would pin him down, unmask the charade of his play-acting, and commit him to a measurable goal against which he might fail.

In the absence of a concrete plan, all that the people can do, or need to do, is "to band together as an elite in order to take from others what we want for ourselves," which too commonly takes the form of "biological self-defense" (or as we called it in a prior chapter, biopopulism).[17] His "arguments or pseudoarguments" offer little more than "extreme nationalism" and exaltation of "free enterprise, individualism, protective tariffs, and simple flagwaving."[18] He is congenitally suspicious of international organizations as sacrifice of sovereignty and capitulation to the powers and interests of foreigners. The American institution he loves the most is the military. And when the people have won? Then authoritarian populism will be complete:

> The agitator takes it for granted that after the purge the populace will withdraw to their homes and leave the government in the hands of the "patriotic remnant." In his eyes the masses remain essentially passive.

---

[15] Lowenthal and Guterman, *Prophets of Deceit*, 91–92, emphasis added.
[16] Ibid., 92.
[17] Ibid., 95.
[18] Ibid., 97.

The agitator's quarrel with the government is not at all basic, it merely involves a desire to see it manned by satisfactory personnel.[19]

This means his most loyal supporters, often his close kin.

Lowenthal and Guterman reserve a few words for the followers of the nationalist/populist agitator. They are the "simple Americans," Nixon's silent majority, the grassroots, the people "of sound instincts and, he is happy to say, little sophistication." But this tribute to the masses leads to anti-intellectualism and conformism "as a moral principle."[20] Further, while the agitator wishes the people to wake up from their lethargy and reclaim what is theirs, to make America great again, in the end they "are invited, not to organize rational responses, but to act out their impulses."[21] At its worst, this "hysteria" breeds "sadistic fantasies," in which the "verbal fury of the agitator is only a rehearsal of real fury."[22]

Returning finally to the agitator, his success rests on cleverly portraying himself as one of the common folk yet far above the common folk. He trades on his reputation as "the indefatigable businessman" or "the rugged frontiersman" but always "a suffering martyr" who gives up much—his wealth, his empire—to serve the people and therefore "deserves special privileges and unlimited ascendancy over his followers." A salesman (if not a huckster), he "does not hesitate to advertise himself":

He could hardly trust anyone else to paint his self-image in such glowing colors. As the good fellow who has nothing to hide, whose effusiveness and garrulousness know no limit, he does not seem to be inhibited by considerations of good taste from openly displaying his private life and his opinions about himself.[23]

The performance of the agitator thus tends to fall into one of two basic categories—"one in a minor key establishing him as a 'great little man,' and the other in a major key as a bullet-proof martyr who despite his extraordinary sufferings always emerges victorious over his enemies."[24] Either way, he conveys unequivocally that "he is an exceptionally gifted man who knows and even admires his own talent."[25] To be sure he is a "tough guy ... physically powerful and something of a terrorist to boot," but he also "has access to secret and highly important information, the source of

---

[19] Lowenthal and Guterman, *Prophets of Deceit*, 101.
[20] Ibid., 109.
[21] Ibid., 112.
[22] Ibid., 115.
[23] Ibid., 118.
[24] Ibid., 119.
[25] Ibid., 124.

which he is careful not to disclose. He quotes mysterious 'sources'" (sometimes just what "many people" say) and cryptically refers to information he will reveal in some indefinite future.[26]

In sum, then, in all he says and does, the agitator "engages in an essentially ambiguous activity":

> He never merely says; he always hints. His suggestions manage to slip through the nets of rational meaning—those nets that seem unable to contain so many contemporary utterances. To know what he is and what he says, we have to follow him into the underground of meaning—the unexpressed or half-expressed content of his hints, allusions, doubletalk. Always, then, the agitator appeals to those elements of the contemporary malaise that involve a rejection of traditional western values. As we have seen in the previous chapter, he directs all of his themes to one ultimate aim: his followers are to place all their faith in his person—a new, externalized, and brutal superego.[27]

The Authoritarian-Following Personality

The crowning achievement of the aforementioned "Studies in Prejudice Series" was Theodor Adorno et al.'s *The Authoritarian Personality*. It is a nearly one-thousand-page quantitative inquiry into what they call "the authoritarian type of man." As we gathered from our brief survey of the 1950s-era literature above, Adorno's project has a decidedly psychological, even Freudian, slant, investigating the personality (literally, among other issues, the childhood experiences, parent-child relationships, and depth-psychology—id, superego, etc.) variables in this authoritarian man and his opposite, the liberal man. The data for the study come from questionnaires, interviews, and clinical research (such as projective tests like the Thematic Apperception Test). It contains pages and pages of test protocols and tables of data, aimed at developing reliable measurement scales, particularly a Fascism scale which is subsequently correlated to other variables like education and religiosity. Some of this theory and methodology is dated and dubious, but the analysis still yields interesting results.

As the authors explain early in the volume, the focus of the work is "the *potentially fascistic* individual," though not the fascist *leader* as we might well expect but instead the person "whose [personality] structure is such as to render him particularly susceptible to antidemocratic propaganda."[28] Now it becomes apparent that the "authoritarian type of

---

[26] Lowenthal and Guterman, *Prophets of Deceit*, 132.

[27] Ibid, 140–41.

[28] Theodor W. Adorno et al., *The Authoritarian Personality* (New York: Harper & Row, 1950), 1.

man" is the *follower*, not the leader, that is, the person who submits to, on many occasions selects and approves of, the antidemocratic leader. (The book, like many of its kind, tends to slide uncritically between terms like antidemocratic, fascist, prejudiced, and authoritarian, which are not synonymous.) Because of the abundance of potential fascist/antidemocratic personalities in the United States, the authors caution that "it is up to the people to decide whether or not this country goes fascist."[29]

By the second chapter we are told that the prime issue is not prejudice, which is too limited, but the general attitude of *ethnocentrism*, which they define as "provincialism or cultural narrowness; it meant a tendency in the individual to be 'ethnically centered,' to be rigid in his acceptance of the culturally 'like' and in his rejection of the 'unlike.'"[30] One perennial expression of prejudice and ethnocentrism is anti-Semitism, but they contend that the ethnocentric individual evinces an aversion to "aliens" in general, which anti-Semitism is just one expression. In the ethnocentric mentality, the Other—they mention races, ethnic minorities, refugees, and putatively "inferior nations"—is "regarded as backward, immoral, and threatening. The superiority of the American nation justified a policy of destruction and subordination of others."[31] Plumbing the heart of ethnocentrism as a collective exclusionary attitude (our group versus their group), they assert that "submissiveness and obedience to the ingroup are regarded as primary virtues, and a punitive attitude" is taken toward outgroup members (other races, ethnicities, nationalities, religions, etc.) as well as toward ingroup members who deviate from or betray their own kind.[32]

The authors propose two initial hypotheses. First, as already noted, one "primary characteristic of ethnocentric ideology is the *generality* of outgroup rejection"; that is, ethnocentrists and proto-fascists do not object merely to some particular other but to all others.[33] Second—and they do not flatter themselves to claim they are the first to notice it—political conservatism tends to correlate with ethnocentrism, whereas political liberalism correlates to "relative freedom from prejudice." To distinguish the traditional conservative, the patriotic small-government pro-business type, from the ethnocentric conservative, they introduce the term "pseudoconservative" whose ideology displays "a tendency antithetical to democratic values and traditions":

---

[29] Adorno et al., *The Authoritarian Personality*, 10.
[30] Ibid., 103.
[31] Ibid., 116.
[32] Ibid.
[33] Ibid., 147.

[H]is politico-economic views are based on the same underlying trends—submission to authority, unconscious handling of hostility toward authority by means of displacement and projection onto outgroups, and so on—as his ethnocentrism. It is indeed paradoxical that the greatest psychological potential for antidemocratic change should come from those who claim to represent democratic tradition. For the pseudoconservatives are the pseudodemocrats, and their needs dispose them to the use of force and oppression in order to protect a mythical "Americanism" which bears no resemblance to what is most vital in American history.[34]

Much later in the proceedings, they conclude:

The goal toward which the pseudoconservative mentality strives—diffusedly and semiconsciously—is to establish a dictatorship of the economically strongest group. This is to be achieved by means of a mass movement, one which promises security and privileges to the so-called "little man" (that is to say, worried members of the middle and lower middle class who still cling to their status and their supposed independence), if they join with the right people at the right time.[35]

Before they arrive there, they have some other observations to share. For instance, the ethnocentrist, also a pseudopatriot and militarist, believes that America "should either keep out of world affairs altogether (isolationism) or we should participate—but without losing our full sovereignty, power, and economic advantage (imperialism). And in either case we should have the biggest army and navy in the world."[36] Essential to the ethnocentric mentality is a personalization of every issue and problem, attributing every setback of "ours" to an individual or group of "them," inevitably stereotyped. Both alternative perspectives—perceiving individuals in all their diversity and complexity and a universalist humanitarianism that embraces all people as basically alike—are beyond their grasp. And all relations and interactions are viewed through the lens of *power*: hierarchy is in operation at all times, and any gain in the power of another group is a loss in power of ours. Power is how the authoritarian personality maintains unequal social relations, by pushing other groups down and supporting leaders who will act the same.

Finally, the authors construct their Fascism scale, characterized by such variables as

---

[34] Adorno et al., *The Authoritarian Personality*, 182.
[35] Ibid., 685.
[36] Ibid., 147.

- conventionalism or rigid traditionalist thinking
- authoritarian submission: "Submissive, uncritical attitude toward idealized moral authorities of the ingroup"
- authoritarian aggression
- anti-intraception or resistance to subjectivity or tenderness (i.e., lack of self-awareness and of empathy)
- superstition and stereotypy
- power and "toughness": "Preoccupation with the dominance-submission, strong-weak, leader-follower dimension; identification with power figures; overemphasis upon the conventionalized attributes of the ego; exaggerated assertion of strength and toughness"
- destructiveness and cynicism
- projectivity: "The disposition to believe that wild and dangerous things go on in the world; the projection outwards of unconscious emotional impulses"
- and last but not least, a fixation on other people's sexuality.[37]

Armed with this trait list, the authors spend the rest of the book unpacking the fascist/authoritarian personality. To it they ascribe idealization of the parents, which is a first step in the blind acceptance of authority; a moralistic animosity to all expressions of the "id" (mostly sex); an equally moralistic condemnation of people who are different from them; punitiveness and inclination to blame others for their problems; exploitation and manipulation; self-glorification; pseudo-masculinity and macho boastfulness; and a "distortion of outside reality." Summarizing the data on individuals who score high on the Fascism scale, they judge that these potential fascists, these submissive authoritarians, share a rigidity of thought, an intolerance of ambiguity, a pseudoscientific or antiscientific outlook, a lack of introspection or insight into their own mind and emotions, suggestibility and gullibility, and unrealistic thinking.[38]

At this point, they offer a typology of fascistic personalities, of which the authoritarian is only one. Among these types are "surface resentment," wracked by "justified or unjustified social anxieties" and desirous of someone or something who will bring relief. The "conventional" type, perhaps the most common and benign, is committed to existing conventions and opposes or fears the new and different. The "tough guy" is likened to the psychopath: asocial, his pleasure comes from shows of strength and endurance and sadistic persecution of the weak and different. The "crank" has "largely replaced outward reality by an imaginary inner

---

[37] Adorno et al., *The Authoritarian Personality*, 228.
[38] Ibid., 461.

world"; the authors do not use the term "conspiracy theorist," but it probably fits here. The "manipulative," the most dangerous in their estimation, divides the world into "empty, schematic" categories and values only ends over means.[39]

In blatantly psychoanalytic terms, they hold the authoritarian type to be closest to the basic portrait of a high-scorer on the Fascism scale. Invoking Fromm, they dub the authoritarian a "sadomasochistic character" who, overcome by superego, "achieves his own social adjustment only by taking pleasure in obedience and subordination."[40] Aggression seems to rule the authoritarian's world, turned outward against others and turned inward against the self, which inclines him to surrender himself to an equally belligerent figurehead. Without pity, with disdain for the weak and the poor, the "identification of the 'authoritarian' character with strength is concomitant with rejection of everything that is 'down'"[41]—and that, if they have their way, will stay down.

On the Origin of Totalitarian Species

A year after the publication of *The Authoritarian Personality*, Hannah Arendt released her magisterial study, *The Origins of Totalitarianism*. This first title in a distinguished career of insightful political analysis, which produced *The Human Condition* (1958), *Eichmann in Jerusalem* and *On Revolution* (1963), and *Crises of the Republic* (1972) among others, explores the rise of communism and Nazism in a more inclusive historical context. The book's more than five hundred pages are divided into three thematic sections— anti-Semitism, imperialism, and totalitarianism. She links these three phenomena as one moral for mankind, that the only way to prevent such brutalities in the future is through the

Fig. 10 Hannah Arendt, 1933

---

[39] See Adorno et al., *The Authoritarian Personality*, 753–67 for a thorough discussion of these fascistic types.

[40] Ibid., 759.

[41] Ibid., 762.

precise opposite of authoritarianism and populism, that is, through "a new political principle ... whose validity must comprehend the whole of humanity while its power must remain strictly limited."[42]

Twentieth-century totalitarianism, she asserts, has a much older lineage, one preceded by anti-Semitism and imperialism and premised on major political-historical changes like the rise of the modern nation-state and of bourgeois capitalism. It was from the demands for regular national incomes and secure finances with the waning of monarchies that Jewish financiers moved to a place of prominence and precarity in Europe, and after a series of scandals, frauds, and financial disasters that impacted the lower middle class most harshly, this class "now suddenly turned anti-Semitic." Anti-Jewish parties appeared in the unprecedented setting of the coalescing nation-state, which only exists, she theorizes, because "no single group was any longer in a position to wield exclusive political power."[43] In other words, because Schmittian sovereignty was evaporating, there was a scramble for political organization and political legitimacy. The critical symptom was the rise of parties, including anti-Semitic parties, that claimed that "they were not a party among parties but a party 'above all parties,'" seeking "to become the representative of the whole nation, to get exclusive power, to take possession of the state machinery, to substitute themselves for the state."[44]

Imperialism is a child of the same circumstances. Industrial capitalism had (and has) but one imperative—*expansion*—which is not "political" but drags politics along with it: where the economy goes, the politics must go. The economy could theoretically grow indefinitely, as long as production and demand permit, but imperialism appeared when and because the capitalist class discovered that the needs of capitalism exceeded national borders. Capitalism outgrew the nation in the immediate sense (i.e., coveting resources and markets that lie outside the country), but also in the sense that the nation, understood as a group bound by ties of blood, land, and culture, cannot in principle grow like capital does: capital may entangle other peoples, but they remain *other peoples*. And, as some other scholars have also opined, it was domestic or continental imperialism in Europe that exacerbated political irritations more than overseas conquest. German, Russian, Serbian and other strivings for political unification and then for living space spawned pan-national "tribalism" characterized by "contempt for liberal individualism, the ideal of mankind and the dignity of man."[45]

---

[42] Hannah Arendt, *The Origins of Totalitarianism*, second enlarged ed. (Cleveland, OH and New York: The World Publishing Company, 1958 [1951]), ix.

[43] Ibid., 38.

[44] Ibid.

[45] Ibid., 235.

Almost inevitably, this anti-liberalism and anti-universalism entailed a blatant "disregard for law and legal institutions": "Contempt for law became characteristic of all movements" in this political climate.[46] As parliaments and elected governments proved themselves feckless, political institutions lost legitimacy, and citizens lost faith in them. At the worst, members—especially those disposed to authoritarian attitudes as described by Adorno—came to revile the state, and Arendt maintains that there "are no movements without hatred of the state."[47] The tribalist, antidemocratic parties and the governments ruled by such parties in power favored the executive decree over the parliamentary process, since the decree requires no "general principles," provides no justifications, and accepts no limits. Even better for the arbitrary ruler, the populations "ruled by decree never know what rules them."[48] The effect is a Kafkaesque world of eternal ambiguity and *permanent exception*. It is hard to disagree with Arendt that, by the late nineteenth century, "man," that is, the abstract denationalized concept enshrined in principles like "the rights of man," had "hardly appeared as a completely emancipated, completely isolated being who carried his dignity within himself without reference to some larger encompassing order, when he disappeared again into a member of a people."[49]

With that, the table is set for totalitarianism. The first difference between totalitarian and other movements is that the former are not class or interest-group based but rather "mass" movements aimed at mobilizing and organizing the nation—especially those who, she contends, have not been or could not be previously organized. Such movements, like later populisms, "placed themselves outside and against the party system as a whole," appealing to the disenfranchised who had given up on other parties "as too apathetic or too stupid."[50] Believing, with like thinkers of her time, that totalitarian movements reached primarily "atomized, isolated individuals" (see Hoffer below), these socially detached or alienated people were ripe for personal attachment—and more, for "total, unrestricted, unconditional, and unalterable loyalty" to a leader. It might be an overstatement to insist that movement partisans were people with no friends or family, but Arendt is probably correct when she argues that the success of totalitarianism exploded the illusions of democratic government. It is a fantasy, she writes, that the majority of the population is necessarily in accord with the parties and the more general institutions of the society; they may grant no more than their "silent approbation and tolerance" to those parties and institutions, which neither represent nor serve the majority. In other words, it is painfully

---

[46] Arendt, *The Origins of Totalitarianism*, 243.
[47] Ibid., 259.
[48] Ibid., 244.
[49] Ibid., 291.
[50] Ibid., 311.

obvious that "a democracy could function according to rules which are actively recognized by only a minority."[51] But woe unto the system when the previously silent and passive masses do rise.

Among the tactics employed to both awaken and prod the masses, according to Arendt, are propaganda and terror, but the perverse fact is that terror "continues to be used by totalitarian regimes even when its psychological aims are achieved: its real horror is that it reigns over a completely subdued population."[52] This is one great irony of totalitarianism, that the masses are roused only to be immediately tranquilized. And since totalitarianism is a strange sort of war against one's own society, and since the first casualty of war, as they say, is truth, it makes sense that truth has little place in a totalitarian system. Propaganda substitutes for truth, and the "truths" of the old discredited regime as well as any rivals and enemies of the new regime are nothing but hypocrisy and corruption. Besides, as time has proven, the masses do not want facts, "not even invented facts," but "only the consistency of the system of which they are presumably part."[53] A vital aspect of this consistency and of the imperviousness to truth is the claim by the leader, and the belief by the follower, of the leader's infallibility. Once the leader has established his perfection, he and his propaganda machine "can outrageously insult common sense" and "conjure up a lying world of consistency which is more adequate to the ends of the human mind than reality itself."[54] Incredibly but with great relevance, Arendt chronicles occasions when "members of the movement knew very well that [the leader] lied, and trusted him more than ever because he apparently was able to fool public opinion and the authorities."[55]

What in the end are totalitarianism and its vast propaganda and terror machine for? In Arendt's analysis, it comes down simply to organizing and disciplining the people for the *further accumulation of power*. Having divided first the society and then the world into "two gigantic hostile camps" and recruited everyone into the (often or eventually quite literal) war effort, it marches toward ever grander power in sneering defiance of all legal restrictions, of the very notion of "positive law" (i.e., laws created by human institutions like legislatures and courts). Far from arbitrary or ungrounded, though, the totalitarian's

> defiance of positive laws claims to be a *higher form of legitimacy* which, since it is inspired by the sources themselves, *can do away with petty legality*. Totalitarian lawfulness pretends to have found a way to

---

[51] Arendt, *The Origins of Totalitarianism*, 312.
[52] Ibid., 344.
[53] Ibid., 351.
[54] Ibid., 352–53.
[55] Ibid., 383.

establish the rule of justice on earth—something which the legality of positive law admittedly could never attain.[56]

This "higher form of legitimacy" could be, and in prior historical periods has been, divine or revealed law, but for twentieth-century totalitarianism it has tended to be the inescapable law of Nature and/or History—for instance, the natural "survival of the fittest" and superiority of the master race (Nazism) or the historical inevitability of a dictatorship of the proletariat (Bolshevism). In the end, then, Arendt posits that a key difference between normal "lawful" government (not necessarily but especially democracy) and totalitarianism is the attitude toward positive (read: man-made, imperfect, ever-changing) law:

By lawful government we understand a body politic in which *positive laws are needed* to translate and realize the immutable *ius naturale* [natural law] or the eternal commandments of God into standards of right and wrong. Only in these standards, in the body of positive laws of each country, do the *ius naturale* or the Commandments of God achieve their political reality. In the body politic of totalitarian government, *this place of positive laws is taken by total terror, which is designed to translate into reality the law of movement of history or nature....*If lawfulness is the essence of non-tyrannical government and lawlessness is the essence of tyranny, then terror is the essence of totalitarian domination.[57]

Beware the True Believer

Unlike the tightly argued case of Arendt or the data-driven analysis of Adorno et al., Eric Hoffer's short treatise (less than 170 pages) is an impressionistic, almost aphoristic sociology of mass movements. Although the title implies religion, Hoffer hardly mentions religion and is really interested in the person who devotes his/her true belief to a cause like communism or Nazism.

Following the footsteps of theorists of crowds and collective behavior like Charles Mackay and Gustave Le Bon and anticipating the work of Elias Canetti, who consistently assess crowds and masses as inherently irrational and pestilent, Hoffer states in his preface that all mass movements, regardless of the details of their ideology, "breed fanaticism, enthusiasm, fervent hope, hatred, and intolerance"; "all of them demand

---

[56] Arendt, *The Origins of Totalitarianism*, 462, emphasis added.
[57] Ibid., 464.

blind faith and singlehearted allegiance."[58] For Hoffer, a mass movement is first and foremost about *action* rather than thought, and the true believer is "the man of fanatical faith who is ready to sacrifice his life for a holy cause."[59]

It goes without saying that mass movements look forward to change, and the twentieth century has been noted for its *pathos of the real*, its firm conviction that society (if not the whole world) can be engineered for the better, regardless of the human cost. The century is littered with projects to deconstruct and reconstruct society in its entirety according to some ideal master-plan (going back to the anarchists of the nineteenth century like Nechayev, who were pleased to burn society down to the ground), usually littering the affected territory with corpses. What these movements reflect, in Hoffer's mind, is "faith in the future" and discontent if not disgust with the present. But more—in his psychological diagnosis of the movement and its adherents—movement enthusiasts "crave to be rid of an unwanted self," to discard their feelings of loss and self-loathing and to restore "pride, confidence, hope, a sense of purpose and worth by identification" with something bigger and more perfect than themselves.[60] A large chunk of his book is committed to describing this cast of characters, whom he lists as the poor, misfits, "the inordinately selfish," "the ambitious facing unlimited opportunities," minorities, the bored, and sinners. Echoing Fromm and many others, he reasons that too many members of society suffer from freedom, which presents too much choice and too little guidance and ultimately "places the whole blame of failure on the shoulders of the individual."[61] The mass movement is a Frommian escape from freedom, offering the consolation of a "refuge ... from the anxieties, barrenness, and meaninglessness of an individual existence."[62]

Hoffer concurs with the consensus on political movements and political actors that reality and truth are peripheral matters: when it comes to participating in the movement and envisioning the future, "make-believe plays perhaps a more enduring role than any other factor."[63] Predictably, then, the appeal and efficacy of a movement derives not from its veracity or any particular interpretation of its doctrine but from the sheer weight of its *certitude*. This is crucial for the leadership of the movement. The most effective leader displays "iron will, daring, and vision." The ideal movement leader

---

[58] Eric Hoffer, *The True Believer: Thoughts on the Nature of Mass Movements* (New York: HarperPerennial, 1966 [1951]), xi.

[59] Ibid., xii.

[60] Ibid., 21.

[61] Ibid., 35.

[62] Ibid., 44.

[63] Ibid., 65.

personifies the certitude of the creed and the defiance and grandeur of power.... He stages the world of make-believe so indispensable for the realization of self-sacrifice and united action ... *Exceptional intelligence, noble character and originality seems neither indispensable nor perhaps desirable.* The main requirements seem to be: audacity and a joy in defiance; an iron will; *a fanatical conviction that he is in possession of the one and only truth*; faith in his destiny and luck; a capacity for passionate hatred; contempt for the present; a cunning estimate of human nature; *a delight in symbols (spectacles and ceremonials)*; *unbounded brazenness which finds expression in a disregard of consistency and fairness;* a recognition that the innermost craving of a following is for communion and that there can never be too much of it; a capacity for winning and holding the utmost loyalty of able lieutenants.[64]

The leader's job is to identify (or manufacture) a complaint, discredit the existing social-political order, and assemble a cohort of the disgruntled, and then direct them into action. For the purpose of collecting and agitating his followers, the leader exploits a standard set of "unifying agents" or strategies, including hatred, suspicion, imitation, persuasion, and coercion. Of all these, Hoffer deems hatred the most potent, and the focal point of organized hatred is the enemy, the Schmittian essence of politics. In semi-religious language, Hoffer declares that mass movements "can rise and spread without belief in a God, but never without belief in a devil," although that devil is often, if not always, a very worldly adversary, for example another party, nationality, race, religion, etc.[65]

As mentioned, action is the fuel that feeds the movement. The figures who initiate a movement may be intellectuals, people of thought and words, but the figures who transport a movement to power are more often people of action. And Hoffer understands that collective action, of whatever sort, is a tool of unifying and integrating the group in the first place. An active membership "tends toward uniformity"; action—including or especially rallying, marching, and breaking things—functions "to strip its followers of their distinct individuality and render them more soluble in the collective medium."[66] Give them slogans to chant and signs—or guns—to carry, and it is all the better; give them uniforms to wear and symbols to rally around, and it is better still. The one thing you should not give them, however, is a very specific and attainable goal. "A mass movement with a concrete, limited objective is likely to have a shorter activity period than a

---

[64] Hoffer, *The True Believer*, 105–6, emphasis added.
[65] Ibid., 86.
[66] Ibid., 121.

movement with a nebulous, indefinite objective"[67] and for two comprehensible reasons: if the movement reaches its goal, it may disband, and if it does not reach its goal, it may abandon the movement and the leader as failures and fakes.

Trump, Agitator, Authoritarian

This thicket of terminology—fascist, totalitarian, dictator, authoritarian, and the like—and the leaders, parties, and publics it implicates return to the foundational question of political theology, namely, the relation between power and law, how law commissions or constrains power and how power erects, evades, or erodes law. With or without reference to religion (and on plenty of occasions with, at most, metaphorical reference to religion), the tension between power and law endures. Fascism, authoritarianism, etc. only underscore the irresolvable Schmittian paradox of power and law: law cannot absolutely define and delimit power, because law cannot foresee every political circumstance and because ultimately *power makes law*, but power cannot absolutely slip the bounds of law, because even in the most autocratic of governments, alternative sites of power survive in the law and because power tends in the long run to settle back into law.

The question remains where Trump belongs in the authoritarian landscape. Hopefully, readers have had no difficulty glimpsing his silhouette in the portraits of the agitator, the authoritarian, and the leader of true believers. In one of the rare recent writings to cite Lowenthal and Guterman, Panayota Gounari ranks Trump as a latter-day American agitator, the source of a "neofascist, authoritarian turn." In fact, Gounari, a scholar of linguistics and education, criticizes the term "right-wing populism" as a substitute for what she prefers to call *neofascist authoritarianism* and blasts Trump—his administration and his Twitter storms—for fitting the description of a neofascist authoritarian. This profile features a "high degree of concentration and centralization" of power, a politics of fear and demonization of the Other, "purposeful ideological confusion," authoritarian leadership style with extensive personalization of politics, and a "propaganda machine that distorts reality and historical facts, produces fake news stories, and is at war with intellectualism and scientific knowledge."[68] Play-actor, propagandist, anti-pluralist, flag-waving divider and destroyer, irrationalist, and self-promoting tough guy—these qualities all describe Trump the campaigner and Trump the president. Punitive, non-empathetic, anti-scientific, defiant of law in answer to a putative higher authority (Christian god, American

---

[67] Hoffer, *The True Believer*, 142.

[68] Panayota Gounari, "Authoritarianism, Discourse and Social Media: Trump as the 'American Agitator,'" in *Critical Theory and Authoritarian Populism*, ed. Jeremiah Morelock (London: University of Westminster Press, 2018), 210–11.

people, his own ego, or whatever), unintelligent and ignoble but brimming with certainty, he is the epitome of Hoffer's movement leader, if not Arendt's totalitarian.

But perhaps it is less important to decide what Trump *is* on the spectrum or from the selection of anti-democratic leaders and, taking a cue from Marlies Glasius, better to consider what authoritarian things he *does*. Advocating a practice approach to authoritarianism, Glasius urges us to attend less to authoritarian leaders or followers and more to *authoritarian practices*, defined as "patterns of action that sabotage accountability to people over whom a political actor exerts control, or their representatives, by means of secrecy, disinformation, and disabling voice."[69] Recall from the last chapter that Paula Diehl also put accountability front and center in the analysis and critique of populism; Mark Bovens adds a useful definition of accountability when he calls it "a relationship between an actor and a forum, in which the actor has an obligation to explain and justify his or her conduct, the forum can pose questions and pass judgment, and the actor may face consequences."[70] Bovens' forum could be the legislature and the courts, the media, or public opinion expressed through (dis)approval ratings and re-election (or not).

In normal democracy, an elected official, in this instance the president, not only should but wants to explain and justify conduct (although these explanations and justifications are not always honest), making the case for policy decisions, declarations of war, and other actions. The office-holder ordinarily subjects him/herself to questioning from the media (press briefings, interviews, etc.) and from constituents, and of course the holder may subsequently lose office through electoral or other means (e.g., impeachment). But there are many authoritarian actions, Glasius emphasizes, that a democratically-elected leader can take to squelch questioning, avoid consequences, and negate accountability. The most obvious is *secrecy*, keeping unfavorable information away from the forum; an example in mid-2020 was Trump's efforts to "classify" every conversation he has ever had as president, for present purposes to prevent former national security advisor John Bolton's "tell-all" book from being published (a ploy that failed). Another practice, or set of practices, is *misinformation* which includes outright (in Trump's case, extravagant) lying. If information leaks into the legislative, judicial, media, and/or public realms, the authoritarian has a battery of practices to elude consequences. One set involves *disabling questioning*, for instance terminating press conferences, refusing interviews, and attacking (verbally or otherwise, as

---

[69] Marlies Glasius, "What Authoritarianism Is…and Is Not: A Practice Perspective," *International Affairs* 94, no. 3 (2018), 517.

[70] Mark Bovens, "Analysing and Assessing Accountability: A Conceptual Framework," *European Law Journal* 13, no. 4 (2007), 450.

with police searches, lawsuits, and tax investigations or, in the worst cases, arrest and torture) anyone who does or might dare to raise a question or objection. Finally, the authoritarian can interfere with the application of consequences by *disabling passing of judgment*, which tends to require more muscular maneuvers like disbanding legislatures, ignoring or co-opting courts, or canceling elections.

Provocatively, Glasius proposes that *authoritarian* practices are distinct from *illiberal* practices, defined as "a pattern of actions, embedded in an organized context, infringing on the autonomy and dignity of the person," which might feature "interference with legal equality, legal recourse or recognition before the law; infringement of freedom of expression, fair trial rights, freedom of religion and the right to privacy; and violations of physical integrity rights."[71] The contrast between authoritarian and illiberal is probably important although not total: some practices, like "subversion of the separation of power" and "election fraud," are clearly authoritarian, while others (Glasius offers the examples of Rodrigo Duterte of the Philippines who supports the death penalty for drug users, or Russia's Vladimir Putin—or for that matter Trump—who seeks to deprive LBGTQ citizens of their rights) are demonstrably illiberal. In political reality, the difference between the practices, and their effects, is frequently hard to maintain. Glasius admits that illiberal practices can have the goal of "suppressing the voices of those who constitute a threat to power-holders," which is an authoritarian goal; for instance, if you imprison, deport, or exterminate members of society, you have also eliminated their voice and their vote.

It is plain to see that many of Trump's practices are authoritarian, illiberal, or both without having to conclusively assign him and his regime to the categories authoritarian or illiberal as a whole. In fact, separating the authoritarian/illiberal democrat into a congeries of practices frees us to assess a particular leader or government as *more or less* authoritarian or illiberal. It also directs us to make further differentiations within the category of authoritarian itself. In a series of writings, Steven Levitsky and various co-authors have done precisely this, insisting that "authoritarian" is too rigid a concept, especially in the fluid twenty-first century. Recent decades, he explains, have produced a variety of "hybrid political regimes" with both democratic and authoritarian qualities; old-fashioned bare authoritarianisms or totalitarianisms are comparatively rare, though not unknown. Assorted terms have been suggested for these political systems, including semi-democracy, virtual democracy, semi-authoritarianism, and, as discussed in the previous chapter, illiberal democracy. For a particular kind of regime, he advances the label *competitive authoritarianism*. In a

---

[71] Glasius, "What Authoritarianism Is," 530.

competitive authoritarian government, "formal democratic institutions are widely viewed as the principal means of obtaining and exercising political authority. Incumbents violate those rules so often and to such an extent, however, that the regime fails to meet conventional minimum standards for democracy."[72] That is, competitive authoritarianisms hold elections, but they take strenuous measures to ensure that the incumbent government never loses.

Levitsky and his collaborators argue rightly that competitive authoritarianism is not "full-scale authoritarianism" while certainly not normal democracy. Completely authoritarian governments may not hold elections at all, or they may conduct only sham elections which the incumbents always win by a landslide. Such elections are obviously not intended to reflect the public will but to *shape* the public will, convincing those who are convinced by such subterfuge that the autocrat's rule is legitimate. The true import of the existence of competitive authoritarianism is its revelation that regimes "may mix authoritarian and democratic features in a variety of ways"; among these ways are "'exclusive republics' (regimes with strong democratic institutions but highly restrictive citizenship laws" and "'tutelary' or 'guided' democracies—competitive regimes in which nondemocratic actors such as military or religious authorities wield veto power."[73] No matter what the form, given Glasius' separation of authoritarianism from illiberalism (and in the previous chapter, of democracy from liberalism), it appears that authoritarianism "may coexist indefinitely with meaningful democratic institutions."[74] This is so, however, only if we consider the electoral aspect of such governments to the exclusion of other authoritarian/illiberal practices as identified by Glasius. There is much more to a government, liberal/democratic or illiberal/authoritarian, than voting.

Finally, Levitsky and Way recognize more than one path to competitive authoritarianism. Contrary to some opinion, history shows that it is not necessarily a step on the road to democracy. Two of the routes to competitive authoritarianism begin with a fully authoritarian system, which either weakens to the point where it must accept at least some democratic practices, or it collapses and is replaced by a competitive variation. Belarus, a former Soviet republic, presents a case of this sort. After the fall of

---

[72] Steven Levitsky and Lucan A. Way, "Elections without Democracy: The Rise of Competitive Authoritarianism," *Journal of Democracy* 13, no. 2 (2002), 52. For extended discussions of the concept and comparative surveys of over three dozen recent regimes, see Steven Levitsky and Lucan A. Way, *Competitive Authoritarianism: Hybrid Regimes after the Cold War* (New York: Cambridge University Press, 2010) and Steven Levitsky and Daniel Ziblatt, *How Democracies Die* (New York: Crown Publishing, 2018).

[73] Levitsky and Way, "Elections without Democracy," 54.

[74] Ibid., 59.

communism, democratic elections were held in 1994, won by Alexander Lukashenko; surviving an impeachment effort in 1996, he amended the country's constitution and convened a new parliament of loyal legislators. (Western governments refused to recognize the legitimacy of this new government, which gave Lukashenko the opportunity to accuse the liberal democracies of conspiring against him, a typical authoritarian ploy.) In 2020, after his fifth consecutive term as president, he won re-election largely because—and here is the competitive authoritarian part—in July he prohibited his two most serious political rivals from running against him. Vicktor Babariko was arrested in June for money laundering, and Valery Tsepkalo was disqualified for failing to obtain a sufficient number of valid signatures to get on the ballot. (Naturally, both men dispute the accusations against them.) Another candidate, Sergei Tikhanovsky, is in jail for allegedly attacking a police officer, and his wife Svetlana took his place on the ballot but ceased active campaigning out of fear. With no real competition, Lukashenko was virtually assured a sixth term, although domestic and international outrage followed his political stunt.

The third path, worrisomely, results from the decay of a democratic regime, in which "deep and often longstanding political and economic crises created conditions under which freely elected governments undermined democratic institutions—either via a presidential 'self-coup' or through selective, incremental abuses—but lacked the will or capacity to eliminate them entirely."[75] In their essay on Alberto Fujimori, Levitsky and James Loxton (discussed in Chapter 3) advance Peru as a model of competitive authoritarianism following a relatively functional democracy; we previously discussed how Fujimori corrupted the polling process, shut down the legislature, and rewrote the constitution to preserve his executive power. Esen and Gumuscu explicitly detect the rise of competitive authoritarianism in Turkey. They report that the country transitioned from a secular democracy to a tutelary democracy managed by the military to competitive authoritarianism under Erdoğan and his Justice and Development Party (AKP). Turning the institutions, the media, and the resources of the country into weapons for the government, the AKP promulgated election laws that shorten the campaign period so that opposition parties cannot disseminate their messages effectively, obstructed those parties from holding rallies and other events, used pliant media to support the AKP while burdening or closing independent media, intimidated journalists, employed extensive surveillance, filed lawsuits against critics, and, at some extreme moments, indulged in physical violence against rivals.[76] Viktor Orbán's Hungarian illiberal democracy has pulled all the same tricks to secure an electoral

---

[75] Levitsky and Way, "Elections without Democracy," 61.

[76] Berk Esen and Sebnem Gumuscu, "Rising Competitive Authoritarianism in Turkey," *Third World Quarterly* 37, no. 9 (2016), 1586–92.

supermajority for his Fidesz party and to sweep away any effective opposition.

If we ask, then, whether Trump engages in authoritarian and illiberal practices, keeping full awareness of the documented possibility of a democracy slipping into competitive authoritarianism, we cannot help but acknowledge the presence of such troubling practices. He has attempted, with some success, to centralize power around himself, although America's institutions are not yet utterly degraded and reputedly his own staff intercedes against his most pernicious inclinations. He spurns Congress and state governments at every opportunity and excoriates the courts when they rule against him, as the Supreme Court, filled with a conservative majority and two of his own appointees, did in two June 2020 decisions on LGBTQ rights and the Deferred Action for Childhood Arrivals (DACA, or "Dreamers") program. He circumvents law with executive orders and abuses the Constitution to exercise his executive privilege and pardon authority. He keeps secrets and (to put it politely) exudes misinformation. He disables questioning by vilifying the media, condemning unfavorable facts (or even recommendations like wearing face masks to prevent viral infection) as anti-Trumpism, and militarizing the response to legal protest. And, in continuation of tactics not exclusively owned by him or by conservatives but overwhelmingly utilized by him and them, he aims to insulate himself from electoral consequences through voter suppression, gerrymandering, blocking mail-in balloting (openly and accurately denouncing mail-in voting, that is, enhanced voter participation, as "the greatest risk" to his re-election[77])— even "joking" that he may seek and deserve a third (unconstitutional) term or intimating that his base might react to a re-election loss (no doubt fraudulent and stolen) with violence if not revolution.

Is the United States sliding into authoritarianism, competitive or otherwise? It might be alarmist to suggest so, and it is a sign of social health that the immune system of the American body social responds forcefully (but so far not very effectively) against such an invasion. And the body may well expel it. But the transformation has happened, and is happening, elsewhere, despite seventy-plus years of tracking authoritarians, totalitarians, and agitators by generations of theorists.

---

[77] Alex Isenstadt, "'My Biggest Risk': Trump Says Mail-In Voting Could Cost Him Reelection," *Politico*, June 19, 2020, https://www.politico.com/news/2020/06/19/trump-interview-mail-voting-329307.

5

Who Trump's Supporters Are—
and Are Not

The one thing that has confused and frustrated scholars, pundits, and journalists—mostly educated and fair-minded if not liberal-minded sorts that they are—is the character of the Americans who voted for Donald Trump in 2016 and who continued to endorse him through his term. It is facile and appealing to dismiss them as ignorant screaming rubes, Hillary Clinton's so-called "basket of deplorables" with their "racist, sexist, homophobic, xenophobic, Islamophobic" views.[1] No doubt these people, communities, and movements exist in the United States, and Trump is popular among them, as right-wing agitators and demagogues have been throughout our history. But even if they were Trump's main base, we could not dismiss them given their sheer numbers and political clout. Fortunately, Clinton was more accurate when she proceeded to identify "that other basket of people" who are not inherently deplorable but who "feel that the government has let them down, the economy has let them down, nobody cares about them, nobody worries what happens to their lives and their futures, and they're just desperate for change."[2]

This chapter will try to make sense of Trump's supporters, who are sometimes collectively if not condescendingly dubbed Trump Country or Trumpland. It is well known that he was especially enthusiastically received by whites and evangelical Christians, the latter of whom remain his most dependable constituency. Other variables such as class, education, and geography (i.e., rural residents) are often touted as keys to his success. And while these factors remain significant, a closer inspection of Trump's people paints a more complicated picture of Trump supporters, Republicans, Christians, and Americans in general in the early twenty-first century. Political theology perhaps plays a part for some of these citizens, but as we argued in the introduction of this book, theology is neither the question nor the answer for many who handed Trump the reins of power.

---

[1] Katie Reilly, "Read Hillary Clinton's 'Basket of Deplorables' Remarks About Donald Trump Supporters," Time.com, September 10, 2016, https://time.com/4486502/hillary-clinton-basket-of-deplorables-transcript.

[2] Ibid.

Race and Class in Trump Country

It is a truism that race and class played a major role in Trump's 2016 victory. He carried the white vote by twenty-one points (fifty-eight percent versus thirty-seven percent for Clinton) while losing the black vote by eighty points (eight percent to eighty-eight percent) and the Hispanic vote by thirty-six points.[3] As dramatic as those results are, they are consistent with party preferences over recent decades; Mitt Romney won fifty-nine percent of the white vote in the previous election, almost identical to Trump's performance, so Trump's racial success is not exceptional at all. Less significant but still measurable was the education effect: Trump dominated the less-educated population (no college degree) by eight percent, and college-educated voters preferred Clinton by nine. At the intersection of these variables, "Trump's margin among whites without a college degree is the largest among any candidate in exit polls since 1980. Two-thirds (67%) of non-college whites backed Trump.... In 2012 and 2008, non-college whites also preferred the Republican over the Democratic candidate but by less one-sided margins (61%–36% and 58%–40%)."[4] Again, although impressive, the 2016 outcome is consistent with historical trends.

Many observers have diagnosed from these numbers a rampant racism in Trumpland. Racism is nothing new in the United States, as we recounted in early chapters and as all informed Americans know. Combined with education, a common determinant of class, much attention and cultural worry has been focused on the "white working class" as a significant (if not noxious) voting bloc. Andrew Whitehead, Samuel Perry, and Joseph Baker stress that studies of Trump supporters have concentrated on "five key factors: white working class economic anxieties, misogyny, anti-black prejudice, fear of Islamic terrorism, and xenophobia"[5]—disturbingly similar to Clinton's deplorables checklist. However, when evaluating the race/class nexus, Sophie Bjork-James concludes that "Trump did not have a particular appeal among the white working class. In fact, only around 35 percent of his supporters had incomes below $50,000. His support didn't cluster around a class demographic, but did cluster around a racial one."[6]

---

[3] Alec Tyson and Shiva Maniam, "Behind Trump's Victory: Divisions by Race, Gender, Education," Pewresearch.org, November 9, 2016, https://www.pewresearch.org/fact-tank/2016/11/09/behind-trumps-victory-divisions-by-race-gender-education.

[4] Ibid.

[5] Andrew L. Whitehead, Samuel L. Perry, and Joseph O. Baker, "Make America Christian Again: Christian Nationalism and Voting for Donald Trump in the 2016 Presidential Election," *Sociology of Religion* 79, no. 2 (2018), 149.

[6] Sophie Bjork-James, "Americanism, Trump, and Uniting the White Right," in *Beyond Populism: Angry Politics and the Twilight of Neoliberalism*, ed. Jeff Maskovsky and Sophie Bjork-James (Morgantown: West Virginia University Press, 2020), 42.

Lilliana Mason, Julie Wronski, and John Kane make a very convincing case for the influence of racial out-group animosity as a prime motivator for Trump supporters. For instance, relating Trump's approval ratings to changes in attitudes toward non-whites, they find that "when feelings toward Blacks are cold and grow increasingly colder over time, approval for Trump increases"; conversely, if their feelings toward African Americans improved, "their feelings toward Trump in 2017 declined."[7] Results are the same when considering other racial and ethnic minorities. Increased acceptance of Hispanics between 2011 and 2017 correlates to decreased approval of Trump, just as a decline in acceptance of Hispanics leads people to be "significantly more approving of Trump." Likewise in regard to Muslims, only more so: increased coldness or hostility toward Muslims leads to seventy percent approval of Trump (and this trend also applies to non-ethnic others like gays and lesbians: negative attitudes lead respondents to a fifty-five percent Trump approval rating). Predictably, "feelings toward these groups largely predict Democratic Party affect as well. These results are positive and significant for changes in affect toward Blacks, Hispanics, Jewish people, Muslims, and lesbian and gay people";

Fig. 11 Donald Trump speaking with supporters at a campaign rally at the South Point Arena in Las Vegas, Nevada, February 22, 2016.

contrary to what many conservatives expect, "changing feelings toward Whites and Christians do not predict Democratic Party affect."

Despite the undeniable racial dimension of Trump support, it remains the case that more than one-third of white voters chose Clinton over Trump, whereas at least eight percent of black voters were somehow attracted to his rhetoric. The situation with Hispanics is more complex. Clinton garnered sixty-six percent of the Latino vote nationally (less than Obama's seventy-one percent in 2012), leaving Trump still able to claim twenty-eight percent (statistically insignificantly different than Romney's 2012 twenty-seven percent).[8] Drilling down into

[7] Lilliana Mason, Julie Wronski, and John Kane, "Ingroup Lovers or Outgroup Haters? The Social Roots of Trump Support and Partisan Identity" (paper presented at the Conference of the Midwest Political Science Association, Chicago, IL, May, 2019).

[8] Jens Manuel Krogstad and Mark Hugo Lopez, "Hillary Clinton Won Latino Vote but Fell Below 2012 Support for Obama," Pewresearch.org, November 29, 2016, https://www.pewresearch.org/fact-tank/2016/11/29/hillary-clinton-wins-latino-vote-but-falls-below-2012-support-for-obama.

those numbers, Cuban Americans, disproportionately located in Florida, conspicuously split from their Latino compatriots in *favoring* Trump by fifty-four percent compared to a mere twenty-six percent of Florida's non-Cuban Hispanics. In Florida overall, Trump still claimed more than one-third (thirty-five percent) of Latino votes, which was actually *less* than Romney's success with thirty-nine percent.

Why would Hispanics vote for Trump, especially given some of the horrific slurs that he aimed toward them during the campaign and his master-plan to build a barricade against them? Quinn Galbraith and Adam Callister ask this question too, reminding us first that Hispanic Americans are a diverse category and that many of them are conservative and strongly Christian. Second, Hispanic American voters in 2016 tended to be older, more male, and more likely to be born in the U.S. (including Puerto Rico) than those who did not cast a vote, all increasing their odds of leaning conservative.[9] The really remarkable discovery is that those voters, compared to the ones who sat out the election, "had a significantly higher mean support for Trump's plan to build a wall, a significantly lower mean perceived increase in discrimination since Trump's election, and a significantly higher proportion of people who agreed with the statement that, generally, all illegal immigrants should be deported."[10] Nearly three-quarters (seventy-four percent) of Hispanic Trump voters *approved of* deporting illegal immigrants, demonstrating profound intra-ethnic non-empathy and profound concurrence with white conservative sentiment.

Looking beneath the statistics begins to shed light on the actual beliefs and values that motivated not only Hispanic Trump support but support in the wider populace. For this purpose, ethnographic research reveals what "big data," for all their wonders, cannot. Ariana Hernandez-Reguant spent time in the Cuban American community of Miami during the 2016 campaign, where she found:

> [Trump's] discourse of power and nation has resonated with many immigrants' yearning for a nation, at ease with a hierarchical model of society led by a strongman. At the same time, Trump's personal story has validated the myth of the American dream that inspired many immigrants in their journey. In Miami, while Cuban Americans and a middle class might support Trump on the basis of his economic

---

[9] Quinn Galbraith and Adam Calllister, "Why Would Hispanics Vote for Trump? Explaining the Controversy of the 2016 Election," *Hispanic Journal of Behavioral Sciences* 42, no. 1 (2020), 84.

[10] Ibid., 85.

prescriptions, first generation immigrants might also find an appeal in his ideology of national destiny.[11]

Particularly among the *exilio histórico*, the post-Castro exile community, "support for Trump was a given." Visiting radio stations and attending rallies, she reports that many locals liked Trump as "a man who wears the pants," not a weakling like Clinton *la vieja esa* ("the old hag") or Obama before her. Rather than being put off or offended by his inflammatory style, "It was Trump's bravado that made him appear as a leader," and his whiteness even worked in his favor:

> Trump's white male authority signifies a restoration of order in a fragmented Cuban society still finding its place within the United States. As a businessman whose supporters refuse to see as less than successful, he is the embodiment of the American dream and a living proof that neoliberal tax policies allow just about anyone to pull themselves up by their bootstraps and reach the top. Thus, to new cohorts of Cuban immigrants, Trump represents hope better than Obama, because he promises self-reliance.[12]

For these Hispanic citizens, as for many others we will meet subsequently, Trump combines macho with American-Dream aspiration, leavened with a dose of nostalgia in "proposing a continuity with a past vision of the future; the vision that the Founding Fathers and other gentle folk were said to have imagined for the country's greatness. In this sense, Trump's view is essentially utopian"[13]—and better yet, a no-place that diverse races and ethnicities can potentially inhabit.

Other research illustrates just how incongruous Trump's support can be. Myles Lennon met three unlikely Trump voters who underscore "the fascinating contradictions and inconsistencies" in American society and politics and thus the danger of generalizing about the Trump type. The first is a woman who, under normal circumstances, should have been a Democrat voter based on her many "left-leaning positions." Yet despite being relatively liberal, "she disdained 'liberal smugness' … [and] felt that Trump had been treated 'unfairly'": "'I voted for him as push back,' she added, repeating this refrain several times. 'Push back,' that is, against the

---

[11] Ariana Hernandez-Reguant, "Miami Cubans 4 Trump and the Battle for the Nation," cubacounterpoints.com, accessed May 11, 2020, https://cubacounterpoints.com/archives/4399.html.

[12] Ibid.

[13] Ibid.

smugness and arrogance and 'unfairness' of the media and her neighbors."[14] In other words, she backed a candidate many of whose policies she disapproved because she disliked the style of the Democrats more.

More bizarre is Joseph, a gay porn actor, who voted for Trump,

> not to throw his support behind a candidate who represents his views but instead to explicitly embrace and call attention to such ideological tensions. Joseph supports a radical redistributionist political agenda and a queer liberation ideology at odds with the Republican platform, but he was compelled to vote for Trump as a retaliation against the Democratic National Committee (DNC) and what he viewed as its corrupt politics and neoliberal ideology embodied, in his mind, by its candidate, Hillary Clinton. While he finds Trump's views reprehensible—the antithesis of what he believes in and stands for—in voting for Trump he sought to expose the chasm between his political ideals and the country's political reality, as he perceives it.[15]

As more than a few Trump partisans would gladly admit, Joseph liked Trump's forthrightness (he says what he means and means what he says— even if what he says and means is reprehensible and antithetical to the listeners' interests) and swagger, forgiving Trump as an imperfect being.

Finally, Ian the "decorated military officer" is a bit more predictable Trump fan, although he had resisted political partisanship for most of his life. However, perceiving lately "a fervent anti-white, anti-male, and anti-conservative stance" in American culture, Ian felt compelled to overcome his hesitation to affiliate with his white "tribe" in "direct response to the 'tribalism' of other races and cultures." He does not love Trump, but in his mind supporting Trump "is a private backlash to the new 'anti-white' mainstream," even if it is "a degeneration of the shared patriotic norms of civic life."[16]

What these three instances tell us is, first, not everyone who voted for Trump actually agrees with him on all or most issues and, second, political behavior, as suggested in our introduction, is often non-rational and inconsistent. Human political actors, like humans in all their actions, are "by no means ideologically coherent, and contradictions, illegibility, and inconsistencies" often characterize their opinions and decisions.[17] In that

---

[14] Myles Lennon, "Revisiting 'The Repugnant Other' in the Era of Trump," *HAU: Journal of Ethnographic Theory* 8, no. 3 (2018), 442.

[15] Ibid., 445.

[16] Ibid., 451–52.

[17] Ibid., 442.

regard, Trump may be the embodiment of "the incoherence and absurdity of this moment" in American life.[18]

Even that elusive creature "the white working class" is not as monolithic as we often imagine. As we have noted, one conventional indicator of class in the last election was education, namely, the possession or lack of a college degree. However, comparing two very different versions of the "white working class," Christine Walley discerns that their issues and their identities can diverge substantially. One version resides in Louisiana, where a region formerly associated with southern Democrats now identifies as Republican; they are

> self-defined conservatives with a sense of identity bound up for many with Cajun ethnicity, strong religious sensibilities, and a resentment about the perceived disdain of coastal liberals. Ironically, the desire to roll back government stemmed in part from a weak and corrupt Louisiana government, with its failures perceived as further reason to starve rather than support it.[19]

Much of this description is common Republican fodder today. But the unique history of the South with its slave- and plantation-owner heritage and the absence of a middle class left a tendency toward poor whites "identifying up" to wealthy whites, which "strengthened support for 'pro-business' (if anti-Wall Street) Tea Partiers and for Donald Trump." This same heritage created an odd variety of racism, in which locals

> deny charges of racism, which they defined as personal hatred, yet many were deeply skeptical about the existence of structural racism. And they often perceived President Obama as Other, as not a real American and probably a Muslim, symbolizing a changed America where interlocutors considered themselves increasingly and unfairly overlooked and … "strangers in their own land." While not all … became Trump supporters, many did, and Trump rallies became almost a kind of religious revival event for affirming a white identity politics in a context of perceived national marginalization.[20]

Walley's second version of the white working class occupies the Midwest and its "Rust Belt" district, where traditional factory jobs have evaporated. The social history of this region made folks "less inclined to 'identify up'" or close ranks along race rather than class lines. Race also played out

---

[18] Lennon, "Revisiting 'The Repugnant Other' in the Era of Trump," 440.

[19] Christine J. Walley, "Trump's Election and the 'White Working Class': What We Missed," *American Ethnologist* 44, no. 2 (2017), 233.

[20] Ibid.

differently, with whites and non-whites (African Americans and more recent immigrants) competing for the same manufacturing jobs. With the demise of factory work, those who were able, both black and white, escaped to the suburbs; consequently, in an area "once known for the male 'family wage,' married women often continued in, or reentered, the workforce in service positions after the closing of the mills. Men faced a particularly difficult time finding work."[21] Several of these states went blue during Obama's two election campaigns, and in 2016, both disruptive candidates—Trump and Bernie Sanders—were popular. With Sanders off the general election ballot, Trump took five of the Rust Belt states, including some traditionally loyal to Democrats, which Walley understands as follows:

> The flipping of the Rust Belt simultaneously underscores three important phenomena: the centrality of economic concerns for many white voters, the "white privilege" of those who could register economic grievances by voting for Trump without having to fear the bigotry his campaign was unleashing, and the channeling of economic resentments against Others. Trump, like industrial managers of old, had split the diverse industrial and postindustrial-working classes along ethnic and racial lines.[22]

Race, Rurality, and Resentment

Race is an omnipresent element of American society. But the "fact" of race is not an automatic vote for Trump or even a ticket to enlisting in Ian's racial tribe. Other forces, especially grievances (real or perceived), must interact with racial differences to transform them into mobilization and votes.

Hernandez-Reguant's and Lennon's subjects give us some clues as to what those forces are. First and importantly, a vote for Trump (and possibly continuing support for him) is not always a vote *for Trump* as much as a vote *against a specific Democrat/liberal candidate*. For various reasons—her husband, the previous eight years of the Obama administration, her alleged failings as Secretary of State, her personal email server, or her very femaleness—many Americans could not stomach a vote for Hillary Clinton.

But the distaste felt by many Trump advocates goes beyond any one Democrat rival. More than a few express a discomfort or an actual loathing toward liberals on the whole, viewed as remote, and particularly *urban*, elites. Morgan Ramsey-Elliot, in the course of studying truck-owning families in Texas and Colorado for a consulting firm, chronicles a distinct pre-political style that sets many voters at odds with Democrats in principle.

---

[21] Walley, "Trump's Election," 234.
[22] Ibid.

This distinct set of "small-town America community values" that Trump, intentionally or accidentally, was able to activate includes "an intense sense of duty to the whole or 'team,' an attention to individuals that is at once concrete and extremely personal and, in upholding these two simultaneously, a sense of exceptionalism that often defies the rules they've set out for themselves."[23] Because of their sustained and intimate social knowledge of and bonds with each other, they highly value loyalty, a trait that is also dear to Trump. Many of these small-town folk voice insensitive racist (and sexist and homophobic) opinions, to be sure, simultaneously exempting individuals selectively from their judgment: "One of the truck drivers with whom I spent time during my fieldwork described a member of his construction crew as 'a Mexican, but a good Mexican,' for example."[24] But it is not race that primarily defines their politics or their attraction to Trump; rather, while his biography bears little resemblance to theirs, and he has spent little or no time in small-town America,

> his persona—straight-shooting, unpretentious, seemingly benevolent and both individual and familiar in his celebritydom—struck a familiar chord for the Americans who frequent them. Trump lacks the poise and polish of traditional political elites, but rather than garnering disdain, this allowed him to be understood as more "genuine" and "local" by many of the small-town Americans I met. Whereas voters across the political spectrum frequently expressed a lack of "trust" in Hillary, for these rural Americans, Trump seemed more proximate and more predictable—vices and all.[25]

As for people who promote liberal causes like racial or same-sex equality, Ramsey-Elliot's informants disparage them as selfish, demanding "special privileges," which offends their communal sensibilities. He concludes that, "Until the coasts develop a more nuanced understanding of everyday life in rural America—how values like service, duty, generosity, and authenticity are actually experienced—we will continue to have a reductive view of Trump's supporters."[26]

Katherine Cramer, writing on the eve of the presidential election but with Wisconsin's conservative governor, Scott Walker, in mind, develops this theme further, pinpointing "a significant rural-versus-urban divide" in

---

[23] Morgan Ramsey-Elliot, "From Trucks to Trump: The Role of Small-Town Values in Driving Votes," *Anthropology Now* 9, no. 1 (2017), 54.

[24] Ibid., 55.

[25] Ibid., 56.

[26] Morgan Ramsey-Elliot, "An Ethnographer Has a New Explanation for Donald Trump's Support in Small-Town America," *Quartz*, September 22, 2016, https://qz.com/787948/why-is-donald-trump-so-popular-in-rural-america.

the United States that speaks to basic "ideas about who gets what, who has power, what people are like, and who is to blame."[27] From the perspective of rural Wisconsin, it feels like urban elites "routinely ignore rural places and fail to give rural communities their fair share of resources," as well as that "rural folks are fundamentally different from urbanites in terms of their lifestyles, values, and work ethic."[28] These three features typify what Cramer calls the "rural consciousness." But together and over time, especially as the fortunes and futures of small-town America grow dire, Cramer insists that this consciousness turns bitter, into resentment— resentment against urbanites, against those whom they interpret as getting more (more money, more rights, more attention) than they deserve, and against the liberal establishment that sides with the undeserving (as we observed in Chapter 3, a standard populist narrative). The result is a "politics of resentment," a volatile blend of identity (importantly but not exclusively racial), emotion, and economic insecurity for people who interpret "their circumstances as the fault of guilty and less deserving social groups, not as the product of broad social, economic, and political forces."[29]

Arlie Hochschild, based on her fieldwork in rural Louisiana, distills this rural consciousness to what she calls the "deep story" of America, a composite tale as follows:

> You are patiently standing in the middle of a long line stretching toward the horizon, where the American Dream awaits. But as you wait, you see people cutting in line ahead of you. Many of these line-cutters are black—beneficiaries of affirmative action or welfare. Some are career-driven women pushing into jobs they never had before. Then you see immigrants, Mexicans, Somalis, the Syrian refugees yet to come. As you wait in this unmoving line, you're being asked to feel sorry for them all. You have a good heart. But who is deciding who you should feel compassion for? Then you see President Barack Hussein Obama waving the line-cutters forward. He's on their side. In fact, isn't he a line-cutter too? How did this fatherless black guy pay for Harvard? As you wait your turn, Obama is using the money in your pocket to help the line-cutters. He and his liberal backers have removed the shame from taking. The government has become an instrument for redistributing your

---

[27] Katherine J. Cramer, *The Politics of Resentment: Rural Consciousness in Wisconsin and the Rise of Scott Walker* (Chicago and London: The University of Chicago Press, 2016), 5.
[28] Ibid., 6–7.
[29] Ibid. 9.

money to the undeserving. It's not your government anymore; it's theirs.[30]

This plotline, she assesses, indicts what she dubs "line-cutters" who take what is not theirs and accordingly, for hardworking white folks, "reflects pain; you've done everything right and you're still slipping back. It focuses blame on an ill-intentioned government. And it points to rescue: The Tea Party for some, and Donald Trump for others."[31] Ominously, when she read it back to her interlocutors, they immediately recognized themselves in it. And she also locates another appeal of the story: although small-town folk tend to castigate welfare recipients and other beneficiaries of government dole, Trump offers to redirect and restrict government handouts "to real Americans," which "offers the blue-collar white men relief from a taker's shame: If you make America great again, how can you not be proud." This, she reasons, "solves a white male problem of pride."

As discussed in the introduction and revisited in previous chapters, at bottom, the experience of many disaffected Americans who voted for and persist in supporting Trump is *loss—losing money, losing status, losing power, and, in sum, losing America.* Rory McVeigh and Kevin Estep take the crucial but often neglected next step of linking these complaints to the very broad social/economic forces that the voters themselves usually miss. This broader horizon also elucidates some anomalies in the voter statistics. Trump's march to power began in the Republican primaries, which is where McVeigh and Estep direct their attention. As already acknowledged, Trump did better during those early contests in counties with lower incomes and lower college graduation rates, and the researchers determine that "an increase in just 1 percent of college graduates in a county reduces the Trump vote by about .3 percent."[32] However, the writers sagely attribute this effect not to the stupidity of non-college graduates but to their lack of "credentials to thrive in a global economy." For instance, he outperformed his rivals in places where more workers were employed in retail, as those voters were shut out of better-paying jobs; he did less well where a higher proportion of workers still enjoyed manufacturing jobs—as they did not share his, and their retail-worker neighbors', anxiety about American manufacturing. He was also less appealing in counties with higher numbers of women in the workplace. Even overall unemployment was not an automatic boon for

---

[30] Arlie Hochschild, "I Spent 5 Years with Some of Trumps Biggest Fans: Here's What They Won't Tell You," Mother Jones (2016), accessed May 12, 2020, http://www.motherjones.com/politics/2016/08/trump-whiteblue-collar-supporters.

[31] Ibid.

[32] Rory McVeigh and Kevin Estep, *The Politics of Losing: Trump, the Klan, and the Mainstreaming of Resentment* (New York: Columbia University Press, 2019), 106.

Trump: his message stuck most when high unemployment was conjoined with low college education, signaling that those voters were the most left behind by the new high-skill, high-tech economy.[33] More acutely, the recovery from the 2008 global economic crisis and recession "almost exclusively benefited those with a college degree, particularly if they lived in cities where available jobs matched their education"; this excluded much of Trump's eventual constituency.[34]

Nevertheless, the large segment of citizens who did cleave to Trump were the ones whose economic disadvantages were aggravated by "a sense of political impotence"; they "felt their political power waning"—which also meant their numerical power as the traditional white majority of the country.[35] They were thereby ripe for a crusader like Trump: "he alone seemed willing to defend them—sometimes artlessly—from their cultural enemies, and they hoped that he might deliver policies that would restore their status where his more cautious predecessors had failed."[36]

It was not inevitable, but heavily overdetermined, that this regional resentment would exhibit a racial tinge. Lennon's portrait of Ian above exemplifies how that would happen. Individuals like Ian, or the good citizens of Louisiana or Texas or Wisconsin, see "others" cutting in line ahead of them for the benefits of American society. These others are often racially or ethnically othered: they are African Americans, Hispanics, or overseas foreigners stealing their jobs and their standing in the world. Ian represents the endpoint of a journey—a journey that some white people did not initially want to make—toward seeing themselves, in the words of Nicholas Valentino, Fabian Neuner, and Matthew Vanderbroek, as an "embattled and even disadvantaged group, and this has led to both strong in-group identity and a greater tolerance for expressions of hostility toward out-groups."[37] This is why Jeff Maskovsky weighs Trump's politics as "a new form of racial politics that I am calling white nationalist postracialism," composed of two discordant goals—"to reclaim the nation for white Americans while also denying an ideological investment in white supremacy."[38] Of course, more than a few Trump fans have foregone the nicety of denying white supremacy, some wearing it boldly and defiantly, but Trump himself and arguably the majority of his camp do not openly

---

[33] McVeigh and Estep, *The Politics of Losing*, 108.

[34] Ibid., 131–32.

[35] Ibid, 132.

[36] Ibid., 169.

[37] Nicholas A. Valentino, Fabian G. Neuner, and L Matthew Vanderbroek, "The Changing Norms of Racial Political Rhetoric and the End of Racial Priming," *The Journal of Politics*, 80, no. 3 (2017), 768.

[38] Jeff Maskovsky, "Toward the Anthropology of White Nationalist Postracialism: Comments Inspired by Hall, Goldstein, and Ingram's 'The Hands of Donald Trump,'" *HAU: Journal of Ethnographic Theory* 7, no. 1 (2017), 433.

avow white supremacy and may condemn it. But Maskovsky's white nationalist postracialism is facilitated by "Trump's excoriation of political correctness, his nostalgia for the post–WWII industrial economy, his use of hand gestures, and his public speaking about race [which] work together to telegraph a white nationalist message to his followers without making them feel that he is, or they are, racist."[39] By word and deed—and the meaning is not lost on his audience, as our discussion has amply proven—when he conjures the image of an America made great again, his images "define white male workers as the virtuous majority," as the America that was great and will be great once more; in so doing, he draws a portrait of African Americans, Hispanics, and other immigrants "both as government dependents for whom [he and his followers] hold disdain, and as preferred recipients of government largess"[40]—a faithful paraphrase of Hochschild's deep story.

We come then full-circle to the enmeshed issues of race and class, many disadvantaged, undereducated, and underemployed or unemployed, especially small-town and rural, whites perceiving themselves as victims of inattentive government, reverse discrimination, outsourcing and offshoring, and a general onslaught of "others" who aim to "replace them," as the white marchers at Charlottesville chanted. Measuring the variables of socioeconomic status, education, and racism (and also sexism), Brian Schaffner, Matthew MacWilliams, and Tatishe Nteta reckon that "while economic considerations were an important part of the story, racial attitudes and sexism were much more strongly related to support for Trump; these attitudes explain at least two-thirds of the education gap among white voters in the 2016 presidential election."[41] Lower education and dissatisfaction with one's social status were indeed correlated with Trump support (and with each other), but "these effects were dwarfed by the relationship between hostile sexism and denial of racism [that is, asserting that there is racism in American society] and voting for Trump."[42] In the final analysis, when racism and sexism were controlled statistically, the effect of lack or possession of a college degree faded to less than one-third its original significance, to the level "it had been in every election since 2000."[43]

So in many ways, the 2016 election was consistent with Republican-versus-Democrat contests of recent years, but in a few ways it was unique. Trump collected a lot of the traditional and predictable

---

[39] Maskovsky, "Toward the Anthropology," 433.

[40] Ibid., 435.

[41] Brian Schaffner, Matthew MacWilliams, and Tatishe Nteta, "Understanding White Polarization in the 2016 Vote for President: The Sobering Role of Racism and Sexism," *Political Science Quarterly* 133, no. 1 (2018), 9–10.

[42] Ibid., 24.

[43] Ibid., 30.

Republican voters—not enough to gain a majority of the popular vote, mind you—while losing some and attracting a number of atypical supporters. But we cannot overlook one other factor, noticed by Valentino, Neuner, and Vanderbroek in their statement above: a greater tolerance for expressions of hostility toward out-groups. If there is one quality that distinguishes the Trump enthusiasts who showed up for his rallies and that distinguishes the current moment in American politics and society, it is anger. Like many of the right-wing populists and demagogues met in an earlier chapter, Trump radiates anger and outrage, which is undiluted by the customary political tact and decorum. David Norman Smith and Eric Hanley parse the data to assert that, without discounting educational and economic differences, "Trump's supporters voted for him mainly because they share his prejudices, not because they're financially stressed."[44] A closer glimpse at the numbers highlights the forgotten fact that the majority of Trump's voters were suburban (sixty-three percent), not rural (thirty-five percent).[45] Further, from the primaries on, Trump's constituents actually had *higher* average incomes than either Clinton or Sanders supporters, and among households earning less than $50,000, both Clinton and Sanders polled better than Trump.[46] And of course, most of Clinton's voters were white too (sixty percent), nineteen percent rural and fifty-seven percent without a college degree.

The variable to which Smith and Hanley return is prejudice and anger, of a specific sort that they characterize as authoritarian: "negatively, they target minorities and women; positively, they favor domineering and intolerant leaders who are uninhibited about their biases"; in fact, "once we take these biases into account, demographic factors (age, education, etc.) lose their explanatory power."[47] Interestingly, they describe this authoritarian personality differently from the classic model of the submissive individual who, as in Hoffer's or Adorno et al.'s interpretation, is prepared to surrender his/her will to an authority. Smith and Hanley's authoritarian followers are driven by aggression rather than submission; they "follow domineering leaders less for the pleasure of submission," of jettisoning an unwanted self, "than for the pleasure of forcing moral outsiders to submit." Their chosen leader "must be punitive and intolerant," someone who "will 'crush evil and take us back to our true path.'"[48] But aggression and

---

[44] David Norman Smith and Eric Hanley, "The Anger Games: Who Voted for Trump in the 2016 Election, and Why?," *Critical Sociology* 44, no. 2 (2018), 195.

[45] Pew Research Center, "An Examination of the 2016 Electorate, Based On Validated Voters," Pewresearch.org, August 9, 2018, https://www.people-press.org/2018/08/09/an-examination-of-the-2016-electorate-based-on-validated-voters.

[46] Nate Silver, "The Mythology of Trump's 'Working Class' Support," FiveThirtyEight, May 3, 2016, https://fivethirtyeight.com/features/the-mythology-of-trumps-working-class-support.

[47] Smith and Hanley, "The Anger Games," 195.

[48] Ibid., 196.

submission are not contraries; instead, "'Authoritarian aggressiveness' takes aim at despised groups, and 'authoritarian submissiveness' prompts support for leaders who target those same groups."[49] Ultimately, Trump may appeal more to white Americans than non-white Americans, but this white base, Smith and Hanley judge, "is more readily found among voters who want domineering and intolerant leaders than among voters of any particular class background."[50] If this approach is accurate, it would resolve some mysteries of Trump support, such as why some non-whites voted for him, why many whites did not, and, most improbably of all, why many of both remain ardent champions after almost four years of Trump's bombastic and often ugly performance as president.

Evangelicals and Christian Nationalism

[Donald Trump] will be president because God has chosen him …
Donald John Trump; is the last Trump in symbolism, and his voice/Shofar/trump sounds for 7 years to 10 years from some starting point in the future. However, I believe that that starting point and countdown has begun and Oct 3, 2016 was the launching date!!!
Also, Trump is the Rams horn which is last trump blown as the final last warning, where Gods people are the preliminary in unison silver trumpets blowing alongside Trumps, and calling Gods people to wake up!
The Shofar is associated with the LEFT horn of the Ram as 'the first trump' (i.e., *warning, wake up call, and represents Democrats, CNN, Hillary, Obama, and the rest*) and the RIGHT horn as 'the last trump' (*Which is DJT, and he is the Ace of Spades, Trump Card, and Victor!*)….
The Donald is speaking prophetic words from the bible like Jesus to point to himself (*i.e. Psalm 2:1 that Jesus was fulfilling scripture*) now inserting himself into Donald J. Trump the rich somewhat bold indiscrete man.[51]

It would be nice to think that no one actually believes that Trump is a divine figure, but Myra Cook's totally over-the-top vision of Trump as some kind of prophetic fulfillment tells us otherwise. Granted, she is an amateur writer with a fairly fringe view of her president and her preferred scriptures—most of Trump's people are not professional scholars and writers, and most professional scholars and writers are not Trump's people—but that is beside

---

[49] Smith and Hanley, "The Anger Games," 197.
[50] Ibid.
[51] Myra Cook, *Donald 'MESSIAH' Trump: The Man, the Myth, the Messiah?* (Oregon: American Freedom Publishing, 2016).

the point; the electorate is full of amateur and fringe elements. More serious and disturbing is that other more reputable and influential sources, including sometimes Trump himself, either believe that Trump is a savior and messiah or at least deploy language that activates such notions in followers' minds. For instance, on August 21, 2019 Trump retweeted extreme comments by talk show host Wayne Root, who had said that, based on Trump's support for Israel, it is "like he's the King of Israel. They love him like he is the second coming of God" (notwithstanding that Jews do not believe that their god, or the messiah, has come once yet). Trump has rolled out the loaded term "the chosen one" in reference to himself, forcing some religious supporters to scramble to excuse his remarks as jokes or hyperbole while others like Ms. Cook no doubt accept them as gospel.

One of the most astonishing facets of the Trump election and administration has been the staunch backing he has received from American Christians, especially evangelicals. Comprising almost a quarter of the American population, evangelical Christians are a major voting bloc, and they have been faithful Republican voters for at least four decades. Still, it is incredible enough that Trump captured eighty-one percent of the evangelical vote in 2016, given his overtly un-Christian biography and campaign conduct; more incredibly, by most counts, he has retained high popularity with this segment of society.

As with demographic factors such as class and education dissected above, a look inside the numbers tells a more complex tale. First and foremost, race and religion intersect meaningfully in American society. Almost forty percent of American evangelicals are non-white, half of those African American, and Philip Gorski reports that "most non-white evangelicals did *not* vote for Trump."[52] In fact, Harry Enten maintains that in late mid-2019, only twenty-nine percent of nonwhite evangelicals approved of Trump and a mere seven percent of black evangelicals.[53] What we have, then, is a case where the race of the evangelical community makes a huge difference and where members "did not vote as whites or as evangelicals but rather as *white evangelicals*."[54]

Still more confusing, but enlightening, is the apparent fact that it was not religion alone that drove these believers into the arms of Trump. One interesting reality is that he was not as popular among religionists in the primary races as in the general election: a survey by the Public Religion Research Institute calculates that Trump "never polled above 50 percent

---

[52] Philip S. Gorski, "Christianity and Democracy after Trump," *Political Theology* 19, no. 5 (2018), 361.

[53] Harry Enten, "White Evangelicals Love Trump. Religious Voters? Not so Much," CNN, January 1, 2020, https://www.cnn.com/2020/01/01/politics/evangelical-support-trump/index.html.

[54] Gorski, "Christianity and Democracy after Trump," 361.

favorability with white evangelical-Protestants during the primaries," his popularity weirdly building over time.[55] Stranger still, Enten and Gorski both emphasize that it is not religion as such that attracts people to Trump. Among Americans who attend church regularly and do not identify as born-again evangelicals, only forty-six percent approved of Trump in 2019, and more of them (forty-nine percent) disapproved.[56] This trend held for born-again evangelicals too: when we consider only those who attend church at least weekly, their approval of Trump dropped to sixty percent—impressive, yes, but not the full eighty percent. Even if we factor race back in, Gorski concludes that "amongst white evangelicals, there was an *inverse* correlation between churchgoing and Trump-supporting": "In other words, the more often an evangelical attended, the less likely they were to prefer Trump. For #alwaysTrumpers, one suspects, 'evangelical' was more of an identity marker than a faith commitment. They were not Christians so much as Christianists."[57]

Finally, a widely unknown subset of evangelicals actively opposes Trump. These dissenting evangelicals only came to prominence in late 2019 when Mark Galli, holder of a Master of Divinity from Fuller Theological Seminary and editor-in-chief of the evangelical magazine *Christianity Today* (founded by Billy Graham in 1956), published an editorial bluntly titled "Trump Should Be Removed from Office." Written during the impeachment proceedings, the piece acknowledges the fact that, despite the Democrats having "had it out for him from day one," the "president of the United States attempted to use his political power to coerce a foreign leader to harass and discredit one of the president's political opponents," actions that are both unconstitutional and "profoundly immoral."[58] Galli condemns Trump's Twitter rants as "a near perfect example of a human being who is morally lost and confused," admits that the impeachment hearings "illuminated the president's moral deficiencies for all to see," and passes sentence that his removal from office "is not a matter of partisan loyalties but loyalty to the Creator of the Ten Commandments."[59] A month later, the International Bonhoeffer Society, named after the estimable theologian Dietrich Bonhoeffer, issued a similar statement, warning that the "policies of the Trump administration both threaten and disempower the most vulnerable

---

[55] Kit Kirkland, "Politics Before God: How America's Political Divisiveness Is Trumping Religious Identity," *Journal of the British Association for the Study of Religions* 20 (2018), 169.

[56] Enten, "White Evangelicals Love Trump."

[57] Gorski, "Christianity and Democracy after Trump," 361–62.

[58] Mark Galli, "Trump Should Be Removed from Office," *Christianity Today*, December 19, 2019, https://www.christianitytoday.com/ct/2019/december-web-only/trump-should-be-removed-from-office.html.

[59] Ibid.

members of our society," conjuring memories of the Third Reich, and advocating "the ending of Donald Trump's presidency."[60]

That this is a minority sentiment among American evangelicals is an understatement, but it does reflect the position of a small but vocal portion of that category. As Brantley Gasaway describes in a historical survey of the "progressive evangelical" movement, it traces its origins in the United States to the late 1960s, around the time that other socially-conscious forms of Christianity emerged, including liberation theology. In documents like the 1973 "Chicago Declaration of Evangelical Social Concern," progressives declared that "the Bible calls Christians to care as much about combatting poverty, ending racism, working for peace, defending human rights, and protecting the environment as they do about abortion and same-sex marriage."[61] Various arms of the progressive evangelical movement arose, such as the magazine *Sojourners*, the Red Letter Christians, and Evangelicals for Social Action. The antics and election of Trump were a particular offense to this group of liberal Christians. During the early days of the campaign, in April 2016, they published the document "Called to Resist Bigotry—A Statement of Faithful Obedience," which declared that Trump had already created "a moral and theological crisis."[62] This action was followed by a Change.org petition and articles in *Christianity Today* and *Sojourners*, and once he was elected, over eight hundred Christians signed a public letter calling on Trump to govern better than he campaigned (a vain hope). Several leaders even let themselves get arrested for civil disobedience outside the White House. Some evangelicals like Russell Moore went so far as expressing embarrassment at being evangelical in his *Washington Post* opinion piece "Why This Election Makes Me Hate the Word 'Evangelical.'" In 2018, spokespersons revisited the 1973 founding document with "The Chicago Invitation: Diverse Evangelicals Continue the Journey," reaffirming their "commitment to 'biblical justice' and active resistance to racism, patriarchal sexism, homophobia, economic injustice, and all forms of dehumanizing oppression"[63]—the most appalling attitudes circulating inside and outside Trump's administration, then and now.

It goes without saying that this counsel did not sway the vast majority of American evangelicals, who remain steadfast in their dedication to Trump. The crucial question that must be answered is, how did and do so

---

[60] Jim Wallis, "International Bonhoeffer Society Calls for 'Ending Donald Trump's Presidency' in 'Statement of Concern'," *Sojourners*, January 16, 2020, https://sojo.net/articles/international-bonhoeffer-society-calls-ending-donald-trumps-presidency-statement-concern.

[61] Brantley W. Gasaway, "Making Evangelicals Great Again? American Evangelicals in the Age of Trump," *Evangelical Review of Theology* 43, no. 4 (2019), 296.

[62] Quoted in ibid., 298.

[63] Ibid., 310.

many evangelicals reconcile their unwavering support with Trump's un-Christ-like words and deeds? Marcia Pally uses the apt but stinging concept of "triage" to decipher the work that they have done to insulate their politics from their morality. She concedes that Trump's evangelical base may be stirred by their beliefs, but the most relevant beliefs "may not be the *religious* beliefs associated with evangelicals, such as opposition to abortion and to gay marriage. Evangelicals weigh these along with other priorities, including economic and way-of-life concerns."[64] In an essay that is about populism as much as or more than evangelicalism, Pally contends that over half (fifty-nine percent) of "self-identified evangelicals" cast their 2016 vote not on religious but on economic grounds; almost half (forty-eight percent) were roused by immigration or national security, but only thirty-one percent listed abortion as their main issue and sixteen percent named gay/lesbian rights. In other words, evangelicals were basically similar to the typical American voter, particularly the typical Republican voter, with their anti-government and pro-business stance.

To be sure, Trump has delivered some of the goods for evangelical and other Christian backers, not the least placing conservative judges in the Supreme Court and lower federal courts and championing "religious freedom" such as threatening to nullify the Johnson Amendment that bans political proselytizing from the pulpit. But these gains are complicated by his decidedly non-evangelical persona. Here, triage takes two forms, one more political, the other more theological. Politically, as Pally phrases it, evangelical Christians have become adept at "bracketing disapproval of what they saw as Trump's immoral personal life for economic policies they believe will better society."[65] She sees this as less than a Faustian bargain, since adherents get both political/economic and religious benefits. According to Kit Kirkland, some were moved by their Christian charity to give Trump-the-sinner a second chance, relieving them of their "squeamishness over his style or moral scruples about his behavior."[66] Ironically, one consequence is that whereas evangelicals used to be among the most unforgiving of moral failures, only thirty percent of white evangelicals believing in 2011 that an immoral individual could still be a decent public official, within five years they had reversed themselves completely, more than seventy percent *now forgiving the public servant for his personal sins*, such that "white evangelicals are now more tolerant than average Americans of elected officials' immoral behavior."[67] I would wait to

---

[64] Marcia Pally, "Why is Populism Persuasive? Populism as Expression of Religio-Cultural History with the U.S. and U.S. Evangelicals as a Case Study," *Political Theology* (2020), 13.

[65] Ibid., 16.

[66] Kirkland, "Politics Before God," 171.

[67] Ibid., 182.

see whether this new-found generosity applies equally to *all* elected officials, like the next Democratic president, whoever s/he may be.

But while Trump and his ilk may get a second chance, a key part of Trump's rhetoric was and is that America will not get another chance. The Trump-Clinton showdown was "repeatedly labeled as conservative Christians' 'last chance' for citizens to protect America's religious heritage and win back a chance at securing a Christian future."[68] Trump openly admonished voters that such an opportunity would never happen again, that if they abandoned him and allowed the liberal elite to keep the White House, then all would be lost (typical apocalyptic rhetoric). According to Kirkland's analysis of the Public Religion Research Institute data, two-thirds of Trump's people agreed that it was now or never, putting the urgency of the message ahead of the odiousness of the messenger.[69]

Of course, there are always those, Smith and Hanley's aggressive authoritarians, who actually like what they observe in Trump. They are represented by Tony Perkins, president of the conservative Family Research Council, who trivialized the allegations of porn star Stormy Daniels as a "mulligan" for which Trump was entitled to a "do-over" (no such clemency for Bill Clinton, we notice!). More important,

Fig. 12 Tony Perkins of the Family Research Council with Vice-President Mike Pence, at a 'Voice Your Values in Washington' event in Washington, DC on April 7, 2017.

Perkins told a *Politico* interviewer, is that he and his followers "were tired of being kicked around by Barack Obama and his leftists. And I think they are finally glad that there's somebody on the playground that is willing to punch the bully."[70] This shockingly unbiblical outlook goes a long way to explaining the charm of the "baddest hombre" in the 2016 presidential field, not to mention the immediate political advantage: Trump may not have been the first choice of evangelicals in the primaries or their ideal candidate or president, but "just letting them get closer to that steering wheel is more than they were about to get from Trump's opponents."[71] Without making excuses

---

[68] Whitehead, Perry, and Baker, "Make America Christian Again," 153.

[69] Kirkland, "Politics Before God," 174.

[70] Edward-Isaac Dovere, "Tony Perkins: Trump Gets 'a Mulligan' on Life, Stormy Daniels," *Politico*, January 28, 2018, https://www.politico.com/magazine/story/2018/01/23/tony-perkins-evangelicals-donald-trump-stormy-daniels-216498.

[71] John C. Stackhouse, Jr., "American Evangelical Support for Donald Trump: Mostly American and Only Sort-of-'Evangelical'—a Response," Religion & Culture

for him, Jerry Falwell, Jr. knighted Trump the evangelical "dream president," and CBN's David Brody gushed that he is "the most evangelical-friendly United States president ever."[72]

Such fans need no apology for their enthusiasm, but for others, evangelical theology offers a variety of resources to assuage their doubts about Trump the man and their guilt for endorsing him. Just as their moral standards for leadership have slipped, so have their demands for a godly state. Trump stalwart Robert Jeffress, pastor of an evangelical congregation in Dallas, in a rather stunning reversal of traditional fundamentalist/evangelical policy, now holds the position that it is "out of place … to force Gospel principles on the state"; in explanation of this startling stance, he professes that, "While Scripture commands individual Christians and churches to show mercy to those in need, the Bible never calls on government to act as a Good Samaritan." So as not to be misunderstood, he continues, "A Christian writer asked me, 'Don't you want the president to embody the Sermon on the Mount?' … I said absolutely not."[73]

The political theology underpinning this opportunistic embrace of a character like Trump is a variation of Martin Luther's famous "two kingdoms" theory. Minimally, this means that government cannot be expected to display the virtues of the heavenly realm; more ambitiously, it allows the faithful to positively revel in an imperfect if not verifiably sinful leader. Referring to scripture, some evangelicals liken Trump to Cyrus of Persia, who facilitated the return of ancient Israel to its land and the reconstruction of its temple; the prophet Isaiah went so far as to honor Cyrus—no Israelite, to be sure—as a messiah. At the extreme,

> only a pagan ruler who knows nothing of the God of Israel—and who was in fact just as happy to finance the building of pagan abominations as part of a general policy of restoring the local religious observances his predecessors had uprooted—can restore the righteous remnant to the Promised Land.[74]

Forum, February 2, 2018, https://voices.uchicago.edu/religionculture/2018/02/02/american-evangelical-support-for-donald-trump-mostly-american-and-only-sort-of-evangelical-a-response.

[72] Gasaway, "Making Evangelicals Great Again," 299.

[73] David R Brockman, "The Little-Known Theology Behind White Evangelical Support for Donald Trump," *Texas Observer*, Marcy 29, 2018, https://www.texasobserver.org/the-little-known-theology-behind-white-evangelical-support-of-donald-trump.

[74] Adam Kotsko, "The Political Theology of Trump: What Looks Like Hypocrisy is the Surest Possible Evidence that God is in Control," Nplusone, November 6, 2018, https://nplusonemag.com/online-only/online-only/the-political-theology-of-trump.

In this counterintuitive if not schizophrenic theology, it becomes *desirable* that the leader is a flawed person, a wicked sinner, and a bad hombre. God glorifies himself by selecting such a person as a "vessel" for his sovereignty:

How could it be clearer that God's hand is guiding events than to witness a man who has never darkened the door of a church calling for greater public recognition of Christianity? What looks like hypocrisy, or at least deep irony, from the outside appears from within the evangelical perspective as the surest possible evidence that God is in control.[75]

Only one last task remains for us, which is to reconnect this mutated theology to the American experience of race. Everything we have discussed in this chapter points to a certain intersection of religion, class, nationalism, and race. It is only too obvious that if Trump is a savior at all, he "is the savior not simply of America but of a particularly Christian America"[76] (of course, only Christians acknowledge saviors; secularists do not). And this Christian America is not just demographic but idealized and racialized. Without necessarily going all the way to Christian Identity, many Americans—especially conservative Republican Christians—conceptualize America as a *white Christian nation.* Whitehead, Perry, and Baker are the most explicit in forging the link between Trump and white Christian nationalism:

[G]reater adherence to Christian nationalist ideology was a robust predictor of voting for Trump, even after controlling for economic dissatisfaction, sexism, anti-black prejudice, anti-Muslim refugee attitudes, and anti-immigrant sentiment, as well as measures of religion, sociodemographics, and political identity more generally. These findings indicate that Christian nationalist ideology—although correlated with a variety of class-based, sexist, racist, and ethnocentric views—is not synonymous with, reducible to, or strictly epiphenomenal of such views. Rather, Christian nationalism operates as a unique and independent ideology that can influence political actions by calling forth a defense of mythological narratives about America's distinctively Christian heritage and future.[77]

They evaluate this Christian nationalism as a worldview that connects America and biblical Israel as peoples who are "commanded to maintain

---

[75] Kotsko, "The Political Theology of Trump."

[76] Viefhues-Bailey, Ludger. "Looking Forward to a New Heaven and a New Earth Where American Greatness Dwells: Trumpism's Political Theology," *Political Theology* 18, no. 3 (2017), 194.

[77] Whitehead, Perry, and Baker, "Make America Christian Again," 147.

cultural and blood purity, often through war, conquest, and separatism," which necessarily entails "exclusion of other religious faiths or cultures" and "cultural purity with racial or ethnic exclusion."[78] And although perennially embattled in their prison of the city of the world, Christian nationalists feel acutely besieged today by liberals, secular elites, non-whites and immigrants, and their own diminishing numbers: as Kirkland documents, whereas white evangelicals were recently as much as twenty-one percent of the population, they had declined to 15.3 percent around election time.[79]

Such a religious-national identity system has long operated in the United States, but what is unique and pernicious about the present moment, as we have established, is that contemporary pro-Trump Christian nationalism

> can be unmoored from traditional moral import, emphasizing only its notions of exclusion and apocalyptic war and conquest. Trump represents a prime example of this trend in that he is not traditionally religious or recognized (even by his supporters) to be of high moral character, facts which ultimately did little to dissuade his many religious supporters.[80]

Quite to the contrary, Whitehead, Perry, and Baker find a powerful correlation between Christian nationalism and Trump support, with every unit of increased Christian nationalism amounting to a nine percent greater likelihood of a Trump vote.[81]

Some critics brand Trump himself as a white Christian nationalist, or a white nationalist with or without a Christian twist, but Gorski offers that Trump is best understood "as a secularized version of white Christian nationalism" whose rhetoric and leadership style "resonat[e] powerfully with the evangelical narrative."[82] In the end, it may not matter much whether Trump is them or they are Trump, as both have entered into a political-theological alliance and bargain, Faustian or otherwise. What is most disquieting is that a large body of twenty-first century American evangelicals "sees no moral confusion in associating their Christian faith with racism and nativism, nor no shame in seeking the political protection of a man such as Trump."[83] For white evangelicals in 2016, "theology came

---

[78] Whitehead, Perry, and Baker, "Make America Christian Again," 150.
[79] Kirkland, "Politics Before God," 170.
[80] Whitehead, Perry, and Baker, "Make America Christian Again," 150–51.
[81] Ibid., 163.
[82] Gorski, "Christianity and Democracy After Trump," 361.
[83] Kirkland, "Politics Before God," 182.

second to their bluntly expedient needs,"[84] and they seem content to hold Trump's hand as long as they are both winning.

As a closing thought, Smith and Hanley identify eight attitudes or values that predict an American's pro-Trump position: "conservative identification; support for domineering leaders; fundamentalism; prejudice against immigrants, African Americans, Muslims, and women; and pessimism about the economy."[85] Whether there is an inevitable connection between these eight mostly malignant attitudes, they characterize a depressingly large segment of the American population. Smith and Hanley indict religion again when they single out the four of these attitudes that distinguish strong Trump supporters from mild ones—economic pessimism, preference for domineering leaders, anti-immigrant sentiment, and Christian fundamentalism. Here is the portrait of an American constituency in pain and anger, reaching out for an antidote like Trump.

---

[84] Kirkland, "Politics Before God," 174.
[85] Smith and Hanley, "Anger Games," 205–6.

6

All the King's Hoaxes
and All the King's Mendacity:
Trump as Will and Representation

> The ideal subject of totalitarian rule is not the convinced Nazi or the convinced Communist, but people for whom the distinction between fact and fiction (i.e., the reality of experience) and the distinction between true and false (i.e., the standards of thought) no longer exist.
>
> —Hannah Arendt[1]

"The world is my idea/representation": so declares Arthur Schopenhauer in the opening sentence of his monumental *The World as Will and Representation*. Schopenhauer (1788–1860) philosophizes in and against the German tradition of Kant and Hegel. In his 1781 *Critique of Pure Reason*, Kant argues that our knowledge of the world, the world as we know it, is a synthetic product of whatever "the world" is in itself (Kant termed the object beyond sense-perception the *Ding-an-sich* or thing-in-itself) and the mental categories that humans bring to experience, such as time and cause; the world-as-known is always and inescapably an artifact of the knower. Hegel, on the other hand, asserts that the world is a materialization of the absolute and divine will or spirit (*Geist*) which comes to know and express itself through history, through humanity, and most perfectly—and as a consummate political theology—through the state and the "great men" who personify the state, like Napoleon or the Prussian king Friedrich Wilhelm III.

In a sort of contradiction yet extrapolation of Kant and a secularization of Hegel, Schopenhauer avers that the world is indeed the product of a will—a human, not a superhuman, will, full of embodied desires and interests. Our will and our idea of the world (*Vorstellung* in German can mean idea, representation, presentation, image, etc.) are one and inseparable; our will shapes the world as we know it. "The world is my

---

[1] Hannah Arendt, *The Origins of Totalitarianism*, second enlarged ed. (Cleveland, OH and New York: The World Publishing Company, 1958 [1951]), 474.

idea/representation" therefore summarizes Schopenhauer's philosophy; it could just as easily be a campaign slogan or epitaph for Trump.

There is room to debate whether Trump is an authoritarian, a populist, an autocrat and demagogue. But there is no disputing that he is a liar, a profligate and promiscuous liar. Everyone lies, politicians more than most, but the scale and brazenness of Trump's dishonesty is truly breathtaking. According to *The Washington Post*, by early April 2020, having served in office for 1,170 days, he had spoken eighteen thousand "false or misleading claims," averaging fifteen lies, exaggerations, or misstatements per day.[2] (This does not include the ridiculous and dangerous things he has said, like that people should consider ingesting or injecting bleach or Lysol to fight the coronavirus.) In the seventy-five days immediately prior to that report, which corresponds to the height of the coronavirus crisis, his lying actually *increased* to twenty-three lies per day. Many of these lies have been repeated more than once, even when they have been thoroughly rebutted: at his return-to-campaign-mode rally in Tulsa, Oklahoma in June 2020, he once again claimed that he passed the Veterans Choice bill, which was enacted during Barack Obama's administration. Almost two hundred times he has taken false credit for the largest tax cut in American history, and almost three hundred times he made the vague but inaccurate assertion that the American economy is better than it has ever been. Frequently, he denies saying something that he is clearly on the record saying. And when he is caught in a lie, he barges ahead, ignoring the charge, denying it, or attacking fact-checkers and the media as "fake news" and "Trump enemies."

Nor is Trump's perfidy some late discovery. His biography of deceit and flimflam goes back to the beginning of his business career: in the 1970s and 1980s, he was renowned for making wild assertions about his business success, overstating his wealth and holdings and understating his debts and losses. That could all be excused as the braggadocio of a New York real estate developer, but it indicates a lifelong habit acquired in the trenches of business and carried to the Oval Office.

According to James Pfiffner, Trump stands out from other public figures not only for the number but the nature of his lies. Pfiffner organizes these fabulations into four categories—trivial lies, exaggerations and self-aggrandizing lies, lies to deceive the public, and egregious lies. Among Trump's trivial lies are his claim that Trump Tower has sixty-eight stories (it has fifty-eight) or that he was featured on the cover of *Time* magazine more often than anyone else (Richard Nixon appeared on the cover much more

---

[2] Glenn Kessler, Salvador Rizzo, and Meg Kelly, "President Trump Made 18,000 False or Misleading Claims in 1,170 Days," *The Washington Post*, April 14, 2020, https://www.washingtonpost.com/politics/2020/04/14/president-trump-made-18000-false-or-misleading-claims-1170-days.

often). For self-aggrandizement, he exaggerated his Electoral College victory and the size of his inaugural audience. For disputing or twisting facts to mislead the public, he maintains that several million fraudulent votes cost him the majority of the popular vote in 2016 (which he therefore sort of won by default) and that the United States has—at least had prior to his tax cuts—the highest tax rates in the world (whereas, in reality, it has one of the lowest rates in the developed world).

Then there are the egregious lies, including his dogged "birther" slanders against Obama (e.g., that Obama was born outside the United States

and thus disqualified to be president), his bizarre claim that Obama founded ISIS, or blatant lies that he told to Canadian Prime Minister Justin Trudeau (saying to Trudeau's face that the United States has a trade deficit with Canada, which it does not). This kind of lying illustrates "the cynicism with which Donald Trump approaches political leadership. It is one thing to spin news or to make exaggerated claims for

Fig. 13 Protesters against Trump's Lying, outside the White House the day after the firing of FBI Director James Comey, May 10, 2017

credit for positive trends in the country, but it is quite another to make statements that are factually wrong and to persist in making the inaccurate claims."[3] Finally, much of Trump's equivocation is circularly self-confirming, that is, "1. Trump makes a false statement. 2. His followers believe it, and others hear it from a source credible to them. 3. When asked how he could make a claim with no evidence, Trump says 'a lot of people agree' or 'many people are saying'"—or more simply, "He makes a false claim; people believe him; Trump concludes it is true."[4]

One often wonders if Trump himself believes his nonsense. Much of it falls squarely within the domain of what Harry Frankfurt memorably (and in 1988, long before Trump's march to the White House began) dubbed *bullshit*. Frankfurt makes a tantalizing distinction between lying and bullshitting. The liar, he reckons, operates in the universe of truth: "In order to invent a lie at all, he must think he knows what is true"; by comparison,

---

[3] James P. Pfiffner, "The Lies of Donald Trump: A Taxonomy," in *Presidential Leadership and the Trump Presidency: Executive Power and Democratic Governance*, ed. Charles M. Lamb and Jacob R. Neiheisel (Cham, Switzerland: Palgrave Macmillan, 2019), 27.

[4] Ibid., 25.

a person who undertakes to bullshit his way through has much more freedom. His focus is panoramic rather than particular. He does not limit himself to inserting a certain falsehood at a specific point, and thus he is not constrained by the truths surrounding that point or intersecting it. He is prepared to fake the context as well, so far as need requires....[T]he mode of creativity upon which it relies is less analytical and less deliberative than that which is mobilized in lying.[5]

For the bullshitter, "the truth-values of his statements are of no central interest to him; what we are not to understand is that his intention is neither to report the truth nor to conceal it"; unlike the liar, "he is neither on the side of the true nor on the side of the false. His eye is not on the facts at all.... He does not care whether the things he says describe reality correctly. He just picks them out, or makes them up, to suit his purpose."[6] In a word, the purveyor of bullshit could not care less what is true, which makes bullshit more destructive than lies, Frankfurt concludes.

Surely no one in his right mind, or under the glaring light of public scrutiny, would sink to bullshitting. But right-wing personality and MAGA "life coach" Brenden Dilley self-consciously and pompously professes that "he doesn't care about the truth of the things he says and that he has no problem 'making shit up'"; "I don't give a fuck about being factual.... I make shit up all the time."[7] And why would anyone be so indifferent to the truth of his statements? Because he is not in the business of informing but of warring: "My objective is to destroy Democrats, OK? To destroy liberals, liberalism as an idea, Democrats, and anything that opposes President Trump."[8] Remember how Alex Jones of Infowars fomented the silly conspiracy of Pizzagate, stirring a listener to carry a gun to the pizza joint to liberate the abused kids. Trump as much as admitted to bullshitting with Trudeau: he later explained to some donors that "I didn't even know ... I had no idea. I just said, 'You're wrong.'"[9]

Quinta Jurecic appreciates the link between Trump's dissimulation and political theology when she reasons that his truth deficiency "is also intimately connected with his possible role as an extra-constitutional Schmittian President"; an executive who habitually disregards and mocks the truth "is functionally identical to ... a sovereign unconstrained by law":

---

[5] Harry G. Frankfurt, *On Bullshit* (Princeton, NJ: Princeton University Press, 2005), 51–52.

[6] Ibid., 55–56.

[7] Kyle Mantyla, "Brenden Dilley Doesn't 'Give a F*ck About Being Factual,'" *Right Wing Watch*, May 27, 2020, https://www.rightwingwatch.org/post/brenden-dilley-doesnt-give-a-fck-about-being-factual.

[8] Ibid.

[9] Pfiffner, "The Lies of Donald Trump," 9.

The character of a person who habitually peddles bullshit and the character of a person who lacks a foundational respect for the Constitution and the rule of law to the point of perhaps considering the office of the President as "extra-constitutional" are, if not identical, at least very closely related.[10]

This is why it is so vitally important to recognize lying not as error or pathology (although possibly also that) but as a social act and, when coming from a politician, a political act, and when coming from a leader, a political-theological act. More, like most if not all social acts—and like linguistic "performatives" as described by J. L. Austin in his groundbreaking *How to Do Things with Words*[11]—speaking is less often than we imagine about transmitting information and more about performing an action *and about inviting or provoking a reaction in others*. That fellow master of lies, Josef Goebbels, knew it well when he taught, "We do not talk to say something, but to obtain a certain effect."[12]

Our job in this chapter, then, is not merely to criticize or correct Trump's falsehoods—that has been done sufficiently elsewhere, although with predictably little impact—but, as Carole McGranahan pleads in her essay on "An Anthropology of Lying," to "understand lies and liars in cultural, historical, and political context so that we see clearly *the work of lies*."[13] And for that task, we must take a tour of the wider universe of doubt and ignorance, of which lying and bullshitting are one part and of which both politics and religion have been consistently guilty.

Agnotology and Agnomancy:
Studying Ignorance, Conjuring Ignorance

For too long scholars and pundits assumed that the possession and perseverance of false ideas and beliefs were simply a matter of lack of information. If people only knew the facts, they would surely dump their wrongheaded thinking and welcome true knowledge. Instead, we are frustrated to discover that false notions are stubborn and, more importantly, that ignorance of the facts is often not the default position (i.e., we do not know, then we learn the facts, then we know) but an achieved status, a social

---

[10] Quinta Jurecic, "Donald Trump's State of Exception," Lawfare, December 14, 2016, https://www.lawfareblog.com/donald-trumps-state-exception.

[11] J. L. Austin, *How to Do Things with Words* (Oxford: Clarendon, 1962).

[12] Quoted in N. J. Shallcross, "Social Media and Information Operations in the 21st Century," *Journal of Information Warfare* 16, no. 1 (2017), 1.

[13] Carole McGranahan, "An Anthropology of Lying: Trump and the Political Sociality of Moral Outrage," *American Ethnologist* 44, no. 2 (2017), 243, emphasis added.

construction by means of which we are rendered and kept ignorant. Among the first to realize and confront this problem, understandably, were educators, who face the challenge not just of filling empty minds but of refurnishing cluttered ones. For instance, Clark Chinn and William Brewer describe how students handle "anomalous data," that is, information that contradicts their prior ideas and beliefs. They identify seven possible reactions, *only one of which entails changing one's mind*, including ignoring the information, rejecting it as false, excluding it as irrelevant, postponing dealing with it, reinterpreting it to fit pre-existing convictions, and making peripheral changes to beliefs while clinging to their core.[14]

As early as 1854, James Ferrier recognized that ignorance is not a residual category, not pure emptiness, but is a worthy topic in its own right, for which he coined the term "agnoiology."[15] Neither the term nor the project got any traction at the time, and it took more than a century for another scholar to revive the subject. In 1989, Michael Smithson published a fairly technical book where he argues that ignorance has been unhelpfully "treated as either the absence or the distortion of 'true' knowledge" but that instead we should approach it as a complicated social construct resulting from a plethora of innocent and not-so-innocent practices. In his scheme, ignorance consists of two main branches, *error* and *irrelevance*. Irrelevance, the simpler of the two, can be further decomposed into *untopicality* (data that are off-topic), *undecidability* (matters that cannot, at least for the moment, be settled), and *taboo*, to which we will return later. Error designates a much more elaborate epistemological space, characterized by *distortion* or *incompleteness*. Distortion of knowledge embraces both *confusion* and *inaccuracy*. Incompleteness of knowledge can result from *absence* of knowledge or from *uncertainty*, itself a result of *vagueness, probability,* or *ambiguity*. Lies do not figure explicitly in his system, but we can see a number of sites where they might fit, for instance by making questions undecidable, by distorting or withholding the facts, and by causing confusion, inaccuracy, or ambiguity.[16]

It would be another twenty-five years before a name was attached to the study of ignorance, and Robert Proctor and Londa Schiebinger would supply that name—*agnotology*, from the roots *a-* (no, without) and *gnosis* (knowledge) and related to agnosticism. In the introduction to their 2008

---

[14] Clark A. Chinn and William F. Brewer, "The Role of Anomalous Data in Knowledge Acquisition: A Theoretical Framework and Implications for Science Instruction," *Review of Educational Research* 63, no. 1 (1993), 4.

[15] James F. Ferrier, *Institutes of Metaphysics: The Theory of Knowing and Being* (Edinburgh and London: William Blackwood and Sons, 1854).

[16] Michael Smithson, *Ignorance and Uncertainty: Emerging Paradigms* (New York: Springer-Verlag, 1989).

edited volume *Agnotology: The Making and Unmaking of Ignorance*, Proctor posits that ignorance is not only rampant but also diverse and socially consequential. It is "more than a void" and often anything but natural or accidental. He proposes three ways to construe ignorance: as a state or a "resource," as a "lost realm" (i.e., that which was known and subsequently forgotten, sometimes by choice), and as "a deliberately engineered and *strategic ploy* (or active construct)."[17] He adds that ignorance overlaps with a myriad of other terms and social practices such as "secrecy, stupidity, apathy, censorship, disinformation, faith, and forgetfulness."[18]

The case studies in Proctor and Schiebinger's volume signal the initial interests of the researchers exploring agnotology—climate science, public health (particularly tobacco), sexuality and contraceptives, race, and history. Indeed, most of the work emerging around that time, much of it by investigative journalists, was focused on corporations and the convergence of science and ignorance (or the corruption of science into ignorance). For Gerald Markowitz and David Rosner, the particular culprit is companies that make lead-based paint and polyvinyl chloride for plastics.[19] For Naomi Oreskes and Erik Conway, it is a congeries of industries and interest groups engaged in misinformation about tobacco, pesticides, and environmental hazards like acid rain, global warming, and the depleted ozone layer.[20] David Michaels, focusing on health risks such as smoking and workplace toxins, blows the whistle on what he calls "manufacturing uncertainty," quoting a tobacco executive who states directly, "Doubt is our product since it is the best means of competing with the 'body of fact' that exists in the minds of the general public. It is also the means of establishing a controversy."[21] Ignorance, many businesses recognize, helps them sell products and evade culpability for the negatives of production (e.g., worker health exposure, waste disposal) and use (e.g., consumer health exposure, product failure, accidents, addiction, etc.) of those products.

Stressing the sociology of ignorance, a laudable counterpart to the better-established sociology of knowledge, Shannon Sullivan and Nancy

---

[17] Robert N. Proctor, "Agnotology: A Missing Term to Describe the Cultural Production of Ignorance (and Its Study)," in *Agnotology: The Making & Unmaking of Ignorance*, ed. Robert N. Proctor and Londa Schiebinger (Stanford, CA: Stanford University Press, 2008), 3.

[18] Ibid., 2.

[19] Gerald Markowitz and David Rosner, *Deceit and Denial: The Deadly Politics of Industrial Pollution* (Berkeley, CA: University of California Press, 2002).

[20] Naomi Oreskes and Erik M. Conway, *Merchants of Doubt: How a Handful of Scientists Obscured the Truth on Issues from Tobacco Smoke to Global Warming* (New York: Bloomsbury, 2010).

[21] David Michaels, *Doubt is Their Product: How Industry's Assault on Science Threatens Your Health* (New York: Oxford University Press, 2008), x.

Tuana speak for the rest when they contend that all knowledge and all knowers and non-knowers are situated in a specific time and place and that the identities and interests of knowers and non-knowers are always relevant. Particular social actors are able to know and to enable others to know or to prevent them from knowing. Further, if knowledge is power, then non-knowledge is disempowerment (with a few exceptions, discussed below); in fact, looking closely at the cases presented in the various studies listed above shows that "a lack of knowledge or an unlearning of something previously known often is actively produced for purposes of domination and exploitation," especially when there are riches of money, power, and status at stake, which is true in every reported example.[22]

Without having a word for it, what much of this research describes is *agnomancy*, the more-or-less (and often quite a bit more) intentional creation or conjuring of ignorance. Agnomancy is one branch or subtopic, but a very sizeable one, of agnotology, but the two are not synonymous. The relationship between agnomancy and agnotology is analogous to that between crime and criminology: crime is the commission of illegal acts, and criminology is the study of crime (among other subjects, such as policing, prisons, rehabilitation, and the like). A criminal might benefit from knowing some criminology, but they usually do not. Another more germane analogy for our purposes would be the relation between politics and political science: politics is the commission of political acts, and political science is the study of such acts (among other subjects, such as law, institutions, international relations, and the like). Agnomancy, then, is the commission of acts of ignorance-making, whereas agnotology is the general study of ignorance, including agnomancy and other topics.

Research on corporations and other actors has unveiled an impressive and time-tested battery of tricks and tactics available to the agnomancer. The key to agnomancy is to erect barricades against potentially-disruptive information, to flood believers with misinformation and disinformation, and to sow confusion, doubt, and suspicion. Primary among these tactics is impugning any source of information that contradicts their claims and imperils their interests. Agnomancers may argue, for instance, that there is no scientific consensus or that the science is incomplete. They may stress that scientists were wrong in the past, so how can we trust them now? They may exaggerate disagreement or inconclusiveness on small or tangential matters while conveniently overlooking the consensus on the main or fundamental matters. At their most corrosive, they may question the quality or the very truth of facts while accusing the bearers of those facts of bias or self-interest. They may, for

---

[22] Shannon Sullivan and Nancy Tuana, eds., *Race and Epistemologies of Ignorance* (Albany: State University of New York Press, 2007), 1.

instance, vilify scientific findings as little more than opinion or majority rule, relegating scientific conclusions to the level of opinion.

One crafty act of modern agnomancers is to sponsor "research" by their own "experts" and circulate those results as what has come to be called "alternative facts." Tobacco companies notoriously pursued this line of attack by paying scientists to argue that cigarette smoking was not harmful, indeed maybe even healthy. The point, of course, as Michaels reminds us, is that "the public is in no position to distinguish good science from bad. Create doubt, uncertainty, and confusion. Throw mud at the [real] research under the assumption that some of it is bound to stick. And buy time, lots of time, in the bargain."[23] On complex issues where ordinary folks cannot distinguish between valid information and propaganda, or on any issue where reasoning is highly motivated and driven by ideological or pecuniary commitments (for example, Holocaust denial, evolution denial, or climate-change denial), these "alternative facts" give the partisans a license to reject information that they dislike and to disbelieve further information that emanates from the same sources. And agnomancers of all stripes comprehend that repeating a claim, including a false claim, over and over confers a kind of legitimacy, consciously or unconsciously exploiting cognitive biases like the confirmation bias (audiences selecting the data that supports their pre-existing beliefs) and the basic tendency to remember and believe things that we have heard many times (variously known as the availability cascade, the mere exposure effect, or most pointedly the illusory truth effect).

When appropriate to the matter or industry at hand, agnomancers may shift responsibility from the product to the user. This is a common maneuver for "vice" industries, also known as "unhealthy commodity industries" such as alcohol, fast food, and gambling, as well as for the gun lobby. Agnomancers respond to information about the hazards of their fare by insisting that alcoholism or obesity or gambling addiction are complex issues and/or that the problem is not their product but how the consumers (mis/ab)use it. Corporations commonly offer to police themselves and to provide support services for users (alcohol and gambling counseling, for instance); what they do *not* want is labeling (that is, *information* for the consumer), taxation, and regulation, which might hurt their sales.

Further agnomancy ploys include establishing false equivalencies, for instance insisting that schools or media present "both sides" of "controversies" like evolution, climate change, or the Holocaust. Accomplished agnomancers also understand that strong emotion affects (and impedes) thinking, especially negative emotions such as anger and fear. Not entirely irrationally, anger toward individuals or groups and their ideas

---

[23] Michaels, *Doubt is Their Product*, 9.

makes people close their ears and minds to them, and fear spawns boundary formation and defense and risk aversion. Ample studies confirm that fear tends to inspire in-group solidarity, obedience to authority, and resistance to change or "support for the 'way things are.'"[24] This effect is so concrete that asking experimental subjects to imagine that they have superpowers (thereby enhancing their invulnerability to risk and danger) renders them more open to change. Conversely, it is no wonder that agnomancers frequently scream and threaten and scare, agitating their targets to close ranks and minds.

The agents of agnomancy need not be anything as centralized as a regime or a board room. Any constituency that is dedicated to hierarchy and to "identity-protective cognition" may be inclined to deny knowledge that jeopardizes its interests, and research indicates that, at least in the United States, the most prominent denialists are conservative white males.[25] Examining attitudes toward global warming specifically, Aaron McCright and Riley Dunlap find that conservative white males are more than twice as likely as other Americans to discount global warming, and ironically (or not), these same men "are more confident in their knowledge of climate change than are other adults, even as their beliefs conflict with the scientific consensus"—(over)confidence compensating for, if not accounting for, their error.[26] Ultimately, cognitive exertions to defend their status and to preserve the system in which they enjoy that status "lead them to reject information from out-groups (e.g., liberals and environmentalists) they see as threatening the economic system, and such tendencies provoke strong emotional and psychic investment, easily translating into (over)confidence in beliefs."[27]

Finally, there might be value not only in keeping others ignorant but in keeping *oneself* ignorant—or being able to feign ignorance. Linsey McGoey clarifies how pharmaceutical companies among many others practice "strategic ignorance" to shield themselves from liability. An "ignorance alibi" is "any mechanism that obscures one's involvement in causing harm to others, furnishing plausible deniability and making unawareness seem innocent rather than calculated."[28] Drug manufacturers,

---

[24] Jaime L. Napier, Julie Huang, Andrew J. Vonasch, and John A. Bargh, "Superheroes for Change: Physical Safety Promotes Socially (but not Economically) Progressive Attitudes among Conservatives," *European Journal of Social Psychology* 48, no. 2 (2018), 188.

[25] Dan M. Kahan, Donald Braman, John Gastil, Paul Slovic, and C. K. Mertz, "Culture and Identity-Protective Cognition: Explaining the White-Male Effect in Risk Perception," *Journal of Empirical Legal Studies* 4, no. 3 (2007), 465–505.

[26] Aaron M. McCright and Riley E. Dunlap, "Cool Dudes: The Denial of Climate Change among Conservative White Males in the United States," *Global Environmental Change* 21, no. 4 (2011), 1167.

[27] Ibid.

[28] Linsey McGoey, *The Unknowers: How Strategic Ignorance Rules the World* (London: Zed Books, 2019), 56.

for instance, can allege that they did not know the risks of their products; they can also blame any bad outcomes on consumer abuse (say, in the case of opioids), underlying conditions, or drug interactions (trotting out again the "complexity" argument, that it is impossible to assign causal responsibility to just one variable). Of course they may be lying about their ignorance, but this ignorance can be real if deliberate: they may rush a drug to market before it has been thoroughly tested, or they may keep themselves or regulators blissfully ignorant by not conducting certain tests and collecting relevant information in the first place or suppressing unfavorable information. Therefore, McGoey insists that, unlike secrecy which "hides," strategic ignorance *"creates*: constructing plausible rationale ... for why problems should not exist, and therefore do not require closer investigation or penalization."[29]

Agnomancy in Politics and Government

Research on agnotology and agnomancy has concentrated on corporations, but agnomancy practices are not limited to business. In the only previous use of the term of which I am aware, William Clough, writing in a vastly different context, directly refers to questioning, misrepresenting, or lying about knowledge "for social, political, economic, or religious purposes."[30] Likewise, McGoey describes a cycle of ignorance—individual or "micro-ignorance leading to larger, more structural forms of macro-ignorance, which in turn compels individual forms of micro-ignorance"—which is "common *to all religious and secular thought systems.*"[31] But presumably no reader requires convincing that politicians and governments are accomplished agnomancers or what McGoey calls "masters of ignorance." As long as there have been leaders and governments, there has been political dishonesty: as Karl Popper reminds us in his *The Open Society and Its Enemies*, Plato actually advised rulers against political openness:

> It is one of the royal privileges of the sovereign to make full use of lies and deceit: [Plato wrote that] "It is the business of the rulers of the city, if it is anybody's, to tell lies, deceiving both its enemies and its own citizens for the benefit of the city, and no one else must touch this privilege....If the ruler catches anyone else in a lie ... then he will

---

[29] McGoey, *The Unknowers*, 294.
[30] William R. Clough, "The Role of Agnomancy in the Creation and Perpetuation of Conflict," in *Visions of Conflict: International Perspectives on Values and Enmity*, ed. Brian C. Alston (Lihue, HI: Brian C. Alston, 2010), 83.
[31] McGoey, *The Unknowers*, 12–13, emphasis added.

punish him for introducing a practice which injures and endangers the city."[32]

No doubt the philosopher-king accused that civilian liar of liberal bias and fake news. Infamously, Machiavelli also counseled the prince to break his word whenever expedient through "shrewdness and cunning," instructing that "occasionally words must serve to veil the facts. But let this happen in such a way that no one become aware of it; or, if it should be noticed, excuses must be at hand to be produced immediately."[33]

Plato and Machiavelli, plus the entire political history of humanity, justify Arendt's clear-eyed deduction that "truth and politics are on rather bad terms with each other, and no one, as far as I know, has ever counted truth among the political virtues. Lies have always been regarded as necessary and justifiable tools not only of the politician's or the demagogue's but also of the statesman's trade."[34] It is essential to accept that politics and governing are not principally about informing the public; they are at best about mobilizing, and at worst about manipulating, the public. Politics and governance are a call to action (not necessarily a call to thought) of a society, whether that action is voting for a candidate or enlisting in a war, and truth is not always the ideal motivator.

More than occasionally, political leaders flat-out lie, either through commission or omission. After the Yalta conference near the end of World War II, Franklin Roosevelt unscrupulously misrepresented the terms of his agreement with Soviet leader Joseph Stalin, terms which would have been unpalatable to Americans, like conceding Eastern Europe to Stalin or endorsing the Soviet claim to Outer Mongolia or South Sakhalin Island.[35] Another Democrat, John Kennedy, lied about the details of the Cuban missile crisis settlement (denying that the United States agreed to remove missiles too, from Turkey), and his assistant secretary of defense for public affairs, Arthur Sylvester, articulated duplicity as policy: "It's inherent in [the] government's right, if necessary, to lie to save itself.... News generated by the actions of the government ... [is] part of the arsenal of weaponry that a President has."[36] Kennedy's successor, Lyndon Johnson, ruined his presidency and much of the country's faith in government by lying about the

[32] Karl Popper, *The Open Society and Its Enemies, Volume 1 The Age of Plato* (New York and Evanston, IL: Harper Torchbooks, 1945), 150–51.

[33] Niccolo Machiavelli, *The Historical, Political, and Diplomatic Writings of Niccolo Machiavelli*, vol. 4 (Boston, MA: J. R. Osgood and Company, 1882), 422.

[34] Hannah Arendt, "Politics and Truth," Wordpress.com, accessed June 23, 2020, https://idanlandau.files.wordpress.com/2014/12/arendt-truth-and-politics.pdf. Originally published in *The New Yorker*, February 25, 1967.

[35] Eric Alterman, *When Presidents Lie: A History of Official Deception and its Consequences* (New York and London: Viking, 2004), 38–39.

[36] Quoted in ibid., 92.

escalation of the Vietnam War after the so-called "Gulf of Tonkin" incident, which has been condemned as a "mixture of self-deception and deliberate dishonesty."[37]

Richard Nixon was chased from office for his involvement in crimes and cover-ups surrounding the Watergate break-in, and Ronald Reagan could have been impeached for his dirty dealings and subsequent lies about funneling aid to the Nicaraguan Contras by illegally selling weapons to Iran. Writes Eric Alterman:

> The Contra aid program was clothed in falsehoods from its inception. CIA director William Casey believed in lying to Congress as a matter of principle and genially referred to its denizens as "those assholes on the Hill." Whenever he had planned covert operations involving sensitive information in the past, his instincts were to dissemble, deny, and disappear.[38]

Fig. 14 President Lyndon Johnson signing the 'Gulf of Tonkin' Resolution, August 10, 1964, starting the Vietnam War based on a lie.

In late 1982, Reagan faithlessly signed a congressional bill banning American funds from being spent to overthrow the Nicaraguan government; "And once again, the CIA simply ignored it, conducting Nicaraguan affairs as Casey saw fit."[39] Reagan went so far as to open an Office of Public Diplomacy for express agnomancy purposes, such as "offering privileges to favored journalists, placing ghostwritten articles over the signatures of Contra leaders in the nation's leading opinion magazines and op-ed pages, and generally publicizing negative stories about the Sandinistas, whether true or not."[40]

To this ancient history can be added the flurry of untruths told by American and British leaders on the road to war with Iraq in 2003. Not only did the George W. Bush administration make unjustified and demonstrably untrue assertions that the 9/11 terrorists were associated with Iraq and that Iraq possessed weapons of mass destruction (but then what country does not?)—statements that were "later judged to be false by the president's own weapons inspections team"—but Bush's Department of Justice told the Supreme Court that the government demanded the freedom "to give out false

---

[37] Alterman, *When Presidents Lie*, 213.
[38] Ibid., 262.
[39] Ibid., 266.
[40] Ibid., 269–70.

information … incomplete information and even disinformation whenever it deemed necessary."[41]

Blatant lying to the citizenry is not the only trick in the political agnomancy playbook. To a significant extent, governments depend on secrecy, especially but not exclusively in the area of national security and defense. A country does not want its enemies knowing its true strengths and weaknesses nor its military plans and resources. Governments often enter into secret negotiations—not wanting the public to know about the talks lest the talks fail—and secret treaties (a practice much decried after World War I but hardly curtailed).

A useful way to keep secrets is "classifying" documents, thereby taking them out of circulation. Granted, some knowledge is too dangerous to circulate freely among the population, like directions for nuclear weapons and recipes for chemical weapons. Brian Balmer shares the case of a nerve gas designated VX, arguing that the classification of knowledge as secret-sensitive is an act of "anti-epistemology" that "does not so much deny knowledge, as it fractures and disrupts the topography of knowledge—providing particular geographically restricted accounts of the world. In this sense, secrecy acts as a spatial epistemic tool in the exercise of power."[42]

Censorship is another tactic that can be narrowly targeted or broadly and bluntly enforced. According to Elizabeth Purdy writing in *The First Amendment Encyclopedia*, censorship occurs when "individuals or groups try to prevent others from saying, printing, or depicting words and images"—and therefore to prevent third parties from seeing, reading, *and knowing* those things.[43] Censorship is thus, like classification, an anti-epistemological practice: a censor intends "to limit freedom of thought and expression by restricting spoken words, printed matter, symbolic messages, freedom of association, books, art, music, movies, television programs, and internet sites") and one that is not limited to governments. It can have moral motivations (e.g., censoring pornography and obscenity) as well as political ones, particularly when the censored materials are believed to be treasonous or seditious, a loose standard that can cover principled opposition to government policy, like criticism of war or the government in general. Censorship can be done directly, by a government office, or indirectly, through control or intimidation (fines, taxes, license revocations, threats, arrests, and more) of information outlets such as newspapers, television and

---

[41] Alterman, *When Presidents Lie*, 296.

[42] Brian Balmer, "A Secret Formula, A Rogue Patent, and Public Knowledge about Nerve Gas: Secrecy as a Spatial-Epistemic Tool," *Social Studies of Science* 36, no. 5 (2006), 695.

[43] Elizabeth R. Purdy, "Censorship," The First Amendment Encyclopedia, accessed June 23, 2020, https://www.mtsu.edu/first-amendment/article/896/censorship.

radio stations, and social media platforms (e.g., Facebook or Google)—a favorite move of authoritarians.

One devious means to choke the flow of information is never to collect that information at all. We mentioned in Chapter 2 how previous administrations have blinded government by defunding or understaffing data-collecting agencies like the Census Bureau, the Bureau of Justice Statistics, and the National Center for Health Statistics. In recent days, Trump has ordered that coronavirus data bypass the Centers for Disease Control, the agency most qualified (in fact, created) to handle it, and go directly to the Department of Health and Human Services, headed by a Trump appointee. Presidents have also undermined the government's capacity to acquire and act on information by appointing heads of agencies who are hostile to the mission of those departments, like Anne Gorsuch (the mother of Trump's Supreme Court justice pick Neil Gorsuch) who was tapped by Reagan to direct the Environmental Protection Agency despite— or because of—her opposition to the very regulations that the EPA was designed to enforce. Reagan also instituted the Orwellian-named Office of Information and Regulatory Affairs *to impede* federal agencies from informing and regulating. On many other occasions, presidents have seated industry leaders or industry-friendly experts in high positions or on advisory boards and/or given corporations the right to review, challenge, or prevent the dissemination of data. Staying the course of strategic ignorance and calculated non-knowing, Trump has

> removed or obscured information about climate change from Web sites, dismissed scientific advisory panels, blocked scientists who receive EPA grants from advisement, and put a political appointee in charge of scientific grants. [Scott] Pruitt now plans to sponsor a public "red team/blue team" debate to artificially litigate settled questions in climate science.[44]

Apparently during the COVID-19 pandemic, several states have been underreporting their testing results and hospitalization data, giving residents of those states and of the country an unrealistically positive sense of well-being (precisely what Trump rips China for doing).

Finally, governments roll out a variety of communication practices to uninform, misinform, and disinform their own citizens and other

---

[44] Leif Fredrickson, Christopher Sellers, Lindsey Dillon, Jennifer Liss Ohayon, Nicholas Shapiro, Marianne Sullivan, Stephen Bocking, Phil Brown, Vanessa de la Rosa, Jill Harrison, Sara Johns, Katherine Kulik, Rebecca Lave, Michelle Murphy, Liza Piper, Lauren Richter, and Sara Wylie, "History of US Presidential Assaults on Modern Environmental Health Protection," *American Journal of Public Health* 108, no. 52 supplement 2 (2018), S100.

countries. We are too acquainted with political-speak or the fine art of talking without saying anything. Politicians (and leaders in other capacities, including corporate executives) often speak in generalities, platitudes, and indirections to avoid answering questions or saying anything for which they could be held responsible later. Political talk can also take advantage of framing and language co-optation to corrupt public knowledge and manage public opinion. Operators like Republican consultant Frank Luntz recognize that the very words we choose are little arguments that can influence people's understanding and attitude. In his notorious "14 Words Never to Use," he guides Republicans, "Sometimes it is not what you say that matters but what you don't say. Other times a single word or phrase can undermine or destroy the credibility of a paragraph or entire presentation....So from today forward, YOU are the language police."[45] Among his recommendations was to call the estate tax a "death tax" because the majority of people favor the former but oppose the latter—although it is the same thing. Other recent examples of words that act as hammers or fences for or against thought are "socialist," "climate change" (instead of global warming), "welfare queen," and of course "fake news" and "liberal media."

Governments have developed much more sophisticated skills, mostly directed against rival governments but always available to aim at one's own people. Under the heading of "organized persuasive communication," we find a number of practices, the most sinister of which is *strategic communication*. According to Paul Cornish, Julian Lindley-French, and Claire Yorke, strategic communication is a "systematic series of sustained and coherent activities, conducted across strategic, operational, and tactical levels, that enables understanding of target audiences and identifies effective conduits to promote and sustain particular types of behavior."[46] This weaponization of knowledge and non-knowledge has predictably caught the attention of the military, which in the United States defense community has become known as *information operations*, "the integrated employment, during military operations, of information-related capabilities in concert with other lines of operation *to influence, disrupt, corrupt, or usurp the decision making of adversaries and potential*

---

[45] Frank Luntz, *The Frank Luntz Rethug Playbook, Unauthorized Edition: How to Scare the American Public into Voting Republican* (Luntz Research Companies), accessed February 22, 2020, https://joshuakahnrussell.files.wordpress.com/2008/10/luntzplaybook2006.pdf.

[46] Paul Cornish, Julian Lindley-French, and Claire Yorke, "Strategic Communications and National Strategy" (London: The Royal Institute of International Affairs, 2011), 3–4.

adversaries while protecting our own"—which is synonymous with "disinformation campaign."[47]

In their report about information operations for and by Facebook, Jen Weedon, William Nuland, and Alex Stamos add that information operations are communication practices intended "to distort *domestic* or foreign political sentiment, most frequently to achieve a strategic and/or geopolitical outcome" consisting of "false news, disinformation, or networks of fake accounts (false amplifiers aimed at manipulating public opinion)."[48] Worrisomely, many observers have judged Russia to be far ahead of most countries in information operations, which are termed "reflexive control" in Russia. Reflexive control is a program to analyze the ideas and decision-making processes of the enemy and use that knowledge against them—tricks like "camouflage (at all levels), disinformation, encouragement, blackmail by force, and the compromising of various officials and officers" in order "to influence his combat plans, his view of situation, and how he fights."[49] It demonstrated its worth in Russia's recent adventuring in Ukraine.

Agnomancy in Religion

If by far most of the work in agnotology and agnomancy has centered on corporations and much less on governments and politicians, virtually none has touched the thorny subject of religion. Whether this is because no one has thought to look there or because they respect or fear religion too much or for some other reason, this oversight cannot be permitted. Like any other social and cultural domain, religion is a field of knowing, non-knowing, and unknowing.

Indeed, just as closer inspection refutes the idealistic notion that clear and honest communication is the essence of politics, so investigation dashes the assumption that truth is the mission of religion. All religions in all times and places have had a heart of darkness, secrecy, and ignorance. Maybe the most universal of all religious conceptions is *taboo* or that which must not be done, said, or known. Understanding religion as beliefs and practices of power makes it easy to see how some objects, actions, or knowledge are too frightening to approach at all or may be approached only in the correct ritual condition. Violating a taboo may unleash dangerous forces and/or damage the tabooed object/place/word/being through pollution and profanation. Meyer Fortes conveys the centrality of taboo in Tallensi

---

[47] Catherine A. Theohary, "Defense Primer: Information Operations" (Washington, DC: Congressional Research Service, 2018), 1, emphasis added.

[48] Jen Weedon, William Nuland, and Alex Stamos, "Information Operations and Facebook" (Facebook, 2017), 5.

[49] Timothy Thomas, "Russia's Reflexive Control Theory and the Military," *Journal of Slavic Military Studies* 17, no. 2 (2004), 241–42.

(northern Ghana) society, religion, and morality. *Kyiher* or "taboo custom" was enforced through "the likelihood of mystical retribution" and—as an instance of tribal political theology—was "accepted as absolutely binding":

> The observance of a taboo signifies submission to an internal command which is beyond question.... Transgression is tantamount to repudiating one's identity, or one's identification with a locality or office of status ... [Such] taboos ordain rules of conduct that are binding on the individual, in the first place because he is the person he is in the situation he is in. Compliance with them means that he identifies himself with, appropriates to himself, the capacities, the rights and obligations, the relationships and the commitments that devolve upon a normal person of his status in his situation. He has, it must be remembered, been cast in these roles or in roles preparatory to them since childhood. Being with him all the time taboos keep him aware of his enduring identity, as a person in contraposition to other persons.

He finishes by pronouncing that Tallensi taboos "represent acknowledgement of a particular form of dependence ... to bonds that amount to inescapable bondage."[50]

Taboos may be binding on all members of a society or on all but the most spiritually powerful and informed members. Certain religious knowledge is not so much taboo as restricted or secret-sacred. Such knowledge may be kept and guarded by the elders or priests of the group. Other knowledge may be available only to the initiated. For instance, initiation among Australian Aboriginals commenced a lifetime of increasingly deep ritual and mythical knowledge, much too complex and much too potent for the young to handle. Religious knowledge was also highly distributed: different individual men or clans of men enjoyed rights to different knowledge, and women were generally excluded from male secret-sacred knowledge, although, as Diane Bell and others gradually came to realize, Aboriginal women also possess their own gender-specific knowledge and associated ritual.[51]

Because religious words, actions, and objects are not meaningful in themselves, simply being exposed to them does not immediately confer knowledge. People must be prepared and trained to "know" what the words, actions, and objects mean, which may never happen. Stanley Tambiah, for example, observes that monks in a Thai Buddhist village chant to lay inhabitants but, because the laypeople have not been instructed in the

---

[50] Meyer Fortes, *Religion, Morality, and the Person: Essays on Tallensi Religion* (Cambridge: Cambridge University Press, 1987), 125–57.
[51] Diane Bell, *Daughters of the Dreaming* (Minneapolis: University of Minnesota Press, 1983).

religion and do not speak the arcane ritual language, the experience is not "informative" for them. The entire point, according to Tambiah, is that Buddhist chants "are meant to be heard but paradoxically they are not understood by the majority of the congregation (nor by some of the monks themselves), because the sacred language is the dead Pali language"; in what Tambiah astutely dubs "the virtue of listening without understanding," Thai laity are "emphatic that through listening to the chants the congregation gains merit, blessings, and protection"—but *not knowledge.*[52] The same situation obtained for most lay Catholics hearing the traditional Latin mass. In the light of cross-cultural incomprehension of much religious speech and action, Frits Staal takes the next step and declares that religious ritual (and much religious talk) is literally "meaningless" in the sense that it is not intended to transmit information in the first place; its appeal and efficacy come from the brute fact that it must be performed.[53]

It is not usually recognized that history in the Judeo-Christian tradition begins with an act of agnomancy—the proscription of knowledge (specifically of good and evil) under penalty of death. Like any human autocrat, the god of Eden desires not informed subjects but obedient ones and punishes them extravagantly for acquiring the resources of independent thought and behavior, for becoming social and moral agents in their own right. Later, when Job dares to request reasons and justifications from an evidently unjust god, rather than provide those answers, the deity berates Job for the audacity to ask the questions.

When biblical divinity is not actively reprimanding humanity for its wish to know, he is strangely and confusingly silent. At the best of times, he is mysterious and inscrutable, but he often seems capricious if not altogether absent: he does not respond to prayers, relieve suffering, or appear in times of need. The Hebrew scriptures chronically struggle with a god who intentionally *hides* from mankind:

- (God speaking to Moses): "Then my anger shall be kindled against them in that day, and I will forsake them, and I will hide my face from them." (Deuteronomy 31:17)
- "Truly, you are a God who hides himself, O God of Israel, the Savior." (Isaiah 45:15)
- "Wherefore hidest thou thy face, and holdest me for thine enemy?" (Job 14:24)
- "Why standest thou afar off, O Lord? Why hidest thou thyself in times of trouble?" (Psalsm 10:1)

---

[52] Stanley J. Tambiah, *Buddhism and the Spirit Cults in North-East Thailand* (Cambridge and New York: Cambridge University Press, 1970), 195.
[53] Frits Staal, "The Meaninglessness of Ritual," *Numen* 26, no. 1 (1979), 2–22.

- "Wherefore hidest thou thy face, and forgettest our affliction and our oppression?" (Psalms 44:24)

Nor were the Hebrews the first or only people to lament their inconsistent or missing god. The ancient Greek thinker Theognis expressed his dismay with Zeus:

Dear Zeus, you baffle me. You are king of all; the highest honor and greatest power are yours, you discern what goes on in each man's secret heart, and your lordship is supreme. Yet you make no distinction between the sinner and the good man, between the man who devotes himself to temperate and responsible acts and the man who commits deeds of hubris. Tell me, son of Cronus, how can you deal such unfairness?[54]

Theologians, philosophers, apologists, prophets, and keen layfolk have conceived a plethora of agnotological solutions to the problem of "divine hiddenness" or the "hiddenness of god." As implied in Deuteronomy above, a god may withdraw from human sight out of anger, as vengeance for unrighteousness or unbelief. Some writers have speculated that a god may not want to curtail human free will or compel belief by obvious demonstrations of power or may prefer that followers undertake an arduous trek to faith. Some reckon that a god's hiddenness or absence leaves space for the cultivation of higher moral qualities such as courage, generosity, and altruism, while others simply stop at the assertion that the human mind is too feeble to grasp the supreme mind. Thus, a god reveals himself as he/she/it sees fit.

One strategy for grappling with the incomprehensibility, potentially the unknowability, of a god is negative theology, which defines divinity precisely in terms of *what cannot be said or known of it*. Unknowability may itself be an essential quality of the deity, what Philo calls divine "luminous darkness." Augustine characterizes his god as *aliud, aliud valde*—other, completely other. John Scotus Erigena (ninth century) explains: "We do not know what God is. God Himself does not know what He is because He is not anything. Literally God is not, because He transcends being."[55] (Can a god be ignorant of his/her own being and nature?) Or godhead may simply be beyond human language, all of our words failing to do it justice; the best we can achieve is to utter that the deity is not this or that (e.g., good, just, powerful, loving, etc.) because every formulation is insufficient. This view

---

[54] Philip Wheelwright, ed., *The Presocratics* (New York: The Odyssey Press, 1966), 29–30.

[55] Quoted in William Indick, *The Digital God: How Technology Will Reshape Spirituality* (Jefferson, NC: McFarland and Company, 2015), 179.

has been shared by other religions and not only theisms. Indeed, the opening lines of the *Tao Te Ching* teach, "Tao (the Way) that can be spoken of is not the constant Tao. The name that can be named is not a constant name." Thus, the best knowledge we can have of deity or ultimate reality is non-knowledge.

By the mid-twentieth century, after the unspeakable horror of the Holocaust, the torment of divine hiddenness became too acute for some to bear. New strategies for comprehending their god's inaction were sought, leading to "death of God" theology. Dating back at least to Nietzsche's epochal announcement of God's death, theologians and scholars made lemonade out of the lemon of godly silence, as in Thomas Altizer's *The Gospel of Christian Atheism*: the old god, or at least the old concept of god, truly had died, and Christianity could go on without him/it (like government goes on without the old sovereign), making room for a god-after-god, a god-beyond-god.[56] For Paul Tillich, "god" became not a being but the ground of being which would not be expected to intervene in human affairs. And most recently, Richard Kearney proposes a theology of *anatheism*, a coming-back-around-to-theism premised on a convenient but unsatisfying "powerlessness of the divine," of a "nonsovereign, nonmetaphysical God" who is "vulnerable and powerless," incapable of relieving either misery or injustice.[57]

Given the insurmountable theological problem of god-knowledge, it is little wonder that the Judeo-Christian tradition has frequently valorized ignorance. Ecclesiastes 1:18 teaches that "in much wisdom there is much grief, and increasing knowledge results in increasing pain," demeaning and threatening "the fool" who rejects the deity. The New Testament more often and forcefully admonishes the believer to be a fool and a child and scorns human knowledge: "For the wisdom of this world is foolishness in God's sight," says 1 Corinthians 3:19.

Early church fathers echo and elaborate this theme, none more energetically than Tertullian (155–220 CE). In *The Prescription Against Heretics*, Tertullian writes, "After Jesus Christ we have no need of speculation, after the Gospel no need of research. When we come to believe, we have no desire to believe anything else; for we begin by believing that there is nothing else which we have to believe."[58] He goes on to rhapsodize:

---

[56] Thomas J. J. Altizer, *The Gospel of Christian Atheism* (Philadelphia, PA: Westminster Press, 1966).

[57] Richard Kearney, *Anatheism: Returning to God After God* (New York: Columbia University Press, 2010), 66.

[58] Quoted in Ed L. Miller, ed., *Classical Statements on Faith and Reason* (New York: Random House, 1970), 5.

My first principle is this. Christ laid down one definite system of truth which the world must believe without qualification, and which we must seek precisely in order to believe it when we find it.... You must seek until you find, and when you find, you must believe. Then you have simply to keep what you have come to believe, since you also believe that there is nothing else to believe, and therefore nothing else to seek, once you have found and believed what he taught who bids you seek nothing beyond what he taught.... I warn people not to seek for anything beyond what they believe, for that was all they needed to seek for.[59]

Tertullian concludes that the Rule of Faith (the Christian credo) "allows of no questions among us," such that "it is better for you to remain ignorant for fear that you come to know what you should not know. For you do know what you should know."[60]

Christianity has been resolute in subordinating reason to faith in the work of Augustine (354–430) and beyond. Augustine (Sermon 43.7, 9) affirms that belief precedes knowledge when he insists *Crede, ut intelligas* (Believe in order that you may understand), even arguing that faith is a kind of knowledge. Anselm (1033–1109) nearly quotes Augustine when he confesses *Credo, ut intelligam* (I believe in order that I might understand). But Augustine's stance on knowledge and reason is much harsher. In his classic *Confessions* (chap. XXXV, 54), he denounces the "temptation of curiosity":

For besides that concupiscence of the flesh which lieth in the gratification of all senses and pleasures, wherein its slaves who "are far from Thee perish," there pertaineth to the soul, through the same senses of the body, a certain vain and curious longing, cloaked under the name of knowledge and learning.... This longing ... originates in an appetite for knowledge.

Later Protestant thinkers share the same dim view of knowledge. Martin Luther castigates reason as "God's worst enemy"—"the devil's bride," which "faith must trample under foot." "There is," he opines, "on earth among all dangers no more dangerous thing than a richly endowed and adroit reason," which "must be deluded, blinded, and destroyed."[61] Likewise for Luther's contemporary, John Calvin, who teaches that human reason has been "partly weakened and partly corrupted" by sin and that knowledge (of God at least, which is the only kind of knowledge that matters) is "open only

---

[59] Miller, *Classical Statements*, 7.

[60] Ibid., 9–10.

[61] Quoted in Walter Kaufmann, *The Faith of a Heretic* (Garden City, NY: Doubleday & Company, 1961), 75.

to him whose mind has been made new by the illumination of the Holy Spirit."[62] "Thus we can see," he judges, "that the reason of our mind, wherever it may turn, is miserably subject to vanity."[63]

A present-day stream of theology transforms the obstacle of non-knowledge of the Christian god into a non-problem, if not a virtue. Rejecting the burden of supporting Christian claims with argument and evidence, Alvin Plantinga's "reformed epistemology" is an unabashed exercise in religious agnomancy. Because all efforts to secure Christian beliefs with fact and logic have failed, Plantinga insists that Christianity requires none. Most fully in his *Warranted Christian Belief* he boldly contends that belief in the existence of the Christian god is warranted, if not self-evidently true, because such belief is "properly basic." Like sight or hearing, it needs no inferences or proofs; it is immediately obvious. Notwithstanding the naivety of his phenomenology (i.e., sense perceptions are not perfectly self-evident or pre-theoretical as Edmund Husserl and Maurice Merleau-Ponty established decades ago), Plantinga liberates himself by "starting from an assumption of the truth of Christian belief and from that standpoint investigating its epistemology, asking whether and how such belief has warrant."[64] Of course, if you assume that a claim is true, then that assumption *is* your warrant to believe it, but Plantinga goes the extra mile by assuring us that his god installs in humans a *sensus divinitatis*, a sense of the divine, which automatically detects him when the mind is functioning properly. The circularity of this argument is not only awe-inspiring (and condescending) but also self-defeating: any other religion could maintain that *its* god or such being(s) installs its own automatic detection system and that failure to "know" that being is a symptom of mental malfunction.

Simply stipulating that your beliefs are true without regard to facts is one means to immunize religion against "anomalous data." Yet the toolkit of religion burgeons with other agnomancy practices, many shared by secular authorities. One is censorship: members can be forbidden to read and thus know certain things, as with the Catholic Church's *Index Librorum Prohibitorum* (Index of Forbidden Books). For stronger measures, those books can be confiscated and burned. Individuals who profess unorthodox and false doctrines, or dispute the truth of orthodox ones—heretics and blasphemers—can be cursed, excommunicated, and persecuted (even unto death). And the faithful can be shielded from discomfiting knowledge by separation from outsiders, withdrawing into closed (anti-)epistemological communities. At worst, religious zealots can invade and subvert information-imparting institutions like public schools, as documented by

---

[62] Quoted in Miller, *Classic Statements on Faith and Reason*, 75.

[63] Ibid., 81.

[64] Alvin Plantinga, *Warranted Christian Belief* (New York: Oxford University Press, 2000), xiii–xiv.

Eric Cernyar in his study of the Child Evangelism Fellowship: targeting primary school students, CEF trains children under twelve years of age to resist education "by attacking scientific evidence of origins, encouraging disrespect for the teachers who teach it, and actively intimidating children from critical thinking. Invidiously, the curriculum discourages students from becoming close friends with their disbelieving classmates."[65] Ideally such movements would replace secular public schools with sectarian religious institutions (as would Christian Reconstruction, discussed in an earlier chapter).

Other religions have their own versions of ignorance concepts and practices. In Islam, *jahiliyya*, usually translated as ignorance or barbarism, refers commonly to pre-Islamic society before the knowledge of Islam and the Qur'an was available; in extreme cases, as with the Taliban, all remnants of those dark and evil times should be eliminated, like the Bamiyan Buddhist statues destroyed in Afghanistan. Islam also confronts its own problem of divine hiddenness, the medieval philosophy Ibn 'Arabi (1165–1240) concurring that unknowability is a trait of deity:

> The being of the Essence is beyond being known, it is the most hidden secret (*aktam al-sirr*). As the absolutely absent being (*al-ghayb al-ghuyub*), no one can know God in Himself but Himself. No one can perceive the divine essence but God Himself. The Gnostics can perceive divine self-disclosure, which is His revelation, but they cannot perceive God Himself unless they become annihilated. The divine essence will never be found and cannot be sought.[66]

Finally, the Sanskrit term *avidyā* (literally not-knowing, not-perceiving, not-understanding) denotes ignorance in Hindu and Buddhist (Pali, *avijjā*) traditions, but according to Alex Wayman, the word has more religion-specific connotations. He would translate it as "unwisdom," stressing that it is not an empty state, a mere lack of knowledge, but also a condition of delusion, obscuration, and error, for instance mistaking impermanence for permanence and selflessness (*anatta*) for self.[67] As we would suspect, religions construct ignorance in relation to their own notions of truth.

---

[65] Eric W. Cernyar, *Protecting Public Elementary School Children from Emotional and Psychological Harm by Outside Groups* (Intrinsic Dignity, 2013), 2.

[66] Quoted in Ebrahim Azadegan, "Ibn 'Arabi on the Problem of Divine Hiddenness," *Journal of the Muhyiddin Ibn 'Arabi Society* 53 (2013), 51.

[67] Alex Wayman, "The Meaning of Unwisdom (Avidya)," *Philosophy East and West* 7, no. 1/2 (1957), 21–25.

Trump's Mendacity as Political Theology

We're an empire now, and when we act, we create our own reality. And while you're studying that reality—judiciously, as you will—we'll act again, creating other new realities, which you can study too, and that's how things will sort out. We're history's actors ... and you, all of you, will be left to just study what we do.[68]

These words were reported by Ron Suskind, *The New York Magazine* writer, attributed to an aide of George W. Bush (often held to be Karl Rove, although Rove denies it) who slammed journalists and other truth-seekers as "the reality-based community" who "believe that solutions emerge from your judicious study of discernible reality." If the words are authentic—and Suskind stands by them—they are an unusually flagrant admission of a normally shrouded Schmittian truth: politics, and not just imperial politics, does not limit itself to describing today's facts but equally or more so aspires to invent tomorrow's. The more authoritarian the government, the more unashamed is this fact-invention. Politics is inherently future-oriented; it is about crafting policies that will bear fruit in days and years ahead, about laying down laws and institutions that will affect behavior tomorrow and beyond, about persuading the governed to act in certain ways from now on.

Further, as our sojourn through political and religious agnomancy has demonstrated, falsehood and ignorance are as effective for the exercise of power as truth and probably more so. As much as we want to believe that politics is defined by "rational, deliberative and civil processes that should ideally empower meritocratic professionals and technocrats" and that "civility and consensus around truth" are "the rules of the game,"[69] we must accept that those are not the *only* rules of the game and that the game's rules can be ignored, abused, and sabotaged anyhow.

Lying is always a social practice; the lying of leaders (corporate, governmental, or religious) is a political practice; and the lying of authoritarian leaders is *an authoritarian practice*. The authoritarian practice of lying, as theorized by Glasius in the previous chapter, is perfectly suited to exempt the leader from accountability in all four ways identified by Glasius—keeping information from the public, serving misinformation to the public, restricting the ability to question, and impairing the capacity to judge and impose consequences.

---

[68] Ron Suskind, "Faith, Certainty and the Presidency of George W. Bush," *The New York Times Magazine* (October 17, 2004).

[69] Olivier Jutel, "Civility, Subversion and Technocratic Class Consciousness: Reconstituting Truth in the Journalistic Field," in *Post-Truth and the Mediation of Reality: New Conjunctures*, ed. Rosemary Overell and Brett Nicholls (Cham, Switzerland: Palgrave Macmillan, 2019), 178.

In more detail, there are five effects or benefits for Trump in his policy of prevarication.

1. *A sign of authenticity to his followers.* As perverse as it may sound to Trump non-supporters, when his lying is acknowledged (and it is not always acknowledged), it is often perceived as a good thing. For followers of a certain ilk, Trump's lies verify his contempt for "political correctness" and prove that he is not a regular politician who minces words to curry political favor. He "says what he means," they will cheer. And he will not be gagged by the "reality-based community," who are, after all, only conspiring with alleged "facts" to undermine him and his populist agenda.

In an eye-opening paper, Oliver Hahl, Minjae Kim, and Ezra Zuckerman Sivan try to make sense of "the authentic appeal of the lying demagogue." They reason that when a constituency has given up on the political system as hopelessly corrupt and/or deaf to their interests, "a lying demagogue can appear as a distinctively *authentic champion* of its interests"; he may be appreciated for "bravely speaking a deep and otherwise suppressed truth," one that is more true or at least more relevant than ordinary mainstream truth.[70] Of course, the liar must withstand the fury of the establishment that calls out his lies, but "his willingness to antagonize the establishment by making himself *persona non grata*" is part of the appeal; it "lends credibility to his claim to be an authentic champion for those who feel disenfranchised by that establishment" by proving that he is not one of *them* but one of *us*.[71] Worse for his opponents, every attack on his pretenses reinforces the prejudice among his base that the system is out to get him and cannot be trusted, making it appear that his critics are the liars and not him.

Just as Trump's lying is a performance of faithfulness to his people (who are, after all, *the* people), couched in the vernacular and vulgarity of the common folk, so his people's assent to those lies is a performance of faithfulness to him. In a study whose title sums up the situation—"They Might Be a Liar But They're My Liar"—Briony Swire-Thompson et al. describe how Trump supporters presented with facts that correct the misinformation uttered by Trump tend to continue to trust his lies, but even if they surrender their belief in the misinformation, they do "not change their voting preferences nor feelings towards him."[72] It is as if they say to themselves, "Yes, he was wrong/lying, but he is still my guy." (Equally

[70] Oliver Hahl, Minjae Kim, and Ezra W. Zuckerman Sivan, "The Authentic Appeal of the Lying Demagogue: Proclaiming the Deeper Truth about Political Illegitimacy," *American Sociological Review* 83, no. 1 (2018), 3.

[71] Ibid., 8.

[72] Briony Swire-Thompson, Ullrich K. H. Ecker, Stephan Lewandowsky, and Adam J. Berkinsky, "They Might Be a Liar But They're My Liar: Source Evaluation and the Prevalence of Misinformation," *Political Psychology* 41, no. 1 (2020), 21.

distressing, in another study the same team finds that a week after the test-subjects are given facts that disconfirm Trump's lies, they have begun to "re-believe" him and to forget the true facts of the matter.[73]) Jennifer Hochschild and Katherine Levine Einstein pass along a comment by a Tea Party member who says it succinctly when asked about Trump's fallacious insistence that Barack Obama was born outside the United States:

> The birther issue definitely isn't part of our core values, but what Donald Trump is doing is questioning things and saying, "Why do we have to just accept everything?" ... To hold the birther view is to affiliate oneself with an attitude, not a truth claim....Your average Trump supporter may think that the proper attitude to have toward America's politicians is contempt.[74]

2. *A show of power.* The lies of a leader like Trump make him appear not only authentic to certain audiences but also dominant. As Pfiffner posits, "Telling lies and expecting others to believe or at least to accept false claims can also be an assertion of power."[75] First, they make him look like a tough guy, someone who will not concede to anyone; he will not be deterred by experts, elites, or any denizens of the reality-based community. Second, every time he survives an onslaught from the fact-police, he has illustrated once again his strength and the strength of his convictions. He has shown, in a word, that he can lie and get away with it, which licenses him to lie again. He is, as they said of Reagan, Teflon.

Various observers have noted that today's populist figures, almost all of them male (with the exception of France's Le Pen), typically exude machismo, which is part of what Miguel Diaz-Barriga and Margaret Dorsey dub the "dictator aesthetic." Lying is just one element of this role, which also features "loud, gaudy, imposing, and golden" speech and actions like, in the estimation of Diaz-Barriga and Dorsey, Trump's "beautiful" border wall.[76] Along with sexism, the dictator aesthetic is marked by "cruelty, menace, violence and arbitrariness," including arbitrariness with the facts, all of which "is meant to impress and express absolute power."

Tellingly, Masha Gessen, the author of several books on Russia and Vladimir Putin, calls this complex of behaviors the "Putin paradigm." "Both

---

[73] Briony Swire, Adam J. Berinsky, Stephan Lewandowsky, and Ullrich K. H. Ecker, "Processing Political Misinformation: Comprehending the Trump Phenomenon," *Royal Society Open Science* 4 (2017), 11.

[74] Jennifer Hochschild and Katherine Levine Einstein, "Do Facts Matter? Information and Misinformation in American Politics," *Political Science Quarterly* 130, no. 4 (2015/2016), 608–9.

[75] Pfiffner, "The Lies of Donald Trump," 11.

[76] Miguel Diaz-Barriga and Margaret Dorsey, "Trump's Wall and the Dictator Aesthetic," *Anthropology News* 58, no. 4 (2017), e84.

Trump and Putin," Gessen concludes, "use language primarily to communicate not facts or opinions but power: it's not what the words mean that matters but who says them and when. This makes it impossible to negotiate with them and very difficult for journalists to cover them."[77] In a prophetic essay written before Trump's inauguration, Gessen notes Trump's "admiration" for strong men like Putin, which has only been repeated in his bromance with Kim Jong Un and his praise for Jair Bolsonaro and Rodrigo Duterte. As for truth, in a paraphrase of Marshall McLuhan, "Lying is the message. It's not just that both Putin and Trump lie, it is that they lie in the same way and for the same purpose: blatantly, to assert power over truth itself."

In addition to a direct display of power, inveterate lying has an indirect power-effect: it keeps opponents off-balance and distracted by countering lies, leaving the executive to get on with his agenda in the fog of fiction. Trump is routinely accused of using distraction to misdirect attention, yet he continues to succeed at it as fact-checkers lag behind, debunking his last round of falsehoods while he moves on to the next.

3. *Control and construction of reality.* As just suggested by Gessen, authoritarian lying strives for more than power over policy and populations; it reaches for power over truth. Speaking of Putin but thinking of Trump, Gessen holds that the master of lies announces that he is "able to say what he wants, when he wants, regardless of the facts. He is president of his country and king of reality."

All of the 1950s theorists visited in a previous chapter agree that an Orwellian control over truth and memory is a key device of the tyrant and totalitarian. Whether sincerely or cynically, the authoritarian leader conjures an alternative reality, full of alternative facts, because frankly the leader does not care *what is true today, but only what will be true tomorrow.* Hence, as Arendt cautions, "Before mass leaders seize the power to fit reality to their lies, their propaganda is marked by its extreme contempt for facts as such, for in their opinion fact depends entirely on the power of a man who can fabricate it."[78] This is the imperial mindset expressed at the opening of this section of the chapter, of the world-makers who are creating the reality that the rest of us must inhabit. The only surprise is that it surprises so many Americans, after Peter Berger and Thomas Luckmann taught us more than a half-century ago that reality is socially constructed;[79] each of us constructs

---

[77] Masha Gessen, "The Putin Paradigm," New York Review of Books, December 13, 2016, https://www.nybooks.com/daily/2016/12/13/putin-paradigm-how-trump-will-rule.

[78] Arendt, *The Origins of Totalitarianism*, 350.

[79] Peter Berger and Thomas Luckmann. *The Social Construction of Reality: A Treatise in the Sociology of Knowledge* (Garden City, NY: Doubleday & Company, 1966).

reality in small ways, politicians in greater ways, and authoritarian and totalitarian politicians greatest of all. Deconstructionists, postmodernists, postcolonialists, critical theorists, and such all predate Trump in comprehending that reality is not solid but highly malleable—more so to the person willing to wield a big hammer—but they did not *make* the world fluid, they only discovered its fluidity. More, they believe—and hope—that this discovery will enhance liberty and justice. Do they not understand that it can be used for the very opposite purpose?

If we think of political lying as a practice of strategic communication, of information operations, of Russian-style reflexive control, much of the mystery of Trump's act dissipates. The only novelty, in scale anyhow, is how it is directed at the American people rather than America's enemies. But recall that Schmitt locates the essence of politics in the distinction between friend and enemy and that the authoritarian populist believes that *much of his own society, and certainly its institutional framework, is the enemy.* Then we must recognize that *Trump treats much of American society as if it is his enemy.* The point, as with international information operations, is to influence, disrupt, corrupt, or usurp the decision making of *both the opposition and one's own followers* and to promote and sustain particular types of behavior, namely, the types that the authoritarian wants. From this perspective, as Ruth Marcus opines in an early 2017 article in *The Washington Post*, Trump is not so much a "post-truth" president as a "pre-truth" one, in the sense that truth does not exist *until he speaks it into existence*: it is not that Trump denies reality, "it is that he bends it to his will. In this Trump tower of dreams, if he tweets it, the truth—or some asserted version thereof—will come."[80]

This mastery of reality has one other valuable application. It inoculates the leader against any potential criticism. A pre-emptive strike on competing realities, Trump tweeted in February 2017 that "any negative polls are fake news," and Trump loyalist Representative Matt Gaetz of Florida protested in May 2020 that fact-checking Trump's remarks amounts to "interfering with an election," as if the truth is an unwelcome guest— which it is.

4. *Embedding the habit of lying/non-reality in society.* Trump may think he is clever, using strategic communication so effectively against his own populace, but these final two points emphasize the lasting damage that such cavalier disregard for truth can and will have on America. Adam Hodges argues that Trump's lies "serve to prop up the problematic

---

[80] Ruth Marcus, "Forget the Post-Truth presidency. Welcome to the Pre-Truth Presidency," *The Washington Post*, March 23, 2017, https://www.washingtonpost.com/opinions/welcome-to-the-pre-truth-presidency/2017/03/23/b35856ca-1007-11e7-9b0d-d27c98455440_story.html.

worldview he peddles to his base," a worldview that might otherwise collapse under the weight of reality.[81]

> Factual fidelity is superseded by ideological fidelity to one or more axioms that undergird the system of beliefs of Trumpism....
>
> Trump's lying does valuable political work. The lies build a compelling narrative of "the way things are," reinforcing a picture of reality that accords with what Trumpian conservatives already know and accept as true regardless of what the facts say. In other words, Trump's lies confirm a set of beliefs by promulgating "alternative facts" that remain ideologically faithful even if they lack factual verifiability.[82]

At a bare minimum, so shielding their worldview from disconfirmation sanctions Trump's minions to slumber in their (anti-)epistemological daydream. Worse yet, it invites them to join him in ignoring and denouncing reality—and in ignoring and denouncing the "reality-based community" of journalists, scientists, and anyone else who disagrees—which short-circuits any possibility of a civil and reasoned debate and of potentially changing supporters' attitudes. And of course, Trump is far from alone in perpetuating this attack on and delegitimation of opponents and of civil discourse itself. Fox News has been pumping perfidy into the body social for years, softening it for a character like Trump; according to a 2015 analysis, fully sixty-percent of the "information" featured on Fox News was false, from mostly false (twenty-one percent) to totally false (thirty-one percent) to blatantly false (nine percent).[83] By comparison, CNN reporting was eighty percent half-, mostly- or completely-true, a finding that Fox and Trump fans would no doubt decry as another sign of elite/liberal bias and fakery. But thanks to Fox, Infowars, and the likes of Brenden Dilley, as Claire Wardle puts it, the information "ecosystem is so polluted" that we do not know how, or if, we can clean it up.[84]

A polluted information ecosystem has the deleterious effect for society but advantageous effect for Trump of scrambling public judgment and discernment. After a carpet-bombing of lies, denials, hoaxes, and other agnomancy practices, people are rendered unable to discern what is true or false and whom to trust. On such unstable ground, trust itself may seem

---

[81] Adam Hodges, "How Trump's Lying Affirms a Worldview," *Anthropology News* 59, no. 1 (2018), e189.

[82] Ibid., e189–90.

[83] Aaron Sharockman, "MSNBC, Fox, CNN Move the Needle On Our Truth-o-meter Scorecards," Politifact, January 27, 2015, https://www.politifact.com/article/2015/jan/27/msnbc-fox-cnn-move-needle-our-truth-o-meter-scorec.

[84] Claire Wardle, "Fake News. It's Complicated," First Draft, February 16, 2017, https://medium.com/1st-draft/fake-news-its-complicated-d0f773766c79.

impossible or unwise. And despite his protestations about fact-checkers, Trump probably understands that the uprising of critics and checkers benefits him by forcing them to spin their wheels chasing after each whopper of a lie, putting those critics in permanent reactive mode.

Trump also attracts and promotes extremists and absurdists. Steve Bannon was one of the early fringe figures on the Trump team. Then there is Dr. Stella Immanuel, praised by Trump for advancing his discredited promotion of hydroxychloroquine as a "cure" for COVID-19 while dismissing the use of masks (since there is a cure!). This same physician, we learn, has attributed gynecological conditions to sex with demons ("demon semen"), alleged that extraterrestrial DNA is used in mainstream medical treatments and that scientists are devising a vaccine to prevent religion, and repeated the bizarre conspiracy that the government is run by reptilians.

Worst of all, Trump's model inspires political imitators. The complicity of formerly relatively sensible figures like Lindsey Graham is incomprehensible enough, but others have more dishonorably hopped the unreality train. One truly reprehensible example is Cynthia Brehm, a Texas county Republican Party chairperson, who actually posted on Facebook that the death of George Floyd at the hands of the police, which launched weeks of street protests, was a "staged event." Previously, Republicans and conservatives have questioned the reality of school shootings, as in Newtown, Connecticut (Alex Jones called the Sandy Hook shooting "synthetic, completely fake with actors") and in recent days politicized the wearing of preventative face masks against the coronavirus as an infringement on their rights—if the coronavirus is not a hoax altogether, despite the rising numbers of infections, hospitalizations, and deaths. Elsewhere, Republican governor of West Virginia Jim Justice, a billionaire businessman with no political experience, forced the resignation of long-time state health officer, Dr. Cathy Slemp, on the grounds that she was overreporting COVID-19 cases and impeding his efforts to accelerate the reopening of the state. Meanwhile, in late 2019, a Texas Republican Party plot was uncovered to purchase domain names similar to those of their Democratic rivals and hijacking traffic to decoy websites stocked with false and inflammatory (dis)information.[85] In the end, if Trump is successful, we can expect to see more Trump-like politicians and tactics in his footsteps. In fact, Matthew Rosenberg and Jennifer Steinhauer despair that the "QAnon candidates" are already here, marching in the footsteps of Trump: Angela

---

[85] Andrea Zelinski, "Texas Republican Party Plans to Build Phony Campaign Websites Loaded with Negative Information About Democrats," *Houston Chronicle*, November 26, 2019,
https://www.houstonchronicle.com/news/politics/texas/article/Texas-Republican-Party-plans-to-build-phony-14863988.php?fbclid=IwAR2_westK_-GEUk8f_pEPLGGaIPXnAgFnx31NtRb9eAWVINryaIRTc1NL7w.

Stanton-King (congressional candidate, Georgia) has tweeted about "global elite pedophiles" and a supposed child-trafficking ring operated by an online furniture store (shades of Pizzagate!); Lauren Boebert (congressional candidate, Colorado) praised QAnon, saying, "Everything I've heard of Q— I hope this is real"; Jo Rae Perkins (senatorial candidate, Oregon) trumpeted, "I stand with Q and the team" and swore the QAnon "digital soldier oath"; and Marjorie Taylor Greene (congressional candidate, Georgia) lauded the "once-in-a-lifetime opportunity to take this global cabal of Satan-worshipping pedophiles out."[86]

5. *Erosion of democratic standards and institutions.* Americans who are proud and protective of the country's political traditions and institutions are aghast at how Trump disparages both, blaming his political abnormality on ignorance or ego. Narcissism and non-knowledge are probably part of the story, but our study of populism, authoritarianism, and agnomancy suggests another factor at work: populist/authoritarian leaders *want* to violate and impoverish those traditions and institutions that impede (in their populist rhetoric) the will of the people and that more pertinently impede the will of the leader. If there are two barriers to unrestrained sovereignty, they are *institutions and reality.* Reality commonly if usually does not conform or conduce to the leader's vision and plan, and so it must be subdued and replaced with fantasy and wish-fulfillment. Less stubborn than reality, institutions are more easily assaulted and more defenseless against assault; as an alleged tool of the mainstream/elite betrayal of the people, institutions *deserve* to be assaulted. Besides, previous chapters have tried to sort out the difference between "democratic" and "liberal" practices and institutions. It is the liberal ones—the ones that ensure equal rights and lawful processes— that are most disagreeable to the populist authoritarian (although all institutions are constraining). An articulate populist authoritarian can maintain that liberal institutions *interfere with and mediate between* the leader and "the people" and therefore stifle democracy. An agnomancer lies to and about institutions; a Schmittian sovereign transgresses them; and a Schoperhauerian imposes his own will on them.

Trump: Schmittian or Schoperhauerian?

Most of this book has considered political theology in general and Trump specifically through the lens of Carl Schmitt, forgivable since Schmitt revived and reconceived the notion of political theology. But Schmitt may not get us all the way to twentieth- and twenty-first-century populism, authoritarianism, and totalitarianism, nor all the way to Trump.

---

[86] Matthew Rosenberg and Jennifer Steinhauer, "The QAnon Candidates Are Here. Trump Has Paved Their Way," *The New York Times*, July 14, 2020, https://www.nytimes.com/2020/07/14/us/politics/qanon-politicians-candidates.html.

Schmitt fruitfully directs our attention away from conventional matters of religion (e.g., of church and state) and stresses the power and authority of a leader to make decisions that *break or make the law*, as he wishes. In modern parlance, he identifies the social construction of law. But refracted through the experiences that produced the 1950s literature surveyed in the previous chapter and the subsequent insights from that literature, together with an examination of agnomancy as a political and authoritarian practice, political theology looks different than Schmitt describes it—different and more Schoperhauerian.

Schmitt rightly accentuates the effect of decision, but he seems not to have pondered *how* and *why* a sovereign makes any specific decision. He perhaps assumes that the sovereign makes informed, benevolent, and above all realistic decisions, although we have seen no reason for such optimism and plenty of reason for pessimism. The stoutest sovereigns of the past century have been the *least* informed, the *least* benevolent, and the *least* realistic of political actors. Their decisions have been driven by unproven theory (e.g., Marxism), venality, and/or arrogance. In most cases, however, empirical reality has supported neither their diagnosis of society's ills nor their recommended remedy. Since reality is seldom with the leader, the leader is seldom with reality.

So Schmitt seems to overlook the very real possibility, if not the near-inevitability, that the sovereign must be an enemy not only of liberalism but of literalism, not only of rights but of facts. After all, in a perfectly rational world—the sort envisioned by America's Founding Fathers and by Habermas—the decisions of the executive would be consistent with the guidelines of institutions and the proscriptions of reality. In that case, the executive would be a bureaucrat and hardly sovereign at all, governing as any leader, legislator, or logician would in his place. Is it possible, then, that sovereignty of the Schmittian kind only obtains *insofar as it frees itself from and actively, even gratuitously and excessively, trespasses and nullifies natural and positive law*? How would we recognize sovereignty *unless* it acted *against* norm and truth?

Lying from this perspective is not a mistake or ignorance or character flaw but a vital and indispensable component of (Platonic, Machiavellian, Leninist-Stalinist, Trumpian) sovereign performance. Schmitt has not carried his political theology to its logical conclusion, to its communist and Nazi conclusion and, more mildly, to its right-wing populist and authoritarian conclusion, let alone accounted for the leader marked by mendacity, mean-spiritedness, or mental illness. A sovereign not only exposes the inherent weakness and contingency of institutions and law but confirms that "unpredictability, raging narcissism, novel vulgarity, demagoguery, and contempt for the rules of the game" are inherent in sovereignty.[87] The sovereign, like Nietzsche's overman, decides beyond good and evil, beyond truth and falsity, and *good, evil, truth, and falsity are outcomes of his decisions*. In so saying, we are transported from Schmitt's world to Schopenhauer's. Schopenhauer, not generally taken as a political philosopher, delivers us to the next level where the leader not only decides but *wills reality*. A more fully god-like character, a Schopenhauerian sovereign does not decide whether it is light or dark but *makes it light* ("Let there be light"). For such a sovereign, the reasons for a decision are never clear, probably never provided (as Job heard it from his god, you have no right to ask), and at best "illegible"; in the human political world, this means that there can be no mechanism for self-correction, since the very causes and effects of decisions are decisions.

Russell Muirhead and Nancy Rosenblum, in a book bearing one of Trump's favorite dodges in its title (*A Lot of People are Saying*), add that such behavior not only, because it must, erases "standards of verification" but "prepare[s] the ground for popular acceptance of extreme actions" by the leader and themselves" and results in "disorientation … from the steady barrage of its fabulist claims"; by their "special kind of attack on what it means to know something," Schopenhauerian sovereigns "claim to own reality and to impose this reality on the nation."[88]

So as we transcend traditional political theology, seeing Trump as less Schmittian than Schopenhauerian—less a sovereign who decides than a will who (mis)represents an idea of the world into existence—in the final two chapters, we transcend traditional Christianity to weigh other religious sources and resources for perspective on Trump and political theology.

---

[87] Jutel, "Civilty, Subversion, and Technocratic Class Consciousness," 184.

[88] Russell Muirhead and Nancy L. Rosenblum, *A Lot of People are Saying: The New Conspiracism and the Assault on Democracy* (Princeton, NJ: Princeton University Press, 2019), 120–21.

7

Myth America and Alt-Rites:
Political Theology Beyond Belief

"The truth, the whole truth, and nothing but the truth" would thus be a perverse and paralyzing policy for any worldmaker. The whole truth would be too much; it is too vast, variable, and clogged with trivia. The truth alone would be too little, for some right versions are not true— being either false or neither true nor false—and even for true versions rightness may matter more.

—Nelson Goodman[1]

In the preceding chapters, we have explored primarily the political side of political theology, examining Trump as president, populist, and prevaricator. Our tour, which began with Carl Schmitt's propitious thoughts on sovereignty, exception, and decision, has pushed the edges of Schmitt's theory and seasoned it with twentieth and twenty-first century experiences of authoritarianism and totalitarianism. As the last chapter came to a close, we interrogated the applicability of truth as a political standard and expectation when encountering a Schmittian sovereign or a Schoperhauerian will. We exposed Trump, an American authoritarian and plutocratic populist, as fundamentally unconcerned with, if not contemptuous of, truth in his project to distort perception and dominate reality. As Nelson Goodman remonstrates, truth is not the business of a worldmaker: truth comes *after* the worldmaking, not before. If we liken truth to law, it is not a cause of the sovereign's willful deciding but an effect.

Reflecting on worldmaking brings us back to religion, where the ultimate acts of worldmaking are told. It is because religion provides the exemplars of the greatest power, the highest authority and freest decision-making and will, the total eruption of the miraculous (sovereignty) into the mundane (law and legal institutions), that Schmitt reckons modern political concepts are secularized religious concepts. We could not and need not accept that analysis as given, and just as we were compelled to push the political side of political theology, in the remaining chapters we must push the theological side. Prior to Schmitt's reform (and often subsequent to it as

---

[1] Nelson Goodman, *Ways of Worldmaking* (Indianapolis, IN: Hackett Publishing Company, 1978), 19.

well), political theology is too narrowly focused on the literal relationship between god(s) and government, between religion and the state. But as government and state are not identical, neither are god(s) and religion.

In a word, theology is too narrowly associated with and defined by Christianity. Theology is not synonymous with religion, since many religions do not include the god-concept, although theology is frequently glossed as religion. For instance, Owais Khan, appreciating that political theology "is largely a field of study within Christian theology," asserts that there "is no academic field called 'Islamic political theology.'"[2] That is to say, even other theisms do not necessarily feature political theology, let alone non-theistic religions.

Anthropologists and many religion scholars realize that Christian concepts cannot be imposed on other religions, although such imposition has certainly been tried; we could say that until recently, it was the norm. The comparative study of religions, as a Western enterprise, has regularly viewed non-Western religions through the prism of Christianity, or worse, of Protestant Christianity. "Religion" is not only assumed to entail god(s)—ideally *one* god—but to have a few other essential characteristics: it is scriptural/text-based, morality-oriented, personal or internal to the individual, and a single coherent system. Above all, the Christian perspective presumes that religion is about "belief," but as to this bedrock assumption there is room for doubt. A half-century ago, Rodney Needham investigated a wide range of non-Western and tribal religions and found that in many of these religions and their indigenous languages, there is no word equivalent to the English/Christian notion of "belief."[3] E. E. Evans-Pritchard's classic study of Nuer (east Africa) religion provides similar evidence of the absence of a word for an avowal like "I believe": when the Nuer say that they *ngath* their god/spirit *kwoth*, Evans-Pritchard insists that *ngath* should be translated as "trust" rather than "believe in" in an epistemological/ontological way.[4]

More interesting yet, the Akha of highland Burma have a word (*tjhŷa*) commonly translated as "belief" and a word (*zán*) translated as "religion." According to Deborah Tooker, though, *zán* is not a topic of belief: "For the Akha, you cannot believe or not believe in *zán*."[5] Rather,

---

[2] M. Owais Khan, "100 Years of Political Theology: An Islamic Perspective," Political Theology Network, February 6, 2014, https://politicaltheology.com/100-years-of-political-theology-an-islamic-perspective-by-m-owais-khan.

[3] Rodney Needham, *Belief, Language, and Experience* (Chicago, IL: The University of Chicago Press, 1972).

[4] E. E. Evans-Pritchard, *Nuer Religion* (New York and Oxford: Oxford University Press, 1956).

[5] Deborah Tooker, "Identity Systems of Highland Burma: 'Belief,' Akha Zan, and a Critique of Interiorized Notions of Ethno-Religious Identity," *Man* (new series) 27, no. 4 (1992): 804.

zán is something to *do*, a way of life more than a belief system, including elements we would count as religion but others we would not, such as the proper way to plant rice, build a house, or boil an egg. Rather than *believing in* it, the Akha say that they "carry" *zán*. Behaviors may be proper (*zán-tsha-e*, "*zán*-ish") or improper (*zán ma tsha-e*, "un- *zán*-ish") by *zán* standards but not "true" or "false." Despite the fact that their worldview includes spirits, they "do not say anything like *neq djan-e* ('to believe in spirits')."[6] If one is Akha, one carries *zán*; if one is not Akha, one does not carry *zán*; and if one stops carrying *zán*, one ceases to be Akha.

In Western languages and in Christianity, belief is no less contested. In a noteworthy essay on "Christians as Believers," Malcolm Ruel avers that the Hebrew term translated as belief (*'mn*) denotes not assent to a proposition but participation in a relationship; the word signifies "the reliability or trustworthiness of a servant, a witness, a messenger, or a prophet" as well as a god.[7] Propositional belief became a preoccupation of Christianity during the era of official creeds like the Nicene Creed, which opens, *Credo in unum Deum*, "I believe in one God" (and divergence from which could spell punishment or worse). The Protestant Reformation, Ruel says, emphasized the personal "adventure of faith rather than belief as a body of doctrine"; either way, he concludes that there is "little evidence that there is anything equivalent to Christian belief in other world religions," let alone ancient and tribal religions like Nuer and Akha.[8] Jean Pouillon adds that the modern French verb *croire* is polysemous: to say *je crois* is to "state a conviction" but also to admit doubt, while to say *je crois á* is to believe that something exists, *je crois en* is to have confidence in something, and *je crois que* is to represent something in a certain way.[9] Posing still more trouble for Christian belief, Pouillon speculates that "belief" may be an outsider's concept rather than the experience of the "believer" herself:

The believer not only need not say that he believes in [*croire á*] the existence of God, but he need not even believe in [*croire á*] it; precisely because in his eyes there can be no doubt about it: the existence of God is not believed in [*crue*], but perceived. On the contrary, to make God's existence an object of belief, to state this belief, is to open up the possibility of doubt—which begins to clarify the ambiguity with which

---

[6] Tooker, "Identity Systems," 802.

[7] Malcolm Ruel, *Belief, Ritual, and the Securing of Life: Reflexive Essays on Bantu Religion* (Leiden: E. J. Brill, 1997), 38.

[8] Ibid., 50–51.

[9] Jean Pouillon, *Between Belief and Transgression: Structuralist Essays in Religion, History, and Myth*, ed. Michel Izard and Pierre Smith, trans. John Leavitt (Chicago, IL: The University of Chicago Press, 1982), 1–2.

we started. So one could say that it is the unbeliever who believes that the believer believes in [*croire á*] the existence of God.[10]

Predictably, forcing other religions through the screen of Christian categories has unfortunate consequences for understanding and tolerance. Geoffrey Oddie discusses how Protestant/Christian assumptions biased Western views of "Hinduism," the name suggesting a monolithic identity that Indian religious concepts and practices lacked. Among early scholars and missionaries, the "most important unquestioned assumption appears to be that there was one Hindu religious system" with a body of sacred texts (the Vedas and perhaps the Upanishads), a cadre of priests (the Brahmans, of whom the Western observers tended to disapprove), and a Hindu "creed" or "faith."[11] Westerners were frustrated and angry when Hinduism failed to conform to their Christian model. Likewise, Zoroastrianism in India and Persia left nineteenth-century Europeans unimpressed because it lacked consistent doctrine and "moral profundity"; its prayers, like those of Tambiah's Thai Buddhists, were uttered in a language obscure to the speakers, and "their meaning unknown to those who repeat them, cannot be supposed to have much influence on the conduct of life."[12] Hinduism, Zoroastrianism, and most other religions cried out for reform in the eyes of Western/Christian travelers, to make them more scriptural, more moralistic, more propositional and personal but most assuredly *less mythical and less ritualistic*.

The present chapter starts the job of moving political theology beyond Christian theology, resuscitating two specific deprecated religious categories, myth and ritual, both marginalized in Western/Christian (again, particularly Protestant) thought as false and futile. Myths are the mistaken and ridiculous beliefs of others, and rituals are their impractical and pointless behaviors. These sentiments reflect a presupposition about what is true (i.e., one's own religion), but they may also, in keeping with the previous chapter, indicate a misapplication of the standard of "truth" altogether. As impartial analysts rather than partisans of any one religion, we join anthropologist A. R. Radcliffe Brown who states that the social and political significance of a religion "is independent of its truth or falsity, that religions which we think to be erroneous or even absurd and repulsive ...

---

[10] Pouillon, *Between Belief and Transgression*, 2.

[11] Geoffrey A. Oddie, *Imagined Hinduism: British Protestant Missionary Constructions of Hinduism, 1793–1900* (New Delhi, Thousand Oaks, CA, and London, 2006), 98–99.

[12] Monica M. Ringer, *Pious Citizens: Reforming Zoroastrianism in India and Iran* (Syracuse, NY: Syracuse University Press, 2011), 90.

may be important and effective parts of the social machinery."[13] The importance of religions, including unloved aspects of religion such as myth and ritual, is not their truth-status but instead "the contribution that they make to the formation and maintenance of a social order."[14] Summing this position in one word, the key to religion is its *efficacy*, not its facticity. Our task here, then, is to consider how the nearly universal religious concepts of myth and ritual can expand political theology and explain Trump and other contemporary authoritarian populists.

Myth: Words that Create

Myth is a term that most Christians do not care for and definitely do not care to have attached to *their* religion. (Myth is always someone else's—and therefore false—religion, whereas religion is the myth that you believe in.) In everyday usage, "myth" tends to mean a false belief, not necessarily religious in nature, such as the myth of Atlantis or ten myths about retirement. Scholars of religion do not use the term this way. In ancient Greek, *mythos* simply designated speech or story received by word of mouth (that is, something "heard") as opposed to knowledge that was derived from research and reasoning (*logos*). Unluckily, *logos* was absorbed by Christianity as the divine word, an essence or instantiation of deity itself, leaving nothing good for myth. But in Greek culture, both *mythos* and *logos* were accepted and valued.

For contemporary thinkers, who sidestep the issue of veracity, myth is simply narrative, one manifestation of humans' propensity for story-telling and story-making. What sets myth apart from other narratives is that myths normally have supernatural or at least superhuman (e.g., culture heroes like Gilgamesh) characters; they recount the adventures of beings greater than ourselves. As the comparative religionist Mircea Eliade defines it:

> Myth narrates a sacred history; it relates an event that took place in primordial Time, the fabled time of the "beginnings." In other words, myth tells how, through the deeds of Supernatural Beings, a reality came into existence, be it the whole of reality, the Cosmos, or only a fragment of reality—an island, a species of plant, a particular kind of human behavior, an institution. Myth, then, is always an account of a "creation"; it relates how something was produced, began to *be*. Myth

---

[13] A. R. Radcliffe-Brown, *Structure and Function in Primitive Society* (New York: The Free Press, 1965 [1952]), 154.
[14] Ibid.

tells only of that which *really* happened, which manifested itself completely. The actors in myths are Supernatural Beings.[15]

The key to this passage, and the mystery and power of myth, is *how a reality came into existence*. Myths are, in Eliade's estimation, always about *creation*, or if not creation then *precedent*. As stories about the acts and the actors that formed the world as we know it, myths chronicle their creative activity and the sacredness (or simply the supernaturalness) of their works. "In short, myths describe the various and sometimes dramatic breakthroughs of the sacred (or the 'supernatural') into the World. It is this sudden breakthrough of the sacred that really *establishes* the World and makes it what it is today."[16] Eliade refers to this eruption of the sacred into the mundane as a hierophany (from the Greek "sacred"-"to show/reveal").

To ask whether a myth is "true" is almost to ask a nonsense question. People who subscribe to a myth presumably accept it as true, but they do not submit it to empirical proof; rather, the myth is self-evidently and circularly true "because the existence of the World is there to prove it."[17] Among the Warlpiri of central Australia, the physical features of their environment, as well as the cultural features of their society, were established by ancestral beings in The Dreaming or Dreamtime (*jukurrpa*); the "proof" is the presence of those features—hills, river beds, and water holes, and language, kinship, and technical skill. The issue for myth, though, is not whether it is true but that *it is formative*. It tells how the world, humanity, and society began, and Eliade emphasizes the "prestige of beginnings" implicit in myth. "Force and fullness"—creativity, potency, fertility, authority—"are at the beginning" when the greatest of beings were active.[18] This does not mean that the work is complete. In most if not all societies and religions, creation must be sustained through human effort, which includes reiterating, *reliving*, the myth. For the Warlpiri, *jukurrpa* is not merely in the past, in some genesis-time, but is "everywhen" and eternal. The myth, as an account of power, is powerful itself, and the telling of it (although societies often do not "tell" a myth in the sense of sitting down and repeating a story; rather, they chant and/or re-enact parts of it, with the "story" of the myth as a kind of background knowledge) is a making-present of those formative events and actors.

So we are not quite justified in regarding myth as an "explanation," as a just-so story of how this or that aspect of reality started. Bronislaw Malinowski, a father of British social anthropology, demands that myth "is

---

[15] Mircea Eliade, *Myth and Reality*, trans. Willard R. Trask (Prospect Heights, IL: Waveland Press, 1998 [1963]), 5–6.

[16] Ibid., 6.

[17] Ibid.

[18] Ibid., 51.

not a savage speculation about origins of things born out of philosophic interest. Neither is it the result of the contemplation of nature—a sort of symbolic representation of its laws."[19] In what is his probably most-cited passage, he contends:

> Studied alive, myth ... is not symbolic, but a direct expression of its subject matter; it is not an explanation in satisfaction of a scientific interest, but a narrative resurrection of a primeval reality, told in satisfaction of deep religious wants, moral cravings, social submissions, assertions, even practical requirements. Myth fulfills in primitive culture an indispensable function: it expresses, enhances, and codifies belief; it safeguards and enforces practical rules for the guidance of man. Myth is thus a vital ingredient of human civilization; it is not an idle tale, but a hard-worked active force; it is not an intellectual explanation or an artistic imagery, but a pragmatic charter of primitive faith and moral wisdom.[20]

Malinowski is remembered for this "charter" approach to myth, in which myth is a founding document of society, a constitution if you will, a record of the past decisions of beings with the right and power to make such decisions and impress them on the rest of us and on the world itself.

Among the precedents that a myth can constitute, form, or authorize is the political system of the society. For example, John Beattie shares a Bunyoro (Uganda) myth concerning the roots of hierarchy and kingship. The first human father, Kintu or "the created thing," had three sons. The three boys were given two tests. First, six objects were placed where the boys would find them—an ox's head, a cowhide thong, a bundle of cooked millet and potatoes, a grass head-ring (for carrying loads on the head), an axe, and a knife.

> When the boys come upon these things, the eldest picks up the bundle of food and starts to eat. What he cannot eat he carries away, using the head-ring for this purpose. He also takes the axe and the knife. The second son takes the leather thong, and the youngest takes the ox's head, which is all that is left. In the next test the boys have to sit on the ground in the evening, with their legs stretched out, each holding on his lap a wooden milk-pot full of milk. They are told that they must hold their pots safely until morning. At midnight the youngest boy begins to nod, and he spills a little of his milk. He wakes up with a start, and begs his brothers for some of theirs. Each gives him a little, so that his pot is full

---

[19] Bronislaw Malinowski, *Magic, Science, and Religion and Other Essays* (Garden City NY: Doubleday Anchor Books, 1948), 83–84.
[20] Ibid., 101.

again. Just before dawn the eldest brother suddenly spills all his milk. He, too, asks his brothers to help fill his pot from theirs, but they refuse, saying that it would take too much of their milk to fill his empty pot. In the morning their father finds the youngest son's pot full, the second son's nearly full, and the eldest sons' quite empty.[21]

These decisions settled the status and fate of the sons and their descendants. The first son and his line would be servants and farmers, laboring for his younger brothers and their descendants; he was named "Kairu" or peasant. The second son and his descendants would have the elevated status of cattle herders; he was called "Kahmua," little cowherd. The youngest son was named "Kakama," little Mukama or ruler, and his descendants became the kings of Bunyoro.

It is plain to see that myth, although recording potent events in the past, contains potency in the present. In one of his most acclaimed essays, anthropologist Claude Lévi-Strauss describes how myth is used by the Cuna (sometimes spelled Kuna, recently revised to Guna) of Panama in shamanic healing. A sick woman undergoes a curing ceremony in which the healer never touches her. Instead, he sings a song from the inventory of myth referring to "supernatural monsters and magical animals."

> The sick woman believes in the myth and belongs to a society which believes in it.… The sick woman accepts these mythical beings or, more accurately, she has never questioned their existence. What she does not accept are the incoherent and arbitrary pains, which are an alien element in her system but which the shaman, *calling upon myth, will re-integrate within a whole where everything is meaningful.*[22]

Lévi-Strauss opines that the cure works by replacing the illness with a socially-sanctioned "language" of mythical wellness. Fascinatingly but controversially, he likens the mythical curing situation to Freudian psychoanalysis, where a personal/biographical narrative of wellness substitutes for a neurotic one.

> Both cures aim at inducing an experience, and *both succeed by recreating a myth which the patient has to live or relive.* But in one case, the patient constructs an individual myth with elements drawn

---

[21] John Beattie, *Bunyoro: An African Kingdom* (New York: Holt, Rinehart, and Winston, 1960), 11–12.

[22] Claude Lévi-Strauss, *Structural Anthropology*, trans. Claire Jacobson and Brook Grundfest Scheepf (New York: Basic Books, 1963), 197, emphasis added.

from his past; in the other case, *the patient receives from the outside a social myth which does not correspond to a former personal state.*[23]

It is further critical to grasp myth as one species of religious language—religious language itself a genus of language in general (along with and overlapping political language)—that transmits not only, or mostly, information but, as Lévi-Strauss conveys in the title of the chapter describing the mythical cure, *effectiveness*. In a previous chapter, we introduced J. L. Austin's analysis of linguistic "performatives," utterances that do not describe a reality but *constitute* a reality; examples would be promises, apologies, marriage pronouncements, and many more. Other religious examples would be a spell, a curse, or an incantation. Of course, religious language faces its own unique challenges, not the least of which is the invisibility, silence, and possibly absence of the supernatural communication partner (the spirit, god, demon, etc.); Webb Keane attributes to these problems the nature of religious speech—repetitive, formal, standardized, and formulaic—with the additional devices of noise, pageantry, and material offerings.[24]

All religious, political, and social experience teaches us that words are powerful and not primarily for the information they carry. Among the Hasidic Jews studied by Simon Dein, "a word and the thing it refers to are held to be spiritually linked, and because of this, the manipulation of words can effect change in the physical world."[25] Like the Cuna/Guna, religious words are resources in Lubavitcher Hasidic cures: auspicious words from prayers and psalms are administered to patients, and a standard prescription for ailments like headache and sore throat is to learn and recite the Torah. We saw Stanley Tambiah explain in an earlier chapter that words need not be understood to be efficacious. Nor must they be heard or spoken. In many cultures and religions, from Islam to Sikhism, scrolls and books are objects of power. Religious specialists in Berti (Sudan) society fashion amulets containing scraps of verses from the Qur'an; wearing a Qur'anic amulet (like a Jewish phylactery or *tefillin* containing Torah texts) brings the individual in contact with divine energy. More dramatically, a Berti religious expert may also write verses on a wooden slate, wash the words off with water, and have people drink the liquid (*mihai*). Individuals consume the liquid words routinely as religious precautions, and the entire society drinks together to ward off disasters and misfortunes like drought, fire, locusts, or diseases. For the Berti, the Qur'an "is considered to have an immense power which

---

[23] Lévi-Strauss, *Structural Anthropology*, 199, emphasis added.

[24] Webb Keane, "Religious Language," *Annual Review of Anthropology* 26 (1997), 47–71.

[25] Simon Dein, "The Power of Words: Healing Narratives among Lubavitcher Hasidim," *Medical Anthropology Quarterly* 16, no. 1 (2002), 42.

guarantees the well-being of those who have internalized it"—and not just internalized it "intellectually."[26]

Ritual: Acts that Transform

If possible, Protestant Christianity has a still more jaundiced opinion of ritual. Ritual is pure empty form, mindless unproductive activity, whereas "true religion" dwells in texts and ideas and "beliefs." Nevertheless, all religions intimately involve some form of ritualized conduct, if only ritually attending church on Sundays to read scriptures and hear sermons. Early scholar R. R. Marett went so far as to conclude that religion is largely "something not so much thought out as danced out."[27]

Ritual has been defined in many ways, most highlighting its qualities of "formality, fixity, and repetition."[28] All agree that it is not "practical" or utilitarian, in the sense that there is no causal link between the action and the stated effects (e.g., rain rituals do not really cause rain), and most concur that there is some element of "communication" involved. Tambiah characterizes it as "a culturally constructed system of symbolic communication" composed of "patterned and ordered sequences of words and acts,"[29] whereas for Anthony Wallace, insofar as communication occurs in ritual, it is

> communication without information: that is to say, each ritual is a particular sequence of signals which, once announced, allows no uncertainty, no choice, and hence, in the statistical sense of information theory, conveys no information from sender to receiver. It is, ideally, a system of perfect order and any deviation from this order is a mistake.[30]

As such—and like mythical language—ritual behavior "is potent in itself in terms of cultural conventions ... or alternatively behavior which is directed

---

[26] Ladislav Holy, *Religion and Custom in a Muslim Society: The Berti of Sudan* (Cambridge: Cambridge University Press, 1991), 33.

[27] R. R. Marett, *The Threshold of Religion* (London: Methuen & Co., 1909), ix, xxxi.

[28] Catherine Bell, *Ritual Practice, Ritual Theory* (New York: Oxford University Press, 1992), 92.

[29] Stanley J. Tambiah, *A Performative Approach to Ritual* (London: The British Academy and Oxford University Press, 1979), 119.

[30] Anthony F. C. Wallace, *Religion: An Anthropological View* (New York: Random House, 1966), 233.

towards evoking the potency of occult powers even though it is not presumed to be potent in itself."[31]

Ritual is absolutely central to one of the most influential theorists of religion, sociologist Émile Durkheim. In his groundbreaking *The Elementary Forms of Religious Life*, originally published in 1912, Durkheim searches for the world's most "elementary" or non-elaborated religion and thinks that he finds it in Australian Aboriginal cultures. The irreducible idea behind religion, he maintains, is "the sacred," in contrast to "the profane." But where do humans get the idea of the sacred: what is more powerful than the individual, exists before and apart from the individual, survives the individual, and makes the individual dependent upon it? His answer is the social group: "this power exists, it is society."[32] The group—not just the society but its internal organization, featuring clans or other such kinship groups—is a "social" fact and the most real fact. The elementary form of religion, then, is a spiritual association between social groups and the natural world, including non-human beings and forces (plants, animals, the sun, the wind, etc.), which has been called *totemism*. He concludes that the "god of the clan, the totemic principle, can therefore be nothing else than the clan itself, personified and represented to the imagination under the visible form of the animal or vegetable which serves as totem."[33]

But in the formation and perpetuation of the social group out of disparate individuals, ritual plays the vital role. Ritual makes of a collectivity of humans an integrated and *moral* community, a social group that shares common norms, values, and morals. This identity and cohesion is achieved through the effectiveness of ritual. Ritual activity operates at a deep psychological level through what he calls "effervescence":

> When they are together, a sort of electricity is formed by their collecting which quickly transports them to extraordinary degree of exaltation. Every sentiment expressed finds a place without resistance in all the minds, which are very open to outside impressions; each re-echoes the others, and is re-echoed by the others. The initial impulse thus proceeds, growing as it goes, as an avalanche grows in its advance. And as such active passions so free from all control could not fail to burst out, on every side one sees nothing but violent gestures, cries, veritable howls, and deafening noises of every sort, which aid in intensifying still more the state of mind which they manifest.... So it is in the midst of these

---

[31] Edmund Leach, "A Discussion of Ritualization of Behavior in Animals and Man," *Philosophical Transactions of the Royal Society of London. Series B, Biological Sciences* 251, no. 772 (1966), 403.

[32] Émile Durkheim, *The Elementary Forms of Religious Life* (New York: The Free Press, 1965 [1912]), 257.

[33] Ibid., 236.

effervescent social environments and out of this effervescence itself that the religious idea seems to be born.[34]

This theory has naturally been challenged, but it does raise ritual to a prominence far grander than mere empty behavior.

Religious studies scholars have proposed various classifications of rituals. Wallace surmises that there are five main types:

- Technical, intended to achieve natural or supernatural effects through "technique," the more or less mechanical manipulation of objects and words (many would call this "magic")
- Therapeutic/anti-therapeutic, for purposes of curing or causing illness and misfortune (including "witchcraft" and "sorcery")
- Salvation, functioning to alter the personal qualities of the individual (e.g., expiation rituals to expel sin; trance or spirit possession)
- Ideological, rites of natural and social control (e.g., rites of social intensification like funerals to preserve social integration in times of loss and tragedy; taboos; rites of kingship) as well as "rituals of rebellion" or *anti*-ideological rituals where social norms are intentionally set aside, like Carnival or Mardi Gras
- Revitalization, to effect changes in society including the inauguration of new social orders (e.g., messianic or millenarian rituals)

Catherine Bell assembles a somewhat different typology, featuring calendrical or commemorative rituals, rites of exchange and communion, rites of affliction (healing, exorcism, purification), rites of feasting, fast, and festival, "political rituals"—to which we will return below—and rites of passage or life-crisis rituals.[35]

Although Bell places rites of passage among the types of rituals, Victor Turner argues that they exemplify the very structure of the "ritual process." Turner observes that many rituals around the world occur at key moments in the life of individuals, groups, or society. Rituals appear when social facts and relations are changing or threatening to change in some way, such as puberty, adulthood, marriage, childbirth, and death. But more than accompanying these changes, the rituals help or serve to *effect* the change; along the lines of Austin's linguistic performatives or the effectiveness of

---

[34] Durkheim, *The Elementary Forms*, 247.

[35] Catherine Bell, *Ritual: Perspectives and Dimensions* (Oxford and New York: Oxford University Press, 1997).

mythical speech, the ritual facilitates change rather than simply acknowledging or celebrating it.[36]

Turner's ritual process proceeds through three stages, the middle of which draws the bulk of his attention. Before the ritual commences, the individual/group/society is in a certain condition or state (juvenile, unmarried, alive, etc.). The ritual process opens with the *separation* of the party undergoing change; this may be construed or achieved through the capture or (symbolic) death of the subject of the ritual. In the case of coming-of-age initiations, adult men may enter the community and seize the young males while their mothers wail that they will never see their boys again; in a manner of speaking, they are correct. The adolescents may be sequestered from the rest of society for the duration of the ritual or for weeks or months, while they are put through trials including physical operations like circumcision or scarification, shown sacred objects, and instructed in religious knowledge. Or there may be little such "training." The Gisu of Uganda practiced an initiation ritual in which males aged eighteen to twenty-five were circumcised in public and then given gifts signifying new manhood. What they did *not* receive was any specific teaching. The main function of the ritual, other than to announce maturity, was to generate a particular emotional or psychological trait in the men, called *lirima*. *Lirima* was the manly quality of violent emotion, connected with anger, jealousy, hatred, and resentment. It was not totally wild emotion, though; it also implied or required self-control, strength of character, bravery, and will. It was the quality or substance that enabled men to overcome fear (the ritual itself was a test of overcoming fear), but it was also a dangerous power, one that produced aggressiveness in men that even the Gisu themselves regretted.[37]

Like a butterfly in a chrysalis, the actual transformation of the individual/group/society happens during the second or "liminal" (from the Latin *limen*, threshold) stage of ritual. This is a condition that Turner describes as "betwixt and between," not another status but a non-status. It is the absence of status, a social no-place, but a condition of potential. It is the doorway or portal between statuses, the road that links the origin and destination. This non-status takes a variety of symbolic forms, often symbolized as death, wilderness, return to the womb, even bisexuality. It is without name, rank, or social identity. Occupants of this threshold may be deprived of possessions including clothes; they came into life naked, so they must enter their new life naked. They are often required to be obedient,

---

[36] Victor Turner, *The Ritual Process: Structure and Anti-Structure* (Chicago, IL: Aldine Publishing, 1969).

[37] Suzette Heald, "The Ritual Use of Violence: Circumcision among the Gisu of Uganda," in *The Anthropology of Violence*, ed. David Riches (Oxford: Basil Blackwell, 1986), 70–85.

passive, receptive, and non-assertive. In other cases, including periodic rituals partaken by adults, the language of liminality may involve opposites, doing things "backward" or "upside down," and other forms of contradiction or violation of everyday behavior.

In a way, the liminal condition is a lowly one, conceptually outside of society altogether. In another way, though, it is sacred—special, potent, and perhaps dangerous. Liminality combines all these features in the elimination of distinctions, social and otherwise. It is an unnamed state, the circumstance when all things are equal but therefore unstructured. Turner calls this condition *communitas*, an undifferentiated and structureless existence. There are no children or adults, no males or females, no kings and commoners. As an example, when Muslim pilgrims undertake the *hajj* or journey to Mecca, they shed their markings of nationality or rank and don the same white robes, signaling the shared (and therefore homogeneous) status of pilgrim.

Liminality is a creative state, but it is also an unstable one. Neither individuals nor society can endure there for long. In other words, "all sustained manifestations of *communitas* must appear as dangerous and anarchical, and have to be hedged around with prescriptions, prohibitions, and conditions."[38] Interestingly, Turner locates this *communitas* experience in other social locations besides the liminality of ritual passage, including the status of "hippies," monks, prophets, jesters/comedians, and no doubt poets and artists—all those people who are at the margins or the bottom of society. Structured society tolerates them, even benefits from them, but their "anti-structure" always poses a risk to social order. They also represent the creative edge from which new social orders will emerge. Thus, ultimately, society, via religion and ritual, is a cycle or dialectic of *communitas* and differentiation, anarchy and order.

Political Myth, Political Ritual, Political Theology

It is not difficult to recognize how myth and ritual address and, from the perspective of the adherents of those religions, solve the central problems of political theology. They posit the source of original and ultimate power and authority, lodged in the primordial actions and decisions of beings much higher than today's humans. They thereby legitimize natural and social arrangements as humans find those arrangements (including, significantly, political relationships and institutions). Here is a crucial aspect of religion regularly overlooked or minimized by religion scholars. Roy Rappaport urges that the key to religion is not any specific beliefs and doctrines but the requisite attitude of members/believers, which is *commitment*.

---

[38] Turner, *The Ritual Process*, 109.

For Rappaport, religion and its mythic and ritual performance (for myths are ordinarily performed too) have two "offices." The first is acceptance: to do or participate in a myth or rite is to publicly accept its right (to be performed) if not its rightness (to be true). He is adamant that acceptance is not "belief" and can happen separately from or without belief. The point is to embrace the *obligation* that comes with myth, ritual, religion, and culture as a whole. When people take part in a ritual, they communicate that such behavior is the "proper thing to do" and that those who lead the ritual have the prerogative to do so. This institutes not only obligation but authority. The second office, then, is the establishment of convention, of those "proper things to do." Once established, the convention is endowed with importance, with "sacredness," which makes it *obligatory*. Hence, the obligatoriness of the conventional behavior *becomes morality*: "Breach of obligation may, then, be the fundamental immoral act.... [F]ailure to abide by the terms of an obligation is universally stigmatized as immoral."[39] This insight makes comprehensible Kant's insistence that the essence of morality is *duty*; it does not especially matter *what* we are bound to do as long as we are bound to do it.

Myth and ritual, simply put, get things done and make things real (if not "true"). They are, thus, although their source and location are "religious," indispensable parts of politics. We might say that myth and ritual fulfill Schmitt's profile of sovereignty. Through eruption into the mundane world, the characters of myth bring or "ordain" order in the first place; through their violation of law, they inscribe law. Ritual reaffirms and recreates this order and law in the present and future, stressing the human obligatory role in perpetuating natural and social constancy. But, like a Schmittian sovereign, the mythical beings can always interrupt or alter everyday order, with either singular acts of law-exception ("miracles") or enduring acts that inaugurate new institutions and laws—which may be overturned and replaced by another sovereign mythic or ritual act someday. Indeed, in all their religious glory, myth and ritual may provide a more perfect political theology than anything Schmitt conceives.

The efficacy of myth and ritual is not yet exhausted. First, both myth and ritual have their secular counterparts; there are obviously religious founding stories and ritual acts and non-religious founding stories and ritual acts. Or, perhaps more accurately, religious myths and rituals are special cases of the more general categories of narrative and ritualized action. (This applies to every other province that religion seeks to monopolize; as religion-friendly psychologist William James had to concede, there are no objects, acts, or feelings that are solely "religious": "These are each and all of them special cases of kinds of human experience of much wider scope.

---

[39] Roy Rappaport, *Ritual and Religion in the Making of Humanity* (Cambridge: Cambridge University Press, 1999), 132.

Religious melancholy, whatever peculiarities it may have qua religious, is at any rate melancholy. Religious happiness is happiness. Religious trance is trance."[40] And religious music is music, religious feasting is feasting, *ad infinitum.*)

One other point must be made before we proceed. The traditional approaches to both myth and ritual accentuate their static nature, their conservatism, at worst their immutability. But closer inspection finds that this quality is exaggerated; it is a piece of the *ideology* of myth and ritual but not their reality. Anthropologists, folklorists, and religion scholars observe myths change *when the social facts they explain and legitimize change.* For instance, a myth might recount the supernatural origins of a tribe's four clans; however, if over time a clan divides so that there are now five clans, the myth uncannily adapts to recount the supernatural origins of the tribe's *five* clans. Among Durkheim's most primitive and elementary peoples, the Australian Aboriginals, the Dreaming is not a closed canon; the ancestral beings can always, and sometimes do, reveal previously-unknown mythic or ritual knowledge in dreams. But no Aboriginal would consider this to be religious innovation; the knowledge is eternal, just never accessible to humans before. Rituals too are much less rote and much more situational and improvisational than usually granted. Practitioners may critique, change, or cease a ritual (e.g., animal sacrifice); they may invent new rituals; and rituals, however well-aged and well-performed, may fail.

Political Myth:
Stories to Live (and Govern) By

Delving deeper into myth first, it is clear that *religious* myth suggests the possibility of other kinds of myth, including *political myth.* Two political thinkers, in equally short books published three decades apart, insert the notion of myth into political science. Henry Tudor contends that a myth is political if its subject-matter is politics; the Bunyoro myth of kingship above would be a simultaneous or overlapping religious and political myth. He further argues that a political *narrative* becomes a political *myth* when it is conveyed in "dramatic form" as the tale of "a critical event by reference to which men can order their present experience but the events in question are thought of as taken place in the past."[41] Unlike ordinary history, political myth is accepted ("believed") whether true or false, and more consequentially, it serves a "practical argument," i.e., it offers guidance if not demands submission on a current political question. His three examples of political myth are the foundation myth of Rome, the millennium myth of

---

[40] William James, *The Varieties of Religious Experience: A Study in Human Nature* (New York: The New American Library, 1958 [1902]), 37.

[41] Henry Tudor, *Political Myth* (London: Pall Mall Press, 1972), 16.

Christianity, and the race myth of Aryanism. Thirty years later, Christopher Flood concurs that "mythmaking is a normal feature of political life," although he unfairly distinguishes political myth from "sacred myth" by insisting that political myth lacks sacredness.[42] In this chapter and in previous chapters, we have seen that this is not entirely true; a *purely* political myth may be shorn of any sacrality, but in many instances, political myth retains the aura of the sacred—sometimes literally invoking gods and spiritual power, unfailingly carrying a sense of importance, strongly convincing and motivational, and untouchable or unquestionable by present-day people. Based on examples like Charles DeGaulle and female Cherokee chief Wilma Mankiller, Flood's concept of political myth can be summarized as "ideology cast in the form of history."[43]

Chiara Bottici has more fully conceptualized political myth, particularly in her 2007 *A Philosophy of Political Myth*. She holds that a political myth is a narrative "which grants significance to the political conditions and experiences of a social group"; a historical or political story becomes a political myth when it "coagulates and reproduces significance," when "a given group shares in it," and when "it can address the specifically political conditions in which a given group lives."[44] Several elements of this hypothesis deserve comment. By coagulate, Bottici presumably means something like the often-mentioned capacity of myths, and of symbols generally, to "condense" meaning.

Further, Bottici appreciates that the social group of a political myth—usually a national polity but also a sub-national group like a race or class or a trans-national group like "Islam," "Western civilization," or "the international proletariat"—is not just a target of political myth but a potential *product* of myth, that is, the myth may assemble and integrate a political group and identity around itself, and may be used, with more or less sincerity, by leaders to accomplish that assemblage and integration. But the real significance of political myth lies in its ability to address current political circumstances. It does so, like all myths and symbols, by acting as a lens through which the present moment is viewed and interpreted. As Geertz memorably says of religion, a political myth is a source of both a model *of* reality and a model *for* reality, showing us what the world *was* like and what it *should be and will be* like.[45]

---

[42] Christopher G. Flood, *Political Myth: A Theoretical Introduction* (London and New York: Routledge, 2002), 12.

[43] Ibid., ix.

[44] Chiara Bottici, "Towards a Philosophy of Political Myth," *Iris: European Journal of Philosophy and Public Debate* 3, no. 5 (2011), 39. See also Chiara Bottici, *A Philosophy of Political Myth* (Cambridge and New York: Cambridge University Press, 2007).

[45] Clifford Geertz, *The Interpretation of Cultures* (New York: Basic Books, 1973), 94.

For this very good reason, Bottici declares that a political myth is not a proposition to be proven but *a prophecy* to be realized. That is, while a political (or any other) myth references the past, it is really about the present *and the future*. She offers the instance of Georges Sorel's theory of the general strike, the primary tool of the working class. The general strike does not aim to *explain* anything; it is a response to Marx's insistence that we stop explaining the world and start changing it. In Bottici's words, Sorel's general strike is not a proposition but "a determination of the will."[46] This is her prophetic quality of political myth, which is (hopefully for the proponents of the myth) a self-fulfilling prophecy. Or, as Roland Boer puts it in his study of political myth and biblical themes, following Alain Badiou, the grammar of political myth is "the future perfect": by "forcing of a truth" through the promotion of political myth, at some time in the future the message of the myth "will have been true."[47]

We can see that political myth is as much political as mythical. As myth, it summons a past, but as politics, it musters action—organization, decision-making, institution-creation, sometimes violence—in the present in pursuit of a horizon informed by, continuous with, that past. To make more progress on the topic, we must refine our concept of myth still more. A myth may be a complete story, with beginning, middle, and end. Even when it is, though, it is not usually "told" like a story; instead, sections of the myth are typically sung, chanted, or enacted. Or the myth may be tacit knowledge behind our behaviors; for instance, at Thanksgiving dinners, Americans do not narrate the account of "the first thanksgiving" (which few Americans know and which truly *is* mythical, Thanksgiving being an invented tradition with only the loosest association with the Pilgrims). The myth need not be a full narrative at all but discrete scenarios or metaphors—in the American case, "manifest destiny" or "the frontier" or "a shining light on a hill." Members of the society may not, and may not be able to if they were inclined to, verbalize these mythic scenes, but although unnarrated, the snippets and scenes underwrite and rationalize our present actions, ideas, and experiences. What is mythical about myths, then, is arguably less their narrative quality than their *temporal* quality: the events of myth are in the (primordial or formative) past, but those events, like the Aboriginal Dreamtime, are also atemporal, timeless, everywhen, both then and now (and possibly more so tomorrow). History, mundane *political* time, moves and churns, lurches forward and back, while myth—the truth underneath events—moves slowly, if at all.

---

[46] Chiara Bottici, "Philosophies of Political Myth, a Comparative Look Backwards: Cassirer, Sorel, and Spinoza," *European Journal of Political* Theory 8, no. 3 (2009), 372.

[47] Roland Boer, *Political Myth: On the Use and Abuse of Biblical Themes* (Durham, NC: Duke University Press, 2009), 17.

As not just narration but also scenes, themes, and tacit knowledge, political myth is part of what Maurice Halbwachs calls "social memory," and therein lies its efficacy.[48] No living Americans were present at the first thanksgiving or the signing of the Declaration of Independence or the Battle of Gettysburg, but we "remember" them as our shared collective inheritance. And the preservation and transmission of a society's collective, political memory is not left to chance. Much political will and many social resources are invested in collective memory, which is "stored" in, recovered from, and practiced in numerous social sites, often of political intensity, including national/patriotic holidays, songs, speeches, parades, stories and legends, books and textbooks (schools are a prime site of collective memory, as are libraries), movies and television programs, and the very landscape itself (consider Mount Rushmore).

We have already learned (see Chapter 3) that political myths are immanent in contemporary politics; the trope of the "sacred nation" illustrates that, contrary to Christopher Flood, a political myth can be plenty sacred. A brilliant instance of political myth comes in Victor Shnirelman's investigation of contemporary Russian radical nationalists, who promote a myth of "Hyperborea." Like Eastern European societies, after the fall of communism, many Russians faced a political and an identity crisis; some turned to a dream "of a 'pure Russian country,' or at least of the privileged status of ethnic Russians within the Russian state."[49] Such a national aspiration is fertile ground for political mythmaking. Suspecting, as conspiracy theorists are wont to do, that official and Western historians had distorted or suppressed Russian history, many nationalists were attracted to a national/racial myth—a literal Aryan myth (forgetting somehow that the German Aryans despised the eastern Slavs)—which portrayed modern-day Russians as descendants of an "ancient people," romanticized as "robust, noble, reliable, truthful, courageous, generous, skillful, knowledgeable and wise."[50] These idealized ancestors built a great civilization and culture in the far north, on a polar island called Arctida or Hyperborea. On a more grandiose scale, the original Russians or Russes, also the original Aryans, were "the forefathers of the White Race, and all the other 'white people' are viewed as their younger brothers."[51] Naturally, the white Russes were contrasted to, and actually opposed by, their southern dark-skinned neighbors, who were driven south to Africa.

---

[48] Maurice Halbwachs, *On Collective Memory*, ed. and trans. Lewis A. Coser (Chicago and London: The University of Chicago Press, 1992 [1952]).

[49] Victor Shnirelman, "Hyperborea: The Arctic Myth of Contemporary Russian Radical Nationalists," *Journal of Ethnology and Folkloristics* 8, no. 2 (2014), 121.

[50] Ibid., 124.

[51] Ibid., 127.

This preposterous but all-too-familiar political myth has several happy implications for its proponents. First, it legitimates Russian racial superiority to non-white people; more, it elevates white Russians over other white people too, placing Russians at the root of the whole white race. That alone could entitle Russians to a (racially-exclusive) national state. But the myth has further ambitions. In some versions, ancestral Russians once occupied most or all of the northern hemisphere; hence, the myth establishes that "all Eurasian territory between the Baltic Sea and the Kuril Islands is their historical heritage. The myth does not stop at that and points to the Slavic Aryan expansion into Europe, North Africa, the Middle East, India, China and even the Americas."[52] In an especially odious turn, the myth sometimes proclaims that the vanquished and displaced black race "went to America to be slaves there in order to take revenge upon the White Race today for defeat in the prehistoric past."[53] And curiously,

Fig. 15 Russian nationalist poster in Odesa, Ukraine, June 2013, reading 'In the matter of literature, Slavic-Russian language has indisputably supremacy to all European languages.'

while the epic struggle was ostensibly between whites/Russians and blacks, somehow the Jews get swept up in the narrative, anti-Semitism being more prominent than anti-Africanism. On the fringe of the myth/movement, Jews are depicted as "a product of some experiment carried out by Egyptian priests. [Radical nationalists] present them as an artificial population, or bio-robots. Thus, they deprive them of human nature and, especially, of positive moral qualities."[54] All of the ensuing national pride could be achieved without any reference to religion whatsoever, but the supernatural has also been worked into the myth, producing a genuine sacred-political myth in which the Russian people are construed as "the major and necessary integral part of the All-Cosmic evolution of God and God-like in unrealized reality."[55] (Nor is this the wackiest contemporary post-socialist political

---

[52] Shnirelman, "Hyperborea," 127.
[53] Ibid.
[54] Ibid., 128.
[55] Ibid., 134.

myth: recall from Chapter 3 how some Hungarian nationalists believe that the Hungarian people originated on the distant star Sirius.)

Shnirelman's case of the primordial and cosmic Russes is a prime example of one recurrent, near-universal political (and religious) myth or myth-element, which Ramy Magdy, in a discussion of Egypt, dubs the "foundation myth," the "political myth narrating the foundation story of a state or republic or a regime and the values that should be learned from it."[56] In a real sense, most if not all myths are foundation myths, but political foundation myths specifically relate the origin of a people and/or their polity (society or state). This echoes and extends Bottici's point that political myths refer to or target certain political/identity groups, the value of the myth being "its ability 'to ignite' political expectations in its target groups who will be its social force" and to give those expectations precise shape.[57] As always, a foundation myth is "transcendentally true," whether it can be empirically verified (and the attempt to verify or falsify the myth is often taken as part of the conspiracy to suppress the truth and oppress the people.)

Raoul Girardet proposes that there are elements of political myth that are, if not exclusive to, then central to modern populist movement.[58] The four political myths identified by Girardet are *the conspiracy myth, the myth of unity, the myth of the savior*, and *the myth of the golden age*. At least three of these are observable in Schnirelman's Russian material (he does not mention a particular Russian savior, although some might see Putin in that role), and we encountered all four in our survey of global right-wing populism. The conspiracy myth claims that some malevolent group is and/or has been throughout history obstructing and persecuting "us" and taking what is rightfully "ours"; this group (liberals, socialists, immigrants, Jews, the party system, the establishment, the "deep state"—the list goes on) must be identified, opposed, stripped of power, and in the worst case liquidated. The myth of the golden age is the dream in retrospect, the vision of the perfect pure people and culture in some vague past, which we once were *and which we will be again*. The myth of the savior, of course, is the ideal leader who will then deliver us to this promised land, and the myth of unity is that there is a single monolithic "us" to deliver.

Mihnea Stoica insists that modern populism promotes all of these myths, placing the conspiracy myth at the core around which all the others revolve.[59] The former claim is indisputably true, although the latter is

---

[56] Ramy Magdy, "Mythos Politicus: A Theoretical Framework for the Study of Political Myths," *Athens Journal of Mediterranean Studies* 6, no. 2 (2020), 157.

[57] Ibid., 167.

[58] Raoul Girardet, *Mythes et Mythologies politiques* (Paris: Éditions de Seuil, 1986).

[59] Mihnea S. Stoica, "Political Myths of the Populist Discourse," *Journal for the Study of Religions and Ideologies* 16, no. 46 (2017), 63–76.

debatable; one could imagine a populism that does not entail conspiracy at all, however unlikely. And Girardet's four myths do not complete the arsenal of contemporary populism. Fundamental to populism is the notion of "the will of the people," which Albert Weale argues is a still deeper and more essential political myth than conspiracy.[60] The myth of the will of the people presumes (1) that "the people" possess a single will which (2) the leader can hear or intuit and act upon such that (3) there is an immediate and unmediated synchrony, an almost mystical union, between the leader and the people. As discussed in the chapter on populism, the notion of the sovereignty of the people, which tends toward anti-institutionalism and a cult of the leader as the voice if not the embodiment of the people, has it that the will of the people can be and should be converted directly into political action. But the myth of the will of the people rests on the bedrock myth of "the people" as such. The myth of "the people" imagines an entity called "the people" that is externally bounded, i.e., clearly distinguished from "the other," and internally homogeneous *so that it is capable of possessing a single will upon which the populist leader can act* (not to mention that it is wise enough that realizing its will is a good idea).

Finally, while these political mega-myths, these grand political-mythical narratives, are widely distributed through populist and other contemporary politics, there are also innumerable "little" and local political myths that are more or less specific to particular societies and their governments or movements. Croatia exemplifies the myth of victimhood, which is not exactly identical to the conspiracy myth as the forces pitted against the country and its people may have been anything but secret. Croats express this myth in the political phrase *mali narod, velika nepravda* (small nation, great suffering), verbalizing their sense that the nation "has been systematically persecuted, has suffered more than any other, and is consequently innocent of any injustice or crime."[61] More than a century of war in the Balkans has left a landscape littered with battlegrounds and memorials, constant reminders of the nation's survival against the odds—and more essentially, of "who is and who is not a perpetrator, who suffered the most ... who made the most sacrifices, who has to bewail most casualties, and, eventually, who will emerge as the victor of history."[62]

Elsewhere in the world, the Sinhalese and Tamils of Sri Lanka are locked in a mythical competition of first occupation, each staking their claim to the island on the basis of their status as original inhabitants (so much so that each side has been known to destroy ancient archaeological sites of the

---

[60] Albert Weale, *The Will of the People: A Modern Myth* (Cambridge, UK and Medford, MA: Polity Press, 2018).

[61] Michaela Schäuble, *Narrating Victimhood: Gender, Religion, and the Making of Place in Post-War Croatia* (New York and London: Berghahn, 2014), 10.

[62] Ibid., 137.

other, to erase the evidence of their historical presence); each even has a national epic/myth to "document" its claim (the Sinhalese *Mahāvamsa* and the Tamil *Yalpana Vaipara Malai*). Turanism is a political myth in Turkey, the ideology that the Turks are part of a great people (sometimes identified culturally, sometimes racially) along with Tatars, Magyars, Finns, and more who are entitled to the "vast and eternal" (and mythic) land of Turan.[63] Hindutva plays the same role in India (see Chapter 3).

The United States has its own set of political myths. Probably the most basic and pervasive is the myth of "American exceptionalism," that the United States is not like any other country. As mentioned, the myth of the shining city on the hill, of America as a beacon and model for the world, is prevalent, as are the myths of the Pilgrims-as-seekers-of-religious-freedom, of manifest destiny, and of the frontier. Conspicuous in many of the political theologies spawned in the United States (and other Christian countries) is the myth of Israel. This is not to say that Israel does not exist today and did not exist in ancient times; Israel as a historical/political fact and Israel as a myth are two different but related ideas. The mythical Israel has been associated with countries, races, and religions that are not "factually" Israeli or Israelite, such as England (Anglo-Israelism), white America (Christian Identity)—both of which repudiate the biological Israelis or Jews—and Mormons and Rastafarians, who like many others fancy themselves as inhabiting the true Zion (see Chapter 1).

Political Ritual:
Powerful Action, Acting Powerful

In June 2008, the king of Nepal abdicated, ending the country's monarchy. Opponents of the royal system defeated it not by bloody revolution but by obstructing the king's ritual functions. For a year prior, republicans in the government had "worked to disrupt and appropriate the king's active calendar of royal rituals," which "effectively prevented him from reproducing his royalty."[64] A typical secular American, and maybe Schmitt himself, would wonder what ritual and the office of king have to do with each other. Anne Mocko's analysis of the Nepalese events, however, perceives that the king was not only, or mainly, a political figure but a ritual figure (sometimes even a spiritual one, claiming to be an incarnation or avatar of the god Vishnu): the king's participation in and leadership of rituals—of two prime kinds, succession rituals (that seat the king on the throne in the first place) and reinforcement rituals (that periodically renew

---

[63] Michael Gunter, *The Kurds in Turkey: A Political Dilemma* (Boulder, CO: Westview Press, 1990), 7.

[64] Anne T. Mocko, *Demoting Vishnu: Ritual, Politics, and the Unraveling of Nepal's Hindu Monarchy* (Oxford and New York: Oxford University Press, 2016), 2.

and restate the king's authority)—*produced* his royal status, marking him "as the person who *could* have access to all the other various practices of monarchy. Ritual, therefore, made him into the person who could be king."[65] Deprived of his ritual roles, he might actually have continued to govern, but he would not be a king; deprived of political power but still allowed to perform his ritual acts, "he would have continued to be king—even if he lost all connection to the government."[66]

Although the notion that ritual makes a leader politically powerful, politically *real*, is foreign to us, our discussion of ritual demonstrates that rituals transform individuals, their relationships and statuses, and the social and natural world around them. In a nearly half-century-old essay on "political ritual," Steven Lukes critiques the social-science bias that ritual merely represents or reaffirms relations and values; ritual portrays "particular models or political paradigms of society and how it functions ... organizing people's knowledge of the past and present and their capacity to imagine the future. In other words, it helps to define as authoritative certain ways of seeing society."[67] He insists that political offices, political institutions, and the very law itself need drama and ceremony in order to be experienced and accepted by members of society.

As mentioned earlier, Catherine Bell includes political rituals in her typology. Political rituals are "those ceremonial practices that specifically construct, display, and promote the power of political institutions (such as king, state, the village elders) or the political interests of distinct constituencies and subgroups."[68] But she goes further, declaring that all ritual is political in the sense that it is "a tool for social and cultural jockeying," as with the Nepalese king and his rivals; "it is a performative medium for the negotiation of power in relationships."[69] It is the "dramaturgy of power" performed in ritual that makes offices, institutions, and laws real, through the standard ritual process of (1) highly formalized action, the sort that has worked in the past, (2) employed to transform individuals by "passing" them from one stage to another (commoner to king, non-office-holder to office-holder, adult to elder, etc.), (3) secured, if the ritual has a religious component, through the invocation or intervention of supernatural or superhuman powers.

Religious-political rituals are most common, and most ornate, in pre-modern chiefdoms and kingdoms. Spectacles of coronation almost always inaugurate the rule of a new king, who is frequently believed to

---

[65] Mocko, *Demoting Vishnu*, 9.

[66] Ibid., 13.

[67] Steven Lukes, "Political Ritual and Social Integration," *Sociology* 9, no.2 (1975), 301.

[68] Bell, *Ritual: Perspectives and Dimensions*, 128.

[69] Ibid., 79.

absorb the spiritual qualities—or literally to become a reincarnation—of the previous king. Beattie writes that the Bunyoro kingdom conducted coronation/succession and reinforcement or "refresher" rites. The current king or *mukama* was always, according to tradition, descended from the original king in an unbroken patrilineal succession (thus establishing the religious charter for kingship, flowing from the first family of humans). When a king died, there was an institutionalized period of chaos and social disturbance, during which sons of the deceased king were supposed to fight to the death for the throne. The king's demise was deliberately concealed to allow time for the succession competition to play out. When the new king was finally installed, his ascension was surrounded with ritual, including "the placing on the throne and the subsequent killing of a 'mock king,' who would, it was believed, attract to himself the magical dangers which attended the transition to kingship, protecting the real king."[70]

For Shilluk (southern Sudan) kings, the violent confrontation was more protracted but also more symbolic, although the conception of a religious continuity of the institution of king was similar. All kings inherited the place and power of the primal great king, Nyikang. In fact, as Evans-Pritchard recounts, "It is not the individual at any time reigning who is king, but Nyikang who is the medium between man and God (Juok) and is believed in some way to participate in God as he does in the king."[71] Accordingly, the installation of a new king entailed a symbolic war between the king-to-be and Nyikang himself, present in effigy. Priests displayed the effigy of Nyikang, which traveled through the northern part of the kingdom, gathering the subjects of the mythical monarch. Finally, the army of Nyikang confronted the army of the king-to-be.

> The army of the king-elect is defeated and he is captured by Nyikang and taken by him to the capital. The kingship captures the king. There Nyikang is placed on the royal stool. After a while he is taken off it and the king-elect sits on it in his stead and the spirit of Nyikang enters into him, causing him to tremble, and he becomes king, that is he becomes possessed by Nyikang.[72]

In an important and symbolic sense, after and thanks to the confusion and disorder, order was re-established—and it was the same order (indeed, the same royal spirit) as before.

But we must be careful not to exaggerate the "symbolic" quality of political rituals like coronation or ascension ceremonies (or any other rites

---

[70] Beattie, *Bunyoro*, 28.

[71] E. E. Evans-Pritchard, *Social Anthropology and Other Essays* (New York: The Free Press, 1962), 201.

[72] Ibid., 205.

for that matter). When subjects coronate a king, they do not see themselves as acting symbolically; rather, they are *making a king*, just as when people seek or perform a shamanic cure, they are not acting symbolically but *trying to get well*. From the performer's and the audience's point of view, a ritual is not symbolic, it is *efficacious*. In the case of pre-modern royal rituals, Giorgio Agamben adds an important insight that is neglected by secular-rationalist politics, including that of Schmitt. In a previous chapter we learned that a king or queen (and to an extent a modern populist leader) is two bodies, his/her physical body and the "body social," which is represented by or superimposed on his/hers. Agamben makes the further distinction between royal *power* and royal *glory*, evident for instance in the Nepalese case above. That is, there is a difference between a king/queen who *reigns* and a political leader who *governs*; these two functions may be combined in any one person or office, or they may not. Either way, there is an analytical distinction between "administration" (what Agamben calls "government") and *sovereignty* (what Agamben calls "kingdom" or "glory"). If the distinction seems incomprehensible, consider the Queen of England, who reigns in majesty over her country *but does not govern*. And like us, Agamben is interested in the "liturgies of political power" through which a person is bestowed the glory of sovereignty, whether the power of government. A liturgy of political power is public "acclamation," an "exclamation of praise, of triumph, of laudation or of disapproval yelled by a crowd in determinate circumstances," including simple acts like shouting "God save the Queen."[73]

Coronations and successions are hardly the only ritual occasions on which sovereigns may display their power and subjects may acclaim that power. At the other end of life, royal or state funerals are potent and fraught political moments, in which a death, the end of a reign, and the commencement of a new reign are all entangled. In between are royal weddings and births. More than a few writers recognize the ritual of sacrifice, including and especially human sacrifice, as a liturgy of extreme political power. In kingdoms and empires from the Dahomey (present-day coastal Benin) to the Hawaiians, from the Aztecs to the Romans, royal/imperial sovereignty was exhibited in the prerogative to conduct sacrifices and maintained by internalizing the life-energy liberated through sacrifice. Dahomey was an extraordinary case of sovereignty through sacrifice. Sacrifice to or for the living king and the deceased kings was paramount, and Dahomean religion and politics "daily required a sacrifice as a matter of routine thank-offering for the King's awakening in health to the

---

[73] Giorgio Agamben, *The Kingdom and the Glory: For a Theological Genealogy of Economy and Government*, trans. Lorenzo Chiesa (Stanford, CA: Stanford University Press, 2011), 169.

new day."[74] This daily ritual demanded the lives of two slaves, one male and one female. Deaths were also sought as a gift to noble ancestors, ten or more at any typical ceremony. Other of the many occasions for human sacrifice included:

> whenever the King gave food to his ancestors, when he authorized a new market to be established, before he went to war, and on his return from a campaign. Sacrifices were also made when a King's palace was built, the heads of these persons being cut off and the blood mixed with the earth of the palace walls. When a well was dug a man and a woman were killed to ask permission of the earth to dig.[75]

However, human sacrifice was most prodigious at the death of a king, "who was said to require a sufficient retinue for the next world to establish in miniature a replica of his kingdom."[76] This called for a representative of each office, craft or occupation, and village to be interred along with him, in addition to his wives (who could number more than one hundred), as well as pallbearers and funeral officiates. Sacrifice also displayed the sovereign's authority over life and death, although as among the Aztecs, the emperor was sometimes required to shed his own blood for ritual, that blood being the most potent of all human blood. Roman emperors commanded that all citizens must offer sacrifices to them and the Roman gods (the refusal thereof got Christians in a lot of trouble).

Even today in many parts of the world, members of society and guests of state are commonly expected to perform ritual acts for the sovereign. Visitors to the royal court might be expected to avert their eyes, bow, prostrate themselves, or kiss the monarch's hand or ring. And political ritual is by no means limited to monarchies, nor does it always have an overt religious component. A transitional case, performed by secular authorities but serving a religious function at a religious site, is the ritual attendance of Japanese authorities at the Yasukuni shrine. Yasukuni, opened in 1869 as a tribute to

Fig. 16 Trump at the political ritual at the Tomb of the Unknown Soldier, Memorial Day weekend 2017

---

[74] Melville Herskovits, *Dahomey: An Ancient West African Kingdom*, v. 2. (New York: J. J. Augustin, 1938), 49.

[75] Ibid., 53.

[76] Ibid.

Japan's war dead, does more than commemorate those souls; it *houses* the souls. Twice a year the shrine is visited by political officials, including the Prime Minister, to honor but also to calm the spirits. Without the official choreographed ritual at the site, the spirits could become restless and dangerous; by executing their sacred duty to the dead, political officials represent and reinforce their own secular and spiritual power. A more thoroughly secular version of this homage to the dead is the American political ritual of laying a wreath at the Tomb of the Unknown Soldier.

In ancient and modern societies alike, political rituals abound, often secular yet emanating specialness if not sacrality. Paul Kosmin interprets the ancient Greek procedure of ostracism, in which a citizen was voted out of the city for a period of time, as a political ritual, an explicitly Turnerian rite of passage that "transforms a dangerous or treacherous politician into a safe member of the Athenian community."[77] In Estonia, song festivals have had political implications since their introduction in the 1860s, reflecting, enhancing, and contesting the politics of the day—from independence to Soviet domination to independence again with the so-called "Singing Revolution" of 1988; these musical ritual events have had the effect of making Estonia a political reality by "singing oneself into a nation."[78] Something similar transpires in Trinidad, where nation-building policies openly endorsed musical and cultural exhibitions and competitions as a strategy of national unity and national pride.[79] Back in the United States, David Greenberg justifiably classifies presidential debates as political ritual (in which the demeanor of the candidates and the "gotcha" moment are more important than any information the candidates might impart).[80] Elections themselves are political rituals, albeit—or exactly—ones that actually do seat individuals in power.

Some critics trivialize or dismiss political ritual as "political theater," but being theater makes it no less significant and real. All politics, indeed all society, is theater in the Goffmanian sense that people play roles in society (we expect the American president to "act" presidential). At the far end of the spectrum, theater can *be* politics, as in Geertz's account of the precolonial Balinese kingdom, which he characterizes as a "theater state" where

---

[77] Paul J. Kosmin, "A Phenomenology of Democracy: Ostracism as Political Ritual," *Classical Antiquity* 34, no. 1 (2015), 124.

[78] Karsten Brüggemann and Andres Kasekamp, "'Singing Oneself into a Nation'" Estonian Song Festivals as Rituals of Political Mobilisation," *Nations and Nationalism* 20, no. 2 (2014), 259–76.

[79] Kevin K. Birth, *Bacchanalian Sentiments: Musical Experience and Political Counterpoints in Trinidad* (Durham, NC: Duke University Press, 2008).

[80] David Greenberg, "Torchlight Parades for the Television Age: The Presidential Debates as Political Ritual," *Daedalus* 138, no.2 (2009), 6–19.

the kings and princes were the impresarios, the priests the directors, and the peasants the supporting cast, stage crew, and audience. The stupendous cremations, tooth filings, temple dedications, pilgrimages, and blood sacrifices, mobilizing hundreds and even thousands of people and great quantities of wealth, were not means to political ends: they were the ends themselves, they were what the state was for. Court ceremonialism was the driving force of court politics; and mass ritual was not a device to shore up the state, but rather the state, even in its final gasp, was a device for the enactment of mass ritual. Power served pomp, not pomp power.[81]

Based on the accompanying political myth of the "exemplary center" in which the capital city and the royal court were "a microcosm of the supernatural order ... and the material embodiment of political order," ritual life portrayed and reified that order.[82] The ritual-state was theater but not only theater: it was also "an argument, made over and over again in the insistent vocabulary of ritual, that worldly status has a cosmic base, that hierarchy is the governing principle of the universe, and that the arrangements of human life are but approximations, more close or less, to those of the divine."[83]

As a reminder that American political ritual is theater but serious theater, the first inauguration of Barack Obama in 2009 included a flubbed recitation of the oath of office by the Chief Justice of the Supreme Court, and some Americans fretted that, since the words were not uttered perfectly, perhaps Obama had not really become president.

Trump: The Man, the Myth, the Ritual

One key discovery in this survey of political myth and ritual is that modern politics is not perfectly rational. The common perception of politics as the realm or practice of rational discourse and deliberation is highly deficient. There remains, and always will remain, much of the pre-rational (which is not concerned with truth or falseness) and the irrational (which wantonly disregards truth and falseness) in today's politics. Indeed, what Nelson Goodman was trying to say in the chapter's opening epigraph is that man does not live by truth alone but by every word of myth and act of ritual.

The beauty of myth and ritual as political performance is that, insofar as Geertz is correct that political myths and rituals are arguments, they make their arguments, as Mocko also discerns in the Nepalese case, "in

---

[81] Clifford Geertz, *Negara: The Theatre State in Nineteenth-Century Bali* (Princeton, NJ: Princeton University Press, 1980), 13.
[82] Ibid.
[83] Ibid., 102.

ways that are extraordinarily difficult to argue against."[84] Because the myth or ritual offers no proposition, there is nothing to test against reality for its accuracy. Nor, as Rappaport explains, does the myth or ritual ask participants or observers to "believe" anything; it merely asks for acceptance, commitment, perhaps complicity. Even if they were inclined, the actors and audiences of myth and ritual "have very few options for outwardly opposing the view of the world put forward"—and could most likely pay a heavy price for such opposition.[85]

Trump, like any leader but particularly like an authoritarian/populist leader, indulges in his share of pre-rational and irrational political myth and ritual. He trades on all of the standard populist myths, starting naturally with the conspiracy myth; there is always a conspiracy afoot, against him personally and against "the people" generally, not just the usual conspiracies of liberals, socialists, and immigrants but very specific conspiracies, for instance, to use coronavirus to discredit him or mail-in voting to defraud him of re-election. Through accusations of the latter, he can delegitimize an electoral defeat, complaining, as he began to do long before the polls opened, that the election was rigged or stolen. We hear in his speeches, and sense behind his policies, the unity myth (that there is an authentic American people whom he faithfully represents), golden age myth (some funhouse mirror version of 1950s America), and savior myth (with himself as the only person who can save America) cards. He also calls up more enduring myths, like American exceptionalism and the will of the people. Then there are his lies, miniature myths and puzzle pieces in his world-making future-perfect program. With the Fox News/Infowars/QAnon myth-machine at his service, he subjects reality to an acid bath and replaces it with his authoritarian narrative. Meanwhile, some followers supply their own mythical filters and justifications, like the myth of Trump as Cyrus of Persia, the sinner savior.

Trump is equally if not more adept at political ritual. His campaign-style rallies are textbook political rituals, as are his clumsy attempts to organize military parades of the Soviet sort, with tanks and missiles rolling throuhg the streets. He has injected himself, in partisan political ways, into regular American political rituals, like his speech at Mount Rushmore for the Fourth of July 2020, where he laid out conspiracy myth cards again, slamming Black Lives Matters protesters as enemies of the people. Key to much of his political theater, as we will discuss again at the end of the final chapter, is inciting anger if not physical violence.

Fortunately, even these performances, as unsavory as they are, pale in comparison to genuine torchlight processions, Nazi-era rallies, and Soviet goose-stepping marches. He has not tried, except in the mildest ways, to foment an actual cult of personality (he may put his name on every property

---

[84] Mocko, *Demoting Vishnu*, 19.
[85] Ibid., 19–20.

and business he owns, but at least he does not hang massive posters of himself on buildings and require us to address him as "dear leader"). His use of political ritual is uglier than we are accustomed to, but it is not exceptional by the standard of twentieth and twenty-first century politicians, and he has introduced no original political myth (other than the myth of Trump himself).

But the point that we want to make in closing is that it is difficult, and not altogether relevant, to "argue against" Trump's myths and rituals, because, like all myths and rituals, they are not advancing rational, testable, and defeasible arguments. They are rather, again like all myths and rituals, making future-perfect statements: if we allow him to proceed, then someday—maybe sooner than we think—American *will have been* the way he defines it in his words, actions, and policies. The alternative to arguing against a myth and ritual is, as Boer advises in his aforementioned book on biblical themes as political myth, to wrest those mythic and ritual resources, *including the Bible and Christianity itself*, from him and to meet him with myths and rituals—not just facts and figures—of our own.

8

Trump, Shaman, Trickster:
Political Theology beyond God

> A point worthy of the most careful attention is the number of clever heroes who are rascals on the other side of the law. This type is a hero who in many respects verges upon being a villain, but still retains the admiration of the people. He is upstart, rebel, lawbreaker, liar, thief, and malefactor; and yet in spite of being so—perhaps because of this—he is a social force. What is the secret of his power?[1]

C onsider this forensic profile:

- "He may not be a good man—indeed, he is usually far from being an exemplar of virtue, nor is he outstanding as a servant of his group."
- "He is supreme for wit, resourcefulness, nimbleness, elusiveness, deceit, impudence, and sense of humor."
- "He does not meet an opponent head-on but prefers to trick him. He is a specialist in triumphant but sometimes shady transactions which, on the whole, amuse people more than they outrage them."
- He sets out to "inflict a loss of prestige on those who oppose him.... It is also important that his opponent should be humiliated in some comic way. 'Insult to injury' is the motto.... Taunting, derision and impudence are an essential part of and a fitting climax to the role."
- He possesses "a mental facility like jiujitsu before which even people of capacity feel discomfited and naïve. Not profundity but a quick shrewdness demonstrated in encounter with others is the mark of a clever hero."[2]

As the last words reveal, this is Orrin Klapp's 1954 sketch of the "clever hero," a recurring motif in the world's folklore and religions. One struggles,

---

[1] Orrin E. Klapp, "The Clever Hero," *The Journal of American Folklore* 67, no. 263 (1954), 21.
[2] Ibid., 23–24.

interestingly, to identify such a character in the New Testament, and most of the qualities of the clever hero are anything but admired in Christianity.

This book launched with three interrelated goals. The first and most obvious was to better understand the Trump phenomenon by examining it through the filter of political theology. The second was to critique and rethink political theology in the light of contemporary (especially populist and authoritarian) politics, and the third was to critique and rethink theology itself as a tool for understanding and organizing politics and society. In the introduction, we previewed the diversity of religious authorizations and legitimations of political rule and prevailing institutions and laws. In the seventh chapter, we considered how Christianity with its fixation on belief may not be the best paradigm for political theology, substituting instead myth and ritual, which are less about telling truly or acting truly than *making truth*, such that what they tell and act *will be* true or *will have been* true at some future time.

Based on the fact that the present day abounds with clever heroes, particularly in the form of populist authoritarian leaders who excel in deceit, boldness, insolence, and harsh humor, and on the fact that the clever hero is absent from Christian mythology—indeed, is a thoroughly non-Christian and anti-Christian figure—this concluding chapter presses the critique of theology all the way to *theos* itself. What if the Christian god is not a good model at all for political theology? What if some other, more universal and mischievous religious character(s) can take us further toward comprehending the nature of power and order—and Trump himself?

Religion without God(s)

Every society justifies its social and political practices and institutions to itself, even if not consciously and nervously, and all accomplish this justification through some application of myth and ritual, even if purely secular political myth and ritual. In the vast majority of societies, social and political legitimation conspicuously and directly entails religion. *In the vast majority of societies, though, social and political legitimation does not entail god(s): in fact, the vast majority of religions have no god-concept at all.*

We have objected repeatedly in this treatise to equating religion with god(s) and therefore have opposed the term "theology" as a cross-cultural religious and political category. The reason, which we will now make abundantly clear, is that god(s) is/are present in one type of religion (theism) but not in all types; actually, it would be more accurate to say that theism is not a "type" of religion but a component of religion, because god(s) can and do occur in religions with other kinds of beings and forces.

Cross-cultural and comparative research on religion informs that the god-concept is frankly rather rare in the world's religions. Most indigenous and tribal religions posit other kinds of entities besides or alongside god(s). The "non-theistic religions" (an oxymoron to some, until they study the subject more carefully) feature alternative ontologies that we can call animism, animatism, ancestor spirits, and ethical nontheism.

Table 8.1 Diversity of Religions/Religious Components

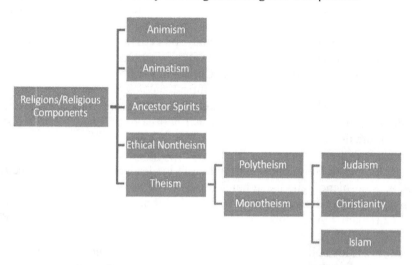

Probably the oldest and most common religious "belief" is that natural/physical phenomena have a "spiritual" constituent as well, which we might call a spirit or soul ("soul" is another troublesome Christian concept with very specific and non-universal traits). Animism refers to this notion that plants, animals, and inanimate things like mountains and rivers, the sun and the moon, perhaps wind and rain, are ensouled. The Ainu of northern Japan, for example, held that plants, animals, and man-made objects like pots and pans were "spirit-owning" or "spirit-bearing" beings who had to be treated with respect. In "life" there were restrictions on how humans could interact with them, as with any persons, and in death these restrictions persisted; Ainu had to maintain a separate location for the disposal of each type of spirit-owning being, called *keyohniusi*, and negligence of their duties toward these beings brought sickness or worse.[3] The North American Huron said that plants, animals, and objects had spirits, which were the same size and shape as their physical bodies. The Dani of New Guinea met spirits of or in natural objects or places like hills, rocks, ponds, and whirlpools. Anutans (south Pacific) spoke of *tupua penua* or land/totemic spirits, associated either with species like the shark, octopus, or sea turtle or with natural

---

[3] Emiko Ohnuki-Tierney, *The Ainu of the Northwest Coast of Southern Sakhalin* (New York: Holt, Rinehart, and Winston, 1974).

features and sites. These spirits were god-like in some ways—with names, individual personalities, and power, bound to particular locations, prayed to, and invoked in song and story—yet also amoral, egotistical, and dangerous.[4]

It is only sensible that animistic beliefs would endow humans with a spirit-part too, and when this spirit-part continues to interact with society after death, the result is an ancestor cult of some sort. We hesitate to say "ancestor worship" because the attitude toward ancestor spirits was not always worshipful. The Dani feared most ancestors as malevolent ghosts, and the Burmese Thai villagers studied by Melford Spiro asserted that the spirits of their dead, called *leikpya*, were a potential source of trouble, especially former government officials who did not like losing their power. As in many cultures, the spirits of those who led wicked lives constituted a special class of evil ghosts, *tasei* or *thaye*. These evil ghosts resided at the edge of villages, especially near burial grounds, eating corpses or sometimes the living.[5] For the !Kung or Ju/hoansi of the Kalahari Desert, the dead, known collectively as the *//gauwasi* or *//gangwasi*, posed a menace to humans not because they were malicious but because they were lonely; they would try to pull their living kin to the land of the dead with them, with unpleasant results for the living.[6] J. H. Driberg goes so far as to assert, based on his experience with African cultures, that purported "ancestor cults" are not *religion* at all. He is adamant that there is "nothing sacred" about reverence for the ancestors; the behaviors directed toward the deceased including ritual obligations like sacrifice are simply "a social recognition of the fact that the dead man has acquired a new status and ... he is still one with [the community]."[7] In societies where age is the critical variable for status and respectability, the ancestors as the *oldest* members of society deserve the highest respect but the same kind of respect paid to living elders.

Animatism, on the other hand, consists of ideas about impersonal spiritual forces, akin to supernatural electricity. A fine example is the Chinese concept of *chi*, a not-altogether "spiritual" energy that flows through all things; the qualities of this energy (in its two modes, *yin* and *yang*) yield the nature of objects, beings, and spaces. Indeed, *chi* as described in the classic text *Tao Te Ching* is a political concept, as it advises how the ruler should govern his kingdom (ideally, by *not* ruling, by "doing nothing and leaving nothing undone"), allowing the (super)natural flow of

---

[4] Richard Feinberg, "Spirit Encounters on a Polynesian Outlier: Anuta, Solomon Islands," in *Spirits in Culture, History, and Mind*, ed. Jeannette Marie Mageo and Alan Howard (New York and London: Routledge, 1996), 99–120.

[5] Melford Spiro, *Burmese Supernaturalism*, expanded edition (Philadelphia, PA: Institute for the Study of Human Issues, 1978 [1967]).

[6] Richard Katz, *Boiling Energy: Community Healing Among the Kalahari Kung* (Cambridge, MA and London: Harvard University Press, 1982).

[7] J. H. Driberg, "The Secular Aspect of Ancestor-Worship in Africa," *Journal of the Royal African Society* 35, no. 138 (1936), 7.

chi to dictate action. Another equally famous animatistic concept is *mana*, common across the Pacific region, which is likewise a religious and political factor (as discussed in our introductory chapter). The Apache of the American Southwest knew a force named *diyi*, which we might define as luck; more remarkably (because nature abhors categories), *diyi* displayed some "personal" attributes, including the ability to seek out certain people and to feel anger. The !Kung or Ju/hoansi acted in regard to a force called *n/um* that pooled in their lower spine and was activated during healing dances; when heated up by a shaman (*n/um kausi* or master/owner of *n/um*), the shaman could effect spiritual journeys and cures.

Ethical nontheism refers to religions like Buddhism, especially in its early Theravada form (although not everyone concedes that Theravada Buddhism is quite a "religion" at all), which concern themselves with right behavior rather than the existence of god(s). The Buddha, therefore, did not pronounce on the question of god(s); at best, if there were gods, those beings were busy with their own enlightenment quests. In some popular versions of Buddhism, gods reappear (as do souls and other ideas rejected by traditional doctrine), but the very interpenetration of humans and gods—humans could become gods, and gods could become humans—contradicts the Christian idea of god.

So, most religions across time and space got along fine without god(s), while others like the !Kung or Ju/hoansi added god(s)—two in their case, *Gao Na* and *Kauha*, each with a wife and children, the first and greater of the two known for his human emotions of passion, frustration, and stupidity—to the universe of animistic spirits, ancestors, and animatistic forces. Worse, it is not certain what sets a god apart from other spirits. Robert Levy, Jeannette Marie Mageo, and Alan Howard opine that gods and spirits fall on opposite ends of a spectrum, from "well-defined, socially encompassing beings at one pole, to socially marginal, fleeting presences at the other," with gods presumably occupying the defined/encompassing pole.[8] Gods, they think, are more fully imagined, more highly moral, and more associated with social order, while spirits are vague, minimally conceived, and typically extramoral. Unfortunately, the cross-cultural evidence does not support this conclusion. Some non-divine spirits are not vague at all but are quite well-articulated, with names and known personalities and histories. Some have complicated and important cults and rituals associated with or directed toward them. Some are more part of daily life than gods, who can be remote and impassive, virtually unknown and almost irrelevant.

---

[8] Robert I. Levy, Jeannette Marie Mageo, and Alan Howard, "Gods, Spirits, and History: A Theoretical Perspective," in *Spirits in Culture, History, and Mind*, ed. Jeannette Marie Mageo and Alan Howard (New York and London: Routledge, 1996), 11.

If we consider a classic definition of god, we will see the problem. Philosopher-theologian Richard Swinburne defines god as "person without a body (i.e., a spirit) present everywhere, the creator and sustainer of the universe, able to do everything (i.e., omnipotent), knowing all things, perfectly good, a source of moral obligation, immutable, eternal, a necessary being, holy and worthy of worship."[9] The first thing we notice is that a god is not different from a spirit but is a species of spirit. However, it soon becomes apparent that this is not a definition of god at all but *a description of a particular god, namely, the Christian god.* For instance, not all gods are creators: some, like Thor, were born after the world was created. This raises a further objection: not all gods are eternal: some are second- or third-generation gods who were obviously not around since the origin of the universe, and some gods die, like the Mesoamerican goddess Coyalxauhqui, killed by fellow god Huitzilopochtli, who was born full-grown from the Mother Goddess Coatlicue. Nor are all gods omnipotent; some have specific limited powers and portfolios, like Mars, the god of war, Aphrodite, the goddess of love, Poseidon, the god of the sea, etc. Nor are all gods omnibenevolent or even morally upright: Zeus behaved badly on more than a few occasions, including cheating on his wife to sire Hermes, about whom we will say much more below. The Azande (central Africa) god Mbori was not morally interested in humans at all; the Piaroa (Venezuela) god Kuemoi was an ugly and insanely violent cannibal, while the god of the Semai (Malaysia) tormented humans as a "vicious ludicrous monster" and "a stupid, incontinent, violent dupe" who merited their "frightened distaste."[10] Some gods were, quite seriously speaking, *clever heroes.*

The Oppressiveness of Order, the Excitement of Exception

In the early 1800s, there was a paroxysm of iconoclasm on Pacific islands as the locals pulled down their sacred buildings, destroyed their ritual objects, and converted en masse to Christianity. Some Christians—missionaries of the era as well as devotees today—no doubt interpret these events as the victory of true religion over idolatry. Few appreciate the fact that Pacific islanders periodically overthrew their "traditional" cults and replaced them with new ones. According to Jeffrey Sissons, Polynesian societies like Tahiti "were characterized by a seasonality of power in that they all had pre-existing traditions of seasonal social renewal during which the political order

---

[9] Richard Swinburne, *The Coherence of Theism* (Oxford: Clarendon Press, 1977), 2.

[10] Robert K. Dentan, *Overwhelming Terror: Love, Fear, Peace, and Violence among Semai of Malaysia* (Lanham, MD: Rowman & Littlefield, 2008), 74, 84.

was annually dissolved and reconstructed."[11] Yearly at the time of the rise of the Pleiades constellation, "god-images and temples were destroyed or desecrated"; Sissons recognizes this as an episode of Turnerian ritual *communitas*, the unmaking of hierarchies and powers. The ensuing season of Pleiades descending was a time of reinstituted hierarchy, during which gods and social structures—sometimes the same ones, sometimes novel ones— were put back into place. In a very real way, the coup against the island's gods and the turn to Christianity was another instance of island traditions, all the more so since chiefs like Tahiti's Pomare perceived a political advantage in embracing Christianity to unify his rule and expand control over neighboring islands (much as Constantine had done a millennium-and-a-half earlier in Rome). Building and consecrating churches was a latter-day version of the Pleiades-descending tradition, the time for restoring sacred spaces and emplacing gods in them, of "re-binding society." However, there was one unforeseen and undesired consequence of the action: once established, Christianity would brook no further upheavals. There would be no more seasonal rebellion against church and chief.

The difference, in short, was that Christian power and Christian truth "knew no seasonality of life"; "relentless and active day and night throughout the entire year," Christianity permitted no alternative or exception, which the islanders found stultifying and positively frightening: "Excessive hierarchy has always been a threat to life and fertility—that is why certain priests and chiefs hid themselves during the revelries of Pleiades above—and now everywhere this threat was recognized in the form of Christian excess."[12] Despite attempts to revive pre-Christian practices and to parody Christian/Western ways, the unremitting presentness of Christianity and the Christian god was a smothering burden of truth.

It is a profound oddity and irony that the religion that underwrites Schmitt's political theology of the exception is, of almost all imaginable religions, *the least able to comprehend or tolerate an exception.* (Islam would be another unlikely candidate, with its concept of *bid'a* or disapproved innovation.) To be sure, Christianity allows—indeed, is founded upon—the hierophanic eruption stressed by Eliade, the intervention of its god in the world (although less so these days) in the form of the miracle, the most miraculous intervention, of course, being the god's own incarnation and resuscitation. But none of that approximates a Polynesian-style iconoclasm, in which religious *power* and religious *truth* are set aside, violated, abolished, perhaps to be re-established—and perhaps not. Once in power and truth, however, Christianity never relinquishes either; in a

---

[11] Jeffrey Sissons, *The Polynesian Iconoclasm: Religious Revolution and the Seasonality of Power* (New York and Oxford: Berghahn Books, 2014), 1.
[12] Ibid., 118.

contradictory totality of Schmittian sovereignty, although there may be more miracles, *there will be no more exceptions.*

The Tahitian discomfort at the realization that periodic overthrow was now overthrown indicates that not all religions lock down truth and power once and for all and forbid possibilities of radical difference and change. For many, the exception is not only a real possibility but a regular practice, an *institution* if you will; that is, many religions and cultures incorporate myths and rituals of exception and violation. A well-documented example is the Swazi (south African) ritual of Ncwala, which featured "sacred *simemo* songs that appear to insult, reject, and generally blaspheme the Swazi king."[13] At other moments in the ceremony, participants abused the king with assertions of hatred and taunts that the king's successor commits incest with his sister. Andrew Apter calls the Ncwala a ritual of "permitted disrespect" which temporally foregrounded the potential for opposition and rebellion but which ridiculed the individual king rather than the office of king. Ideally and usually, the king was reinstated to his kingship: after rounds of "sacred dispraise," the crowd chanted "public support for the king," and

> at the point of maximum separation, when the king is a monster, darkened, and the year is at its turning point, the king represents power, his office authority; the king is impure, his office is pure.... His costume and medicines are removed, burned and washed away by the rains. The king is cleansed for his office, so that power combines with authority, and the king returns to his people, fit to rule.[14]

The religious world outside of Christianity is replete with such moments of *symbolic inversion* or what have been termed *rituals of reversal.* In many such festivities, the high is (temporarily) made low, whether this is a political or racial or gender hierarchy. During the Festival of the Kings observed by Jean Muteba Rahier, Afro-Ecuadorian villagers upended political, racial, and gender statuses in a three-day ceremony organized by women. In a society where men always held political office, the women appointed themselves president, police commissioner, etc., wore pants (unheard of among adult women), and even assaulted or arrested men, imprisoning them in stocks. Participants of both sexes also mimicked and mocked whites (particularly on the festival *dia de la raza blanca* or day of the white race), officials, and clergy. Significantly, by 2002, the local Christian evangelists had put a stop to much of the revelry, prohibiting women from performing their traditional reversals, generally shortening the

---

[13] Andrew Apter, "In Dispraise of the King: Rituals 'Against' Rebellion in South-East Africa," *Man* (new series) 18, no. 3 (1983), 521.
[14] Ibid., 531.

celebration, and substituting approved Christian activities as much as possible.[15]

In rituals of reversal where power is not directly trespassed, other kinds of violations of norm and propriety are permitted. These behaviors may include "role inversion, burlesquing, clowning, inverted speech, scatology, and sexual license" such as cross-dressing, nudity, and public joking and simulation of intercourse or childbirth.[16] In India, where caste inequalities and avoidances structure daily life, "pollution barriers" may be crossed, "pure" and "impure" castes mixing or otherwise impure actions performed.[17] During the rites for the goddess Gangamma in southeast India, men dress as women. Symbolic inversion in this instance is demanded *precisely because Gangamma* is a deity of *ugram* or "excess" or "too much to bear"; if her "excessive hunger/desire is not satisfied, she can be dangerous to humans."[18] Meanwhile, some women devote their lives to the goddess, symbolically marrying her, which rather than truncating their identity awards them "freedom to move across traditional social and spatial boundaries" ordinarily restricting local women.[19]

Some rituals of reversal involve what we might call "upside down" behavior. During the "peyote hunt" of the Huichol Indians (see below), there is a phase when all sorts of comical inversions occur. To "merriment and excitement … chatter and laughter," individuals are given funny false identities—one man becomes the Pope, another a child, one woman a *gringa* (white woman), and so forth—the nose becomes a penis (which makes sneezing particularly hilarious), and pilgrims ultimately walk backwards into the sacred land.[20] Many societies feature a special role for the "ritual clown." This character, "an ambivalent figure of danger and enticement, gravity and hilarity, solemnity and fun," breaks into otherwise serious ceremonial proceedings.[21] More than simple comic relief—which would require explanation in its own right—Don Handelman insists that the sacred clown performs "crucial functions of boundary-dissolution, of processuality,

---

[15] Jean Muteba Rahier, *Kings for Three Days: The Play of Race & Gender in an Afro-Ecuadorian Festival* (Urbana, Chicago, and Springfield: University of Illinois Press, 2013).

[16] Jacob Pandian, "Symbolic Inversions. An Interpretation of Contrary Behavior in Ritual," *Anthropos* 96, no. 2 (2001), 558.

[17] Ibid., 560–61.

[18] Joyce Burkhalter Flueckiger, *When the World Becomes Female: Guises of a South Indian Goddess* (Bloomington and Indianapolis: Indiana University Press, 2013), 2–3.

[19] Ibid., 213.

[20] Barbara C. Myerhoff, *Peyote Hunt: The Sacred Journey of the Huichol Indians* (Ithaca, NY: Cornell University Press, 1974), 147–48.

[21] Don Handelman, "The Ritual-Clown: Attributes and Affinities," *Anthropos* 76, no. 3/4 (1981), 323.

reflexivity, for the organization itself of such rites"[22]—that is, the ribald, sometimes inappropriate and perverse actions of the clown help to make the ritual work and shed light on the processes by which rituals, religion, power, and society are made.

Mikhail Bakhtin famously writes about the complex of rituals known as "carnival," festivities where order and hierarchy evaporate in outbursts of "excessiveness, superabundance, the tendency to transgress all limits, endless enumerations, and accumulation of synonyms."[23] Throughout *Rabelais and His World*, Bakhtin refers to "transgressing the limits"—the limits of power, of language, of the body (e.g., through feasting and sexual indulgence), of truth itself. Carnival, of which American Mardi Gras or Halloween is a faint survival, "celebrated *temporary liberation from the prevailing truths of the established order;* it marked the suspension of all hierarchical rank, privileges, norms and prohibitions. Carnival was the true feast of time, the feast of *becoming, change and renewal.* It was *hostile to all that was immortalized and completed.*"[24]

Like all instances of liminality in Turner's ritual theory, the suspension or inversion of order and truth is risky. Of course, no one can live indefinitely in a liminal state; the transgressive moment will end. And ideally, order and truth are never in mortal danger: the king will be reinstalled, sexual norms will be re-imposed, the gods will be reseated in their temples. The ritual is always, as Terry Eagleton puts it, "a licensed affair in every sense, a permissible rupture of hegemony."[25] After all, the authorities sanction and condone and provide security so that it can happen but not get too rambunctious. Paradoxically, it is the order that allows the inversion, perhaps precisely so that a real revolution does not occur (i.e., rituals of reversal are not necessarily rituals of *rebellion*). People are expected not to carry their transgressions across the line that separates carnival from "real life" (as they say, what happens in Vegas, stays in Vegas); that would be actual disobedience. Instead, symbolic inversion remains a game played on a circumscribed field—a game, potentially, with real and positive effects but one that is not allowed to persist outside of the circumscribed ritual time and place. It is, in the end, a legal illegality, an ordered disorder, a moral immorality, which is why men, authorities, upper castes, etc. usually find the exceptions funny and not offensive.

Despite the fact that carnival reigned throughout the Middle Ages in Europe (including insults and ridicule of the clergy and the Pope), it was a

---

[22] Handelman, "The Ritual-Clown," 321.

[23] Mikhail Bakhtin, *Rabelais and His World*, trans. Hélène Iswolsky (Bloomington, IN: Indiana University Press, 1984 [1965]), 306.

[24] Ibid., 10, emphasis added.

[25] Terry Eagleton, *Walter Benjamin: Towards a Revolutionary Criticism* (London: Verso, 1981), 148.

facet of vernacular religion and never an official teaching of the Church. Protestantism had even less use for it, disapproving of revelry in general and instigating the kind of unrelieved regime of truth experienced by the Polynesians. Crushed under the weight of order, Christianity was deadly serious, unable to laugh at itself. At its worst, any exceeding of the limits specified by authorities was branded as "evil."[26] But if mankind cannot live permanently in liminality, maybe we cannot live permanently *without* a periodic dose of liminality: if Lewis Hyde, to whom we will return shortly, is correct, "Unless they can incorporate internal forces of transgression, organic structures are in danger of dying from their own articulation."[27] To find systems and characters that integrate transgression into structure like the ritual clown, we must look beyond Christianity and its god.

The Shaman:
Mutable Multiplicity

A theology or religious studies that focuses exclusively on god(s) and other spirits is also impoverished because of the wealth of *human* roles in the world's religions; humans are as much religious/spiritual actors as god(s) and spirits, and it is often only through humans that god(s) and spirits are known and felt.

As in any other field of culture, there are some people who enjoy, and suffer, privileged knowledge and power of the spiritual world. These religious specialists are amazingly diverse across cultures, including diviners and oracles, sorcerers and witches, priests and sacred clowns, but among the most widespread around the world, with the most potential to inform on contemporary politics and society, is the shaman.

From the Tungus (Siberia) word *šaman*, the category of shaman covers a rich array of ritual practitioners, most commonly associated with healing and often, colloquially and misleadingly, dubbed witchdoctors or medicine men. Conventionally, a shaman is a person with unique gifts to communicate and interact with the spirit world, perhaps through a "spirit-familiar" like an animal. These personal gifts may be inherited (the talent for shamanism frequently passes along family lines) or idiosyncratic, related to the individual's capacity for spiritual experiences (dreams, visions, out-of-body-experiences, and such); either way, it is usually developed through apprenticeship and initiation. Once fully fledged, the shaman can perform cures by manipulating objects, including the patient's body, and by traveling to the spiritual realm to speak, and sometimes to fight, with afflicting spirits.

---

[26] Agnes Horvath and Arpad Szakolczai, *The Political Sociology and Anthropology of Evil: Tricksterology* (London and New York: Routledge, 2020), xii.

[27] Lewis Hyde, *Trickster Makes This World: Mischief, Myth, and Art* (New York: Farrar, Straus, and Giroux, 1998), 258.

Because of the shaman's ability to detach the spirit or soul from his/her body to send it to the spiritual plane, Mircea Eliade characterizes shamanism as the "technique of ecstasy," not of pleasure, as shamanism is often painful, but of ex-stasis, of standing outside the self (from the Greek *ek*-"out" + *histanai* "place").[28]

The world's shamans include the !Kung or Ju/hoansi master of *n/um*, introduced earlier. Spiritual power was mostly acquired by dancing into trance; those who demonstrated skill at the trance state (*kia*) were said to receive *n/um* from the gods, who put the power in songs and visions; another source for the apprentice was senior shamans, who gave their juniors *n/um* "to drink" by shooting them with invisible arrows of power by snapping their fingers. Fortunately, there was an infinite supply of *n/um* in the world, so about half of men and one-third of women succeeded in their spiritual quest. !Kung shamans began their healing work by singing and chanting until the *n/um* stored at the base of the spine heated and boiled, rising up the spine in a painful manner. They fell, literally, into a trance, the body collapsing on the ground as the soul departed to the spiritual dimension. As a disembodied spirit, they might struggle with the ancestors (*//gauwasi*) or, in the case of especially serious illness, the great god *Gao Na*. Shaman, still in trance, regained their senses and conducted "operations" that included rubbing their own sweat on the patients, with the belief that the sweat of the shaman is spiritually potent. They also practiced a technique called *twe* that entailed pulling the sickness out of the victim. The shaman eventually "swam" back to consciousness.[29]

In Australian Aboriginal societies, the transformation of an ordinary person into a shaman began with alteration to the person's body. For some Aboriginal shamans, the process involved symbolic (although the Aboriginals did not consider it symbolic at all) replacement of internal organs with other substances, such as crystals; significantly, healing also often featured removing intrusive objects like stones or feathers from the bodies of patients. An Inuit shaman-in-training might be symbolically (again, that is *our* interpretation, not theirs) killed and therefore no longer entirely alive as a human.

Ongoing research into shamanism has yielded a much more sophisticated understanding of the social and psychological nature of the role, along with its ontological and political implications. First, the line between the shaman and the priest (and other religious specialists) is a porous one. Two illustrative examples are the Huichol (Mexico) *mara'akame* and Cubeo (northwestern Amazon) *paye* who combine the function of shaman, priest, and leader. As memorably depicted in Barbara

---

[28] Mircea Eliade, *Shamanism: Archaic Techniques of Ecstasy*, trans. Willard R. Trask (Princeton, NJ: Princeton University Press, 1964), 4.

[29] Katz, *Boiling Energy*.

Myerhoff's *Peyote Hunt*, the *mara'akame* provided standard healing services, using divination to determine the cause of illness and relying on his spirit-familiar to access the spirit world and transform himself into animals. But he also acted like a priest during the annual ceremonies of *tuki*, officiated at public ritual events, and guided members on the pilgrimage to Wirikuta, the Huichol spiritual homeland, to hunt for peyote—in these various capacities admonishing, teaching, modeling, explaining, and advocating "all that it means to be Huichol."[30] Meanwhile, the Cubeo *paye* underwent a rather conventional shamanic apprenticeship and performed the familiar shamanic function, but his position and knowledge were not as eccentric as that of classic shamans. Rather, more like a priest, entering and executing the role of *paye* involved mastering a set body of religious doctrine and practice. He was not just a curer but an "authority," possessing and imparting knowledge that he had acquired from older masters and from his own observations. He was, in the words of Irving Goldman, "the trusted investigative reporter, the ethnographer of hidden worlds."[31]

Further, perhaps like every ethnographer, the shaman is not merely a bearer of information from faraway worlds but a transformed person as a result of the experience. Zeljko Jokic makes this point forcefully in his study of the Yanomami shaman or *shapori*. Significantly, the term *shapori* is related to the word *shapono*, a dwelling, both human and supernatural: humans reside in a *shapono*, and *hekura* spirits inhabit one too. In shamanic initiation, the shaman calls various specifically-named *hekura* into himself, inviting them "into the shapori's body"; in so doing, "he also transforms into a hekura or, to say it better, assumes the identity as a living hekura-in-flesh."[32] Or more correctly and profoundly, the shaman changes into multiple hekura, becomes a home for a number of visiting spirits. Consequently, he is no longer an individual but "a unified multiplicity of all of his embodied spirits and also one of the spirits. He is a total but divided being: a fractal multiple 'one.'"[33] He becomes a "living ancestor," an incarnated spirit—or many incarnated spirits. At the same time, his individual body is remade into a "cosmic body—a microcosm of other hekura and a matrix for the full manifestation of the Yanomami macrocosm and any of its constitutive components."[34]

---

[30] Myerhoff, *Peyote Hunt*, 94–95.

[31] Irving Goldman, *Cubeo Hehenewa Religious Thought: Metaphysics of a Northwestern Amazonian People* (New York: Columbia University Press, 2004), 300–1.

[32] Zeljko Jokic, *The Living Ancestors: Shamanism, Cosmos, and Cultural Change among the Yanomani of the Upper Orinoco* (New York and Oxford: Berghahn, 2015), 73.

[33] Ibid., 74.

[34] Ibid., 135.

The Yanomami *shapori*, as an embodied multiplicity of spirits, is unstable, and this may be the real essence of the shaman. The unique shamanic position, and message, consists not only of a shift of consciousness or awareness from the mundane to the spiritual but of life as a *permanent liminal, flux, or chaotic state*. Western civilization and Christianity again tend to value order as the norm and to dread chaos, flux, or fluidity as the (threatening) exception. In other societies like Bugkalot (also known as Ilongot, northern Philippines), reality is "contingent, fragmentary, perpetually assuming a coherence and stability that swiftly dissolves," in which the shaman or *agoy'en* plays a crucial role.[35] Flux or chaos (*gongot*) is a constant trait of the *agoy'en*, which grants him access to the spirits and to magical powers. Through their actions, including telling stories, the specialists "seek to momentarily establish an order of their own within chaos," limiting the ability of the shape-shifting spirits (*be'tang*) to penetrate human bodies and minds.[36] The ethnographer here, Henrik Mikkelsen, astutely suggests that this new view of the shaman challenges traditional cosmology with the alternative of "chaosmology."

The people of the Blackfoot nation (northern Great Plains) also grasp this transformation. Any individual might undertake a vision quest, seeking a spiritual vision. For the ordinary person, this is usually a one-time experience, "a temporary submission of personal agency to agencies of spirits (good or bad), who may visit questers where they sit, take them on soul flight journeys, or even attack them in the night"; however, apprentice shamans "submit so much of their personal agency to spirits through progressive self-sacrifice that they become like the spirits insofar as they are poised in a liminal state between life and death, humanity and Creator."[37] The Blackfoot "Creator," though, is not exactly a being like the Christian god, and "creation" was not a single Genesis-time

Fig. 17 Mongolian shamans preparing for a ritual, Blue Pearl annual ICE festival at Khovsgol Lake, Mongolia, March 3, 2019

---

[35] Henrik H. Mikkelsen, "Chaosmology: Shamanism and Personhood among the Bugkalot," *HAU: Journal of Ethnographic Theory* 6, no. 1 (2016), 189.

[36] Mikkelsen, "Chaosmology," 201.

[37] Shayne A. P. Dahl, "The Vision Quest as a Progressive Self-sacrifice: The Permeable Agency of a Blackfoot Medicine Man" (paper presented at the annual meeting of the American Anthropological Association, Montreal, Quebec, 2011).

event. Rather, the Blackfoot term *Ihtsipaitapiiyo'pa* means "source of life" or, once more, "flux." All reality is flux, and the ascetic feats that attract a vision push a person into this state or process of flux. A human being who assumes this effort repeatedly, like a shaman, "becomes 'near flux' for the remainder of their lifetime"; they become like a spirit and acquire the "ability to see, communicate with and become permeated or possessed by spirits."[38]

What happens when permeation and possession become the condition not of a few select specialists but of an entire society? For the Darhad of Mongolia, as for the Yanomami, the Bugkalot, and the Blackfoot, shamanism is not quite a "religion" in the orthodox sense of a system of beliefs or propositions but rather a worldview or ontology, one specifically and vividly premised on *transition*. The shaman's expertise in Darhad society, explains Morten Axel Pedersen, is to adopt and move between perspectives—worldly and spiritual—that is, to inhabit "fluid and multiple" positions, to perform transformations.[39] The shamanic ontology is "perpetual metamorphosis, malleability, and fluidity expressed in the unpredictable movements of wild animals and the inchoate trajectories of the shamanic spirits."[40] Pedersen suggests that we think of spirits less as "beings" and more as pure movement or transition—"processes" more than "persons."

Indeed, more than pure and eternal flux—or *because* they are pure and eternal flux—the spirits "are comical almost by definition"; the shamanic way "seems to be all about the explosion of dimension and the proliferation of asymmetries through deliberate acts of unbalancing and decentering."[41] In a word, "Play is what shamanic spirits essentially *are*: inherently multiple and labile agents of change, which exist in a state of perpetual transformation."[42] In stark contrast to "the liturgy-heavy rituals of the Catholic Church," or the dogma-heavy sermons of Protestant sects, Darhad shamanism "celebrates the irreducible fluidity of all signification processes" including *meaning and truth.*[43]

Shaman, then, are the humans who are most like the spirits, able to change and transform; they are also "the knot of knots in the community," able to integrate in their persons the multiple and shifting processes of spiritual/social life.[44] And in the traditional context, the shaman could contain that multiplicity and flux to/within him/herself. However, in post-

---

[38] Dahl, "The Vision Quest," 7.

[39] Morten Axel Pedersen, *Not Quite Shamans: Spirit Worlds and Political Lives in Northern Mongolia* (Ithaca, NY and London: Cornell University Press, 2011), 67.

[40] Ibid., 164.

[41] Ibid., 205.

[42] Ibid., 206.

[43] Ibid., 211.

[44] Ibid., 165.

socialist Mongolia—and in ever more of the twenty-first century world—people confront "a growing sense of confusion and uncertainty," resulting in declining standards of living and accelerating and seemingly arbitrary changes of lifestyle.[45] For people with a shamanic mindset, coping with the retreat of the state in the wake of globalization and neoliberalism and thrown upon the untender mercies of the free market, "the spirits and the market were both variations on one immanent state of transition."[46] Unseen and incomprehensible forces seem to emerge from the void to swarm the individual, the family, and the society. The "market" and the "state" have no face yet many faces, and they are as uncanny as any spirit. Especially compared to the almost suffocating stability of communism, capitalism and democracy exhibit a "lability and capriciousness of forms" that curiously resemble shamanic reality. For the Darhad vulnerable to the modern global system, "the restless spirits simply *were* uncertainty as such; they were materializations, actualizations, instantiations, and condensations of the all-pervasive state of cosmological turmoil variously called 'democracy,' 'transition,' or 'the age of the market.'"[47] This situation might be manageable if there were competent shamans among the people, able to absorb and control the agitated spirits. But there are not enough shamans today, and the ones that exist are "not quite shamans," leaving the population exposed to a world infested by invisible and unstable supra-individual movement.

The Trickster: Chaotic Creator

Eshu-Elegba is a god of the Yoruba (west Africa), associated with a number of diverse but related social spaces—"crossroads, compound entrances, market places, king's palaces, shrines within compounds, and divining sessions."[48] What these places have in common is mystery and liminality, thresholds betwixt and between. It is easy to see how crossroads, entrances, shrines, and ceremonies are liminal, but from the Yoruba viewpoint the market is also a "marginal world, a place where the unexpected can occur and fortunes can be reversed"; there, as in all these locations, "Order is fragile" due to the "welter and diversity of forces for good and ill, of forces of change and transformation—personal and impersonal—that pervade human experience."[49] At such sites, where the "awareness of the unexpected, of the accidental, and of fate, is heightened," that is "where

---

[45] Pedersen, *Not Quite Shamans*, 21.

[46] Ibid., 65.

[47] Ibid., 35.

[48] John Pemberton, "Eshu-Elegba: The Yoruba Trickster God," *African Arts* 9, no. 1 (1975), 22.

[49] Ibid., 25.

Eshu must be acknowledged."[50] Based on this account, John Pemberton concludes that Eshu-Elegba is a *trickster god*, associated with caprice, deception, provocation, and potential harm. He may trip you and trick you, but his trickery "must not be seen simply as deceit; it is a power," specifically the power of "secret action" and unpredictable changes of course.[51]

If there is a religious figure who even better captures or portrays the shifting winds of power, the intrinsic disorderliness of order, the thrilling and fertile randomness of it all, it is the trickster. The trickster is probably also an excellent prototype or paradigm for political theology, especially because, unlike the shaman, the trickster is often (but not always) a god himself. His wicked divinity builds exception into the system—and builds the system out of exception.

The trickster, also known by names like the "sacred fool" and the "clever hero," is a widely distributed trope throughout the world's cultures and religions, so much so that Carl Jung believed he was an archetype. As Norman O. Brown and Lewis Hyde each point out, ancient Greek mythology depicted the trickster in such divine or semi-divine characters as Prometheus and Hermes (Mercury in Roman religion), the latter an illegitimate son of Zeus, messenger of the gods who was able to move between the natural and supernatural realms, "mercurial figure," deity of boundaries whose name derives from the Greek word for stone-heap or boundary stone, and protector of human travelers, merchants—who, in the Greek imagination, "cross the boundary" to do business—and thieves (Brown crowns him the "patron of stealthy action in general").[52] The trickster comes under many guises in Africa and is best represented in Norse mythology by the god Loki.

Also familiar in Native American narrative, the American trickster is usually not a god but an animal, especially the wily coyote, fox, or hare. Michael Carroll reckons that the North American trickster is generally not a clever hero but a "selfish buffoon" because "so much of the trickster's

Fig. 18 Statue of Eshu-Elegbara, from Oyo, southwest Nigeria, c1920

---

[50] Pemberton, "Eshu-Elegba," 25.

[51] Ibid., 26.

[52] Norman O. Brown, *Hermes the Thief: The Evolution of a Myth* (New York: Vintage Books, 1969 [1947]), 8.

activity is oriented toward the gratification of his enormous appetites for food and sex, and 'buffoon' because the elaborate deceits that the trickster devises in order to satisfy these appetites so often backfire and leave the trickster looking incredibly foolish."[53] One of the earliest sustained examinations of the Native American trickster is Paul Radin's 1956 book on the Winnebago character *Wakdjunkaga*, which translates as "the tricky one." In one version of the myth, *Wakdjunkaga* is the chief of the tribe yet strongly anti-social or "desocialized," "an utter fool, a breaker of the most holy taboos, a destroyer of the most sacred objects," a liar and killer; "No ethical values exist for him.... He is still living in his unconscious, mentally a child."[54] But the Winnebago trickster, typical of sacred fools and wicked heroes across cultures, is not all bad; like Prometheus, his treachery brings benefits to mankind:

> Trickster is at one and the same time creator and destroyer, giver and negator, he who dupes others and who is always duped himself. He wills nothing consciously. At all times he is constrained to behave as he does from impulses over which he has no control. He knows neither good nor evil and yet he is responsible for both. He possesses no values, moral or social, is at the mercy of his passions and appetites, yet through his actions all values come into being.[55]

Surely humanity's reaction to such a character is shock and horror? But no, in many if not all places—and as with symbolic inversions and ritual clowning—the prime response is laughter: "Laughter, humor, and irony permeate everything Trickster does. The reaction of the audience in aboriginal societies to both him and his exploits is prevailingly one of laughter tempered by awe."[56]

Harold Scheub compares the trickster and the hero, ranking the "divine trickster" one step beneath the "creator god," combining "the perfection of the gods and the villainy of the nether forces. He comes to embody a period of chaos, upheaval, change" as the "undifferentiated energy of the cosmos."[57] An inferior character, the "profane" or worldly trickster, falls below the "culture hero" and the "epic hero" as the amoral and undomesticated hunger whose only goal is to feed his appetites (and

---

[53] Michael R. Carroll, "The Trickster as Selfish-Buffoon and Culture Hero," *Ethos* 12, no. 2 (1984), 106.

[54] Paul Radin, *The Trickster: A Study in American Indian Mythology* (London: Routledge and Kegan Paul, 1956), 133.

[55] Ibid., ix.

[56] Ibid., x.

[57] Harold Scheub, *Trickster and Hero: Two Characters in the Oral and Written Traditions of the World* (Madison: The University of Wisconsin Press, 2012), unnumbered page.

therefore anti-social just the same). Scheub portrays both tricksters colorfully and usefully:

> The profane or earth-bound trickster is, like the divine trickster, obscene, aggressive, selfish, amoral. In this, he is closest to the basest of humans. He lacks the sublime connection with the gods ... [but] he also creates in the sense that *he creates a world of illusion; he imposes his own corrupt sense of order on the real world.* An agent of chaos, he disrupts harmony; when he establishes harmony, *it is according to his own whim*, his own sense of order. Trickster combines horror and glee: his is the comedy of the grotesque.... [H]e is a grotesque, a rootless, unattached individual *who must secure his own survival and psychological wellbeing in a society that espouses traditional values while actually sanctioning dehumanizing modes of behavior....* [H]e is an outsider [who] undergoes a rude awakening, or initiation, that shocks him into an awareness of what he must do to survive.
>
> The trickster is outrageous. Humans move from one state to another, but the trickster's is the liminal state, the state of betwixt and between. Trickster is undifferentiated energy, *ungovernable*. He may appear tame, but in the next instant he shows that he is not. In the trickster and hero, all is change, transformation. Enormous untamed energy is in the process of being controlled, funneled. *He is always reinventing the world, testing boundaries, relearning the possibilities.*[58]

Consequently, it is futile to impose our "moral framework" on the trickster; a Nietzschean overman, he operates beyond good and evil. Non-normality and exception are his native state; he thrives in "doing things to leaders that we dare not do, saying things that we dare not say. Trickster is amiable at times, brutal at others. He is unpredictable.... He is the clown, who makes one laugh ... but nervously."[59]

For the trickster, Scheub concludes, "everything is identity," and "disguise, deception, and illusion" are his secret weapons. He is "outrageous, obscene, death-dealing, uncaring, ignoble ... ribald, aggressive, selfish, without moral compass."[60] Yet this superficially irredeemable character "also creates in the sense that he establishes a world of illusion; he imposes his own corrupt sense of order on the real world."[61] In him, we can view a deeper truth in the lies: by breaking order, *and only by breaking order*, is making order possible. The trickster is relatively uncivilized, but in his stories, Carroll notes, he is "often the agent responsible for creating the

---

[58] Scheub, *Trickster and Hero*, 6, emphasis added.
[59] Ibid., 7.
[60] Ibid., 34.
[61] Ibid.

conditions that allowed for the development of human civilization."[62] As a disruptor, whether or not a creator or an inventor, he necessarily changes the old structure and replaces it with a new structure, which is our current structure and which depends on a Turnerian voyage through anti-structure and undifferentiation, a crossing of boundaries and thresholds. Whether the change is for the good is a matter of opinion: were humans better off before Prometheus brought us fire, or before, according to Plato, Hermes gave us language, or before, in other traditions, tricksters taught us agriculture or tool-making or other previously unavailable and perhaps forbidden knowledge—including the knowledge of good and evil? (And is Eden's snake the original Judeo-Christian trickster?) It really makes no difference in the end: we have those skills, those resources, that knowledge now because the trickster made it happen. We ultimately live in the trickster's world.

Most importantly, like the shaman, according to Lewis Hyde's extensive analysis (fittingly titled *Trickster Makes the World*), the trickster "is the mythic embodiment of ambiguity and ambivalence, doubleness and duplicity, contradiction and paradox."[63] And like all myth and ritual, as described in the previous chapter, the trickster, while acting in the past, is also a future-perfect character: when he is finished, the world will be or will have been as he left it. This makes him a thoroughly political-theological figure, so much so that Hyde comments, whimsically or not, that the trickster "makes a good politician, especially in a democracy."[64]

The key political-theological insight of the trickster is not just that creation comes from/with destruction, or order from/with chaos, or truth from/with lies; we are all accustomed today to the notion of "creative destruction." The insight is that creation and order can only come *from outside of creation and order*; there is nowhere else for them to come from. Inside, there is nothing but procedure, compliance with laws and norms; outside is where all the alternatives dwell. Bringing a new alternative requires crossing the boundary from outside to inside, and *someone must decide which boundary to cross and what to bring across*. This is what Schmitt really means to say, or should have meant to say, when he talks about the sovereign, the law, and the exception: order, structure, law, power, and their institutional (that is, habitual, settled) forms are mysterious, uncanny, not entirely predictable or explicable. A Schmittian sovereign is like a trickster or shaman, interrupting the normal, making visible the flux that is always there but usually ignored or denied, and demonstrating the fragility and contingency of our truths, political and otherwise.

---

[62] Carroll, "The Trickster as Selfish Buffoon and Culture Hero," 106.

[63] Lewis Hyde, *Trickster Makes This World: Mischief, Myth, and Art* (New York: Farrar, Straus, and Giroux, 1998), 7.

[64] Ibid., 53.

Our contention here is not only that the trickster, along with the shaman, is good for thinking about political theology, but that he is—both of them are—better for thinking about political theology than god(s), especially monotheistic god(s). Indeed, Hyde muses that there are no modern tricksters, precisely because they only exist before theism, or at most in polytheism where a trickster-god can frolic alongside good (but not all-good) deities. Monotheism, a totalizing (if not totalitarian) thought-system, has no tolerance for contradiction and paradox, inconsistency, transformation, flux, and multiplicity. Sure, the monotheistic god works in mysterious ways, and such a god may seem paradoxical to us (that is, when measured by the standard of reality), but a god who is eternal and eternally one disallows multiplicity or serious system transformation. Reality is sealed, set in stone. There are no more rituals of reversal (no joking about the god, no pulling the god down in playful disrespect), no more symbolic inversions, no more Polynesian potential for sanctioned iconoclasm. Deceit, boundary-crossing, wicked fun, even innovation are demonized; there is no category for such behavior other than *evil*; no wonder, as Pemberton mentions, Christian missionaries to West Africa associated Eshu-Elegba with the devil. But Hyde understands that tricksters are not evil, and Satan is not a trickster. They inhabit different worlds.

In the end, the trickster reflects reality more faithfully than does a monotheistic, omnipotent, omnibenevolent god. All experience suggests that the world *is* multiple, fluid, paradoxical, immanently breakable and makeable—that is, vulnerable to a strong and amoral, selfish, or ignorant will. Such wills are a permanent dimension of human society, though they may feel so foreign that they appear to descend from the heavens. Sometimes the trickster's will is entertaining, always thrilling—again the sheer intoxication of the Nietzschean will to power, or minimally the plebeian pleasure of kicking the king. But Agnes Horvath and Arpad Szakolczai in their inspired proposal for a field of "tricksterology" warn that the trickster, the unrepentant rule-breaker, the amoral actor, the *decider*, "presents a permanent threat to any human community—and of the greatest threat, the threat of unreality." We must be on guard, since a trickster "or rather a trickster logic can easily gain the upper hand."[65]

Hail to the (Mis)Chief

In America, one likely candidate for the protagonist of a reborn trickster myth is the confidence man, especially as he appears in literature and film (most actual confidence men don't have the range of imaginary ones, and come to sadder ends). Some have even argued that the

---

[65] Agnes Horvath and Arpad Szakolczai, *The Political Sociology and Anthropology of Evil: Tricksterology* (London and New York: Routledge, 2020), 5.

confidence man is a covert American hero. We enjoy it when he comes to town, even if a few people get their bank accounts drained, because he embodies things that are actually true about America but cannot be openly declared (as, for example, the degree to which capitalism lets us steal from our neighbors, or the degree to which institutions like the stock market require the same kind of confidence that criminal con men need)....

If by "America" we mean the land of rootless wanderers and the free market, the land not of natives but of immigrants, the shameless land where anyone can say anything at any time, the land of opportunity and therefore of opportunists, the land where individuals are allowed and even encouraged to act without regard to community, then trickster has not disappeared. "America" is his apotheosis; he's pandemic.[66]

We began our journey in this book, and modern political theology begins its journey, with Carl Schmitt's pronouncement that the sovereign is s/he who decides on the exception. This formulation presupposes (1) that there is such a person or position in society and (2) that society with its laws and institutions is except-able, that it is possible to come at the law and political-legal institutions from "outside," as it were. It presupposes, in a word, that law is mutable and that this mutability is in human hands. The shaman and the trickster prove that the second presupposition is absolutely true—and they also prove that the person who manages mutability need not be precisely a sovereign. There are many individuals who can see through the illusion of stability and of unity and can, like a mortal Prometheus, bring new light to society.

On that ground, we considered Trump and his administration as the exception, finding that he is more exaggeration, crescendo, and apotheosis than exception. In American history with its enduring republican theology and imperial presidency, in contemporary world politics with its building wave of right-wing populists, and in the pathos of the twentieth century with its authoritarians and totalitarians, Trump is a rather ordinary creature. We even concluded that he is not a particularly distinguished authoritarian and populist—not as extreme as Fujimori, not as sophisticated as Orbán, not nearly as malignant as Hitler or Stalin.

Ultimately, taking seriously Trump's penchant for lying, and transcending conventional academic/Christian preoccupations with belief and god(s) in favor of myth and ritual on the one hand and shamans and tricksters on the other, we arrive at a different angle on Trump, on present-day politics, and on political theology itself. "The sovereign" might not be the ideal concept for interpreting today's politics, if only because no one

---

[66] Hyde, *Trickster Makes the World*, 11.

thinks that Trump is a sovereign (except perhaps Trump himself, but that is more his ignorance of constitutional and liberal democracy than a real grab for absolute power, for example the pretense of presidential jurisdiction over the states which demonstrates that Trump really has no idea what the powers of the presidency are; further, as feeble and limited as the resistance is, American institutions from the Congress to the courts have mounted some opposition, as in denying his protestations of total presidential immunity from investigation) and because the very notion of "sovereign" is a relatively recent one, if by recent we mean a few centuries. Much older, more universal, and more archetypal images may, ironically, take us further in understanding contemporary politics while also emphasizing the inherent frailty and insubstantiality of power and the political systems constructed out of power, the paradoxical and miraculous quality of it all.

No character in religion and folklore reminds us more squarely of the artifice of the real—what Hyde sagely calls the trap of culture—than the trickster. So, if Trump is not a sovereign, is he a trickster? A small number of commentators have ventured the opinion. Rosario Forlenza and Bjern Thomassen, writing before the 2016 election when those with eyes could see Trump for what he was, reject Trump "charisma" in favor of Trump the "political trickster." Rehearsing everything we have learned—that the trickster is grotesque, prankish, dishonest, shadowy, ambivalent but also "a 'second creator'—a nullity, a nobody, a prankster who yet, under special circumstances, creates the world in his image," they draw the connection:

> Trump's statements as well as his political program are trickster-like down to detail. His program is slippery, undefinable. He will defy questions relating to political substance, and he will smoothly change position on key policy areas, cunningly pretending that such a change of opinion never took place. He is proud of his ability to charm women, but he seems unable to commit to lasting relations. His charming laughter and boyish innocence can in a split second freeze into a violent, sinister attack on the interlocutor. His laughter is that of a demonic clown.[67]

Keir Martin and Jakob Krause-Jensen, echoing a point we made in the fifth chapter about the strange appeal of Trump even for people who do not share his positions, add that rather than tainting him, "it is Trump's ability to hold contradictory and mutually exclusive positions together that is the very heart

---

[67] Rosario Forlenza and Bjem Thomassen, "Decoding Donald Trump: The Triumph of Trickster Politics," Public Seminar, April 28, 2016, https://publicseminar.org/2016/04/decoding-donald-trump-the-triumph-of-trickster-politics.

of his appeal."[68] This may be as important and alarming as any specific detail about Trump himself: the trickster resonates with us still, thrills and scares us at once, but for all our vaunted rationality and secularism we are susceptible to his spell and to the general spell of non-rationality and irrationality. Part of the frisson of the trickster is that he "incarnates an oxymoronic mood or a 'fooling around' that plays at the 'unthinkable' and thereby suggests new (im)possible logics."[69] Understanding the Trump phenomenon, they reason, perhaps "means attempting to understand how contradictions and behaviors that appear to render him outside of civilized mainstream behavior from particular perspectives might be central to his appeal to millions of [followers] who feel that the civilized mainstream no longer has anything to offer them."[70] That the present moment makes the trickster alternative seem appealing to many is perhaps the most worrisome point of all.

Corey Pein goes further to assert, hopefully metaphorically, that Trump is not only a latter-day trickster but "the personification of a Norse god named Loki ... god of mischief and lies."[71] (How delicious it is to ponder American Christians, particularly evangelicals, bowing down to a pagan god.) Trump "the Insult Comic Candidate" (the essay was written months before the election) is, like Loki, "a master maligner" and all the more entertaining for it. Pein places Trump in the long line of American tricksters—not exceptional again!—including P. T. Barnum and Tom Sawyer—who reflect and activate "the dark psychic currents of the national experience" but are far from unique to the United States. "Loki has awoken. He walks among us, gaining strength, and he doesn't need your stupid vote, loser."

Of course, Trump is not Loki or any other god; he is not even exactly a trickster. If there is a more twenty-first century character that spares us the theological baggage and tethers Trump more closely to the cultural moment, it is the *troll*, another term borrowed from folklore. Matthew Flisfeder, linking Trump to the proto-fascist and Alt-Right movements, contends that the troll, as "an agent who builds a reputation by tarnishing the reputation of others ... has become one of the primary antagonists of the present, championed heroically by the racists and misogynistic meme culture of the Alt-Right. *For a culture that privileges the*

---

[68] Keir Martin and Jakob Krause-Jensen, "Trump: Transacting Trickster," *Anthropology Today* 33, no. 3 (2017), 5.

[69] Ibid., 6.

[70] Ibid., 8.

[71] Corey Pein, "Donald Trump, Trickster God," The Baffler, March 4, 2016, https://thebaffler.com/magical-thinking/donald-trump-trickster-god.

troll as its antihero, Trump, then, appears as a godsend."[72] Gabriella Coleman offers guidance on the troll motif in her study of the hacker group Anonymous. Manifesting a "desire for leaderless and high democracy," the enigmatic individuals behind Anonymous hold the same dream that prompts populist movements—immediate, unmediated, non-institutionalized action of the people.[73] And like the trickster, one of the main tools or values of the internet troll is laughter and ridicule, known in their circle as *lulz*. Derived from the internet acronym LOL (laugh out loud), Coleman, following Anonymous itself, calls it "dark humor," "a deviant style of humor and a quasi-mystical style of being," "a spirited but often malevolent brand of humor" that typically entails offensiveness, disgust, and more than a touch of cruelty.[74] Online trolls get their jollies from "the targeting of people and organizations, the desecration of reputations, and the spreading of humiliating information."[75] Like the obnoxious mythical creature, trolls "try to upset people by spreading grisly or disturbing content, igniting arguments, or engendering general bedlam,"[76] and the online Encyclopedia Dramatica praises it as "something beautiful, the anguish of a laughed-at victim transformed lol into lulz." While such conduct is anything but honorable—and we have all probably encountered it at times—Coleman expressly relates it to the ancient and venerable tradition of the trickster and his/her "burning desire to defy or defile rules, norms, and laws," in the process—whether it is their intention or not—"allowing norms to be laid bare for folk-philosophical challenge."[77]

The fact that Trump lives and breathes on Twitter like no major politician before him (more like a thirteen-year-old mean girl) makes his troll persona all the more ordinary and comprehensible, but George Hawley brings the discussion of trolling back around to politics in his presentation on the contemporary Alt-Right. Many observers fail to appreciate how far the Alt-Right strays from the mainstream Republican Party and conservatism; it is not just "conservatism-plus" but, according to Hawley, rejects the three normal conservative pillars of "moral traditionalism, economic liberty, and strong national defense. None of these conservative shibboleths seem to interest the Alt-Right."[78] The Alt-Right "despises"

---

[72] Matthew Flisfeder, "'Trump'—What Does the Name Signify? Or, Protofascism and the Alt-Right: Three Contradictions of the Present Conjuncture," *Cultural Politics* 14, no. 1 (2018), 12, emphasis added.

[73] Gabriella Coleman, *Hacker, Hoaxer, Whistleblower, Spy: The Many Faces of Anonymous* (London and New York: Verso, 2014), 106.

[74] Ibid., 2–4.

[75] Ibid., 19.

[76] Ibid., 4.

[77] Ibid., 34.

[78] George Hawley, *Making Sense of the Alt-Right* (New York: Columbia University Press, 2017), 4.

mainstream conservatives, branding them as "cuckservatives" (a portmanteau of cuckold and conservative) and condescendingly labeling anyone who disagrees with them as a "normie"—and their recipe for social change, emblazoned in the title of Angela Nagle's book on Trump and the Alt-Right, is to "kill all normies."[79] Surprisingly secular, even anti-Christian, compared to standard conservatism, Hawley associates the Alt-Right principally with white nationalist and identitarian politics.

In their communication style, we again see the trickster-troll: "An Internet troll is someone who fosters discord online, provoking strong emotional reactions from readers and often changing the topic of conversation."[80] The Alt-Right is a very decentralized entity, but its supporters tend toward the "ostentatiously vulgar and offensive, violating every contemporary taboo related to race, ethnicity, religion, and gender," which includes displaying Nazi symbols and repeating the infamous white nationalist "Fourteen Words" ("We must secure the existence of our people and a future for white children").[81] And, as these tendencies imply, the Alt-Right's program does not end at style but pushes a radically non-conservative agenda, one that appears "willing to reject America—openly desiring the collapse of the country or the creation of a new white-nationalist regime that has nothing in common with the constitutional government the nation has known since its inception."[82] What we have, then, is a rupture from the republican theology of most previous American political theologies from Mormonism to Christian Identity. One of its many spokesmen and theorists, extreme libertarian and "anarcho-capitalist philosopher" Hans-Hermann Hoppe, affiliated with the right-wing Ludwig von Mises Institute, almost gleefully declares that "fundamental doubts concerning the virtues of the American system have resurfaced."[83] Christening democracy as a god, *but one that has failed*, he offers qualified praise for monarchy, arguing that, "*If* one must have a state, defined as an agency that exercises a compulsory territorial monopoly of ultimate decision-making (jurisdiction) and of taxation, then it is economically and ethically advantageous to choose

---

[79] Angela Nagle, *Kill All Normies: The Online Culture Wars from Tumblr and 4chan to the Alt-Right and Trump* (Winchester, UK and Washington, DC: Zero Books, 2017).

[80] Hawley, *Making Sense of the Alt-Right*, 19.

[81] Ibid., 68.

[82] Ibid., 81.

[83] Hans-Hermann Hoppe, *Democracy: The God that Failed* (New Brunswick, NJ: Transaction, 2007), xiii. The foolishness of this philosophy from someone who ostensibly champions private property is almost too painful to laugh at. The monarch may enjoy property rights, but Hoppe the peasant or serf does not, nor do the lower nobles. The monarch can always deprive the nobility of their estates and can commandeer the land, livestock, and even wife of the commoner.

monarchy over democracy."[84] "Give me sovereignty" seems to replace Patrick Henry's historic cry for liberty: a monarchy, or what Hoppe calls "private government ownership" (in which the country's wealth is "the ruler's private estate"), will be better managed and ultimately more successful and orderly than a "publicly owned government" in which "anyone"—that is, the citizens—can "become the government's caretaker."[85]

More pertinent, and truer, is Hoppe's recognition that "the course of human history is determined by ideas, *whether they are true or false*,"[86] and if we add that to his plea for a revival of sovereignty, then we reach the point where Schmitt meets Trump (and Schopenhauer, shamans, and tricksters). It is common knowledge now that when Trump took his opening shots at truth and decency early in his campaign, condemning Mexicans as rapists and drug dealers and promising a beautiful, dictator-style wall, "the Alt-Right believed it had finally found its champion."[87] For his oblique (and sometimes not so oblique) approval of the Alt-Right, as when he commented that there were "very fine people" on both sides of the racist demonstrations in Charlottesville, Virginia or told the white-nationalist Proud Boys during a presidential debate to "stand by," Trump has earned the enthusiasm of the Alt-Right (former KKK leader David Duke just endorsed him again for president in 2020), and the Alt-Right in exchange has been energized by a president whom they believe shares their vision of America.

So, Trump is our presiding troll, our commander-in-(mis)chief with populist and authoritarian leanings, who like a trickster breaks the system because it is fun to break systems. Therefore, criticizing him for lying or undermining the Constitution or violating norms and traditions is futile. Laws, norms, traditions, the Constitution, the truth itself are all the status quo, which is the problem in the first place, and a character like Trump "doesn't want to compromise with the status quo; rather, the trickster wants to destroy the existing political structure."[88] Carried away by his own power, and schooled by a lifetime of dishonesty, resentment, and evasion, his profile is probably more that of a bully, a brute and brawler, a con man and fraudster who gets pleasure from tormenting others and knows full well that his whole career depends on illegality but does not care a whit. It was not only recently that I intuited that Trump probably *wants* to hurt someone, maybe everyone, but certainly anyone he perceives as a threat to this

---

[84] Hoppe, *Democracy*, xx.

[85] Ibid., 46.

[86] Ibid., 43, emphasis added.

[87] Hawley, *Making Sense of the Alt-Right*, 115.

[88] William K. Grevatt, "Confronting the Trickster: Crises and Opportunity in the Time of Trump—A Jungian Perspective," *Psychological Perspectives* 61, no. 1 (2018), 46, DOI: 10.1080/00332925.2018.1422922

authority and ego. He almost itched to deploy troops against the American people, with his military response to unrest in many cities which some fear as the first step toward martial law. Anne Applebaum opines that this action is theatrics, "performative authoritarianism" intended "to transmit a message": attacking protesters serves "to show just how much Trump dislikes 'liberal' Americans, 'urban' Americans, 'Democrat' Americans," just as his policy of separating immigration children from their families at the border was "a performance to show just how much the president dislikes immigrants."[89]

Undoubtedly, it is part show, the Bad Hombre Show, and political ritual. But sometimes the host of the show peeks through the character he plays. Repeatedly, Trump has exuded merriment at the thought of doing harm; for instance, confronted with hecklers at his rallies, he said:

- "I love the old days. You know what they used to do to guys like that when they were in a place like this? They'd be carried out on a stretcher, folks....I'd like to punch him in the face, I'll tell you." (Nevada, February 22, 2016)
- "We had some people, some rough guys like we have right in here. And they started punching back. It was a beautiful thing. I mean, they started punching back." (North Carolina, March 9, 2016)
- "Part of the problem and part of the reason it takes so long [to kick them out] is nobody wants to hurt each other anymore." (St. Louis, March 11, 2016)

True to form, during remarks in Michigan on October 17, 2020 he described police pushing protesters as "a beautiful thing. Then we learn that the coronavirus taskforce headed by his son-in-law, Jared Kushner, may have deliberately withheld critical medical resources because the disease was predominantly hitting Democrat-majority states, causing Americans to suffer and die for the administration's political gain. And Trump himself apparently grasped the severity of COVID-19 early in the pandemic but intentionally downplayed it, dismissing it as a hoax then and irresponsibly cheering that the country was turning the corner on the disease even as it surged to record highs in October 2020.

Meanwhile, his heartiest followers, Smith and Hanley's aggressive authoritarians who lust for a leader who will injure enemies, delight in Trump's performance. On July 24, 2020, Christian radio host Rick Wiles reminded Trump that

---

[89] Anne Applebaum, "Trump Is Putting On a Show in Portland," *The Atlantic*, July 23, 2020, https://www.theatlantic.com/ideas/archive/2020/07/trump-putting-show-portland/614521.

he is now in possession of Obama bullets—two billion 'Bama bullets. You're in possession of them now. You got the 'Bama bullets and you can put down the [insurrection] … you can put it down. You have the 'Bama bullets in your hands. You don't have to tolerate this anymore. They were purchased for the purpose of putting down an insurrection. Well, you got one, so *put the hollow-point bullets to good use and get out there and put down this communist revolution* so the rest of us can live our lives peacefully.[90]

Some, we know, take these admonitions to heart, like the militiamen who allegedly planned to kidnap, try, and execute Democratic Michigan Governor Gretchen Whitmer—to which Trump responded not by condemning the plot but by ridiculing her for doing "a terrible job," as if that somehow justifies the criminal act.

If Trump is merely a performative authoritarian, he is a good (or at least a consistent) one. But I suspect it is more than an act—and that it is a portent of when the trickster becomes the leader, when the fringe moves to the center, and when the exception becomes the norm.

Someday, Trump too shall pass; he may have passed by the time you read these words. In the final analysis, then, the important question is not whether Trump is a trickster, a populist authoritarian, a Schmittian sovereign, or even whether a sovereign is the one who decides the exception. Sovereignty and exceptionalism are a means to an analytical end, not the end itself. If Michael Freeden is correct, the goal of politics itself, and not only of sovereignty, is *finality*, not just *deciding* but *closing the question* so that no further discussion or deciding is to be done. Sovereignty in Schmitt's sense, of which present-day authoritarian populism is one genus, aspires in Freeden's thinking for "decontestation," the end of argument, in the worst case the very end of democratic competition. The essence of political-theological—or of *political-mythical*—decontestation is "reversion back to a starting point," usually if not necessarily a mythical starting point subsequently relived ritually.[91] This starting point Freeden prophetically calls "the 'big bang' of the political," which unlike the physicists' origin of the cosmos "is *the product of will*, either human or—in religious idiom—divine."[92]

---

[90] Quoted in Michael Stone, "Christian TV Host Asks Trump To Use 'Hollow-Point Bullets' On Portland Protesters,' Patheos, July 24, 2020, https://www.patheos.com/blogs/progressivesecularhumanist/2020/07/christian-tv-host-asks-trump-to-use-hollow-point-bullets-on-portland-protesters/?utm_medium=email&fbclid=IwAR1QtYC2HeZie0a0x7Vu6uRyGg0HrzBRMI_uu943YrbGPfDsEKZTpimzU-Q.

[91] Michael Freeden, *The Political Theory of Political Thinking: The Anatomy of a Practice* (Oxford and New York: Oxford University Press, 2013), 94.

[92] Ibid., 95, emphasis added.

But such political decontestation is a fantasy. A decision can be undone, as can the laws, norms, and institutions designed to facilitate *and constrain* decision. Constitutions can be amended or retired, there will be another election someday, and there is always the prospect of revolt and revolution. Politics can never be "finished," even if we put gods back in the political equation. As an "attempt to control equivocal and contingent meaning by holding it constant," the sovereignty solution "imposes a fabricated certainty on inevitable ambiguity, indeterminacy, and vagueness."[93] This is the political lesson of the shaman and trickster and of myth and ritual.

In a post-modern world, infested once again by myths and rituals, by shamans and tricksters and sacred clowns, the essential and irresolvable instability, impermanence, liquidity, flux, paradox, and comic tragedy of law, truth, society, and reality are dramatically on display. Trump may take full advantage and leave devastation in his wake, but he only confirms the perennial wisdom that our most cherished traditions, laws, and institutions are constructed, contingent, and vulnerable to a will that is determined or indifferent to transgressing them.

---

[93] Freeden, *The Political Theory*, 23–24.

Bibliography

Adorno, Theodor W., Else Frenkel-Brunswick, Daniel J. Levinson, and R. Nevitt Sanford. *The Authoritarian Personality*. New York: Harper & Row, 1950.

Agamben, Giorgio. *The Kingdom and the Glory: For a Theological Genealogy of Economy and Government*. Translated by Lorenzo Chiesa. Stanford, CA: Stanford University Press, 2011.

Alterman, Eric. *When Presidents Lie: A History of Official Deception and its Consequences*. New York and London: Viking, 2004.

Altizer, Thomas J. J. *The Gospel of Christian Atheism*. Philadelphia, PA: Westminster Press, 1966.

Ammerman, Nancy T. *Bible Believers: Fundamentalists in the Modern World*. New Brunswick, NJ and London: Rutgers University Press, 1987.

Andersen, Kurt. *Fantasyland: How America Went Haywire—A 500-Year History*. New York: Random House, 2017.

———. "How America Lost Its Mind." *The Atlantic*. December 28, 2017. https://www.theatlantic.com/magazine/archive/2017/09/how-america-lost-its-mind/534231.

Anderson, Nels. *Desert Saints: The Mormon Frontier in Utah*. Chicago and London: The University of Chicago Press, 1966 [1942].

Antal, Attila. "Nationalist Populism and Illiberalism in Hungary: Historical Origins, Current Trajectories." Lecture, Carleton University, Ottawa, Canada, May 9, 2018.

Applebaum, Anne. "Trump Is Putting On a Show in Portland." *The Atlantic*. July 23, 2020. https://www.theatlantic.com/ideas/archive/2020/07/trump-putting-show-portland/614521.

Apter, Andrew. "In Dispraise of the King: Rituals 'Against' Rebellion in South-East Africa." *Man* (new series) 18, no. 3 (1983): 521–34.

Arat-Koç, Sedef. "Culturalizing Politics, Hyper-Politicizing 'Culture': 'White' vs. 'Black Turks' and the Making of Authoritarian Populism in Turkey." *Dialectical Anthropology* 42, no. 4 (2018): 391–408.

Arendt, Hannah. *The Origins of Totalitarianism*, second enlarged ed. Cleveland, OH and New York: The World Publishing Company, 1958 [1951].

———. "Politics and Truth." Wordpress.com. Accessed June 23, 2020. https://idanlandau.files.wordpress.com/2014/12/arendt-truth-and-politics.pdf. Originally published in *The New Yorker*, February 25, 1967.

Association of Religion Data Archives. "Christian Reconstructionism." Accessed May 22, 2020. www.thearda.com/timeline/movements/movement_27.asp.

Atlantic, The. "The Twelve Tribes of American Politics." Accessed July 20, 2020. https://www.theatlantic.com/magazine/archive/2006/01/the-twelve-tribes-of-american-politics/304505.

Austin, J. L. *How To Do Things with Words*. Oxford: Clarendon, 1962.

Azadegan, Ebrahim. "Ibn 'Arabi on the Problem of Divine Hiddenness." *Journal of the Muhyiddin Ibn 'Arabi Society* 53 (2013): 49–67.

Baggini, Julian. *The Edge of Reason: A Rational Skeptic in an Irrational World*. New Haven, CT: Yale University Press, 2016.

Bakhtin, Mikhail. *Rabelais and His World*. Translated by Hélène Iswolsky. Bloomington, IN: Indiana University Press, 1984 [1965].

Balmer, Brian. "A Secret Formula, A Rogue Patent, and Public Knowledge about Nerve Gas: Secrecy as a Spatial-Epistemic Tool." *Social Studies of Science* 36, no. 5 (2006): 691–722.

Barlow, Philip L. "Chosen Land, Chosen People: Religious and American Exceptionalism Among the Mormons." *The Review of Faith and International Affairs* 10, no. 2 (2012): 51–58.

Barrington, Lowell J. "Authoritarianism." In *Ethics, Science, Technology and Engineering: A Global Resource*. 2nd ed, edited by J. Britt Holbrook, 155–58. Boston, MA: Cengage, 2014.

Beattie, John. *Bunyoro: An African Kingdom*. New York: Holt, Rinehart, and Winston, 1960.

Bell, Catherine. *Ritual Practice, Ritual Theory*. Oxford and New York: Oxford University Press, 1992.

———. *Ritual: Perspectives and Dimensions*. Oxford and New York: Oxford University Press, 1997.

Bell, Daniel M., Jr. "Trump as Mirror for the Church: Death and Despair, Hope and Resurrection of the Church." *Religions* 11, no. 3 (2020): 1–17.

Bell, Diane. *Daughters of the Dreaming*. Minneapolis: University of Minnesota Press, 1983.

Bellah, Robert N. "Civil Religion in America." *Daedalus* 96, no.1 (1967): 1–21.

Berger, Peter, and Thomas Luckmann. *The Social Construction of Reality: A Treatise in the Sociology of Knowledge*. Garden City, NY: Doubleday & Company, 1966.

Bíró-Nagy, András. "Illiberal Democracy in Hungary: The Social Background and Practical Steps in Building an Illiberal State." *Illiberal Democracies in the EU: The Visegrad Group and the Risk of Disintegration*. Barcelona: CIDOB Editions (2017): 31–44.

Birth, Kevin K. *Bacchanalian Sentiments: Musical Experience and Political Counterpoints in Trinidad*. Durham, NC: Duke University Press, 2008.

Bjork-James, Sophie. "Americanism, Trump, and Uniting the White Right." In *Beyond Populism: Angry Politics and the Twilight of Neoliberalism*, edited by Jeff Maskovsky and Sophie Bjork-James, 42–60. Morgantown: West Virginia University Press, 2020.

Bloch, Maurice. *Ritual, History, and Power: Selected Papers in Anthropology*. London: The Athlone Press, 1979.

Boer, Roland. *Political Myth: On the Use and Abuse of Biblical Themes*. Durham, NC: Duke University Press, 2009.

Bottici, Chiara. *A Philosophy of Political Myth*. Cambridge and New York: Cambridge University Press, 2007.

———. "Philosophies of Political Myth, a Comparative Look Backwards: Cassirer, Sorel, and Spinoza." *European Journal of Political Theory* 8, no. 3 (2009): 365–82.

———. "Towards a Philosophy of Political Myth," *Iris: European Journal of Philosophy and Public Debate* 3, no. 5 (2011): 31–52.

Bovens, Mark. "Analysing and Assessing Accountability: A Conceptual Framework." *European Law Journal* 13, no. 4 (2007): 447–68.

Bradley, Arthur, and Antonio Cerella. "The Future of Political Theology and the Legacy of Carl Schmitt." *Journal for Cultural Research* 20, no. 3 (2016): 205–16.

Britannica Academic. "Authoritarianism." Encyclopedia Britannica. November 2, 2017. academic-eb-com.aurarialibrary.idm.oclc.org/levels/collegiate/article/authoritarianism/3154.

Brockman, David R. "The Little-Known Theology Behind White Evangelical Support for Donald Trump," *Texas Observer*, March 29, 2018, https://www.texasobserver.org/the-little-known-theology-behind-white-evangelical-support-of-donald-trump.

Brown, Norman O. *Hermes the Thief: The Evolution of a Myth*. New York: Vintage Books, 1969 [1947].

Brüggemann, Karsten, and Andres Kasekamp. "'Singing Oneself into a Nation': Estonian Song Festivals as Rituals of Political Mobilisation." *Nations and Nationalism* 20, no. 2 (2014), 259–76.

Burlein, Ann. *Lift High the Cross: Where White Supremacy and the Christian Right Converge*. Durham, NC and London: Duke University Press, 2002.

Bustikova, Lenka. "Populism in Eastern Europe," *Comparative Politics Newsletter* 26, no. 2 (2016): 15–19.

Canovan, Margaret. *Populism*. New York: Harcourt Brace Jovanovich, 1981.

———. "Trust the People! Populism and the Two Faces of Democracy." *Political Studies* 47, no. 1 (1999): 2–16.

Carroll, Michael R. "The Trickster as Selfish-Buffoon and Culture Hero." *Ethos* 12, no. 2 (1984), 105–31.

Cernyar, Eric W. *Protecting Public Elementary School Children from Emotional and Psychological Harm by Outside Groups*. Intrinsic Dignity, 2013.

Cha, Taesuh. "The Return of Jacksonianism: The International Implications of the Trump Phenomenon." *The Washington Quarterly* 39, no. 4 (2016): 83–97.

Chalcedon Foundation. "The Creed of Christian Reconstructionism." Accessed May 22, 2020. https://chalcedon.edu/creed-of-christian-reconstruction.

———. "What We Believe." Accessed May 22, 2020. https://chalcedon.edu/credo.

Chalmers, David M. *Hooded Americanism: The History of the Ku Klux Klan*. Durham, NC: Duke University Press, 1981 [1965].

Chinn, Clark A., and William F. Brewer. "The Role of Anomalous Data in Knowledge Acquisition: A Theoretical Framework and Implications for Science Instruction." *Review of Educational Research* 63, no. 1 (1993): 1–49.

Churchwell, Sarah. *Behold, America: The Entangled History of "America First" and "The American Dream."* New York: Basic Books, 2018.

Clough, William R. "The Role of Agnomancy in the Creation and Perpetuation of Conflict." In *Visions of Conflict: International Perspectives on Values and Enmity*, edited by Brian C. Alston, 81–100. Lihue, HI: Brian C. Alston, 2010.

CNN. "Trump: 'I'm the Only One That Matters'." Accessed May 24, 2020. https://www.cnn.com/videos/politics/2017/11/03/trump-im-only-one-that-matters-fox-sot.cnn.

Coleman, Gabriella. *Hacker, Hoaxer, Whistleblower, Spy: The Many Faces of Anonymous*. London and New York: Verso, 2014.

Colvin, Jill. "Trump Claims Broad Powers He Does Not Have." Courthouse News Service, May 28, 2020. https://www.courthousenews.com/trump-claims-broad-powers-he-does-not-have.

Cook, Myra. *Donald 'MESSIAH' Trump: The Man, the Myth, the Messiah?* Oregon: American Freedom Publishing, 2016.

Cornish, Paul, Julian Lindley-French, and Claire Yorke. "Strategic Communications and National Strategy." London: The Royal Institute of International Affairs, 2011.

Cramer, Katherine J. *The Politics of Resentment: Rural Consciousness in Wisconsin and the Rise of Scott Walker.* Chicago and London: The University of Chicago Press, 2016.

Cross and the Flag, The. "The Cross and the Flag: In Memory of Gerald l. K. Smith." Accessed May 22, 2020. http://thecrossandflag.com/articles.html.

Dahl, Shayne A. P. "The Vision Quest as a Progressive Self-sacrifice: The Permeable Agency of a Blackfoot Medicine Man." Paper presented at the annual meeting of the American Anthropological Association, Montreal, Quebec, 2011.

de Tocqueville, Alexis. *Democracy in America.* Edited by J. P. Mayer. Translated by George Lawrence. Garden City, NY: Anchor Books, 1969.

de Vries, Hent. "Introduction: Before, Around, and Beyond the Theologico-Political." In *Political Theologies: Public Religions in a Post-Secular World*, edited by Hent de Vries and Lawrence E. Sullivan, 1–88. New York: Fordham University Press, 2006.

Dees, Morris. *Gathering Storm: America's Militia Threat.* New York: HarperCollins Publishers, 1996.

Dein, Simon. "The Power of Words: Healing Narratives among Lubavitcher Hasidim." *Medical Anthropology Quarterly* 16, no. 1 (2002): 41–63.

Dentan, Robert K. *Overwhelming Terror: Love, Fear, Peace, and Violence among Semai of Malaysia.* Lanham, MD: Rowman & Littlefield, 2008.

Diaz-Barriga, Miguel, and Margaret Dorsey. "Trump's Wall and the Dictator Aesthetic." *Anthropology News* 58, no. 4 (2017), e83–86.

Diehl, Paula. "Twisting Representation." In *Routledge Handbook of Global Populism*, edited by Carlos de la Torre, 129–43. London and New York: Routledge, 2019.

Dovere, Edward-Isaac. "Tony Perkins: Trump Gets 'a Mulligan' On Life, Stormy Daniels." *Politico.* January 28, 2018. https://www.politico.com/magazine/story/2018/01/23/tony-perkins-evangelicals-donald-trump-stormy-daniels-216498.

Driberg, J. H. "The Secular Aspect of Ancestor-Worship in Africa." *Journal of the Royal African Society* 35, no. 138 (1936): 1–21.

Durham, Martin. "Christian Identity and the Politics of Religion."
    Totalitarian Movements and Political Religions 9, no. 1 (2008):
    79–91.
Durkheim, Émile. *The Elementary Forms of Religious Life*. New York: The
    Free Press, 1965 [1912].
Eagleton, Terry. *Walter Benjamin: Towards a Revolutionary Criticism*.
    London: Verso, 1981.
Eliade, Mircea. *Shamanism: Archaic Techniques of Ecstasy*. Translated by
    Willard R. Trask Princeton, NJ: Princeton University Press, 1964.
———. *Myth and Reality*. Translated by Willard R. Trask. Prospect
    Heights, IL: Waveland Press, 1998 [1963].
Eller, Jack David. *Introducing Anthropology of Religion*, 2nd ed. Abingdon
    and New York: Routledge, 2015.
Elshtain, Jean Bethke. "Augustine." In *The Blackwell Companion to
    Political Theology*, edited by Peter Scott and William T.
    Cavanaugh, 35–47. Oxford: Blackwell Publishing, 2004.
Enten, Harry. "White Evangelicals Love Trump. Religious Voters? Not So
    Much." CNN. January 1, 2020.
    https://www.cnn.com/2020/01/01/politics/evangelical-support-
    trump/index.html.
Esen, Berk, and Sebnem Gumuscu. "Rising Competitive Authoritarianism in
    Turkey." *Third World Quarterly* 37, no. 9 (2016): 1581–1606.
Evans-Pritchard, E. E. *Nuer Religion*. New York and Oxford: Oxford
    University Press, 1956.
———. *Social Anthropology and Other Essays*. New York: The Free Press,
    1962.
Falcone, Jessica Marie. "Putting the 'Fun' in Fundamentalism: Religious
    Nationalism and the Split Self at Hindutva Summer Camps in the
    United States." *Ethos* 40, no. 2 (2012): 164–95.
Feinberg, Richard. "Spirit Encounters on a Polynesian Outlier: Anuta,
    Solomon Islands." In *Spirits in Culture, History, and Mind*, edited
    by Jeannette Marie Mageo and Alan Howard, 99–120. New York
    and London: Routledge, 1996.
Ferrier, James F. *Institutes of Metaphysics: The Theory of Knowing and
    Being*. Edinburgh and London: William Blackwood and Sons, 1854.
Firth, Raymond. "The Analysis of Mana." *The Journal of the Polynesian
    Society* 49, no. 196 (1940): 483–510.
Fleming, Sandy. "Nothing More Than an 'Ordinary President'." University
    of Kent. March 11, 2019.
    https://www.kent.ac.uk/news/society/21528/new-book-reveals-
    donald-trump-is-nothing-more-than-an-ordinary-president.

Flisfeder, Matthew. "'Trump'—What Does the Name Signify? Or, Protofascism and the Alt-Right: Three Contradictions of the Present Conjuncture." *Cultural Politics* 14, no. 1 (2018): 1–19.

Flood, Christopher G. *Political Myth: A Theoretical Introduction.* London and New York: Routledge, 2002.

Flueckiger, Joyce Burkhalter. *When the World Becomes Female: Guises of a South Indian Goddess.* Bloomington and Indianapolis: Indiana University Press, 2013.

Forlenza, Rosario, and Bjem Thomassen. "Decoding Donald Trump: The Triumph of Trickster Politics." Public Seminar. April 28, 2016. https://publicseminar.org/2016/04/decoding-donald-trump-the-triumph-of-trickster-politics.

Fortes, Meyer. *Religion, Morality, and the Person: Essays on Tallensi Religion.* Cambridge: Cambridge University Press, 1987.

Frankfurt, Harry G. *On Bullshit.* Princeton, NJ: Princeton University Press, 2005.

Fredrickson, Lief, Christopher Sellers, Lindsey Dillon, Jennifer Liss Ohayon, Nicholas Shapiro, Marianne Sullivan, Stephen Bocking, Phil Brown, Vanessa de la Rosa, Jill Harrison, Sara Johns, Katherine Kulik, Rebecca Lave, Michelle Murphy, Liza Piper, Lauren Richter, and Sara Wylie. "History of US Presidential Assaults on Modern Environmental Health Protection." *American Journal of Public Health* 108, no. 52 supplement 2 (2018): S95–103.

Freeden, Michael. *The Political Theory of Political Thinking: The Anatomy of a Practice.* Oxford and New York: Oxford University Press, 2013. Froese, Paul. "Religion and American Politics from a Global Perspective." *Religion* 5 (2014): 648–62.

Froese, Paul, and Christopher Bader. *America's Four Gods: What We Say About God—& What That Says About Us.* Oxford and New York: Oxford University Press, 2010.

Fromm, Erich. *Escape from Freedom.* New York: Farrar & Rinehart, 1941.

Galbraith, Quinn, and Adam Calllister. "Why Would Hispanics Vote for Trump? Explaining the Controversy of the 2016 Election." *Hispanic Journal of Behavioral Sciences* 42, no. 1 (2020): 77–94.

Galli, Mark. "Trump Should Be Removed from Office." *Christianity Today.* December 19, 2019. https://www.christianitytoday.com/ct/2019/december-web-only/trump-should-be-removed-from-office.html.

Gasaway, Brantley W. "Making Evangelicals Great Again? American Evangelicals in the Age of Trump." *Evangelical Review of Theology* 43, no. 4 (2019): 293–311.

Geertz, Clifford, ed. *Old Societies and New States: The Quest for Modernity in Asia and Africa*. New York: The Free Press, 1963.
———. *The Interpretation of Cultures*. New York: Basic Books, 1973.
———. *Negara: The Theatre State in Nineteenth-Century Bali*. Princeton, NJ: Princeton University Press, 1980.
Gentile, Emilio. "The Sacralisation of Politics: Definitions, Interpretations and Reflections on the Question of Secular Religion and Totalitarianism." *Totalitarian Movements and Political Religions* 1, no. 1 (2000): 18–55.
Gessen, Masha. "The Putin Paradigm." New York Review of Books. December 13, 2016. https://www.nybooks.com/daily/2016/12/13/putin-paradigm-how-trump-will-rule.
Girardet, Raoul. *Mythes et mythologies politiques*. Paris: Éditions de Seuil, 1986.
Glasius, Marlies. "What Authoritarianism Is…and Is Not: A Practice Perspective." *International Affairs* 94, no. 3 (2018): 515–33.
Goldman, Irving. *Cubeo Hehenewa Religious Thought: Metaphysics of a Northwestern Amazonian People*. New York: Columbia University Press, 2004.
Goodman, Nelson. *Ways of Worldmaking*. Indianapolis, IN: Hackett Publishing Company, 1978.
Gorski, Philip S. "Christianity and Democracy after Trump." *Political Theology* 19, no. 5 (2018): 361–62.
Gounari, Panayota. "Authoritarianism, Discourse and Social Media: Trump as the 'American Agitator.'" In *Critical Theory and Authoritarian Populism*, edited by Jeremiah Morelock, 207–27. London: University of Westminster Press, 2018.
Greenberg, David. "Torchlight Parades for the Television Age: The Presidential Debates as Political Ritual." *Daedalus* 138, no.2 (2009): 6–19.
Grevatt, William K. "Confronting the Trickster: Crises and Opportunity in the Time of Trump—A Jungian Perspective." *Psychological Perspectives* 61, no. 1 (2018): 43–47.
Guidieri, Remo, and Francesco Pellizi. "Introduction: 'Smoking Mirrors'—Modern Polity and Ethnicity." In *Ethnicities and Nations: Processes of Interethnic Relations in Latin America, Southeast Asia, and the Pacific*, edited by Remo Guidieri, Francesco Pellizi, and Stanley J. Tambiah, 7–38. Austin: University of Texas Press, 1988.
Gunter, Michael. *The Kurds in Turkey: A Political Dilemma*. Boulder, CO: Westview Press, 1990.
Habermas, Jürgen. *Legitimation Crisis*. Translated by Thomas McCarthy. Boston, MA: Beacon Press, 1975 [1973].

Hahl, Oliver, Minjae Kim, and Ezra W. Zuckerman Sivan. "The Authentic Appeal of the Lying Demagogue: Proclaiming the Deeper Truth about Political Illegitimacy." *American Sociological Review* 83, no. 1 (2018): 1–33.

Halbwachs, Maurice. *On Collective Memory*. Edited and translated by Lewis A. Coser. Chicago and London: The University of Chicago Press, 1992 [1952].

Handelman, Don. "The Ritual-Clown: Attributes and Affinities." *Anthropos* 76, no. 3/4 (1981): 321–70.

Hansen, Thomas Blom. "The Political Theology of Violence in Contemporary India." *South Asia Multidisciplinary Academic Journal* special issue 2 (2008): 1–14.

Hawley, George. *Making Sense of the Alt-Right*. New York: Columbia University Press, 2017.

Heald, Suzette. "The Ritual Use of Violence: Circumcision among the Gisu of Uganda." In *The Anthropology of Violence*, edited by David Riches, 70–85. Oxford: Basil Blackwell, 1986.

Herbert, Jon, Trevor McCrisken, and Andres Wroe. *The Ordinary Presidency of Donald J. Trump*. Cham, Switzerland: Palgrave Macmillan/Springer Nature, 2019.

Hernandez-Reguant, Ariana. "Miami Cubans 4 Trump and the Battle for the Nation." cubacounterpoints.com. Accessed May 11, 2020. https://cubacounterpoints.com/archives/4399.html.

Herskovits, Melville. *Dahomey: An Ancient West African Kingdom*, v. 2. New York: J. J. Augustin, 1938.

Hochschild, Arlie. "I Spent 5 Years with Some of Trumps Biggest Fans: Here's What They Won't Tell You." *Mother Jones* (2016). Accessed May 12, 2020. http://www.motherjones.com/politics/2016/08/trump-whiteblue-collar-supporters.

Hochschild, Jennifer, and Katherine Levine Einstein. "Do Facts Matter? Information and Misinformation in American Politics." *Political Science Quarterly* 130, no. 4 (2015/2016): 585–624.

Hodges, Adam. "Trump's Formulaic Twitter Insults." *Anthropology News* 58, no. 1 (2017): e206–10.

———. "How Trump's Lying Affirms a Worldview." *Anthropology News* 59, no. 1 (2018): e189–92.

Höffe, Oftried. *Thomas Hobbes*. Translated by Nicholas Walker. Albany, NY: SUNY Press, 2015.

Hoffer, Eric. *The True Believer: Thoughts on the Nature of Mass Movements*. New York: HarperPerennial, 1966 [1951].

Hofstadter, Richard. "The Paranoid Style in American Politics." *Harper's Magazine* (November 1964): 77–86.

Holtom, Daniel Clarence. *The National Faith of Japan: A Study of Modern Shinto*. New York: Paragon Book Reprint Corp., 1965 [1938].

Holy, Ladislav. *Religion and Custom in a Muslim Society: The Berti of Sudan*. Cambridge: Cambridge University Press, 1991.

Hoppe, Hans-Hermann. *Democracy: The God that Failed*. New Brunswick, NJ: Transaction, 2007.

Horvath, Agnes, and Arpad Szakolczai. *The Political Sociology and Anthropology of Evil: Tricksterology*. London and New York: Routledge, 2020.

Howell, William G. *Power Without Persuasion: The Politics of Direct Presidential Action*. Princeton, NJ and Oxford: Princeton University Press, 2003.

Hummel, Daniel. "Revivalist Nationalism Since World War II: From 'Wake Up, America!' to 'Make America Great Again'." *Religions* 7, no. 11 (2016): 1–18.

Hyde, Lewis. *Trickster Makes This World: Mischief, Myth, and Art*. New York: Farrar, Straus, and Giroux, 1998.

Illing, Sean. "The Conservative Movement Was Destined to Produce Trump." Vox.com. March 9, 2019. https://www.vox.com/policy-and-politics/2019/3/8/18250087/the-reactionary-mind-trump-conservatism-corey-robin.

Indick, William. *The Digital God: How Technology Will Reshape Spirituality*. Jefferson, NC: McFarland and Company, 2015.

Ingersoll, Julie. *Building God's Kingdom: Inside the World of Christian Reconstructionism*. Oxford and New York: Oxford University Press, 2015.

Ionescu, Ghita, and Ernest Gellner. "Introduction." In *Populism: Its Meaning and National Characteristics*, edited by Ghita Ionescu and Ernest Gellner, 1–5. London: Weidenfeld & Nicolson, 1969.

Isenstadt, Alex. "'My Biggest Risk': Trump Says Mail-In Voting Could Cost Him Reelection." *Politico*. June 19, 2020. https://www.politico.com/news/2020/06/19/trump-interview-mail-voting-329307.

James, William. *The Varieties of Religious Experience: A Study in Human Nature*. New York: The New American Library, 1958 [1902]).

Jenkins, Philip. *Mystics and Messiahs: Cults and New Religions in American History*. Oxford and New York: Oxford University Press, 2000.

Jokic, Zeljko. *The Living Ancestors: Shamanism, Cosmos, and Cultural Change among the Yanomani of the Upper Orinoco*. New York and Oxford: Berghahn, 2015.

Jordan, Kayla N., and James W. Pennebaker. "The Exception or the Rule: Using Words to Assess Analytic Thinking, Donald Trump, and the American Presidency." *Translational Issues in Psychological Science* 3, no. 3 (2017): 312–16.

Jurecic, Quinta. "Donald Trump's State of Exception." Lawfare. December 14, 2016. https://www.lawfareblog.com/donald-trumps-state-exception.

Jurecic, Quinta, and Benjamin Wittes. "Being an Actual Authoritarian Is Too Much Work for Trump." *The Atlantic*. April 14, 2020. https://www.theatlantic.com/ideas/archive/2020/04/lazy-authoritarian/609937.

Jutel, Olivier. "Civility, Subversion and Technocratic Class Consciousness: Reconstituting Truth in the Journalistic Field." In *Post-Truth and the Mediation of Reality: New Conjunctures*, edited by Rosemary Overell and Brett Nicholls, 177–202. Cham, Switzerland: Palgrave Macmillan, 2019.

Kahan, Dan M., Donald Braman, John Gastil, Paul Slovic, and C. K. Mertz. "Culture and Identity-Protective Cognition: Explaining the White-Male Effect in Risk Perception." *Journal of Empirical Legal Studies* 4, no. 3 (November 2007): 465–505.

Kahn, Paul W. *Out of Eden: Adam and Eve and the Problem of Evil*. Princeton, NJ: Princeton University Press, 2007.

Kahn, Victoria Ann. *The Future of Illusion: Political Theology and Early Modern Texts*. Chicago and London: The University of Chicago Press, 2014.

Kammen, Michael. *Mystic Chords of Memory: The Transformation of Tradition in American Culture*. New York: Knopf, 1993 [1991].

Kantorowicz, Ernst H. *The King's Two Bodies: A Study in Medieval Political Theology*. Princeton, NJ: Princeton University Press, 1957.

Kasmir, Sharryn. "The Saturn Automobile Plant and the Long Dispossession of US Autoworkers." In *Blood and Fire: Toward a Global Anthropology of Labor*, edited by Sharryn Kasmir and August Carbonella, 203–49. New York and London: Berghahn, 2014.

Katz, Richard. *Boiling Energy: Community Healing Among the Kalahari Kung*. Cambridge, MA and London: Harvard University Press, 1982.

Kaufmann, Walter. *The Faith of a Heretic*. Garden City, NY: Doubleday & Company, 1961.

Keane, Webb. "Religious Language." *Annual Review of Anthropology* 26 (1997): 47–71.

Kearney, Richard. *Anatheism: Returning to God After God*. New York: Columbia University Press, 2010.

Kessler, Glenn, Salvador Rizzo, and Meg Kelly. "President Trump Made 18,000 False or Misleading Claims in 1,170 Days." *The Washington Post*. April 14, 2020. https://www.washingtonpost.com/politics/2020/04/14/president-trump-made-18000-false-or-misleading-claims-1170-days.

Khan, M. Owais. "100 Years of Political Theology: An Islamic Perspective." Political Theology Network. February 6, 2014. https://politicaltheology.com/100-years-of-political-theology-an-islamic-perspective-by-m-owais-khan.

Kirkland, Kit. "Politics Before God: How America's Political Divisiveness Is Trumping Religious Identity." *Journal of the British Association for the Study of Religions* 20 (2018): 169–91.

Klapp, Orrin E. "The Clever Hero." *The Journal of American Folklore* 67, no. 263 (1954): 21–34.

Koenig, Alan P. "'God is Near': American Theocracy and the Political Theology of Joseph Smith." PhD diss., City University of New York, 2016. https://academicworks.cuny.edu/gc_etds/1528/.

Kosmin, Paul J. "A Phenomenology of Democracy: Ostracism as Political Ritual." *Classical Antiquity* 34, no. 1 (2015): 121–62.

Kotsko, Adam. "The Political Theology of Trump: What Looks Like Hypocrisy is the Surest Possible Evidence that God is in Control." Nplusone, November 6, 2018, https://nplusonemag.com/online-only/online-only/the-political-theology-of-trump.

Kovács, András. "The Post-Communist Extreme Right: The Jobbik Party in Hungary." In *Right Wing Populism in Europe: Politics and Discourse*, edited by Ruth Wodak, Majid KhosraviNik, and Brigitte Mral, 223–33. London and New York: Bloomsbury, 2013.

Krogstad, Jens Manuel, and Mark Hugo Lopez. "Hillary Clinton Won Latino Vote but Fell Below 2012 Support for Obama." Pewresearch.org. November 29, 2016. https://www.pewresearch.org/fact-tank/2016/11/29/hillary-clinton-wins-latino-vote-but-falls-below-2012-support-for-obama.

Laclau, Ernesto. *On Populist Reason*. New York: Verso, 2005.

LaFrance, Adrienne. "Nothing Can Stop What is Coming." *The Atlantic* 325, no. 5 (June 2020): 27–38.

Latour, Bruno. *We Have Never Been Modern*. Translated by Catherine Porter. Cambridge, MA: Harvard University Press, 1993 [1991].

Leach, Edmund. "A Discussion of Ritualization of Behavior in Animals and Man." *Philosophical Transactions of the Royal Society of London Series B, Biological Sciences* 251, no. 772 (1966): 403–8.

Lefort, Claude. "The Permanence of the Theologico-Political?" In *Political Theologies: Public Religions in a Post-Secular World*, edited by Hent de Vries and Lawrence E. Sullivan, 148–87. New York: Fordham University Press, 2006.

Lennon, Myles. "Revisiting 'The Repugnant Other' in the Era of Trump." *HAU: Journal of Ethnographic Theory* 8, no. 3 (2018): 439–54.

Lévi-Strauss, Claude. *Structural Anthropology*. Translated by Claire Jacobson and Brook Grundfest Scheepf. New York: Basic Books, 1963.

Levitsky, Steven, and James Loxton. "Populism and Competitive Authoritarianism: The Case of Fujimori's Peru." In *Populism in Europe and the Americas: Threat or Corrective for Democracy?*, edited by Cas Mudde and Cristóbal Kaltwassser, 160–81. Cambridge and New York: Cambridge University Press, 2012.

Levitsky, Steven, and Lucan A. Way. "Elections without Democracy: The Rise of Competitive Authoritarianism." *Journal of Democracy* 13, no. 2 (2002): 51–65.

Levy, Robert I., Jeannette Marie Mageo, and Alan Howard. "Gods, Spirits, and History: A Theoretical Perspective." In *Spirits in Culture, History, and Mind*, edited by Jeannette Marie Mageo and Alan Howard, 11–27. New York and London: Routledge, 1996.

Lifeway Research. "The State of American Theology Study 2016." September 1, 2016. http://lifewayresearch.com/wp-content/uploads/2016/09/Ligonier-State-of-American-Theology-2016-Final-Report.pdf.

Linker, Damon. "Political Theology in America." Cato Unbound. October 10, 2007. https://www.cato-unbound.org/2007/10/10/damon-linker/political-theology-america.

Lowenthal, Leo, and Norbert Guterman. *Prophets of Deceit: A Study of the Techniques of the American Agitator*. New York: Harper & Brothers, 1949.

Lukes, Steven. "Political Ritual and Social Integration." *Sociology* 9, no.2 (1975): 289–308.

Luntz, Frank. *The Frank Luntz Rethug Playbook, Unauthorized Edition: How to Scare the American Public into Voting Republican*. Luntz Research Companies. Accessed February 22, 2020. joshuakahnrussell.files.wordpress.com/2008/10/luntzplaybook2006.pdf.

Lynerd, Benjamin T. *Republican Theology: The Civil Religion of American Evangelicals*. Oxford and New York: Oxford University Press, 2014.

Lyotard, Jean-François. *The Postmodern Condition: A Report on
    Knowledge.* Translated by Geoff Bennington and Brian Massumi.
    Minneapolis: University of Minnesota Press, 1984 [1979].
Machiavelli, Niccolo. *The Historical, Political, and Diplomatic Writings of
    Niccolo Machiavelli.* Vol. 4. Boston, MA: J. R. Osgood and
    Company, 1882.
Magdy, Ramy. "Mythos Politicus: A Theoretical Framework for the Study
    of Political Myths." *Athens Journal of Mediterranean Studies* 6, no.
    2 (2020): 155–78.
Malinowski, Bronislaw. *Magic, Science, and Religion and Other Essays.*
    Garden City NY: Doubleday Anchor Books, 1948.
Manheim, Jarol B. *Strategy in Information and Influence Campaigns: How
    Policy Advocates, Social Movements, Insurgent Groups,
    Corporations, Governments, and Others Get What They Want.* New
    York and London: Routledge, 2011.
Mann, Windsor. "Trump's Lethal Aversion to Reading." The Week. May 21,
    2020. https://theweek.com/articles/915606/trumps-lethal-aversion-
    reading.
Mantyla, Kyle. "Rick Wiles: 'We Are Going to Impose Christian Rule in
    This Country.'" Right Wing Watch. May 17, 2019.
    https://www.rightwingwatch.org/post/rick-wiles-we-are-going-to-
    impose-christian-rule-in-this-country.
———. "Brenden Dilley Doesn't 'Give a F*ck About Being Factual.'"
    Right Wing Watch. May 27, 2020.
    https://www.rightwingwatch.org/post/brenden-dilley-doesnt-give-a-
    fck-about-being-factual.
March, Andrew F. "Genealogies of Sovereignty in Islamic Political
    Theology." *Social Research* 80, no. 1 (2013): 293–320.
Marcus, Ruth. "Forget the Post-Truth presidency. Welcome to the Pre-Truth
    Presidency." *The Washington Post.* March 23, 2017.
    https://www.washingtonpost.com/opinions/welcome-to-the-pre-
    truth-presidency/2017/03/23/b35856ca-1007-11e7-9b0d-
    d27c98455440_story.html.
Marett, R. R. *The Threshold of Religion.* London: Methuen & Co., 1909.
Markowitz, Gerald and David Rosner. *Deceit and Denial: The Deadly
    Politics of Industrial Pollution.* Berkeley, CA: University of
    California Press, 2002.
Marshall, Kimberly Jenkins. *Upward, Not Sunwise: Resonant Rupture in
    Navajo Neo-Pentecostalism.* Lincoln and London: University of
    Nebraska Press, 2016.
Martin, Keir, and Jakob Krause-Jensen. "Trump: Transacting Trickster."
    Anthropology Today 33, no. 3 (2017): 5–8.

Maskovsky, Jeff. "Toward the Anthropology of White Nationalist Postracialism: Comments Inspired by Hall, Goldstein, and Ingram's 'The Hands of Donald Trump.'" *HAU: Journal of Ethnographic Theory* 7, no. 1 (2017): 433–40.

Maskovsky, Jeff and Sophie Bjork-James. "Introduction." In *Beyond Populism: Angry Politics and the Twilight of Neoliberalism*, edited by Jeff Maskovsky and Sophie Bjork-James, 1–19. Morgantown: West Virginia University Press, 2020.

Mason, Lilliana, Julie Wronski, and John Kane. "Ingroup Lovers or Outgroup Haters? The Social Roots of Trump Support and Partisan Identity." Paper presented at the Conference of the Midwest Political Science Association, Chicago, IL, May, 2019.

Mason, Patrick Q. "God and the People: Theodemocracy in Nineteenth-Century Mormonism." *Journal of Church and State* 53, no. 3 (2011): 349–75.

MayflowerHistory.com. "The Mayflower Compact." Accessed May 20, 2020. http://mayflowerhistory.com/mayflower-compact.

Mazzarella, William. "The Anthropology of Populism: Beyond the Liberal Settlement." *Annual Review of Anthropology* 48 (2019): 45–60.

———. "Populism as Political Theology." Lecture, Columbia University, New York, NY, April 23, 2019. https://www.academia.edu/42286798/Populism_as_Political_Theology.

McCright, Aaron M., and Riley E. Dunlap. "Cool Dudes: The Denial of Climate Change among Conservative White Males in the United States." *Global Environmental Change* 21, no. 4 (2011): 1163–72.

McGoey, Linsey. *The Unknowers: How Strategic Ignorance Rules the World*. London: Zed Books, 2019.

McGranahan, Carole. "An Anthropology of Lying: Trump and the Political Sociality of Moral Outrage." *American Ethnologist* 44, no. 2 (2017): 243–48.

McVeigh, Rory, and Kevin Estep. *The Politics of Losing: Trump, the Klan, and the Mainstreaming of Resentment*. New York: Columbia University Press, 2019.

Mead, Walter Russell. "The Jacksonian Tradition and American Foreign Policy." *The National Interest*, no. 58 (Winter 1999/2000): 5–29.

———. *A Special Providence: American Foreign Policy and How It Changed the World*. New York: Routledge, 2000.

Michaels, David. *Doubt is Their Product: How Industry's Assault on Science Threatens Your Health*. New York: Oxford University Press, 2008.

Mikkelsen, Henrik H. "Chaosmology: Shamanism and Personhood among the Bugkalot." *HAU: Journal of Ethnographic Theory* 6, no. 1 (2016): 189–205.

Miller, Ed L., ed. *Classical Statements on Faith and Reason.* New York: Random House, 1970.

Mocko, Anne T. *Demoting Vishnu: Ritual, Politics, and the Unraveling of Nepal's Hindu Monarchy.* Oxford and New York: Oxford University Press, 2016.

Moffitt, Benjamin. *The Global Rise of Populism: Performance, Political Style, and Representation.* Stanford, CA: Stanford University Press, 2016.

———. "The Performative Turn in the Comparative Study of Populism." *Comparative Politics Newsletter* 26, no. 2 (2016): 52–58.

Mounk, Yascha. *The People vs. Democracy: Why Our Freedom is in Danger and How to Save It.* Cambridge, MA and London: Harvard University Press, 2018.

Mudde, Cas, and Cristóbal Kaltwasser. "Populism and (Liberal) Democracy: A Framework for Analysis." In *Populism in Europe and the Americas: Threat or Corrective for Democracy?* Edited by Cas Mudde and Cristóbal Kaltwassser, 1–26. Cambridge and New York: Cambridge University Press, 2012.

Muirhead, Russell, and Nancy L. Rosenblum. *A Lot of People are Saying: The New Conspiracism and the Assault on Democracy.* Princeton, NJ: Princeton University Press, 2019.

Müller, Jan-Werner. *What Is Populism?* Philadelphia: University of Pennsylvania Press, 2016.

Myerhoff, Barbara C. *Peyote Hunt: The Sacred Journey of the Huichol Indians.* Ithaca, NY: Cornell University Press, 1974.

Nagle, Angela. *Kill All Normies: The Online Culture Wars from Tumblr and 4chan to the Alt-Right and Trump.* Winchester, UK and Washington, DC: Zero Books, 2017.

Napier, Jaime L., Julie Huang, Andrew J. Vonasch, and John A. Bargh. "Superheroes for Change: Physical Safety Promotes Socially (but not Economically) Progressive Attitudes among Conservatives." *European Journal of Social Psychology* 48, no. 2 (2018): 187–95.

NBC News. "Trump in 1999." July 8, 2015. https://www.nbcnews.com/meet-the-press/video/trump-in-1999-i-am-very-pro-choice-480297539914.

Neal, Lynn S. "Christianizing the Klan: Alma White, Branford Clarke, and the Art of Religious Intolerance." *Church History* 78, no. 2 (2009): 350–78.

Needham, Rodney. *Belief, Language, and Experience.* Chicago, IL: The University of Chicago Press, 1972.

Nelson, Libby. "'Why We Voted for Donald Trump': David Duke Explains the White Supremacist Charlottesville Protests." Vox.com. August 12, 2017. https://www.vox.com/2017/8/12/16138358/charlottesville-protests-david-duke-kkk.

Newman, Saul. *Political Theology: A Critical Introduction.* Cambridge: Polity Press, 2019.

North, Gary. *Millennialism and Social Theory.* Tyler, TX: Institute for Christian Economics, 1990.

Nussbaum, Martha C. *The Monarchy of Fear: A Philosopher Looks at Our Political Crisis.* Oxford and New York: Oxford University Press, 2018.

Oddie, Geoffrey A. *Imagined Hinduism: British Protestant Missionary Constructions of Hinduism, 1793–1900.* New Delhi, Thousand Oaks, CA, and London, 2006.

Ohnuki-Tierney, Emiko. *The Ainu of the Northwest Coast of Southern Sakhalin.* New York: Holt, Rinehart, and Winston, 1974.

Oreskes, Naomi and Erik M. Conway. *Merchants of Doubt: How a Handful of Scientists Obscured the Truth on Issues from Tobacco Smoke to Global Warming.* New York: Bloomsbury, 2010.

Pack, Jason. "Johnson and Trump Are Trying to Create Sovereign." Al-Jazeera. October 11, 2019. https://www.aljazeera.com/indepth/opinion/johnson-trump-create-sovereign-executives-191010091924052.html.

Packer, George. "The President is Winning His War on American Institutions." *The Atlantic,* April 2020. https://www.theatlantic.com/magazine/archive/2020/04/how-to-destroy-a-government/606793.

Pally, Marcia. "Why is Populism Persuasive? Populism as Expression of Religio-Cultural History with the U.S. and U.S. Evangelicals as a Case Study." *Political Theology* (2020).

Pandian, Jacob. "Symbolic Inversions. An Interpretation of Contrary Behavior in Ritual." *Anthropos* 96, no. 2 (2001): 557–62.

Papazoglou, Alexis. "Trump Has a Peculiar Definition of Sovereignty." *The Atlantic.* September 28, 2019. https://www.theatlantic.com/ideas/archive/2019/09/trumps-undemocratic-obsession-with-sovereignty/598822.

Pappas, Takis S. *Populism and Liberal Democracy: A Comparative and Theoretical Analysis.* Oxford and New York: Oxford University Press, 2019.

Pedersen, Morten Axel. *Not Quite Shamans: Spirit Worlds and Political Lives in Northern Mongolia.* Ithaca, NY and London: Cornell University Press, 2011.

Pein, Corey. "Donald Trump, Trickster God." The Baffler. March 4, 2016.
    https://thebaffler.com/magical-thinking/donald-trump-trickster-god.
Pemberton, John. "Eshu-Elegba: The Yoruba Trickster God." *African Arts* 9,
    no. 1 (1975): 20–27, 66, 70, 90, 92.
Pew Research Center. "Religious Landscape Study." 2014. Accessed May
    19, 2020. https://www.pewforum.org/religious-landscape-study.
———. "An Examination of the 2016 Electorate, Based On Validated
    Voters." August 9, 2018. https://www.people-
    press.org/2018/08/09/an-examination-of-the-2016-electorate-based-
    on-validated-voters.
———. "The Religious Typology." August 29, 2018.
    https://www.pewforum.org/2018/08/29/the-religious-typology.
Pfiffner, James P. "The Lies of Donald Trump: A Taxonomy." In
    *Presidential Leadership and the Trump Presidency: Executive
    Power and Democratic Governance*, edited by Charles M. Lamb
    and Jacob R. Neiheisel, 17–40. Cham, Switzerland: Palgrave
    Macmillan, 2019.
Phillips, Elizabeth. *Political Theology: A Guide for the Perplexed*. London
    and New York: Bloomsbury, 2012.
Plantinga, Alvin. *Warranted Christian Belief*. New York: Oxford University
    Press, 2000.
Popper, Karl R. *The Open Society and Its Enemies, Volume 1 The Age of
    Plato*. New York and Evanston, IL: Harper Torchbooks, 1945.
———. *The Open Society and Its Enemies, Volume 2 The High Tide of
    Prophecy: Hegel, Marx, and the Aftermath*. New York and
    Evanston, IL: Harper Torchbooks, 1945.
Pouillon, Jean. *Between Belief and Transgression: Structuralist Essays in
    Religion, History, and Myth*. Edited by Michel Izard and Pierre
    Smith. Translated by John Leavitt, 1–8. Chicago, IL: The University
    of Chicago Press, 1982.
Proctor, Robert N. "Agnotology: A Missing Term to Describe the Cultural
    Production of Ignorance (and Its Study)." In *Agnotology: The
    Making & Unmaking of Ignorance*, edited by Robert N. Proctor and
    Londa Schiebinger, 1–33. Stanford, CA: Stanford University Press,
    2008.
Purdy, Elizabeth R. "Censorship." The First Amendment Encyclopedia.
    Accessed June 23, 2020. https://www.mtsu.edu/first-
    amendment/article/896/censorship.
Radcliffe-Brown, A. R. *Structure and Function in Primitive Society*. New
    York: The Free Press, 1965 [1952].
Radin, Paul. *The Trickster: A Study in American Indian Mythology*. London:
    Routledge and Kegan Paul, 1956.

Rahier, Jean Muteba. *Kings for Three Days: The Play of Race & Gender in an Afro-Ecuadorian Festival*. Urbana, Chicago, and Springfield: University of Illinois Press, 2013.

Ramsey-Elliot, Morgan. "An Ethnographer Has a New Explanation for Donald Trump's Support in Small-Town America." Quartz. September 22, 2016. https://qz.com/787948/why-is-donald-trump-so-popular-in-rural-america.

———. "From Trucks to Trump: The Role of Small-Town Values in Driving Votes." *Anthropology Now* 9, no. 1 (2017): 53–57.

Rappaport, Roy. *Ritual and Religion in the Making of Humanity*. Cambridge: Cambridge University Press, 1999.

Reilly, Katie. "Read Hillary Clinton's 'Basket of Deplorables' Remarks About Donald Trump Supporters." Time.com. September 10, 2016. https://time.com/4486502/hillary-clinton-basket-of-deplorables-transcript.

Ringer, Monica M. *Pious Citizens: Reforming Zoroastrianism in India and Iran*. Syracuse, NY: Syracuse University Press, 2011.

Robbins, Jeffrey W. *Radical Democracy and Political Theology*. New York: Columbia University Press, 2011.

Robin, Corey. *The Reactionary Mind: Conservatism from Edmund Burke to Sarah Palin*. Oxford and New York: Oxford University Press, 2011.

Rosenberg, Matthew, and Jennifer Steinhauer. "The QAnon Candidates Are Here. Trump Has Paved Their Way." *The New York Times*. July 14, 2020. https://www.nytimes.com/2020/07/14/us/politics/qanon-politicians-candidates.html.

Ross, Andrew. "The New Geography of Work: Power to the Precarious?" *Theory, Culture, & Society* 25, no. 7/8 (2008): 31–49.

Rowland, Christopher. "Scripture: New Testament." In *The Blackwell Companion to Political Theology*, edited by Peter Scott and William T. Cavanaugh, 21–34. Oxford: Blackwell Publishing, 2004.

Ruel, Malcolm. *Belief, Ritual, and the Securing of Life: Reflexive Essays on Bantu Religion*. Leiden: E. J. Brill, 1997.

Rushdoony, Rousas J. *The Institutes of Biblical Law*. Nutley, NJ: The Craig Press, 1973.

Sampat, Preeti. "Make in India: Hindu Nationalism, Global Capital, and Jobless Growth." In *Beyond Populism: Angry Politics and the Twilight of Neoliberalism*, edited by Jeff Maskovsky and Sophie Bjork-James, 61–77. Morgantown: West Virginia University Press, 2020.

Santi, Raffaella. "Legal Thought in Early Modern England: The Theory of Thomas Hobbes." *Economics World* 6, no. 5 (2018): 384–89.

Schaffner, Brian, Matthew MacWilliams, and Tatishe Nteta. "Understanding White Polarization in the 2016 Vote for President: The Sobering Role of Racism and Sexism." *Political Science Quarterly* 133, no. 1 (2018): 9–34.

Schäuble, Michaela. *Narrating Victimhood: Gender, Religion, and the Making of Place in Post-War Croatia*. New York and London: Berghahn, 2014.

Scheub, Harold. *Trickster and Hero: Two Characters in the Oral and Written Traditions of the World*. Madison: The University of Wisconsin Press, 2012.

Scheuerman, William E. "Donald Trump Meets Carl Schmitt." *Philosophy and Social Criticism* 45, no. 9/10 (2019): 1170–85.

Schielke, Samuli. "Second Thoughts about the Anthropology of Islam, or How to Make Sense of Grand Schemes in Everyday Life." Working Papers No. 2, Zentrum Moderner Orient, 2010.

Schlesinger, Arthur M., Jr. *The Imperial Presidency*. Boston. MA: Houghton Mifflin Company, 1973.

Schmitt, Carl. *Glossarium. Aufzeichnungen der Jahre 1947–1951* [*Glossarium. Diaries of the Years 1947–1951*]. Berlin: Duncker & Humblot, 1991.

———. *Political Theology: Four Chapters on the Concept of Sovereignty*. Translated by George Schwab. Chicago: The University of Chicago Press, 2005 [1934].

———. *The Concept of the Political*. Translated by George Schwab. Chicago and London: The University of Chicago Press, 2007 [1927].

Schupmann, Benjamin A. "Emergency Powers and Trump: Lessons from Carl Schmitt." Public Seminar. March 22, 2019. https://publicseminar.org/2019/03/emergency-powers-and-trump-lessons-from-carl-schmitt.

Sen, Atreyee. "The Hindu Goddess in Indian Politics." Political Theology Network. May 29, 2015. https://politicaltheology.com/the-hindu-goddess-in-indian-politics-atreyee-sen.

Shallcross, N. J. "Social Media and Information Operations in the 21st Century." *Journal of Information Warfare* 16, no. 1 (2017): 1–12.

Sharlett, Jeff. *The Family: The Secret Fundamentalism at the Heart of American Power*. New York and London: Harper Perennial, 2008.

Sharockman, Aaron. "MSNBC, Fox, CNN Move the Needle On Our Truth-o-meter Scorecards." Politifact. January 27, 2015. https://www.politifact.com/article/2015/jan/27/msnbc-fox-cnn-move-needle-our-truth-o-meter-scorec.

Shils, Edward. *The Torment of Secrecy: The Background and Consequences of American Security Policies.* Glencoe, IL: The Free Press, 1956.

Shnirelman, Victor A. "Russian Neopaganism: From Ethnic Religion to Racial Violence." In *Modern Pagan and Native Faith Movements in Central and Eastern Europe*, edited by Kaarina Aitamurto and Scott Simpson, 62–76. Durham, UK and Bristol, CT: Acumen, 2013.

———. "Hyperborea: The Arctic Myth of Contemporary Russian Radical Nationalists." *Journal of Ethnology and Folkloristics* 8, no. 2 (2014): 121–38.

Silver, Nate. "The Mythology of Trump's 'Working Class' Support." FiveThirtyEight. May 3, 2016. https://fivethirtyeight.com/features/the-mythology-of-trumps-working-class-support.

Sissons, Jeffrey. *The Polynesian Iconoclasm: Religious Revolution and the Seasonality of Power.* New York and Oxford: Berghahn Books, 2014.

Smith, David Norman, and Eric Hanley. "The Anger Games: Who Voted for Trump in the 2016 Election, and Why?" *Critical Sociology* 44, no. 2 (2018): 195–212.

Smithson, Michael. *Ignorance and Uncertainty: Emerging Paradigms.* New York: Springer-Verlag, 1989.

Spiro, Melford. *Burmese Supernaturalism*, expanded edition. Philadelphia, PA: Institute for the Study of Human Issues, 1978 [1967].

Staal, Frits. "The Meaninglessness of Ritual." *Numen* 26, no. 1 (1979): 2–22.

Stackhouse, John C., Jr. "American Evangelical Support for Donald Trump: Mostly American and Only Sort-of-'Evangelical'—A Response." Religion & Culture Forum. February 2, 2018. https://voices.uchicago.edu/religionculture/2018/02/02/american-evangelical-support-for-donald-trump-mostly-american-and-only-sort-of-evangelical-a-response.

Stern, Kenneth. *A Force upon the Plain: The American Militia Movement and the Politics of Hate.* New York: Simon & Schuster, 1996.

Stoica, Mihnea S. "Political Myths of the Populist Discourse." *Journal for the Study of Religions and Ideologies* 16, no. 46 (2017): 63–76.

Stone, Michael, "Christian TV Host Asks Trump To Use 'Hollow-Point Bullets' On Portland Protesters." Patheos. July 24, 2020. https://www.patheos.com/blogs/progressivesecularhumanist/2020/07/christian-tv-host-asks-trump-to-use-hollow-point-bullets-on-portland-protesters/?utm_medium=email&fbclid=IwAR1QtYC2HeZie0a0x7Vu6uRyGg0HrzBRMI_uu943YrbGPfDsEKZTpimzU-Q.

Sullivan, Shannon and Nancy Tuana, eds. *Race and Epistemologies of Ignorance*. Albany: State University of New York Press, 2007.

Suskind, Ron. "Faith, Certainty and the Presidency of George W. Bush." *The New York Times Magazine* (October 17, 2004).

Swinburne, Richard. *The Coherence of Theism*. Oxford: Clarendon Press, 1977.

Swire, Briony, Adam J. Berinsky, Stephan Lewandowsky, and Ullrich K. H. Ecker. "Processing Political Misinformation: Comprehending the Trump Phenomenon." *Royal Society Open Science* 4 (2017): 1–21.

Swire-Thompson, Briony, Ullrich K. H. Ecker, Stephan Lewandowsky, and Adam J. Berkinsky. "They Might Be a Liar But They're My Liar:
Source Evaluation and the Prevalence of Misinformation." *Political Psychology* 41, no. 1 (2020): 21–34.

Szilárdi, Réka. "Neopaganism in Hungary: Under the Spell of Roots." In *Modern Pagan and Native Faith Movements in Central and Eastern Europe*, edited by Kaarina Aitamurto and Scott Simpson, 230–48. Durham, UK and Bristol, CT: Acumen, 2013.

Tambiah, Stanley J. *Buddhism and the Spirit Cults in North-East Thailand*. Cambridge and New York: Cambridge University Press, 1970.

———. *A Performative Approach to Ritual*. London: The British Academy and Oxford University Press, 1979.

Theohary, Catherine A. "Defense Primer: Information Operations." Washington, DC: Congressional Research Service, 2018.

Thomas, Timothy. "Russia's Reflexive Control Theory and the Military." *Journal of Slavic Military Studies* 17, no. 2 (2004): 237–56.

Tooker, Deborah. "Identity Systems of Highland Burma: 'Belief,' Akha Zan, and a Critique of Interiorized Notions of Ethno-Religious Identity." *Man* (new series) 27, no. 4 (1992): 799–819.

Trump, Donald J. "The Inauguration Speech." Whitehouse.gov. January 20, 2017. https://www.whitehouse.gov/briefings-statements/the-inaugural-address.

Tudor, Henry. *Political Myth*. London: Pall Mall Press, 1972.

Turner, Victor. *The Ritual Process: Structure and Anti-Structure*. Chicago, IL: Aldine Publishing, 1969.

Tyson, Alec, and Shiva Maniam. "Behind Trump's Victory: Divisions by Race, Gender, Education." Pewresearch.org. November 9, 2016. https://www.pewresearch.org/fact-tank/2016/11/09/behind-trumps-victory-divisions-by-race-gender-education.

Valentino, Nicholas A., Fabian G. Neuner, and L Matthew Vanderbroek. "The Changing Norms of Racial Political Rhetoric and the End of Racial Priming." *The Journal of Politics*, 80, no. 3 (2017): 757–71.

Viefhues-Bailey, Ludger. "Looking Forward to a New Heaven and a New Earth Where American Greatness Dwells: Trumpism's Political Theology." *Political Theology* 18, no. 3 (2017): 194–200.

Voegelin, Eric. *The Collected Works of Eric Voegelin: Volume 5, Modernity without Restraint*, edited by Manfred Henningsen. Columbia and London: University of Missouri Press, 2000.

Wade, Wyn Craig. *The Fiery Cross: The Ku Klux Klan in America*. New York: Simon & Shuster, 1987.

Wallace, Anthony F. C. *Religion: An Anthropological View*. New York: Random House, 1966.

Walley, Christine J. "Trump's Election and the 'White Working Class': What We Missed." *American Ethnologist* 44, no. 2 (2017): 231–36.

Wallis, Jim. "International Bonhoeffer Society Calls for 'Ending Donald Trump's Presidency' in 'Statement of Concern.'" Sojourners. January 16, 2020. https://sojo.net/articles/international-bonhoeffer-society-calls-ending-donald-trumps-presidency-statement-concern.

Wardle, Claire. "Fake News: It's Complicated." First Draft. February 16, 2017. https://medium.com/1st-draft/fake-news-its-complicated-d0f773766c79.

Wayman, Alex. "The Meaning of Unwisdom (Avidya)." *Philosophy East and West* 7, no. 1/2 (1957), 21–25.

Weale, Albert. *The Will of the People: A Modern Myth*. Cambridge, UK and Medford, MA: Polity Press, 2018.

Weber, Max. "*Politik als Beruf*" (Politics as a Vocation). *Gesammelte Politische Schriften* (Muenchen, 1921): 396-450.

Weedon, Jen, William Nuland, and Alex Stamos. "Information Operations and Facebook." Facebook, 2017.

Weyland, Kurt. "Clarifying a Contested Concept: Populism in the Study of Latin American Politics." *Comparative Politics* 34, no. 1 (2001): 1–22.

Wheelwright, Philip, ed. *The Presocratics*. New York: The Odyssey Press, 1966.

Whitehead, Andrew L., Samuel L. Perry, and Joseph O. Baker. "Make America Christian Again: Christian Nationalism and Voting for Donald Trump in the 2016 Presidential Election." *Sociology of Religion* 79, no. 2 (2018): 147–71.

Winthrop, John. "John Winthrop Dreams of a City On a Hill, 1630." The American Yawp Reader. Accessed May 20, 2020. https://www.americanyawp.com/reader/colliding-cultures/john-winthrop-dreams-of-a-city-on-a-hill-1630.

Wirth, Louis. "Urbanism as a Way of Life." *The American Journal of Sociology* 44, no. 1 (1938): 1–24.

Woods, Dwayne. "The Many Faces of Populism: Diverse but Not Disparate." In *The Many Faces of Populism: Current Perspectives*, edited by Dwayne Woods and Barbara Wejnert, 1–25. Bingley, UK: Emerald Publishing, 2014.

Wolterstorff, Nicholas. *The Mighty and the Almighty: An Essay in Political Theology*. Cambridge and New York: Cambridge University Press, 2012.

Yabanci, Bilge. "Fuzzy Borders between Populism and Sacralized Politics: Mission, Leader, Community and Performance in 'New' Turkey." *Politics, Religion & Ideology*, 21, no. 1 (2020): 92–112.

Yilmaz, Ihsan, and Galib Bashirov. "The AKP after 15 Years: Emergence of Erdoganism in Turkey." *Third World Quarterly*, 39, no. 9 (2018): 1812–30.

Zakaria, Fareed. "The Rise of Illiberal Democracy." *Foreign Affairs* 76, no. 6 (1997): 22–43.

Zelinski, Andrea. "Texas Republican Party Plans to Build Phony Campaign Websites Loaded with Negative Information About Democrats." *Houston Chronicle*. November 26, 2019. https://www.houstonchronicle.com/news/politics/texas/article/Texas -Republican-Party-plans-to-build-phony- 14863988.php?fbclid=IwAR2_westK_- GEUk8f_pEPLGGaIPXnAgFnx31NtRb9eAWVINryaIRTc1NL7w.

Image Credits

Fig. 1. Image in public domain; Fig. 2. Image in public domain. Fig. 3. Photographic reproduction from *Reminiscences of Joseph, the Prophet* (1893), original in public domain. Fig. 4. United States Library of Congress's Prints and Photographs Division. Fig. 5. Image in public domain. Fig. 6. Photograph by Marc Nozell, Creative Commons Attribution 2.0 Generic license. Fig. 7. Photograph by Jérémy-Günther-Heinz Jähnick, GNU Free Documentation License, version 1.2. Fig. 8. Photograph by European People's Party, Creative Commons Attribution 2.0 Generic license. Fig. 9. Photograph by General Iroh, the Dragon of the West, Creative Commons Attribution-Share Alike 4.0 International license. Fig. 10. Photograph from Elisabeth Young-Bruehl, *Hannah Arendt: For Love of the World*, work in public domain. Fig. 11. Photograph by Gage Skidmore, Creative Commons Attribution-Share Alike 2.0 Generic license. Fig. 12. Image in public domain. Fig. 13. Photograph by Mike Maguire, Creative Commons Attribution 2.0 Generic license. Fig. 14. U.S. National Archives and Records Administration, image in public domain. Fig. 15. Photograph by Yuriy Kvach, Creative Commons Attribution-Share Alike 3.0 Unported license. Fig. 16. Photograph by Arlington National Cemetery, image in public domain. Fig. 17. Photograph by Munkhbayar.B, Creative Commons Attribution-Share Alike 4.0 International license. Fig. 18. Photograph by Humansdorpie, Creative Commons Attribution-Share Alike 3.0 Unported license.

Index

coronavirus 50, 52–53, 65, 68, 161, 174, 190, 223, 252; *see also* COVID-19
COVID-19 51, 53, 65, 110, 174, 190, 254; *see also* coronavirus
Darhad 239–40
"deep story" of America 145–46
Democratic Party 25–26, 29, 37, 49, 55, 63, 68, 137–38, 140–43, 149–50, 152, 155, 171, 190, 252–53; Brendan Dilley's efforts to destroy 163; Trump as member of 56
Duke, David 43, 45, 251
Durkheim, Émile 90, 114, 204, 209
Electoral College 50, 162
Eliade, Mircea 198–99, 231, 236
Erdoğan, Recep Tayyip 78, 85, 94–95, 103–4, 134
Eshu-Elegba 240–1
ethical nontheism 229
ethnocentrism 120–21
evangelicals 2, 20, 24, 26, 28–30, 55–56, 136, 150–8, 248; progressive evangelical movement 152–53
Falwell, Jerry 30, 56; Jerry Falwell, Jr. 156
Fascism scale 119, 121–23
Fidesz 91, 96, 98, 135
Fox News 66, 189, 223
French Revolution 11, 58, 78, 99
Fromm, Erich 112, 114, 123, 128
Fujimori, Alberto 78, 92–94, 97, 100, 134, 246
Geertz, Clifford 91, 210, 221–22
German(y) 52, 91, 111, 124, 160, 212
Goodman, Nelson 194, 222
Graham, Billy 55, 152
Graham, Lindsey 190

Hobbes, Thomas 5–8, 11, 14, 20
Hoffer, Eric 112, 125, 127–31, 149
Hindu(ism) 8, 20, 24, 104–7, 183, 197
Hindutva 105–7, 216
Hispanic(s) 55, 62, 137–40, 146–48
Hofstadter, Richard 61–62, 65
Hungary/-ian 78, 80, 85, 91, 96–99, 107–8, 110, 134, 214
Hyperborea 212–13
illiberal democracy 99–101, 113, 132, 134
India(n) 18, 85, 91, 104–7, 110, 197, 213, 216, 233
information operations 175–76, 188
Islam 9, 13, 95, 183, 202, 210, 231; Islamic political theology 195; Islamic terrorism 137; Islamism 95; Islamophobia 136; *see also* Muslim
Jacksonianism 64
Japan(ese) 10, 93, 220–21, 228
Jeffress, Robert 156
Jesus 3, 9, 24, 26, 74, 150; Jesus camp 106; Ku Klux Klan and 36; Tertullian on 180
Jew(ish) 24, 26, 35–36, 43, 62, 66, 81, 115, 124, 138, 151, 202, 214, 216; Christian Identity and 38–39; "Jews will not replace us" 63; Russian sacred nation narrative and 213
JOBBIK 96
Johnson, Boris 48
Johnson, Lyndon 171–72
Justice and Development Party (AKP) 94–95, 104, 134
Kennedy, John F. 66, 171

CPSIA information can be obtained
at www.ICGtesting.com
Printed in the USA
FSHW020051241220
76860FS